UNCERTAINTY IN INTELLIGENT AND INFORMATION SYSTEMS

ADVANCES IN FUZZY SYSTEMS — APPLICATIONS AND THEORY

Vol. 7: Genetic Algorithms and Fuzzy Logic Systems: Soft Computing Perspectives
(*Eds. E. Sanchez, T. Shibata and L. A. Zadeh*)

Vol. 8: Foundations and Applications of Possibility Theory
(*Eds. G. de Cooman, D. Ruan and E. E. Kerre*)

Vol. 9: Fuzzy Topology
(*Y. M. Liu and M. K. Luo*)

Vol. 10: Fuzzy Algorithms: With Applications to Image Processing and Pattern Recognition
(*Z. Chi, H. Yan and T. D. Pham*)

Vol. 11: Hybrid Intelligent Engineering Systems
(*Eds. L. C. Jain and R. K. Jain*)

Vol. 12: Fuzzy Logic for Business, Finance, and Management
(*G. Bojadziev and M. Bojadziev*)

Vol. 13: Fuzzy and Uncertain Object-Oriented Databases: Concepts and Models
(*Ed. R. de Caluwe*)

Vol. 14: Automatic Generation of Neural Network Architecture Using Evolutionary Computing
(*Eds. E. Vonk, L. C. Jain and R. P. Johnson*)

Vol. 15: Fuzzy-Logic-Based Programming
(*Chin-Liang Chang*)

Vol. 16: Computational Intelligence in Software Engineering
(*W. Pedrycz and J. F. Peters*)

Forthcoming volumes:

Vol. 17: Non-additive Set Functions and Nonlinear Integrals
(*Z. Y. Wang*)

Vol. 18: Factor Space, Fuzzy Statistics, and Uncertainty Inference
(*P. Z. Wang and X. H. Zhang*)

Vol. 19: Genetic Fuzzy Systems, Evolutionary Tuning and Learning of Fuzzy Knowledge Bases
(*O. Cordon, F. Herrera, F. Hoffman and L. Magdalene*)

Advances in Fuzzy Systems — Applications and Theory Vol. 20

UNCERTAINTY IN INTELLIGENT AND INFORMATION SYSTEMS

edited by

B Bouchon-Meunier
LIP6, CNRS, Université Paris VI

R R Yager
Iona College

L A Zadeh
University of California, Berkeley

World Scientific
Singapore • New Jersey • London • Hong Kong

Published by

World Scientific Publishing Co. Pte. Ltd.
P O Box 128, Farrer Road, Singapore 912805
USA office: Suite 1B, 1060 Main Street, River Edge, NJ 07661
UK office: 57 Shelton Street, Covent Garden, London WC2H 9HE

British Library Cataloguing-in-Publication Data
A catalogue record for this book is available from the British Library.

UNCERTAINTY IN INTELLIGENT AND INFORMATION SYSTEMS
Advances in Fuzzy Systems — Applications and Theory, Vol. 20

ISBN 981-02-4364-2

Printed in Singapore by Uto-Print

Contents

Applications

Uncertainty Management

Data Mining by the Self-Organizing Map Method

Teuvo Kohonen
Helsinki University of Technology
Neural Networks Research Centre
P.O. Box 5400, FIN-02015 HUT, Finland
E-mail: teuvo.kohonen@hut.fi

Abstract. The Self-Organizing Map (SOM) method has recently gained an increasing amount of interest in a wide variety of fields ranging from engineering sciences to biology, economics, and knowledge discovery in databases: over 3000 works on it have been published all over the world. This article relates the SOM to the traditional methods in exploratory data analysis and summarizes its main ideas and application areas.

1. Introduction

A multivariate data item may consist of, say, a set of statistical figures. Such a set of values can be conveniently expressed as a *vector* which simply means an ordered set of values. If we associate with every item a set of n values denoted by $x_1, x_2, \ldots x_n$, the vector formed of these values will be denoted by $\mathbf{x}=(x_1, x_2,\ldots x_n)$.

If there are N data items in the data set, the vector corresponding to item k will be denoted by $\mathbf{x}(k)$. In statistics it is customary to call the components of the data vectors *observations* recorded on *variables*. However, according to the general mathematical vector-space terminology, here they will be called *components*. The components may also be called *features* as is customary in pattern recognition literature. In econometric studies the variables are often called *indicators*. In other applications, the names *descriptors* and *attributes* also appear. In the mathematical formalism, the vectors can be interpreted as points in an n-dimensional space.

Several kinds of methods have been developed for illustrating extensive data sets, for example statistical tables or sets of samples of stochastic variables obtained on-line, such as of signals or images. The simplest of these methods produce trivial visual summaries of the sets (cf. Tukey 1977). In this work we shall concentrate on *mapping methods* that can be used for illustrating *metric relations* between masses of multivariate high-dimensional data items.

The traditional mapping methods for the visualization of high-dimensional data items can roughly be divided into *clustering* and *projection* methods, respectively.

2. Clustering Methods

The purpose of clustering is to group similar data items together, whereupon less information is needed to describe the relations between the groups. Such a grouping resembles the way in which human beings process information, and the clustering algorithms are used to automatically construct perceivable categories or taxonomies (Jardine and Sibson 1971, Sneath and Sokal 1973).

The clustering methods (Anderberg 1973, Hartigan 1975, Jain and Dubes 1988, Jardine and Sibson 1971, Sneath and Sokal 1973, Tryon and Bailey 1973) can be divided into two basic types: *hierarchical* and *partitional* clustering.

Hierarchical clustering produces a graph structure of data by merging smaller clusters into larger ones, and splitting larger clusters. The result is a tree of clusters called the *dendrogram* that shows how the clusters are related. When two small clusters are merged, a higher level of representation is created to the dendrogram and the new level is connected to the representations of its constituent clusters at the lower level.

Partitional clustering decomposes the data set into a set of disjoint clusters. The samples are assigned to the various clusters by minimizing some measure of dissimilarity of the samples within each cluster while maximizing the dissimilarity of different clusters.

For the purposes of this work we shall first present the following clustering principle, called the *K-means clustering* (Forgy 1965, Linde et al. 1980, Lloyd 1982) in more detail.

Consider that our goal were to approximate the density $p(\mathbf{x})$ of an open set of input sample vectors $\mathbf{x}$ using a restricted number of suitably selected *model* or *codebook vectors* $\mathbf{m}_i$. One approximation criterion for is that the average *quantization error* is minimized. If the error function between $\mathbf{x}$ and any of the $\mathbf{m}_i$ is in general denoted $d(\mathbf{x},\mathbf{m}_i)$, then, by comparison of $\mathbf{x}$ with all the $\mathbf{m}_i$, one can first identify the model vector $\mathbf{m}_c$ for which $d(\mathbf{x},\mathbf{m}_c)$ is smallest. Let this vector be called the *winner*. Let us now consider a set of given input samples $\mathbf{x}(k)$, k=1,2,..., M. The average quantization error function is then defined as

$$E = \frac{1}{M} \sum_{k=1}^{N} d[\mathbf{x}(k),\mathbf{m}_c] \quad . \tag{1}$$

(Notice that for each $\mathbf{x}(k)$, the index c of the winner is a function of $\mathbf{x}(k)$ and all the $\mathbf{m}_i$.) The choice of all the $\mathbf{m}_i$ that minimizes E then represents the clustering solution.

In practical problems, each cluster should become represented by one or several $\mathbf{m}_i$. The reason for which this method is called the K-means clustering comes from the following consideration. Consider Fig. 1, where a set of $\mathbf{m}_i$ is shown as points in a coordinate system: for simplicity we shall consider two-dimensional vectors. Assume now that $d[\mathbf{x},\mathbf{m}_i]$ is the square of the Euclidean distance between the points $\mathbf{x}$ and $\mathbf{m}_i$. The lines drawn to Fig. 1 divide the plane into regions called the *Voronoi tessellation* (Voronoi 1908).

All those $\mathbf{x}(k)$ vectors that are closest to some $\mathbf{m}_i$ belong to the same division, called the *Voronoi set* around $\mathbf{m}_i$. If this Voronoi set is denoted V_i, then it can be shown (cf. Makhoul et al. 1985, Kohonen 1991) that the average quantization error is minimized when for each V_i ,

$$\mathbf{m}_i = \frac{1}{M_i} \sum_{\mathbf{x}(k) \in V_i} \mathbf{x}(k) \quad . \tag{2}$$

Here M_i is the number of the $\mathbf{x}(k)$ that fall into the respective V_i. In other words, each $\mathbf{m}_i$ shall coincide with the centroid (mean) of those $\mathbf{x}(k)$ that are closest to $\mathbf{m}_i$. Hence the name K-means clustering: if K is the number of the V_i, the density of the $\mathbf{x}(k)$ is described by a set of K local *centroids*, or *means* of subsets of the $\mathbf{x}(k)$.

There exists a classical iterative algorithm for the determination of the K-means clustering. As Linde, Buzo, and Gray (1980) have shown that it works with a wide class of error functions, it is usually called the LBG algorithm.

The learning steps are defined as follows:

1) for the initial codebook vectors $\mathbf{m}_i$, take, for instance, copies of the first training samples $\mathbf{x}$;
2) for each map unit i, collect a list of copies of all those training samples $\mathbf{x}$, whose nearest codebook vector belongs to the neighborhood set N_i of cell i;
3) take for the new value of each new codebook vector the mean over the respective list;
4) repeat from step 2) a few times.

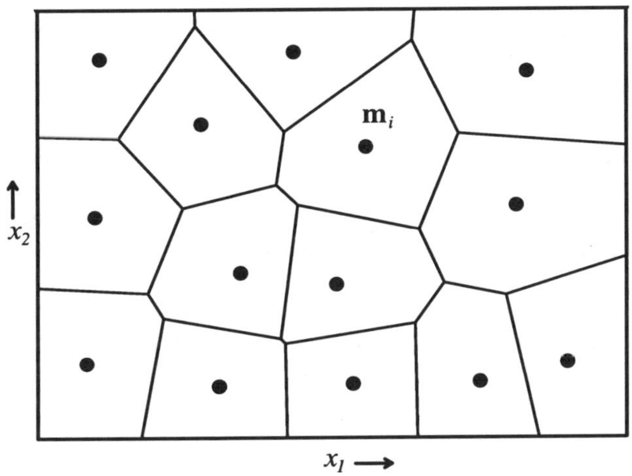

Fig. 1. Voronoi tessellation in a two-dimensional signal space. The sample vectors $\mathbf{x}(k) = [x_1(k), x_2(k)]$ *are distributed over this coordinate system.*

A characteristic potential problem with the K-means clustering is that the choice of the *number* of model vectors may be critical: different sets of model vectors may emerge when K is changed. Good initialization of the model vectors in the iterative LBG algorithm is also crucial; some clusters may even be left empty if the initial model vector values lie far from the distribution of data. The Self-Organizing Map (SOM) algorithm discussed below has turned out to constitute a very good method for the initialization of the K-means clustering (de Bodt and Cottrell 1999). The results of the cluster analysis also need to be validated. Jain and Dubes (1988) present methods for this.

3. Projection Methods

The purpose of the projection methods is to reduce the dimensionality of the data vectors. The projections represent the input data items in a lower-dimensional space in such a way that certain metric relations of the data items are preserved as faithfully as possible. Projections can be used to visualize the data set if a sufficiently small dimensionality, such as one, two, or three, for the output display is chosen.

3.1 Linear Projection Methods

Before proceeding further, we have to introduce the concept of the *subspace*. In the three-dimensional Euclidean space such a subspace can easily be illustrated as being a plane (two-dimensional) or a line (one-dimensional).

As all the possible n-dimensional real-valued vectors $\mathbf{x}=(x_1, x_2,\ldots x_n)$ can be thought to span the n-dimensional *real-space*, we can restrict in this space to a subset or *manifold* of vectors that constitute a *linear subspace* of lower dimensionality. Each vector in an m-dimensional linear subspace ($m<n$) is a *linear combination* of m independently selected *basis vectors*.

The principal-component analysis (PCA) (Hotelling 1933) displays high-dimensional data items as a *linear projection* consisting of points on a much smaller-dimensional subspace such that the variance of the original data is preserved as well as possible. Linear projection simply means that each component of the projected vector is a linear combination of the components of the original data item; the projection is formed multiplying each component by a certain scalar coefficient and summing up the results. There exist mathematical methods for finding optimal coefficients such that the variance of the data after the projection will be maximized, whereby the variance of the projection is also closest to the variance of the original data.

The PCA is a standard method in data analysis. By far every textbook on statistics contains a section on PCA, and most of the general statistical computer programs contain routines for computing it. Even "neural" algorithms for the PCA have been devised (Oja 1983, Oja 1992, Rubner and Tavan 1989, Cichocki and Unbehauen 1993). A demonstration of PCA is presented in Fig. 2.

3.2. Nonlinear Projection Methods

If the data set is high-dimensional and its distribution is highly unsymmetric or otherwise structured, it may be difficult to visualize the structures of its distribution using linear projections.

Several nonlinear methods have been introduced for reproducing high-dimensional structures of data distributions on a low-dimensional display. The most common idea is to find a mapping such that the *distances between the image points* of the data items would be as similar as possible to the distances of the corresponding data items in the original metric space. The various methods only differ in how the different distances are weighted in optimization.

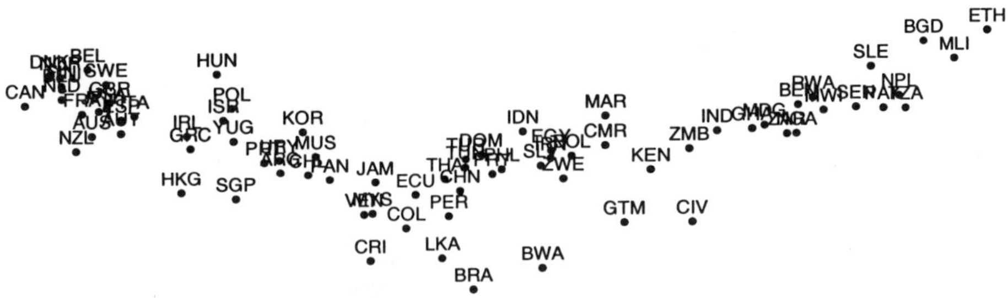

Fig. 2. A data set projected linearly as points onto the two-dimensional subspace obtained with PCA. Each component of the 39-dimensional data items describes a different aspect of the welfare and poverty of one country. The data set consisting of 77 countries, also used in Figs. 3, 4, and 6, was picked up from the World Development Report published by the World Bank (1992). Missing data values were neglected when computing the principal components, and zeroed when forming the projections. The three-letter codes for the countries, abbreviations of their names, may be self-explanatory.

Multidimensional scaling (MDS) signifies a class of methods used widely in behavioral, econometric, and social sciences. There exists a multitude of variants of MDS with slightly different goals and optimization algorithms (Young and Householder 1938; Torgerson 1952; Kruskal and Wish 1978; de Leeuw and Heiser 1982; Wish and Carroll 1982; Young 1985). The methods have been later generalized for analyzing nonmetric data, for which only the order of the distances between the data items is important. A matrix consisting of the pairwise dissimilarities of the entities is assumed to be available.

Preservation of the original metric distances in the projection may not always be the best goal, however. *The nonmetric MDS* (Kruskal 1964, Shepard 1962) introduces a monotonically increasing function f of the original metric distances that tries to preserve the *rank order* of the mapped data in the projection, while allowing deviations in the exact reproduction of the distances. The cost function then reads

$$E_N = \frac{1}{\sum_{k \neq l}[d'(k,l)]^2} \sum_{k \neq l}[f(d(k,l)) - d'(k,l)]^2 \ , \tag{3}$$

where $d(k,l)$ is the distance between the original data items indexed by k and l, respectively, and $d'(k,l)$ is the distance in the two-dimensional space between the corresponding image points. The function $f(\cdot)$ is optimized for each mapping (Kruskal and Wish 1978).

A demonstration of nonmetric MDS, applied to a dimensionality-reduction task, is given in Fig 3.

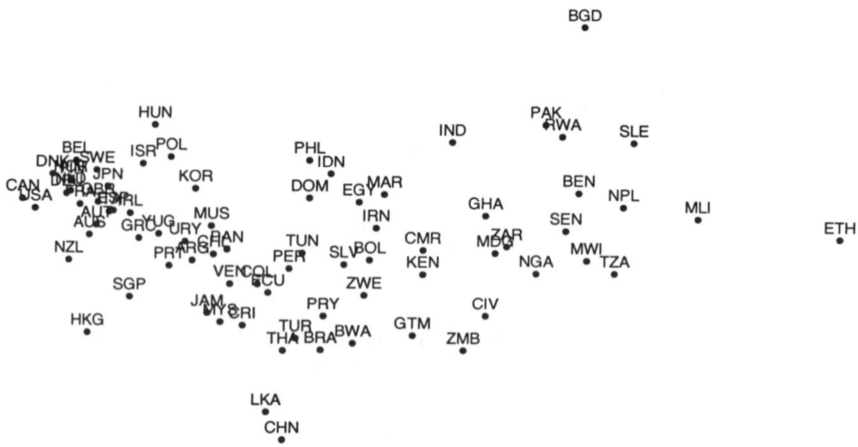

Fig. 3. A nonlinear projection constructed using nonmetric MDS. The data set is the same as in Fig 2. Missing data values were treated by the following simple method which has been demonstrated to produce good results at least in the pattern recognition context (Dixon 1979). When computing the distance between a pair of data items, only the (squared) differences between component values that are available are computed. The rest of the differences are then set to the average of the computed differences.

Another nonlinear projection method is *Sammon's mapping* (Sammon 1969) that also tries to match the pairwise distances of the lower-dimensional representations of the data items with their original distances. The difference between Sammon's mapping and the MDS is that in Sammon's mapping the errors are normalized with the distances in the original data space, which emphasizes small distances. The cost function in Sammon's mapping is (omitting a constant normalizing factor)

$$E_S = \sum_{k \neq l} \frac{[d(k,l) - d'(k,l)]^2}{d(k,l)} \quad . \tag{4}$$

A demonstration of Sammon's mapping is presented in Fig 4. Clearly it spreads the data in a more illustrative way than PCA or MDS.

There also exists a computationally efficient method that may be viewed as a modification of Sammon's mapping, namely, *the curvilinear component analysis* (Demartines 1994, Demartines and Hérault 1997). The data items are first clustered and then the clusters are mapped with a fast algorithm in which the relative emphasis on the large and small distances, respectively, can be regulated.

Principal curves. The PCA can be generalized in the nonlinear domains as forming nonlinear manifolds. While in the PCA a good projection of a data set onto a linear manifold, a "hyperplane", was constructed, the goal in constructing a principal curve or a principal surface is to project the set onto a nonlinear manifold, a curved "hypersurface". The *principal curves* (Hastie and Stuetzle 1989) are smooth curves that are defined by the property that each point of the curve is the average of all data points that project to it, i.e., for which that point is the closest point on the curve. The principal curves are generalizations of principal components extracted using PCA in the sense that a linear principal curve is a principal component.

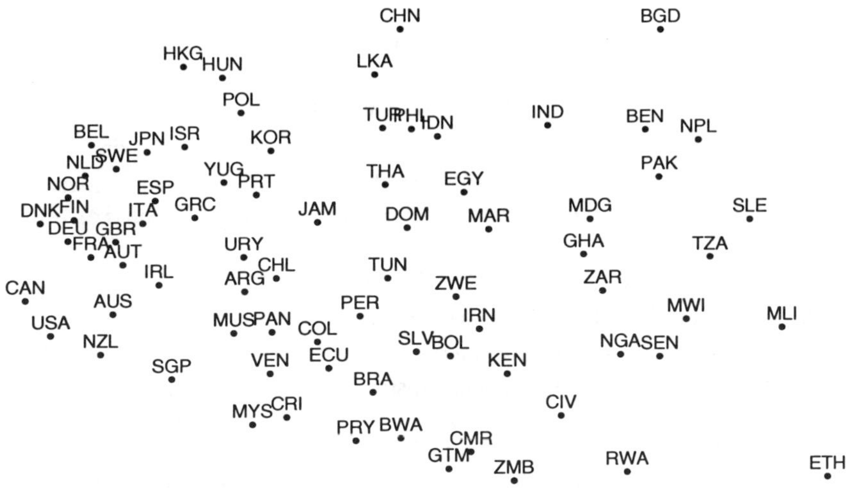

Fig. 4. Sammon's mapping of the same data set that was projected using the PCA in Fig. 2 and nonmetric MDS in Fig. 3. Missing data values were treated in the same manner as in forming the nonmetric MDS.

The conception of continuous principal curves may aid in understanding how principal components could be generalized. The algorithm of Hastie and Stuetzle (1989) proposed for finding discretized principal curves resembles the batch version (Kohonen 1992) of the Self-Organizing Map (SOM) algorithm, although the details are different. To be useful in practical computations, however, the curves must always be discretized. It has turned out (Mulier and Cherkassky 1995, Ritter et al. 1992) that discretized principal curves are then essentially equivalent to the SOMs, introduced long ago before Hastie and Stuetzle (1989) introduced the principal curves. It thus seems that the conception of principal curves is only useful in providing one possible viewpoint to the properties of the SOM algorithm discussed next.

4. The Self-Organizing Map (SOM)

The *Self-Organizing Map (SOM)* (Kohonen 1982a, 1982b, 1990, 1995) combines the clustering and projection operations. The most essential differences with respect to some other methods are: 1. The SOM represents an open set of multivariate items by a *finite* set of model vectors $\mathbf{m}_i$, like in the K-means clustering, 2. The SOM represents the item vectors in an orderly fashion on a two-dimensional regular grid, and the model vectors are then associated with the nodes of the grid, 3. It is not necessary to recompute the whole mapping for every new sample, because, if the statistics can be assumed as stationary, the new sample can be directly mapped onto the closest old model vector.

4.1. The Incremental SOM Algorithm

Assume that the sets of observation samples constitute n-dimensional real *sample vectors*

$$\mathbf{x}(t) = [x_1(t), x_2(t), \dots, x_n(t)] , \tag{5}$$

where t is the index of the sample $(t = 1,2,\dots)$. In other words, one observation is an n-tuple of values, and it is said that the observations span a space that is n-dimensional. Similarly the n-dimensional *model vectors* are denoted as a function of t :

$$\mathbf{m}_i(t) = [m_{i1}(t), m_{i2}(t), \dots, m_{in}(t)] \quad . \tag{6}$$

Every input sample will now be mapped to the closest $\mathbf{m}_i$. This operation is the same as in the classical K-means clustering.

However, unlike in the K-means clustering, in the SOM the model vectors will form a "flexible net" or finite-element "surface" onto which the *projection* of the $\mathbf{x}(t)$ is formed. In the learning process, this "surface" is first put to go through the data, like in regression. The index of the winner at each regression step shall be identified first:

$$\|\mathbf{x}(t) - \mathbf{m}_c(t)\| = \min_i \{\|\mathbf{x}(t) - \mathbf{m}_i(t)\|\} . \tag{7}$$

After that the $\mathbf{m}_i(t)$ are adjusted in the following way:

$$\mathbf{m}_i(t+1) = \mathbf{m}_i(t) + \alpha(t) h_{ci}(t)[\mathbf{x}(t) - \mathbf{m}_i(t)] \quad . \tag{8}$$

That is, the size of the adjustment depends on the mutual distance of $\mathbf{m}_i$ and $\mathbf{m}_c$ measured along the grid and defined by $h_{ci}(t)$ that is called the *neighborhood function*. One can even set $h_{ci}(t) = 0$ for mutual distances exceeding a given limit. Thus the regression step is *local* and usually leaves most of the models intact during one step of adjustment.

The factor $\alpha(t)$ $(0 < \alpha(t) < 1)$ is called the *learning-rate factor* and it is decreasing with t . It can bc combined with $h_{ci}(t)$.

This *Self-Organizing Map (SOM)* algorithm, defined by Eqs. (7) and (8), defines fitting of the "flexible net" to the input density function $p(\mathbf{x})$.

Fig. 5 shows how the "flexible net" has been fitted to data to approximate a structured three-dimensional density function.

There are still a few questions that remain: does the series of the values $\{\mathbf{m}_i(t)\}$ converge, and what is the convergence limit? Is it unique? These are very hard questions, and only a very thorough mathematical analysis (Cottrell and Fort 1989, Cottrell, Fort and Pages 1997) can give some answers to them. Let it suffice to state here that we can be sure of the convergence of the $\mathbf{m}_i(t)$ to reasonably good values $\mathbf{m}_i^*$ if $\alpha(t)$ and $h_{ci}(t)$ are chosen suitably.

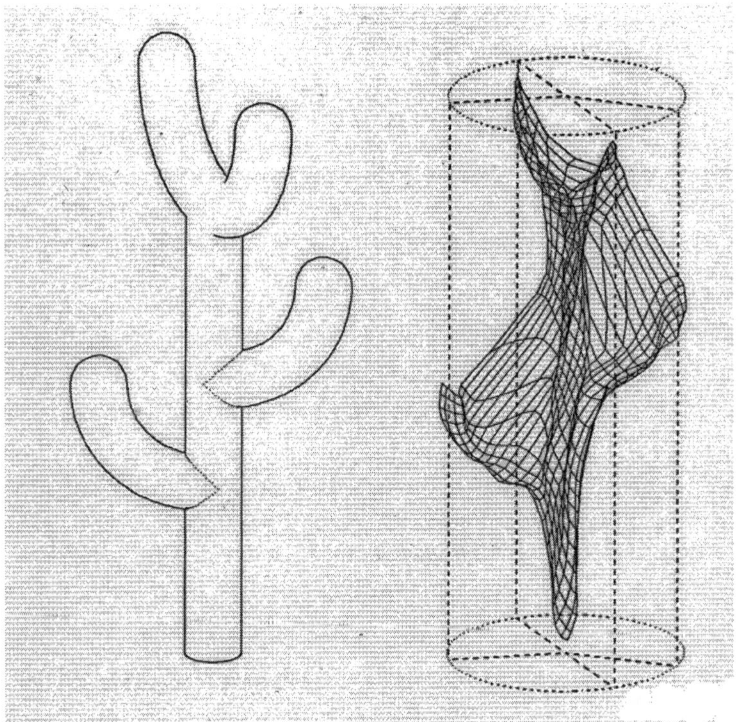

Fig. 5. (a) The density function $p(\mathbf{x})$ of $\mathbf{x}$ in the three-dimensional observation space. Tthis is a hypothetical case: Inside the "cactus" the density has some constant value and is zero outside it. (b) The "flexible net" that approximates the density function.

4.2. The Batch Version of the SOM

The incremental regression process defined by (7) and (8) can often be replaced by the following batch computation version of the SOM, which is significantly faster and does not require specification of any learning-rate factor $\alpha(t)$ (Kohonen 1992).

Assuming that the convergence to some ordered state is true, we require that the expectation values of $\mathbf{m}_i(t+1)$ and $\mathbf{m}_i(t)$ for $t \to \infty$ must be equal, even if $h_{ci}(t)$ were then selected nonzero. In other words, in the stationary state the values $\mathbf{m}_i^*$ must satisfy the equilibrium equation

$$\forall i, \ \mathrm{E}\left\{h_{c(\mathbf{x}),i}(x - \mathbf{m}_i^*)\right\} = 0 \ . \tag{9}$$

In the special case where we have a finite number (batch) of the $\mathbf{x}(t)$ with respect to which (9) has to be solved for the $\mathbf{m}_i^*$, and $h_{c(\mathbf{x}),i}$ represents the time-invariant kernel used during the last phases of the learning process, we can write

$$\mathbf{m}_i^* = \frac{\sum_t h_{c(\mathbf{x}),i}\mathbf{x}(t)}{\sum_t h_{c(\mathbf{x}),i}} \quad . \tag{10}$$

This, however, is not yet an explicit solution for $\mathbf{m}_i^*$, because the subscript $c(\mathbf{x})$ on the right-hand side still depends on $\mathbf{x}(t)$ *and all the* $\mathbf{m}_i^*$. The way of writing (10), however, allows us to apply the *contractive mapping method* known from the theory of nonlinear equations: starting with even coarse approximations for the $\mathbf{m}_i^*$, (7) is first utilized to find the indices $c(\mathbf{x})$ for all the $\mathbf{x}(t)$. On the basis of the approximate $h_{c(\mathbf{x}),i}$ values, the improved approximations for the $\mathbf{m}_i^*$ are computed from (10), which are then applied to (7), whereafter the computed $c(\mathbf{x})$ are substituted into (10), and so on. The optimal solutions $\mathbf{m}_i^*$ are usually obtained in a few iteration cycles, after the discrete-valued indices $c(\mathbf{x})$ have settled down and are no longer changed in further iterations. This procedure is called the *Batch Map* principle.

An even simpler Batch Map principle is obtained if $h_{c(\mathbf{x}),i}$ is defined in terms of the neighborhood set N_c. Let us recall that we defined N_i as the set of nodes that lie up to a certain radius from node i in the array. The union of Voronoi sets V_i corresponding to the nodes in N_i shall be denoted by U_i. Then (10) can be written

$$\mathbf{m}_i^* = \frac{\sum_{x(t)\in U_i}\mathbf{x}(t)}{n(U_i)} \quad , \tag{11}$$

where $n(U_i)$ means the number of samples $\mathbf{x}(t)$ that belong to U_i.

Notice again that the U_i depend on the $\mathbf{m}_i^*$, and therefore (11) must be solved iteratively. The procedure can be described as the following steps:

1. Initialize the values of the $\mathbf{m}_i^*$ in some proper way. (Even random values for the $\mathbf{m}_i^*$ will usually do.)
2. Input all the $\mathbf{x}(t)$, one at a time, and list each of them under the model $\mathbf{m}_i^*$ that is closest to $\mathbf{x}(t)$ according to (7).
3. Let U_i denote the union of the above lists at model $\mathbf{m}_i^*$ and its neighbors that constitute the neighborhood N_i. Compute the means of the vectors $\mathbf{x}(t)$ in each U_i, and replace the old values of $\mathbf{m}_i^*$ by the respective means.
4. Repeat from 2 a few times until the solutions can be regarded as steady.

Also the computation of (10) is further accelerated if one notes that for the different nodes i, the same addends occur a great number of times. It is advisable to first compute the mean $\bar{\mathbf{x}}_j$ of the $\mathbf{x}(t)$ in each Voronoi set V_j and then weight it by the number n_j of samples in V_j and the neighborhood function. Now we obtain

$$\mathbf{m}_i^* = \frac{\sum_j n_j h_{ji} \bar{\mathbf{x}}_j}{\sum_j n_j h_{ji}} \quad , \tag{12}$$

where the sum over j is taken for all units of the SOM.

There is a Matlab SOM Toolbox program package available on the Internet at the address http://www.cis.hut.fi/projects/somtoolbox/, which involves the Batch Map method.

Notice that (12) can be described as an alternation of two steps: 1. One K-means step of the input data, 2. One step of local smoothing of the $\bar{\mathbf{x}}_j$ values over the grid. This may give us a further idea of replacing the K-means step by a more general vector quantization (Makhoul et al. 1985) and developing a better smoothing step that, for example, treats the borders of the SOM array differently.

5. Applications of the SOM

The most promising application areas of the SOM seem to be:

- exploratory data analysis and knowledge discovery in databases (KDD)
- analysis and control of industrial processes and machines
- various tasks in telecommunications
- biomedical analyses and applications.

Some of the applications are described below in more detail.

5.1. Welfare and Poverty Map of the World

When the Self-Organizing Map is being used to project the data displayed in Figs. 2 and 3, the main difference is that now the original data are represented by a set of approximate models that are located at discrete nodes of a two-dimensional regular grid (Kaski and Kohonen 1998).

The clusters in the data set can be visualized by false-color or gray shades as shown in Figure 6; the display is a smoothed version of the so-called U-matrix (Ultsch 1993). Different types of *welfare* and *poverty* are emphasized by light color, whereas the dark color shows where the models are changing more rapidly.

5.2. Analysis of Processes and Machines

The system model of an industrial plant or a complex machine is traditionally described in terms of physical, chemical, or other state variables. The latter are usually distributed spatially and related in a highly nonlinear way. The number of variables may be so high that that they are not identifiable from the measurements. Nonetheless there may exist few characteristic states or state clusters in the system that determine its general behavior and are somehow reflected in the measurements. Such characteristic states or clusters can often be made visible in the self-organizing map, without explicit modeling of the system (Alhoniemi et al. 1999).

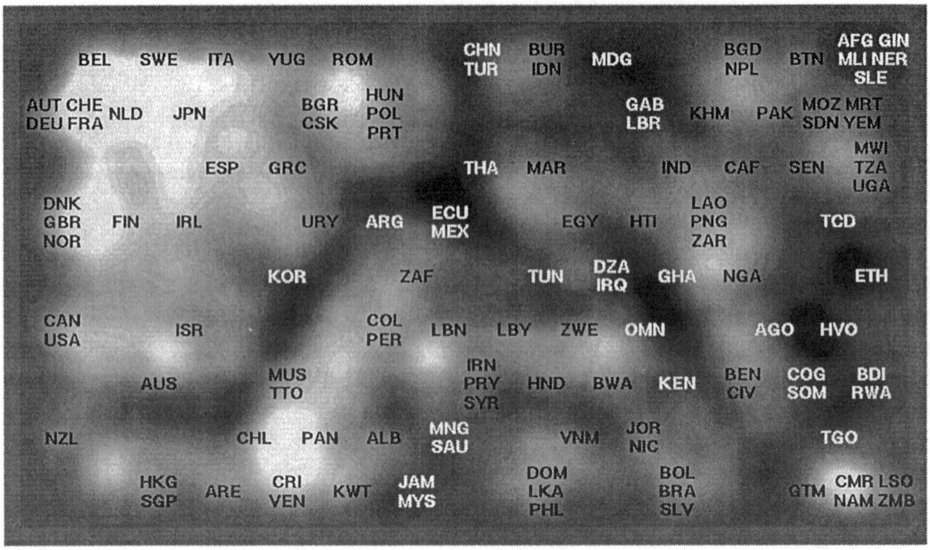

Fig. 6. Structured diagram of the data set chosen to describe the standard of living (Kaski and Kohonen 1998). The order of the abbreviated country names indicates the similarity of the standard of living of the countries, and the colors indicate the degree of clustering. Light areas represent areas of a high degree of clustering and dark areas gaps in the degree of clustering. Different types of welfare and poverty are visible as the clustered (light) areas on the map, separated by the dark "gorges." The symbols or groups of symbols are centered at grid points (not explicitly shown).

Consider a system from which several discrete measurements relating to the system itself as well as to its environment are taken. These measurements and the values of the control variables may be regarded to constitute the data vector $\mathbf{x}$ used as the input to the SOM. Normally the measurements are made in different scales, but a reasonably good strategy to start with has turned out to be to normalize the scales such that the maximum and minimum, respectively, in all scales coincide, or alternatively, the variance of every variable is the same. Assume that the model vectors are $\mathbf{m}_i = [\mu_{i1}, \mu_{i2}, \ldots, \mu_{in}]^{\mathrm{T}}$. The *component plane j* of the SOM is defined as the array of values μ_{ij}, the form of which conforms to the SOM array but which only represents the *j*th components of all the model vectors $\mathbf{m}_i$. The component planes can be displayed as arrays of squares in the same format as the SOM array, colored by shades of gray or pseudocolors according to the values μ_{ij}.

An example of the SOM, or actually only one of its component planes is shown in Figure 7, where a power transformer has been analyzed (Kasslin et al. 1992). In this example, the states relating to the measurements of ten variables (voltages, currents, temperatures, hydrogen content of the insulating coolant) have been followed during a period of 24 hours. The trajectory has been drawn on the component plane that displays the load current of the transformer. Dark gray tones correspond to small and light tones to heavy loads, respectively. It can be seen that the operating point has moved from dark to light areas and back corresponding to the 24 h operation cycle of the system, during which the load was switched on and off.

In addition to visualizing the normal operating conditions of the system or machine by the SOM, one can also illustrate the *fault states*. The main problem is where to get abnormal but still typical measurements from, in order to use them in the training of the SOM. The faults may be rare, and true measurements thus not available. In some cases, real fault situations can be caused during the development and testing of the equipment, but this may become very expensive. Especially with industrial processes and big machines, production of a sufficient number of severe faults might be too costly. Then the faults must be simulated, and the simulated input vectors **x** used for training.

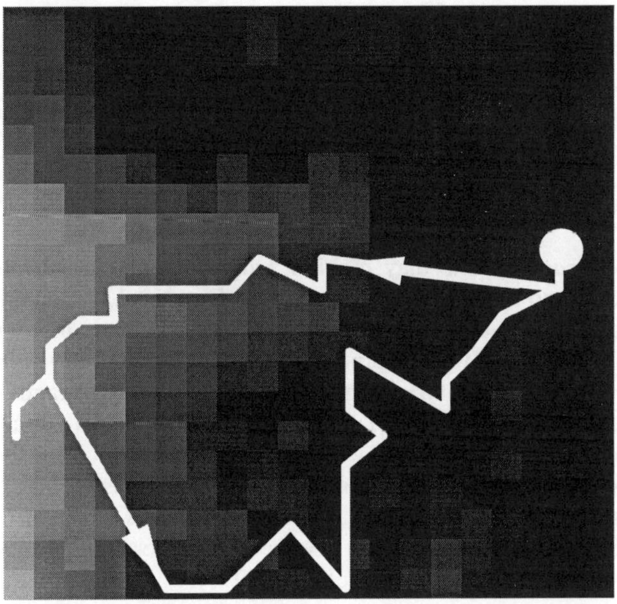

Fig. 7. Each small square represents the value of one component j of some model vector $\mathbf{m}_i$*, in a gray scale. The trajectory drawn in white describes the sequence of "winner" units on the SOM, in response to a sequence of input vectors* $\{\mathbf{x}(t)\}$ *taken over 24 h of operation. This picture describes the load current (white: high, black: low), whereby its values can be read as a function of time from the gray-shade values along the trajectory.*

5.3. Control of Industrial Processes

In the systems-theoretic approach, in order to control a process, a global system model ought to be available, and it must be possible to place a sufficient number of transducers to places where they measure essential process variables. Typical problems are that the most relevant places in the process may not be easily accessible, and the most essential properties of the final product may only be measurable off-line. Therefore, the estimation of process or signal states must often be made indirectly. Elaborate methods such as multivariable analyses or computation of cross correlations and power spectra must frequently be applied; long series of measurements are thereby needed, and still the statistical dependencies may only be obtainable in the linear approximation.

The most characteristic feature in the application of neural networks, and the SOM in particular is that a physically or chemically definable process model is not necessary. The map is solely computed from the set of measurements obtained over a training period (the map can also be made to adapt to new measurements continuously). After this *unsupervised* training period, the display can be labeled by calibration measurements, and it will be possible to monitor the process state by following the trajectory of the operating point on the map. The SOM display facilitates a direct control of the process, e.g., by using control variables that have the largest gradient on the map: the operating personnel will easily learn to spot the most effective control variables in each situation, and to adjust them in such a direction that the trajectory will be guided to the allowed region in the shortest way.

Miscellaneous process applications have been reported in the review article (Kohonen et al. 1996).

5.4. Applications to Telecommunications

In *telecommunications*, one may monitor *telephone traffic* and *telecommunication networks* (Tang and Simula 1996) by the SOM on the basis of their statistics, but there also exist direct tasks in the *telecommunications technology* for which the SOM would bring about viable solutions. One of them is the *quadrature-amplitude modulation (QAM)* in digital communications, especially adaptive demodulation, equalization, and intersymbol and interchannel noise cancellation (Kohonen et al. 1992). Such tasks are commonplace, e.g., in high-definition television (HDTV). Another task for which SOM solutions have been suggested and demonstrated by simulation is efficient *encoding and decoding of images* by a pair of SOMs, which tolerate transmission errors much better than the more traditional vector quantization methods (Kangas and Kohonen 1994).

5.5. Maps of Document Collections (WEBSOM)

Above we used the SOM to describe signals, states, and other metric variables. We shall show in the following that it is possible to perform the clustering of free-text, natural-language documents, too, if their contents are described statistically by the usage of different words in them. Document word statistics can be shown to be very powerful for the discrimination between different documents and their topic areas.

A rather old idea to characterize texts is to use their word histograms for discrimination. However, with the increasing number of documents, and if no restrictions are set to their language, the vocabulary to be taken into account may become huge, e.g., in Internet documents over a million words may be used. A trivial method to reduce the dimensionality of the problem would be to consider histograms of the most important words only, but this requires plenty of manual work, and the discriminatory power of such recduced representations is radically reduced. Nonetheless it will always be a good strategy to omit the words that occur most seldom, and then it is possible to reduce the vocabulary to, say, 100 000 items. But such histograms would still correspond to real vectors of dimensionality 100 000, which means computationally very heavy comparison operations.

The histograms, however, are usually very sparsely occupied: in one document one may use only, say, a few dozen different words (let alone the stopwords). Therefore a simple but still effective method to reduce the dimensionality of the representation vectors, without essentially decreasing their discriminatory power, is to *project* them randomly onto a much lower-dimensional Euclidean space. If the original histogram is denoted by vector **n**, and **R** is a rectangular matrix with random but normalized columns, the vectors $\mathbf{x} = \mathbf{Rn}$ can then have a dimensionality of, say, a couple of hundreds, and can be used in place of the **n** as input data vectors to the SOM, without noticeably reducing the classification accuracy.

In an extensive series of experiments (Honkela et al. 1997, Kohonen et al. 1999) the document-clustering SOM called the *WEBSOM* was shown to produce the visual display of the document collection in the following steps: 1. Some preprocessing of the texts is first carried out, removing nontextual symbols and very rare as well as very common words. A stemmer may be used to transform all word forms into their most probable base forms. 2. The word histogram of each document, in which the frequencies of occurrence of all the, say, 50 000 words of the vocabulary are weighted properly and recorded, is projected randomly onto a space of dimensionality 500, thereby obtaining a new representation vector **x** for each document. 3. A SOM is formed using the **x** as input data. 4. The models $\mathbf{m}_i$ formed at the nodes of the SOM are labeled by all those documents that are mapped onto the said node. The nodes are linked to the document data base by address pointers (indexing). 5. Standard browsing software tools are used to read the documents mapped to the SOM nodes.

Two alternative modes of recall are provided in the WEBSOM: it is possible to use a "key document," or a set of keywords as a search argument to find the best-matching node of the SOM, where the browsing may begin.

We have already implemented WEBSOM systems for the following applications:

- Internet Usenet newsgroups; the largest experiment consisted of 85 newsgroups, with a total of over 1 million documents. The size of the SOM was thereby 104 448 nodes.
- News bulletins (in Finnish) of the Finnish News Agency (Finnish Reuter).
- Patent abstracts (English) that are available in electronic form. The largest demonstration consists of 6 840 568 patent abstracts from the U.S., Japan, and European patent offices and the SOM array consists of 1 002 240 nodes.

An example of HTML pages found in browsing is given in Fig. 8. Demonstrations of various WEBSOM displays are available on the Internet at the address http://websom.hut.fi/websom/, where they can be browsed with standard www browsers.

5.6. Other Application Areas of the SOM

Many applications to *medicine* would be possible, but they have barely started to spread. An important mode of use of the SOM is the *profiling of patients* for their diagnosis and treatment. In the analysis of *brain signals*, EEG and MEG, it has been possible to classify various waking and sleep states on the SOM. Many *biochemical analyses* and interpretations of results in *clinical chemistry* already use SOM methods that have been transferred to practice.

In addition to the four main areas mentioned in the beginning of Chap. 5, there exist numerous applications in *finance*, ranging from the analysis and prediction of time series to the classification and evaluation of macroeconomic systems. We have cooperated with the World Bank, analyzing their socioeconomic data in many ways (Deboeck and Kohonen 1998). Analyses of financial performance (Back et al. 1997) and bankrupts of companies (Kiviluoto 1998) are being made using the SOM method. The reform of the Finnish *forest taxation* in 1992, i.e., an option given to the owners to choose between two taxation policies, one of them based on the surface area of the forest, another on the income from its productivity, was based on a cluster analysis performed by the SOM method.

Also one ought to mention the following examples from other fields of science. The Finnish meteorological institute has used the SOM for the *classification of clouds* (Visa et al. 1991) from infrared satellite images (especially in the nighttime), and the astronomical data produced by the *Hubble space telescope* (Naim et al. 1997) have been analyzed by the SOM method; an earlier unknown classification of thousands of galaxies at moderate red shifts has thereby emerged.

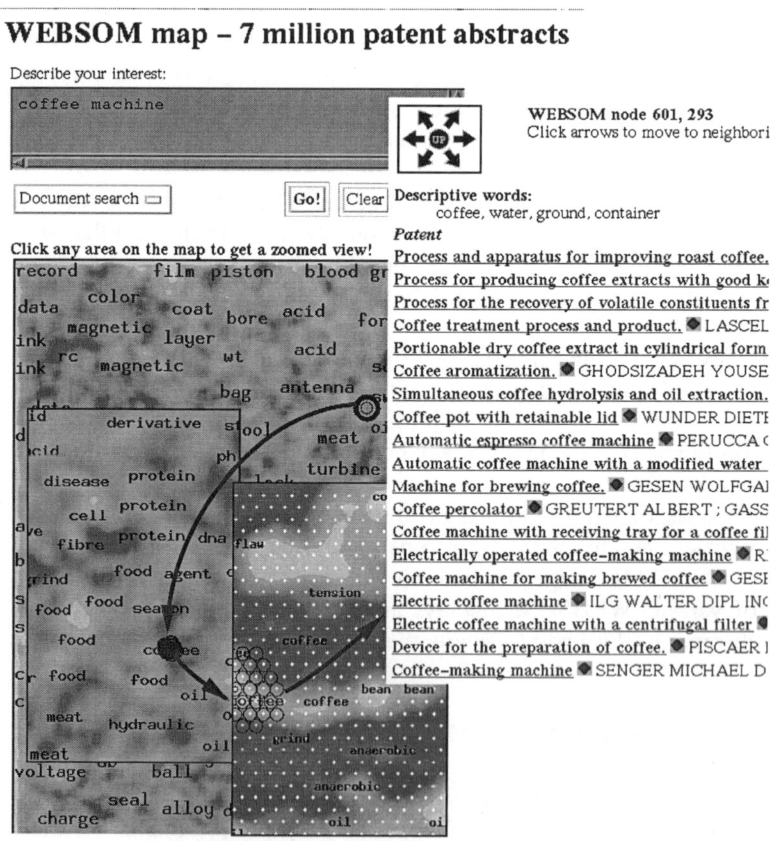

Fig. 8. An example of searching results based on the WEBSOM method.

To survey the whole range of applications of the SOM method in more detail is not possible in this paper. Let it suffice to refer to the list of 3343 research papers as of 1997 on the SOM (Kaski et al. 1998) that is also available at the Internet address http://www.icsi.berkeley.edu/~jagota/NCS/vol1.html.

Acknowledgement. The author wishes to thank Dr. Samuel Kaski for Figs. 2, 3, and 4 and the associated material (Kaski 1997).

References

Alhoniemi, E., Hollmén, J., Simula, O., and Vesanto, J. 1999. Process monitoring and modeling using the self-organizing map. *Integrated Computer-Aided Engineering*, 6:3-14.

Anderberg, M. R. 1973. *Cluster Analysis for Applications*. New York, NY: Academic Press.

Back, B., Sere, K., and Vanharanta, H. 1997. Analyzing financial performance with self-organizing maps. *Proc. WSOM'97, Workshop on Self-Organizing Maps*, Espoo, Finland, pp. 356-361.

Cichocki, A. and Unbehauen, R. 1993. *Neural Networks for Optimization and Signal Processing*. Chichester, England: John Wiley.

Cottrell, M. and J.-C. Fort, 1987. Étude d'un processus d'auto-organisation. *Annales de l'Institut Henri Poincaré*, 23:1-20 (in French)

Cottrell, M., Fort, J.-C., and Pagès, G. 1997. Theoretical aspects of the SOM algorithm. In *Proceedings of WSOM'97, Workshop on Self-Organizing Maps, Espoo, Finland, June 4-6, 1997*, pp. 246-267. Espoo, Finland: Helsinki University of Technology, Neural Networks Research Centre.

de Bodt, E. and Cottrell, M. 1999. Using the Kohonen algorithm for quick initialization of simple competitive learning on algorithm. Prépublications du SAMOS No 112, Université Paris 1.

Deboeck, G. and Kohonen, T., eds. 1998. *Visual Exploration in Finance with Self-Organizing Maps*. Springer-Verlag, London.

de Leeuw, J. and Heiser, W. 1982. Theory of multidimensional scaling. In *Handbook of Statistics*, P. R. Krishnaiah and L. N. Kanal, eds., volume 2, pp. 285-316. Amsterdam: North-Holland.

Demartines, P. 1994. Analyse de données par réseaux de neurones auto-organisés (Data analysis through self-organized neural networks). PhD thesis, Institut National Polytechnique de Grenoble, Grenoble, France.

Demartines, P. and Hérault, J. 1997. Curvilinear component analysis: a self-organizing neural network for nonlinear mapping of data sets. *IEEE Transactions on Neural Networks*, 8:148-154.

Dixon, J. K. 1979. Pattern recognition with partly missing data. *IEEE Transactions on Systems, Man, and Cybernetics*, 9:617-621.

Forgy, E. W. 1965. Cluster analysis of multivariate data: Efficiency vs interpretability of classifications. *Biometrics*, 21:768-769.

Friedman, J. H. 1987. Exploratory projection pursuit. *Journal of the American Statistical Association*, 82:249-266.

Friedman, J. H. and Tukey, J. W. 1974. A projection pursuit algorithm for exploratory data analysis. *IEEE Transactions on Computers*, 23:881-890.

Fyfe, C. and Baddeley, R. 1995. Non-linear data structure extraction using simple Hebbian networks. *Biological Cybernetics*, 72:533-541.

Hartigan, J. 1975. *Clustering Algorithms*. New York, NY: Wiley.

Hastie, T. and Stuetzle, W. 1989. Principal curves. *Journal of the American Statistical Association*, 84:502-516.

Honkela, T., Kaski, S., Lagus, K., and Kohonen, T. 1997. WEBSOM – self-organizing maps of document collections. In *Proc. WSOM'97, Workshop on Self-Organizing Maps, Espoo, Finland, June 4-6*, pp. 310-315. Espoo, Finland: Helsinki University of Technology, Neural Networks Research Centre.

Hotelling, H. 1933. Analysis of a complex of statistical variables into principal components. *Journal of Educational Psychology*, 24:417-441,498-520.

Jain, A. K. and Dubes, R. C. 1988. *Algorithms for Clustering Data*. Englewood Cliffs, NJ: Prentice Hall.

Jardine, N. and Sibson, R. 1971. *Mathematical Taxonomy*. London: Wiley.

Kangas, J. and Kohonen, T. 1994. Developments and applications of the self-organizing map and related algorithms. In *Proc. SPRANN'94, IMACS Int. Symp. on Signal Processing, Robotics, and Neural Networks, Lille, France, April 25-27*, pp. 19-22.

Kaski, S. 1997. Data exploration using self-organizing maps. *Acta Polytechnica Scandinavica, Mathematics, Computing and Management in Engineering Series No. 82*, D.Sc. (Tech.) Thesis, Helsinki University of Technology, Finland.

Kaski, S., Kangas, J., and Kohonen, T. 1998. Bibliography of self-organizing map (SOM) papers: 1981-1997. *Neural Computing Surveys*, 1(3&4):1-176. http://www.icsi.berkeley.edu/~jagota/NCS/vol1.html.

Kaski, S. and Kohonen, T. 1998. Exploratory data analysis by the self-organizing map: Structures of welfare and poverty in the world. In *Neural Networks in Financial Engineering*, A.-P.N. Refenes, Y. Abu-Mostafa, J. Moods, and A. Weigend, eds., pp. 498-507. Singapore: World Scientific.

Kasslin, M., Kangas, J., and Simula, O. 1992. Process state monitoring using self-organizing maps. In *Artificial Neural Networks*, I. Aleksander and J. Taylor, eds., vol. 2, pp. 1532-1534. Amsterdam: North-Holland.

Kiviluoto, K. 1998. Predicting bankruptcies with the self-organizing map. *Neurocomputing*, 21:191-201.

Kohonen, T. 1982a. Self-organized formation of topologically correct feature maps. *Biological Cybernetics*, 43:59-69.

Kohonen, T. 1982b. Clustering, taxonomy, and topological maps of patterns. In *Sixth International Conference on Pattern Recognition*, Munich, Germany, October 19-22, 1982, pp. 114-128.

Kohonen, T. 1990. The self-organizing map. *Proc. IEEE*, 78:1464-1480.

Kohonen, T. 1991. Self-organizing maps: Optimization approaches. In *Artificial Neural Networks*, T. Kohonen, K. Mäkisara, O. Simula, and J. Kangas, eds., Amsterdam, vol. 2, pp. 981-990. Amsterdam: North-Holland.

Kohonen, T. 1992. New developments of learning vector quantization and the self-organizing map. In *SYNAPSE'92, Symposium on Neural Networks; Alliances and Perspectives in Senri, Osaka, Japan*.

Kohonen, T. 1995. *Self-Organizing Maps*. Berlin: Springer.

Kohonen, T., Oja, E., Simula, O., Visa, A., and Kangas, J. 1996. Engineering applications of the self-organizing map. *Proc. IEEE*, 84(10):1358-1384.

Kohonen, T., Kaski, S., Lagus, K., Salojärvi, J., Honkela, J., Paatero, V., and Saarela, A. 1999. Self organization of a massive text document collection. In *Kohonen Maps*, E. Oja and S. Kaski, eds., pp. 171-182. Amsterdam: Elsevier.

Kohonen, T., Raivio, K., Simula, O., and Henriksson, J. 1992. Start-up behaviour of a neural network assisted decision feedback equaliser in a two-path channel. In *Proc. of IEEE Int. Conf. on Communications, Chicago, Illinois, June 14-18*, pp. 1523-1527.

Kruskal, J. B. 1964. Multidimensional scaling by optimizing goodness of fit to a nonmetric hypothesis. *Psychometrika*, 29:1-27.

Kruskal, J. B. and Wish, M. 1978. Multidimensional Scaling. Sage University Paper series on Quantitative Applications in the Social Sciences, number 07-011. Newbury Park, CA: Sage Publications.

Linde, Y., Buzo, A., and Gray, R. M. 1980. An algorithm for vector quantizer design. *IEEE Transactions on Communications*, COM-28:84-95.

Lloyd, S. P. 1957. Least squares quantization in PCM. Unpublished memorandum, Bell Laboratories. (Published in *IEEE Transactions on Information Theory*, 28:129-137, 1982).

Makhoul, J., Roucos, S., and Gish, H. 1985. Vector quantization in speech coding. *Proceedings of the IEEE*, 73:1551-1588.

Mulier, F. and Cherkassky, V. 1995. Self-organization as an iterative kernel smoothing process. *Neural Computation*, 7:1165-1177.

Naim, A., Ratnatunga, K. U., and Griffiths, R. E. 1997. Galaxy morphology without classification: Self-organizing maps. *Astrophys. J. Suppl. Series*, 111, 357-367.

Oja, E. 1983. *Subspace Methods of Pattern Recognition*. Letchworth, England: Research Studies Press.

Oja, E. 1992. Principal components, minor components, and linear neural networks. *Neural Networks*, 5:927-935.

Ripley, B. D. 1996. *Pattern Recognition and Neural Networks*. Cambridge, Great Britain: Cambridge University Press.

Ritter, H., Martinetz, T., and Schulten, K. 1992. *Neural Computation and Self-Organizing Maps: An Introduction*. Reading, MA: Addison-Wesley.

Rubner, J. and Tavan, P. 1989. A self-organizing network for principal component analysis. *Europhysics Letters*, 10:693-698.

Sammon, Jr., J. W. 1969. A nonlinear mapping for data structure analysis. *IEEE Transactions on Computers*, 18:401-409.

Shepard, R. N. 1962. The analysis of proximities: multidimensional scaling with an unknown distance function. *Psychometrika*, 27:125-140; 219-246.

Sneath, P. H. A. and Sokal, R. R. 1973. *Numerical Taxonomy*. San Francisco, CA: Freeman.

Tang, H. and Simula, O. 1996. The optimal utilization of multiservice SCP. In *Intelligent Networks and New Technologies*, J. Norgaard and V.B. Iversen, eds., pp. 175-188. London: Champan & Hall.

Torgerson, W. S. 1952. Multidimensional scaling: I. Theory and method. *Psychometrika*, 17:401-419.

Tryon, R. C. and Bailey, D. E. 1973. *Cluster Analysis*. New York, NY: McGraw-Hill.

Tukey, J. W. 1977. *Exploratory Data Analysis*. Reading, MA: Addison-Wesley.

Ultsch, A. 1993. Knowledge extraction from self-organizing neural networks. In *Information and Classification*, O. Opitz, B. Lausen, and R. Klar, eds., pp. 301-306. London: Springer.

Visa, A., Valkealahti, K., Iivarinen, J., and Simula, O. 1991. Experiences from operational cloud classifier based on self-organizing map. In *Proc. SPIE - The Int. Society for Optical Engineering, Applications of Artificial Neural Networks V*, vol. 2243, pp. 484-495.

Voronoi, G. 1908. Nouvelles applications des paramètres continus à la théorie des formes quadratiques. Deuxième mémoire: Recherches sur les parallélloèdres primitifs. *J. Reine Angew. Math*, 134:198-287.

Webb, A. R. 1995. Multidimensional scaling by iterative majorization using radial basis functions. *Pattern Recognition*, 28:753-759.

Wish, M. and Carroll, J. D. 1982. Multidimensional scaling and its applications. In *Handbook of Statistics*, P. R. Krishnaiah and L. N. Kanal, eds., volume 2, pp. 317-345. Amsterdam: North-Holland.

World Bank 1992. *World Development Report 1992*. New York, NY: Oxford University Press.

Young, F. W. 1985. Multidimensional scaling. In *Encyclopedia of Statistical Sciences*, S. Kotz, N. L. Johnson, and C.B. Read, eds., volume 5, pp. 649-659. New York, NY: Wiley.

Young, G. and Householder, A. S. 1938. Discussion of a set of points in terms of their mutual distances. *Psychometrika*, 3:19-22.

Toward a Theory of Fuzzy Veristic Variables

Ronald R. Yager
Machine Intelligence Institute
Iona College
New Rochelle, NY 10801, USA
yager@panix.com

Abstract: We distinguish between variables having only one solution, possibilistic, and those allowing multiple solutions, veristic. A representation of information contained in statements involving veristic variables is presented. Using this representation we begin to develop a structure for the manipulation of knowledge involving variables that can have multiple solutions. The verity distribution is introduced to capture information about these variables. We show how to combine information involving veristic variables.

1. Introduction

One goal of the work in fuzzy sets has been to provide a formal knowledge manipulation framework can help in the development of artificially intelligent systems. We shall refer to the general framework being developed within the fuzzy set community to accomplish this goal as Approximate Reasoning (AR) [1, 2]. Such a framework must allow for the manipulation of precise numeric information as well as linguistic information, it must allow for the computing with words as well as with numbers [3]. Considerable effort has been focused on the problem of representing imprecise information.

Zadeh [4] indicated some of the different types of variables needed to represent knowledge in AR, in [5, 6] Yager also discussed this issue. Two important classes of variables are possibilistic and veristic variables. Possibilistic variables, which have been widely studied in the approximate reasoning literature, are variables restricted to take one and only one value. Variables such as John's age, your mother's name or the truth value of a proposition are examples of this type of variable, they can only assume one value. While the actual value of a possibilistic variable is unique often our knowledge about the value of these variables is uncertain, here sets and particularly fuzzy sets play an important role in expressing our knowledge about the value of such variables. Let the variable U correspond to John's age, the knowledge ***John is in his twenties***, is represented in the AR framework by a proposition U ***is*** A. Here A = {20, 21, 22, ..., 29}, the set of possible ages of John. In this representation the elements in the subset A are interpreted in a **disjunctive** sense to indicate U = 20 or U = 21 or U = 22 or .... or U = 29. Other knowledge, such as John is young require the use of fuzzy subsets to represent the concept "young". In this case the membership grade in the fuzzy set young allows for a grading in the possibility that U is equal to a particular element, however, here also the use of the fuzzy set is again a disjunctive use. A considerable body of techniques has been developed for the representation and subsequent manipulation of knowledge involving possibilistic variables.

Veristic variables, as opposed to possibilistic ones, are allowed to take any number of solutions from their universes. Variables such as languages spoken by John, Mary's friends and years which I visited Europe are examples of this type of variable. If V is the variable year John lived in Paris we can express the knowledge ***John spent the 1980's in Paris*** in AR as U is B where B = {1980, 1981, 1982 .... 1989}. However, in this case the subset B is used to represent a multiplicity of solutions and is interpreted in a **conjunctive** sense to indicate U = 1980 and U = 1981 and U = 1982 and .... and U = 1989.

Veristic variables have hardly been studied in the literature with a notable exception being a series of articles by Yager [5-9] and work by Dubois & Prade [10]. Our purpose in this work is to help develop a structure useful for manipulating conjunctive information and their associated veristic variables.

2. Representing Veristic Information

First we shall consider the problem of representing knowledge from statements involving veristic variables. Let V be a veristic variable with domain of discourse X. Thus V can take as its solution zero or multiple elements from X. As an example we shall consider the variable **Day John was at work**. In this example our domain is

X = {Monday, Tuesday, Wednesday, Thursday, Friday, Saturday, Sunday}.

Examples of statements that convey information about this veristic variable are

S–1: John worked Monday through Friday.

S–2: John was in work during the early part of the week.

S–3: John worked on the weekend.

S–4: John was not here on Tuesday.

S–5: John worked only Monday and Wednesday.

In each one of these examples we see the centrality of sets in capturing the information about what days John worked. We note the distinction between S–2 and the other statements. In the other statements the boundaries of the associated sets are crisp while in S–2, because of the use of terms of "the early part," we must introduce fuzzy sets. Statement S–4 can be seen to be different from the other statements in that it introduces "negative" information, rather than telling us what days John worked it tells us what days John didn't work, it indicates elements in X which are not solutions to V. Statement S–5 calls our attention to another and perhaps more subtle issue. In this statement we see the inclusion of the term "only" makes this a very strong statement containing a certain exclusionary accept. Compare this with statement S–3, here we don't generally interpret this in an exclusive sense but we interpret this in a inclusive or open way allowing the possibility that he worked other days. This observation requires us to make distinctions between open and closed interpretation.

As a first step toward the formal representation of the knowledge contained in these statements we provide for their expression within the language of AR. Zadeh [1] suggested the symbolic representation of a canonical statement involving the association of a fuzzy subset A with a veristic variable V as V ***isv*** A. Here the copula *isv* is used to indicate that variable is veristic, we note that for possibilistic variables we used the copula *is*.

Based upon our previous observations in addition to denoting that V is veristic we must include information about the manner of association of A with V. By this mean to indicate whether A is to be taken as a set of positive (affirmative) examples of V, as in the case of S-1, or as negative examples of V, as in the case of S-5. In addition we must convey the distinction between a closed (exclusive) or open (inclusive) interpretation of the association. In order to include this information within the approximate reasoning expression we shall use two parameters with the veristic copula *isv*. These parameters are c for closed and n for negative, the lack of appearance of a parameter means its opposite holds. Thus

V *isv* A means open and positive
V *isv(c)* A means closed and positive
V *isv(n)* A means open and negative
V *isv(c, n)* A means closed and negative

As an illustration let V indicate the variable **day John worked** and let B = {Saturday, Sunday) consider the statements

S–7: John worked on the weekend ⇒ V *isv* B
S–8: John worked only on the weekend ⇒ V *isv(c)* B
S–9: John didn't work on the weekend ⇒ V *isv(n)* B
S–10: John only didn't work on the weekend ⇒ V *isv(n, c)* B

Now that we have a means for expressing statements involving veristic variables we now turn to the issue of representing the knowledge contained in these statements in a manner we can manipulatable within the AR system..

Let V be a veristic variable taking values in the space X. We shall associate with V a possibilistic variable V* taking values in the space I^X, the set of all fuzzy subsets of X, it takes as its value one and only one fuzzy subset of X. The value associated with V* is the set of **all** solutions to V. The relationship between V and V*, can best be understood from the following. Let V be the veristic variable "**an** even number less than 13." On the other hand V* is the variable "the **set** of all even numbers less than 13." In this framework the statement V = 8 means that 8 is such an even number. The statement V = 6 and V = 8 means 6 and 8 are such even numbers, we represent this as V *isv* {6, 8}. On the other hand V* is the *set of all* even numbers less then thirteen. In the framework of AR we represent this as

$$V^* \textit{ is } \left(\frac{1}{\{2, 4, 6, 8, 10, 12\}}\right)$$

Thus V is a variable having possibly multiple solutions and V* is the set of all its solutions. The value of V* is a set, whereas the value of V is any of the values in the set.

The information contained in statements involving a veristic variable V, such as S-7 to S-10, tells us something about the value of the associated possibilistic variable V*. Let us now extract this information. Consider first, the canonical statement V *isv* A. What is clear is that the set that is the solution of V* must contain A. For example, the statement John worked on the weekend means that the set consisting of all days John worked must include Saturday and Sunday..Formally this statement induces a possibility distribution Π with respect to the variable V* where for any fuzzy subset $F \in I^X$ $\Pi(F)$ is the degree of containment of A in F. Using Zadeh's definition of containment [11] we get

$$\Pi(F) = 1 \text{ if } A \subseteq F, \ (A(x) \leq F(x) \text{ for all } x)$$

$$\Pi(F) = 0 \text{ if } A \not\subseteq F$$

We see then that the veristic statement expressing V *isv* A is equivalent to an AR statement V* *is* A* where A* is a subset of I^X such that $A^*(F) = 1$ if $A \subseteq F$ and $A^*(F) = 0$ if $A \not\subseteq F$.

Consider now the expression V *isv(c)* A. The statement John worked only on Monday and Wednesday is of this type. This type of statement tells us the exact value of V*, in this case only one set is possible for V*, A. Thus this induces a possibility distribution Π with respect to the variable V* such that $\Pi(A) = 1$ and $\Pi(F) = 0$ for any $F \neq A$. Here again we can associate an AR statement involving the possibilistic variable V^*, V* *is* {A}.

Consider now the expression V *isv(n)* A. This is exemplified by the statement John didn't work on the weekend. This type of statement is telling us which elements from X are not in the solution set of V^*. This type of statement induces a possibility distribution with V* such that

$$\Pi(F) = 1 \text{ if } F \subseteq \overline{A}$$

$$\Pi(F) = 0 \text{ if } F \not\subseteq \overline{A}$$

Thus V *isv(n)* A generates a statement V* *is* A° where A° is a subset of I^X such that $A°(F) = 1$ if $F \subseteq \overline{A}$ and $A°(F) = 1$ if $F \not\subseteq \overline{A}$.

Finally, consider the case V *isv(c, n)* A. This is exemplified by John only didn't work on the weekend. In this case we are again provided with exact information about the value of V*. Here we induce a possibility distribution on V* such that $\Pi(\overline{A}) = 1$ and $\Pi(F) = 0$ for all $F \neq \overline{A}$. Thus the veristic statement V *isv(c, n)* A is equivalent to V* *is* $\{\overline{A}\}$.

In the preceding we have shown how we could convert information about a veristic variable V into information about the associated possibilistic variable V*, corresponding to the set of all solutions to V. One advantage of this is that this allows us to use the well developed machinery of possibilistic variables to manipulate the knowledge. However, it also brings with it a disadvantage, the space I^X on which V* takes its values is much more complicated then the space X on which V takes its values. In the case of the veristic variables we must alternatively work in these two spaces trying as much as possible to work in X.

3. Verity and Possibility Distributions

In the preceding we have shown that statements involving veristic variables induce proposition of the form V* *is* W where V* is a possibilistic variable whose value is the ***set*** of solutions of V and W is a subset of the space I^X. While formally our information is represented in terms of V* we often are required to provide information about the individual elements of X. In order to provide this information we shall introduce two distributions of X, verity and rebuff.

From the statement V* *is* W we induce a verity measure [4, 7, 8] on the space X such that for any $x \in X$

$$Ver(x) = Min_{F \subseteq X}[F(x) \vee \overline{W}(F)]$$

We see that Ver(x) is the minimal degree of membership of x in any subset that can possibly be the collection of all solutions to V. Thus Ver(x) can be seen as the minimal support for x being a solution of V. It is a lower boundary on the truth of the statement "x is a solution of V."

In the special case in which W is a crisp subset the above definition reduces to

$$Ver(x) = Min_{F \in W}[F(x)],$$

Ver(x) is the minimal membership grade in any subset in W.

Let us look at the verity distribution obtained from the primary types of veristic propositions.

1. V *isv* A. This induces V* *is* W where W(F) = 1 if $A \subseteq F$ and W(F) = 0 if $A \subseteq F$ hence

$$Ver(x) = Min_{F \in I^X}[F(x) \vee \overline{W}(F)] = Min_{F \in W}[F(x)],$$

since $F \in W$ if $A \subseteq F$ and F = A is the minimal set such $A \subseteq F$ then Ver(x) = A(x).

2.V *isv(c)* A. This induces the statement V* *is* {A}. Using our definition for $Ver(x) = Min_F[F(x) \vee \overline{W}(F)]$ and since in case W(A) = 1 and W(F) = 0 for $F \neq A$ here again we get Ver(x) =A(x).

3. V *isv(n)* A. Here we have V* *is* W* where W(F) = 1 if $F \subseteq \overline{A}$ and W(F) = 0 if $F \not\subseteq \overline{A}$. With $Ver(x) = Min_{F \in I^X}[F(x) \vee \overline{W}(F)] = Min_{F \subseteq \overline{A}}[F(x)]$. Since the null set, $\varnothing$ is such that $\varnothing \subseteq \overline{A}$ we get $Ver(x) = \varnothing(x) = 0$. For any x, it provides no support. This as it should be for the statement "John didn't work on the weekend" provides no support for any day as one that John worked.

4. V *isv(n, c)* A. We induce the proposition V* *is* W where $W = \{\overline{A}\}$. Using $Ver(x) = Min_F\{F(x) \vee \overline{W}(F)\}$ and the fact that $W(\overline{A}) = 1$ and W(F) = 0 for all $F \neq \overline{A}$ then $Ver(x) = \overline{A}(x)$. Thus here the verity is equal to the negation of A, for example the statement "John only didn't work on the weekend" would provide complete support for the truth of the statement, "John worked on Tuesday."

We now turn to the second distribution over X which we shall use to measure our knowledge about solutions to V, we call this the measure of possibility. Again consider the proposition V* *is* W, W being a subset of I^X. We define Possibility as a mapping $X \to [0, 1]$ such that

$$Poss(x) = Max_F[F(x) \wedge W(F)].$$

It can be seen as a measure of the possibility of x being a solution, it is an upper bound on the truth that x is a solution of V. If W is crisp then $Poss(x) = Max_{F \in W}[F(x)]$.

Let us now consider the prototypical statements involving veristic variables.

1. V *isv* A. This induces V* *is* W where W(F) = 1 if $A \subseteq F$ and W(F) = 0 if $F \not\subseteq A$. With $Poss(x) = Max_{F \in W}[F(x)]$ and since for any A, $A \subseteq X$, and X(x) =1 for all x then Poss(x) = 1. Thus this type of statement offers no refutation about any x, all x are still possible values for V.

2. V *isv(c)* A. This induces V* *is* {A} and therefore

$$Poss(x) = Max_F[F(x) \wedge W(F)] = A(x).$$

3. V *isv(n)*. This induces V* *is* W where W(F) = 1 if $F \subseteq \overline{A}$ W(F) = 0 if $F \not\subseteq \overline{A}$. Thus here we have

$$Poss(x) = Max_F[F(x) \wedge W(F)] = Max_{F \in W}[F(x)]$$

Since $\overline{A}$ is the largest set in W we have $Poss(x) = \overline{A}(x)$.

4. V *isv(n, c)* A. This induces V* *is* $\{\overline{A}\}$. It is easy to see that Poss(x) = 1 - A(x).

Let us in the following summarize these results.

Statement	**Ver(x)**	**Poss(x)**
V *isv* A	A(x)	1
V *isv(c)* A	A(x)	A(x)
V *isv(n)* A	0	1 – A(x)
V *isv(n, c)* A	1 - A(x)	1 – A(x)

Let us consider some special cases of V* *is* W, not necessarily induced by one of our basic type of types. First consider the case in which we have no information, $W = I^X$. Here Ver(x) = 0. and Poss(x) = 1. Consider now the case in which W = ∅. This corresponds to a situation in which the information about V* is conflicting. Here W(F) = 0 for all F, hence $Ver(x) = Min_F(F(x) \vee \overline{W}(F) = 1$ and $Poss(x) = Max(W(F) \wedge F(x)) = 0$.

As we have already shown in the case in which the value of V* is exactly known, W = {A}, we have Verity(x) = A(x) and Poss = A(x). Thus if we know exactly the set of solutions to V then the upper and lower support for the statement x is a solution of V is its membership in the set corresponding to the solutions.

Let us now consider under what circumstances we would get Ver(x) = 1 and Poss(x) = 1. In order to get Ver(x) = 1 we need $1 = Min_F[F(x) \vee \overline{W}(F)]$. Here we see that we need F(x) = 1 for all sets for which W(F) ≠ 0. Thus in order to get Ver(x) = 1, any set that has any possibility of being the solution of V* must have x as a full solution. In order to get Poss(x) = 1 we need $Max_F(F(x) \wedge W(F)) = 1$. This implies that there must exist at least set F in which x is a full member, F(x) = 1, and which is completely possible as a solution to V*. The implication of the condition Ver(x) = 1 and Poss(x) = 1 is x is definitely a solution to V.

Let us now consider under what circumstances we would get Ver(x) = 0 and Poss(x) = 0. In order to get Ver(x) = 0 we need $0 = \text{Min}_F[F(x) \vee \overline{W}(F)]$. This implies that we need at least one F such that $\overline{W}(F) = 1$, F is fully possible as the solution of V* and F(x) = 0, x is not a member of x. In order to get Poss(x) = 0 we need $\text{Max}_F(F(x) \wedge W(F)) = 0$. In particular this requires that for any solution set F that is not impossible, $W(F) \neq 0$, we must have F(x) = 0

In the following we summarize these observations as follows:

Verity(x)	**Poss(x)**	**Implication**
1	1	x is definitely a solution to V
0	0	x is definitely not a solution to V
0	1	we have no information about x
1	0	our information about x is conflicting

4. Combination of Veristic Information

Each piece of knowledge provided by a veristic statement provides partial information about the set of solutions of the variable of interest. For example the statements "Mary and her husband are friends of Bill" and "Tom is a friend of Bill" each provide some information about the people that are friends of Bill. In order to get the totality of information about the friends of Bill we must combine the pieces of information. In this section we consider the issue of combination of veristic propositions. Here we shall see that while we must formally work in the domain of V* our goal is to try and get operations we can perform in the domain of V.

We shall briefly recall some results from AR regarding the combination of possibilistic variables. [1]. If U is a possibilistic variable with domain Y and G_1 and G_2 are two fuzzy subsets over Y then the statement U *is* G_1 ***and*** U *is* G_2 is equivalent to the statement U *is* G where $G = G_1 \cap G_2$, that is $G(y) = \text{Min}[G_1(y), G_2(y)]$. On the other hand the statement U *is* G_1 ***or*** U *is* G_2 is equivalent to the statement U *is* H where $H = G_1 \cup G_2$, that $H(y) = \text{Max}[G_1(y), G_2(y)]$.

Since statements involving a veristic variable V get translated into propositions involving the possibilistic variable V* the process of combining the partial information provided about veristic variables becomes one of combining the statements involving the associated possibilistic variables, a task which we can handle as just noted.

Let us now look at the fusion of different types of veristic propositions. Consider two basic veristic propositions

P_1:V *isv* $A_1 \Rightarrow$ V* *is* W_1

P_2: V *isv* $A_2 \Rightarrow$ V* *is* W_2

Here $W_1(F) = 1$ if $A_1 \subseteq F$ and $W_1(F) = 0$ if $A_1 \not\subseteq F$ and $W_2(F) = 1$ if $A_2 \subseteq F$ and $W_2(F) = 0$ if $A_2 \not\subseteq F$. The conjunction translates into V* *is* $W_1 \cap W_2$ = V* *is* W. We see that W(F) = 1 if $W_1(F) = W_2(F) = 1$ that is if $A_1 \subseteq F$ and $A_2 \subseteq F$.

However $A_1 \subseteq F$ and $A_2 \subseteq F$ implies that $A_1 \cup A_2 \subseteq F$. We see this as follows, $A_1 \subseteq F$ means that $\overline{A}_1 \cup F$.and $A_2 \subseteq F$.means $\overline{A}_2 \cup F$ and their conjunction is $(\overline{A}_1 \cap \overline{A}_2) \cup F$ which means $(A_1 \cup A_2) \subseteq F$. Thus we see that W(F) =1 if $A_1 \cup A_2 \subseteq F$ hence we get that V *isv* A_1 ***and*** V *isv* $A_2 \equiv$ V *isv* $(A_1 \cup A_2)$. Thus the *anding* of two simple affirmative veristic statements results a simple veristic statement whose solution values are the union of the solution values from the individual statements.. This result is actually very intuitive. From the statements "Mary and John are friends of Bill" and "Tom and Ann are friends of Bill" it is natural to consider that the union of these, Mary, John, Tom and Ann are friends of Bill.

Consider now the disjunction of affirmative veristic statements V *isv* A_1 ***or*** V *isv* A_2 this is equivalent to V* *is* $W_1 \cup W_2$ = V* *is* M. Here we see that M(F) = 1 if $W_1^*(F)$ or $W_2^*(F) = 1$, that is if $A_1 \subseteq F$ or $A_2 \subseteq F$. Since $A_j \subseteq F$ is equivalent to $\overline{A}_j \cup F$ we have $(\overline{A}_1 \cup F) \cup (\overline{A}_2 \cup F) = \overline{A}_1 \cup \overline{A}_2 \cup F$ which is equivalent to $A_1 \cap A_2 \subseteq F$. Thus here M(F) = 1 if $A_1 \cap A_2 \subseteq F$. From this we see that V *isv* A_1 ***or*** V *isv* $A_2 \equiv$ V *isv* $(A_1 \cap A_2)$, the *oring* of two basic veristic statements leads to a intersection of their solution sets.

Thus we see that in the case of basic veristic propositions of the type V *isv* A_j the conjunction(anding) and disjunction(oring) of these can be easily carried out at the level of these basic statements

V *isv* A_1 ***and*** V *isv* A_2 ***and*** ....***and*** V *isv* A_n = V *isv* $\cup_j A_j$

V *isv* A_1 ***or*** V *isv* A_2 ***or*** ....***or*** V *isv* A_n = V *isv* $\cap_j A_j$

Because of this we can directly combine the associated verity and possibility distributions. If V *isv* A_j induces Ver_j then the anding of these statements induces a verity distribution Ver such that $Ver(x) = Max_j[Ver_j(x)]$ On the other hand the disjunction(oring) of these statements induces $\widehat{Ver}$ where $\widehat{Ver}(x) = Min_j[Ver_j(x)]$. In addition the possibility distribution resulting from the the combination, conjunction or disjunction, also gives us possibility distribution with one for all x.

Consider now the negative type veristic propositions V *isv(n)* A_1 and V *isv(n)* A_2. It can be shown in a similar manner that

V *isv(n)* A_1 ***and*** V *isv(n)* A_2 = V *isv(n)* $(A_1 \cup A_2)$

V *isv(n)* A_1 ***or*** V *isv(n)* A_2 = V *isv(n)* $(A_1 \cap A_2)$

Thus again we see the reflection of operations.

More generally if V *isv(n)* A_j for j = 1 to q are a collection of negating statements then their conjunction

V *isv(n)* A_1 ***and*** V *isv(n)* A_2 ***and*** ..... ***and*** V *isv(n)* A_q = V *isv(n)* $\cup_j A_j$

while for their disjunction we have

V *isv(n)* A_1 ***or*** V *isv(n)* A_2 ***or*** ..... ***or*** V *isv(n)* A_q = V *isv(n)* $\cap_j A_j$

Again we see the conjunctions and disjunctions of these similar type of pure negating statements can be carried out at the level variable V.

The situation with respect to closed type of veristic propositions is different.

Consider the two propositions V *isv(c)* A_1, and V *isv(c)* A_2 these induce the propositions V* *is* $\widetilde{W}_1$ and V* *is* $\widetilde{W}_2$ where $\widetilde{W}_1 = \{A_1\}$ and $\widetilde{W}_2 = \{A_2\}$. Taking the conjunction of these two pieces of knowledge, V *isv(c)* A_1 ***and*** V *isv(c)* A_2, we get V* *is* $\widetilde{W}_1 \cap \widetilde{W}_2$. We see that if $A_1 = A_2 = A$ then $\widetilde{W}_1 \cap \widetilde{W}_2 = \{A\}$ and we can conclude that V *isv(c)* A ***and*** V *isv(c)* A = V *isv* A. On the other hand if $A_1 \neq A_2$ then $\widetilde{W}_1 \cap \widetilde{W}_2 = \varnothing$ and we get that V *isv(c)* A_1 ***and*** V *isv(c)* A_2 = V* *is* $\varnothing$, we have a conflict in our information.. Taking the disjunction of these statements, V *isv(c)* A_1 ***or*** V *isv(c)* A_2 we get V* *is* $\widetilde{W}_1 \cup \widetilde{W}_2$. If $A_1 = A_2 = A$ we get V *isv(c)* A. If $A_1 \neq A_2$ then we get V* *is* $\{A_1, A_2\}$ In the case of negated closed statement, V *isv(n, c)* A_j the analysis is the same as the preceding with $\overline{A}_j$ replacing A_j.

At this point it is worth pointing out the distinction between three statements: V *isv* $\varnothing$, V *isv(n)* X and V* *is* $\varnothing$. The statement V *isv* $\varnothing$ gets translated into V* *is* W where W is such that W(F) = 1 if $\varnothing \subseteq F$. Since every F satisfies this condition this is equivalent to V^* *is* I^X, it provides no information, it just says all combination of solutions are possible and eliminates no solution. Consider now V *isv(n)* X this translates into V* *is* W when W(F) =1 if $F \subseteq \overline{X}$, where $F \subseteq \varnothing$. Thus this has W = $\{\varnothing\}$, it says the solution to V* is the set $\varnothing$, the empty set. Thus this says that V has no solutions in X. But it is important to emphasize that in this case V* has a solution, $\varnothing$. Consider now V* *is* $\varnothing$ in this case W = $\varnothing$, it says that V* has no solution, since V* is a possibilistic variable and must have at least one solution then it implies a conflict. It should be noted that the statement V* *is* $\varnothing$ should not be representable by a simple veristic proposition but requires the conjunction of at least two propositions.

Thus far we considered the fusion of like veristic statements and have shown we can perform these fusions at the level of the veristic variable V, we don't need to use the variable V*. Let us now look at the situation in which we are combining different modes of veristic statements. Consider V *isv* A_1 and V *isv(n)* A_2. In our situation of John's working days these statements could be "John works on Tuesday and Wednesday" and "John didn't work on Thursday". From the above we get V* *is* W_1 and V* *is* W_2 where $W_1(F) = 1$ if $A_1 \subseteq F$ and $W_1(F) = 0$ if $A_1 \not\subset F$ and where $W_2(F) = 1$ if $F \subseteq \overline{A}_2$ and $W_2(F) = 0$ if $F \not\subset \overline{A}_2$.

Let us consider the conjunction of these statements, V *isv* A_1 ***and*** V *isv(n)* A_2. Here we obtain V_1^* *is* W where $W = W_1 \cap W_2$, $W(F) = 1$ if $W_1(F) = 1$ and $W_2(F) = 1$. One thing that appears clear is that elements appearing in both A_1 and A_2 imply some kind of conflict. Let us define Conf = $\text{Max}_x[A_1(x) \wedge A_2(x)]$. If conflict = 1 then there exists some element, x*, that is both fully supported and fully denied. In this case we note that if $W_1(F) = 1$, then $A_1 \subseteq F$ and hence $F(x^*) = 1$. If $W_2(F) = 1$ then $F \subseteq \overline{A}_2$, $F(x^*) \leq 1 - A_2(x^*)$ and hence $F(x^*) = 0$, this can't exist so we see that in this case $W^* = \varnothing$.

More generally we can consider the following. Consider some arbitrary x where $A_1(x) = \alpha$ and $A_2(x) = \beta$. For any F to satisfy $W_1(F) = 1$ then $F(x) \geq \alpha$ and to satisfy $W_2(F) = 1$ we require $F \subseteq \overline{A_2}$, $F(x^*) \leq 1 - \beta$, hence to satisfy $W(F) = 1$ we require $\alpha \leq 1 - \beta$. Thus if there exists x* such that $A_1(x^*) > 1 - A_2(x^*)$ then $W(F) = 0$ for all F and thus $W = \varnothing$. Consider now the situation in which $A_1(x) \leq 1 - A_2(x)$ for all x. If $W_1(F) = 1$ then $F(x) \geq A_1(x)$ and if $W_2(F) \geq 1$ then $F(x) \leq 1 - A_2(x)$ thus $W(F) = 1$ if $F(x) \geq A_1(x)$ and $F(x) \leq 1 - A_2(x)$

Consider now the verity of x in this case of this mixed conjunction. Using our definition of verity, $Ver(x) = Min_F[F(x) \vee \overline{W}(F)] = A_1(x)$ Consider now Poss, $Poss(x) = Max_F[W(F) \wedge F(x)] = 1 - A_2(x)$

Thus we have the following results for calculating the the values of Ver(x) and Poss(x) for the conjunction V *isv* A_1 ***and*** V *isv(n)* A_2.

1. If $A_1 \not\subset \overline{A_2}$ then the objects are conflicting and $W = \varnothing$. In this case for x $Ver(x) = 1$ and $Poss(x) = 0$

2. If $A_1 \subseteq \overline{A_2}$ then we get $Ver(x) = Ver_1(x)$ and $Poss(x) = Poss_1(x)$

We now have a very simple way of conjuncting multiple statements involving collections of mixed simple affirmative and negative type statements. Let our statements be V *isv* A_j for j = 1 to n and V *isv(n)* B_i for i = 1 to m. We first conjunct all the like type statements, using our previously obtained results. Here we obtain $A = \cup A_j$ and $B = \cup B_i$ Then the overall verity and possibility measures resulting from the fusion are $Ver(x) = A(x)$ and $Poss(x) = 1 - B(x)$

5. Conclusion

We distinguished between variables having only one solution, possibilistic, and those allowing multiple solutions, veristic. A representation of information contained in statements involving veristic variables was presented. This representation allowed us to develop a structure for the manipulation of knowledge involving variables which allow multiple solutions. The verity distribution was introduced to capture information about these variables. We showed how to combine information involving veristic variables.

6. References

[1] Zadeh, L. A, A Theory of Approximate Reasoning, *Machine Intelligence, Vol. 9*, edited by Hayes, J., Michie, D. and Mikulich, L. I., Halstead Press: New York, 1979, pp. 149-194.

[2] Yager, R. R., Deductive Approximate Reasoning Systems, *IEEE Transactions on Knowledge and Data Engineering* 3, 1991, pp. 399-414.

[3] Zadeh, L. A., Fuzzy Logic ≈ Computing with Words, *IEEE Transactions on Fuzzy Systems* 4, 1996, pp. 103-111.

[4] Zadeh, L. A., Toward a Theory of Fuzzy Information Granulation and its Centrality in Human Reasoning and Fuzzy Logic, *Fuzzy Sets and Systems* 90, 1997, pp. 111-127.

[5] Yager, R. R. , Some Questions Related to Linguistic Variables, *Busefal* 10, 1982, pp. 54-65.

[6] Yager, R. R., On Different Classes of Linguistic Variables Defined Via Fuzzy Subsets, *Kybernetes* 13, 1984 , pp. 103-110.

[7] Yager, R. R., Set Based Representations of Conjunctive and Disjunctive Knowledge, *Information Sciences* 41, 1987, pp. 1-22.

[8] Yager, R. R., Toward a Theory of Conjunctive Variables, *Int. J. of General Systems* 13, 1987, pp. 203-227.

[9] Yager, R. R, Reasoning with Conjunctive Knowledge, *Fuzzy Sets and Systems* 28, 1988, pp. 69-83

[10] Dubois, D. & Prade, H, Incomplete conjunctive information, *Computational Mathematics Applications* 15, 1988

[11] Zadeh, L. A., Fuzzy Sets, *Information and Control* 8, 1965, pp. 338-353

A generalizing look at sigma counts of fuzzy sets

Maciej Wygralak

Adam Mickiewicz University
Faculty of Mathematics and Computer Science
Matejki 48/49, 60-769 Poznań, Poland
E-mail: wygralak@math.amu.edu.pl

Abstract: The scalar approach to cardinalities of fuzzy sets is convenient in applications, and therefore favoured by many practitioners. The most commonly used scalar cardinality of a fuzzy set is its sigma count. We like to propose a generalizing axiomatic approach to sigma counts of fuzzy sets. It brings together all standard concepts of scalar cardinality and, moreover, offers us infinitely many new options. The case of fuzzy sets with max and min operations as well as that of fuzzy sets with triangular norm-based operations will be considered.

1. Introduction

At the very beginning, in order to avoid any notational and terminological misunderstanding, we introduce the following conventions. First, fuzzy sets in a universe **M**, i.e. functions $\mathbf{M} \to [0,1]$, will be denoted by single capitals in italic, whereas single bold capitals will denote sets in **M**. In particular, we put $T := 1_\emptyset$ and $M := 1_\mathbf{M}$, where $:=$ stands for 'equals by definition' and $1_\mathbf{D}$ symbolizes the characteristic function of a set $\mathbf{D} \subset \mathbf{M}$. Second, our discussion will be limited to finite fuzzy sets, i.e. to fuzzy sets with finite supports, which play the central role from the viewpoint of applications. Let $\mathrm{FFS} := \{D \in [0,1]^\mathbf{M}\colon \mathrm{supp}(D)$ is finite$\}$ and $\mathrm{FCS} := \{D \in \{0,1\}^\mathbf{M}\colon \mathrm{supp}(D)$ is finite$\}$, i.e. FFS denotes the family of all finite fuzzy sets in **M**, whereas the family of all finite crisp sets in **M** will be denoted by FCS. From now on, if not emphasized otherwise, the phrase 'fuzzy set' will mean 'finite fuzzy set'.

Cardinality seems to be one of the most fascinating and enigmatic aspects of fuzzy sets. If one likes to construct a notion of cardinality for fuzzy sets, the main difficulty and difference in comparison with sets lies in graduation of membership. Generally, counting and cardinal calculus under fuzziness become a challenging task which is more advanced than in the case of sets. Motivations for undertaking that task lie in mathematical theory and multiple applications, e.g. to communication with data bases as well as information and intelligent systems, computing with words, the computational theory of perceptions, decision-making in a fuzzy environment (see e.g. [1, 15, 16]. The subject literature offers many approaches to the notion of cardinality of a fuzzy set (reviews and references can be found e.g. in [1, 10, 12]). The dominating options are in practice those in which the cardinality of $A \in \mathrm{FFS}$ is understood as

(i) a single nonnegative integer or real number,
(ii) a convex fuzzy set in $\mathbb{N} := \{0, 1, 2, \ldots\}$.

The "fuzzy" approach (ii), offering fuzzy perception of cardinality, gives us the most complete and adequate cardinal information about A at the price of relatively high representational and operational complexity. The approach (i), offering scalar perception of cardinality, is simpler and more convenient in every respect and, therefore, favoured by many practitioners despite of obvious disadvantages. In this paper, we focus our attention on the scalar approach (i). Some references to (ii) are made in Section 4.

The most commonly used scalar cardinality of A is the so-called *sigma count*

$$sc_A = \Sigma_{x \in \mathrm{supp}(A)} A(x),$$

possibly rounded to the nearest integer, and its modified forms

$$sc_A^p = \Sigma_{x \in \mathrm{supp}(A)} (A(x))^p \quad \text{with} \quad p > 0.$$

Moreover, the subject literature offers us for instance $|\mathrm{core}(A)|$, $|\mathrm{supp}(A)|$, $|A_{\geq t}|$ and $|A_{>t}|$ with a suitable t as candidates for scalar cardinality of A (see e.g. [2-6, 11, 15]). The following standard notation is used in the above:

$A_{\geq t} := \{x \in \mathbf{M}\colon\ A(x) \geq t\}$ with $t \in (0,1]$, *(t-cut set of A)*

$A_{>t} := \{x \in \mathbf{M}\colon\ A(x) > t\}$ with $t \in [0,1)$, *(sharp t-cut set of A)*

$\mathrm{core}(A) := A_{\geq 1}$, $\mathrm{supp}(A) := A_{>0}$. *(core and support of A)*

In this paper, we like to present an axiomatic approach to scalar cardinalities of fuzzy sets. It brings together the above mentioned concepts and, moreover, offers infinitely many new options. In essence, it leads to a generalizing look at sigma counts in which sums of values of nondecreasing functions of membership values, instead of sums of membership values, are taken as scalar cardinalities. In Section 2, the case of fuzzy sets with the standard max and min operations is considered, whereas Section 3 contains a discussion devoted to fuzzy sets with triangular norms and conorms.

2. Axiomatization of scalar cardinalities of fuzzy sets with max and min operations

In the first step, we like to use the traditional algebra of fuzzy sets: $A \cup B$, $A \cap B$ and $A \times B$, respectively, do symbolize the sum, the intersection and the cartesian product of $A, B \in \mathrm{FFS}$, respectively, defined in the pointwise way via $\vee := \max$ and $\wedge := \min$ operations. The sum of a family $(A_e)_{e \in \mathbf{J}}$ with $\mathbf{J} \neq \emptyset$ as a finite set of indices will be denoted by $\bigcup_{e \in \mathbf{J}} A_e$. So, $A = \bigcup_{x \in \mathrm{supp}(A)} A(x)/x$ with a/x as a singleton supported by x. Finally, A' denotes the standard complement of A ($A'(x) := 1 - A(x)$). Throughout the paper, $A \subset B$ means that A is included in B ($A(x) \leq B(x)$ for each x), whereas the equality $A = B$ denotes the identity $A(x) = B(x)$ at each x.

Definition 2.1. A function σ: FFS$\to[0,\infty)$ is called a *scalar cardinality* if the following postulates are satisfied for each $a, b\in[0,1]$, $x, y\in\mathbf{M}$ and $A, B\in$FFS:

(P1) $\sigma(1/x) = 1$,

(P2) $a \le b \Rightarrow \sigma(a/x) \le \sigma(b/y)$,

(P3) $A\cap B = T \Rightarrow \sigma(A\cup B) = \sigma(A) + \sigma(B)$.

If σ does fulfil (P1)-(P3), then $\sigma(A)$ will be called a *scalar cardinality of* $A\in$FFS.

The system of postulates (P1)-(P3) seem to be quite simple and natural. Let us formulate a few basic properties of scalar cardinalities which are more or less immediate consequences of (P1)-(P3).

Theorem 2.2. *Let* $A, B\in$FFS *and* $A_e\in$FFS *for each* $e\in\mathbf{J}$. *The following properties are then satisfied by each scalar cardinality* σ:

(a) $\sigma(\bigcup_{e\in\mathbf{J}} A_e) = \Sigma_{e\in\mathbf{J}}\, \sigma(A_e)$ *if* $A_e\cap A_{e'} = T$ *for each* $e \ne e'$, *(finite additivity)*

(b) $A\in$FCS $\Rightarrow \sigma(A) = |\operatorname{supp}(A)|$, *(coincidence)*

(c) $\sigma(A) = \sigma(B)$ *whenever there exists a bijection* $\mathbf{b}$: supp$(A)\to$supp(B) *such that* $A(x) = B(\mathbf{b}(x))$ *for each* $x\in\operatorname{supp}(A)$, *(movability)*

(d) $A\subset B \Rightarrow \sigma(A) \le \sigma(B)$, *(monotonicity)*

(e) $|\operatorname{core}(A)| \le \sigma(A) \le |\operatorname{supp}(A)|$, *(boundedness)*

(f) $\sigma(A) + \sigma(B) = \sigma(A\cup B) + \sigma(A\cap B)$, *(valuation property)*

(g) $\sigma(\bigcup_{e\in\mathbf{J}} A_e) \le \Sigma_{e\in\mathbf{J}}\, \sigma(A_e)$. *(finite subadditivity)*

Proof. Indeed, (a) follows from (P3), whereas (b) is a consequence of (a) and (P1). Since (P2) implies $a = b \Rightarrow \sigma(a/x) = \sigma(b/y)$ and both A and B can be viewed as sums of disjoint singletons, (c) follows from (a). As concerns (d), part (a) and (P2) do lead to $\sigma(A) = \Sigma_{x\in\operatorname{supp}(A)}\, \sigma(A(x)/x) \le \sigma(B)$. Since $1_{\operatorname{core}(A)}\subset A\subset 1_{\operatorname{supp}(A)}$, (e) is implied by (d) and (b). As $A\cup B$ and $A\cap B$ are defined via max and min operations, (f) becomes a consequence of (P2) and (a). Finally, (f) implies $\sigma(A\cup B) \le \sigma(A) + \sigma(B)$, which justifies (g). □

So, Definition 2.1 leads us to well-behaving scalar cardinalities. Generally, they are finitely subadditive. For pairwise disjoint fuzzy sets, they are finitely additive. Scalar cardinalities of fuzzy sets being (finite) sets do collapse to the usual cardinalities of those sets. In particular, $\sigma(T) = 0$ and $\sigma(M) = |\mathbf{M}|$ if $\mathbf{M}$ is finite. Any permutation or/and move of membership values does not have any effect on scalar cardinality. Let us formulate a simple characterization of scalar cardinalities.

Theorem 2.3. *A function* σ: FFS$\to[0,\infty)$ *is a scalar cardinality iff*

$$\sigma(A) = \Sigma_{x\in\operatorname{supp}(A)}\, f(A(x)) \quad \text{for each } A,$$

where f: $[0,1]\to[0,1]$ *is such that*

(i) $f(0) = 0$, $f(1) = 1$,

(ii) $f(a) \le f(b)$ *if* $a \le b$.

Proof. If σ: FFS$\to[0, \infty)$ satisfies the postulates (P1)-(P3), then Theorem 2.2(a) implies

$$\sigma(A) = \Sigma_{x\in \mathrm{supp}(A)}\, \sigma(A(x)/x)$$

for each $A\in$FFS. Let f: $[0, 1]\to[0, 1]$ be such that $f(a) := \sigma(a/x)$ with any x (see Theorem 2.2(c)). By Theorem 2.2(b), $f(0) = 0$ and $f(1) = 1$, whereas (P2) says that f satisfies (ii). Conversely, suppose that f fulfils (i)-(ii) and

$$\sigma(A) = \Sigma_{x\in \mathrm{supp}(A)}\, f(A(x))$$

for each $A\in$FFS. By (ii), $\sigma(a/x) = f(a) \le f(b) = \sigma(b/y)$ for $a \le b$, i.e. (P2) is satisfied. (P1) is implied by (i). Since $\mathrm{supp}(A\cup B) = \mathrm{supp}(A) \cup \mathrm{supp}(B)$ and disjoint fuzzy sets do have disjoint supports, (P3) becomes obvious. □

By (i), the summation in the above characterization formula can be extended from supp(A) to the whole universe **M**. Any function f satisfying (i) and (ii) will be called a *cardinality pattern* as it does express our understanding of (scalar) cardinality of a singleton. Moreover, the characterization formula says that the axiomatic approach to scalar cardinalities offered by Definition 2.1 is in essence a generalizing approach to sigma counts. Consequently, the resulting scalar cardinalities can be called *generalized sigma counts*.

Using Theorem 2.3, let us present a few examples of cardinality patterns and derived scalar cardinalities of a fuzzy set $A\in$FFS. The first two examples are examples of integer scalar cardinalities, which without any preassumptions can be applied to fuzzy sets with infinite supports, whereas the others do present generally noninteger scalar cardinalities. Let $D\in$FFS be defined as follows:

$$D = 0.9/x_1 + 1/x_2 + 0.2/x_3 + 0.8/x_4 + 0.5/x_5\,.$$

(A) $f_{1,t}(a) := (1$ if $a \ge t$, else $0)$ with $t\in(0, 1]$. So, we obtain $\sigma(A) = \Sigma_{x\in \mathrm{supp}(A)}\, f_{1,t}(A(x)) = |A_{\ge t}|$. Hence $\sigma(A) = |\mathrm{core}(A)|$ if $t = 1$, which is the smallest scalar cardinality. For instance, $\sigma(D) = 1$ if $t = 1$, $\sigma(D) = 3$ if $t = 0.8$.

(B) $f_{2,t}(a) := (1$ if $a > t$, else $0)$ with $t\in[0, 1)$. Thus, we obtain $\sigma(A) = |A_{>t}|$, i.e. $\sigma(A) = |\mathrm{supp}(A)|$ for $t = 0$ (the largest σ). In this case, $\sigma(D) = 5$ for $t = 0$ and $\sigma(D) = 2$ for $t = 0.8$. One can show that each integer $|A_{>0.5}| \le k \le |A_{\ge 0.5}|$ is the cardinality of a set which is "most similar" to A with respect to the generalized equality in Łukasiewicz logic (see [9, 11]). In this context, the k's are best candidates for integer scalar cardinality of A. Clearly, the nonuniqueness of k disappears if $A(x) \ne 0.5$ for each x. For instance, both the integers 3 and 4 are best integer scalar cardinalities of D.

(C) $f_{3,p}(a) := a^p$ with $p>0$. So, $\sigma(A) = sc^p_A$. Moreover, $\sigma(A)\to|\mathrm{supp}(A)|$ if $p\to0$ and $\sigma(A)\to|\mathrm{core}(A)|$ if $p\to\infty$. For instance, $\sigma(D) = 3.4$ for $p = 1$, $\sigma(D) = 1.8093$ for $p = 6$, and $\sigma(D) = 4.4294$ for $p = 0.25$.

(D) $f_{4,p}(a) := (2^{p-1}a^p$ if $a \le 0.5$, else $1 - 2^{p-1}(1-a)^p)$ with $p>0$. So, $f_{4,2}$ is the classical contrast enhancement operation, whereas $\sigma(A) = sc_A$ if $p = 1$. For instance, $\sigma(D) = 3.48$ if $p = 2$ and $\sigma(D) = 3.4992$ if $p = 4$. Clearly, $f_{4,p}\to\phi$ if $p\to\infty$, where ϕ: $[0, 1]\to[0, 1]$ is such that $\phi(a) = 0$ for $a < 0.5$, $\phi(a) = 1$ for $a > 0.5$, and $\phi(0.5) = 0.5$. Consequently, if $A(x) \ne 0.5$ for each $x\in$**M**, then

$\sigma(A) \to |A_{>0.5}|$ if $p \to \infty$. Finally, $f_{4,p} \to \xi$ if $p \to 0$, where ξ is a cardinality pattern such that $\xi(a) = 0.5$ for each $a \in (0, 1)$.

(E) $f_{5,\lambda}(a) := (a/\lambda$ if $a < 0.5$, $(a+\lambda-1)/\lambda$ if $a > 0.5$, 0.5 if $a = 0.5)$ with $\lambda \geq 1$. So, we get $\sigma(A) = sc_A$ for $\lambda = 1$. For instance, $\sigma(D) = 3.43$ for $\lambda = 1.5$ and $\sigma(D) = 3.47$ for $\lambda = 3$. Again, $f_{5,\lambda} \to \phi$ if $\lambda \to \infty$ (see (D)). Thus, if $A(x) \neq 0.5$ for each x, then $\sigma(A) \to |A_{>0.5}|$ whenever $\lambda \to \infty$.

(F) $f_{6,t,p}(a) := (1$ if $a \geq t$, else $a^p)$ with $t \in (0, 1]$ and $p > 0$. Now, we have $\sigma(A) \to |\mathrm{supp}(A)|$ if $p \to 0$, and $\sigma(A) \to |A_{\geq t}|$ if $p \to \infty$. As one sees, this $\sigma(A)$ with $p = 1$ is a modification of the sigma count sc_A in which "large" (i.e. $\geq t$) membership values are privileged, where t is a given threshold value. For instance, we get $\sigma(D) = 3.7$ if $f = f_{6,0.8,1}$, $\sigma(D) = 4.04$ if $f = f_{6,0.5,2}$, $\sigma(D) = 4.15$ if $f = f_{6,0.8,0.5}$, and $\sigma(D) = 4.51$ if $f = f_{6,0.8,0.25}$.

(G) $f_{6',t,p}(a) := (0$ if $a \leq t$, else $a^p)$ with $t \in (0, 1]$ and $p > 0$. In this case, $\sigma(A) \to |A_{>t}|$ if $p \to 0$, and $\sigma(A) \to |\mathrm{core}(A)|$ if $p \to \infty$. This time $\sigma(A)$ with $p = 1$ is a modification of sc_A which ignores "small" (i.e. $\leq t$) membership values. We have $\sigma(D) = 1.9$ if $f = f_{6',0.8,1}$, $\sigma(D) = 2.45$ if $f = f_{6',0.5,2}$, $\sigma(D) = 1.95$ if $f = f_{6',0.8,0.5}$, and $\sigma(D) = 1.97$ if $f = f_{6',0.8,0.25}$. □

So, very different values of $\sigma(A)$ are generated by various specific cardinality patterns f. The choice of a suitable f is always problem-dependent.

One should ask about two more properties of a scalar cardinality σ which are counterparts of typical properties of sets and their classical cardinalities. Namely, we ask if for each $A, B \in \mathrm{FFS}$ the following equalities hold true:

$$\sigma(A \times B) = \sigma(A) \cdot \sigma(B), \qquad \textit{(cartesian product rule)}$$

$$\sigma(A) + \sigma(A') = |\mathbf{M}|, \quad \mathbf{M} \text{ - finite.} \qquad \textit{(complementarity rule)}$$

Contrary to the valuation property in Theorem 2.2(f), the answer is generally negative. However, one can formulate necessary and sufficient conditions for both properties.

Theorem 2.4. *Let σ be a scalar cardinality, i.e. $\sigma(A) = \Sigma_{x \in \mathrm{supp}(A)} f(A(x))$ for each $A \in \mathrm{FFS}$.*
(a) *σ satisfies the cartesian product rule iff f is such that*

$$f(a \wedge b)) = f(a) \cdot f(b) \quad \textit{for each } a, b \in [0, 1].$$

(b) *If $\mathbf{M}$ is finite, then σ fulfils the complementarity rule iff*

$$f(a) + f(1-a) = 1 \quad \textit{for each } a \in [0, 1].$$

Proof. (a) The implication ($\Leftarrow$) is a consequence of Theorem 2.3 and the equality $\mathrm{supp}(A \times B) = \mathrm{supp}(A) \times \mathrm{supp}(B)$. Suppose $f(a \wedge b)) \neq f(a) \cdot f(b)$ for some a and b. Put $A := a/x$, $B := b/y$ with any x and y. Then $\sigma(A \times B) = f(a \wedge b)) \neq f(a) \cdot f(b) = \sigma(A) \cdot \sigma(B)$, i.e. the cartesian product rule does not hold.

(b) Assume that $\mathbf{M}$ is finite. If $f(a) + f(1-a) = 1$ for each $a \in [0, 1]$, then $\Sigma_{x \in \mathbf{M}} f(A(x)) + \Sigma_{x \in \mathbf{M}} f(1 - A(x)) = |\mathbf{M}|$ for each $A \in \mathrm{FFS}$. So, Theorem 2.3 implies that $\sigma(A) + \sigma(A') = |\mathbf{M}|$.

Suppose that $f(a)+f(1-a) \neq 1$ for some a, and construct $A \in \text{FFS}$ such that $A(x) := a$ for each $x \in \mathbf{M}$. By Theorem 2.3, we get $\sigma(A) = |\mathbf{M}|\, f(a)$ and $\sigma(A') = |\mathbf{M}|\, f(1-a)$, i.e. $\sigma(A) + \sigma(A') \neq |\mathbf{M}|$. □

Applying Theorem 2.4, we easily conclude that the scalar cardinalities in the examples (A) and (B) do satisfy the cartesian product rule. Clearly, the same follows from elementary properties of t-cut sets. The complementarity property is satisfied by the sigma count and, generally, by the scalar cardinalities in (D) and (E) with arbitrary $p \in [0, \infty]$ and $\lambda \in [1, \infty]$, respectively. The other examples of scalar cardinalities do not fulfil the condition in Theorem 2.4(b), i.e. do not satisfy the complementarity rule.

Corollary 2.5. *Assume that the universe* $\mathbf{M}$ *is finite. No scalar cardinality can satisfy at the same time the cartesian product rule and the complementarity rule.*

Proof. Indeed, if a scalar cardinality σ does satisfy the cartesian product rule, then $f(a \wedge b)) = f(a) \cdot f(b)$ for each a and b, i.e. $f(a) = (f(a))^2$ for each a. So, $f(a) \in \{0,1\}$ for each a from the closed unit interval. In particular, $f(0.5) \in \{0,1\}$, i.e. the complementarity rule cannot be fulfilled. □

Since the fulfilment of the cartesian product rule by a scalar cardinality σ does imply that the related (nondecreasing) cardinality pattern f is such that $f(a) \in \{0,1\}$ for each a, we conclude that (A) and (B) are all possible examples of scalar cardinalities fulfilling the cartesian product rule.

Let us define

$$\text{FFS}^* := \{A \in \text{FFS}\colon\ A(x) \neq 0.5 \text{ for each } x \in \mathbf{M}\}$$

and let Φ denote the family of all functions $h\colon [0, 1] \to [0, 1]$ such that

$$h(a) = 0 \quad \text{for } a < 0.5 \quad \text{and} \quad h(a) = 1 \quad \text{for } a > 0.5.$$

So, $\phi \in \Phi$ (see (D)). In reference to the above corollary, one can easily check that if we restrict the discussion to finite $\mathbf{M}$ and to the membership functions from FFS*, then the simultaneous fulfilment of the cartesian product rule and the complementarity rule by a scalar cardinality σ becomes possible. Namely, it holds true iff the σ is such that $f \in \Phi$. Then $\sigma(A) = |A_{>0.5}|$ for each $A \in \text{FFS}^*$.

3. The case of scalar cardinalities of fuzzy sets with triangular operations

Let us recall some basic notions and facts from the theory of triangular norms and conorms (details and further references can be found e.g. in [7, 8]). They will be useful in the main part of the section devoted to scalar cardinalities of fuzzy sets with triangular operations.

A binary operation $\mathbf{t}\colon [0, 1] \times [0, 1] \to [0, 1]$ is a *triangular norm* (*t-norm*, in short) if $\mathbf{t}$ is (i) commutative, (ii) associative, (iii) nondecreasing, and (iv) has 1 as unit. If $\mathbf{s}\colon [0, 1] \times [0, 1] \to [0, 1]$ does satisfy (i)-(iii), and (iv') has 0 as unit, it is called a *triangular conorm* (*t-conorm*, in short). Triangular norms and conorms together will be called *triangular operations* (*t-operations*, in short). If $a\mathbf{s}b = 1-(1-a)\mathbf{t}(1-b)$ for each a and b, we write $\mathbf{s} = \mathbf{t}^*$, and we say that s and **t** are *associated*. A t-norm **t** (t-conorm s, respectively) is called *Archimedean* if it is continuous and $a\mathbf{t}a < a$ ($a\mathbf{s}a > a$, respectively) for each $a \in (0, 1)$. An Archimedean t-operation is called *strict* if it is a strictly increasing function on $(0, 1)\times(0, 1)$.

The following examples of pairs of t-operations will be useful in further discussion:

$a\mathbf{t}_\wedge b := a \wedge b, \quad a\mathbf{s}_\vee b := a \vee b,$

$a\mathbf{t}_a b := ab, \quad a\mathbf{s}_a b := a + b - ab,$ (*algebraic operations*)

$a\mathbf{t}_{S,p} b := (0 \vee (a^p + b^p - 1))^{1/p}, \quad a\mathbf{s}_{Y,p} b := 1 \wedge (a^p + b^p)^{1/p}, \quad p > 0,$

(*Schweizer's t-norm* and *Yager's t-conorm*)

$a\mathbf{t}_E b := ab/(2-a-b+ab), \quad a\mathbf{s}_E b := (a+b)/(1+ab),$ (*Einstein t-operations*)

$a\mathbf{t}_{F,\lambda} b := \log_\lambda(1 + (\lambda^a - 1)(\lambda^b - 1)/(\lambda - 1)),$

$a\mathbf{s}_{F,\lambda} b := 1 - \log_\lambda(1 + (\lambda^{1-a} - 1)(\lambda^{1-b} - 1)/(\lambda - 1)), \quad 1 \neq \lambda > 0,$

(*Frank's t-operations*)

$a\mathbf{t}_{W,\lambda} b := 0 \vee ((a + b - 1 + \lambda ab)/(1+\lambda)),$

$a\mathbf{s}_{W,\lambda} b := 1 \wedge (((1+\lambda)(a + b) - \lambda ab)/(1+\lambda)), \quad \lambda > -1,$ (*Weber's t-operations*)

$a\mathbf{t}_M b := 2/\pi \arccos(1 \wedge (\cos(\pi/2\, a) + \cos(\pi/2\, b))),$

$a\mathbf{s}_M b := 2/\pi \arcsin(1 \wedge (\sin(\pi/2\, a) + \sin(\pi/2\, b))).$ (*Mizumoto's t-operations*)

The operations $\mathbf{t}_{S,1}$ and $\mathbf{s}_{Y,1}$ are called *Łukasiewicz t-operations*. Exceptional limit properties of Frank's t-operations allow us to define $\mathbf{t}_{F,0} := \mathbf{t}_\wedge$, $\mathbf{t}_{F,1} := \mathbf{t}_a$, $\mathbf{t}_{F,\infty} := \mathbf{t}_{S,1}$, $\mathbf{s}_{F,0} := \mathbf{s}_\vee$, $\mathbf{s}_{F,1} := \mathbf{s}_a$, and $\mathbf{s}_{F,\infty} := \mathbf{s}_{Y,1}$. The extended families $(\mathbf{t}_{F,\lambda})_{\lambda \in [0,\infty]}$ and $(\mathbf{s}_{F,\lambda})_{\lambda \in [0,\infty]}$ are called *Frank families* of t-operations.

Theorem 3.1 (*Ling*). *Let* **t**, s: $[0, 1]\times[0, 1] \to [0, 1]$.
(a) **t** *is an Archimedean t-norm iff there exists a strictly decreasing and continuous (additive) generator* g: $[0, 1] \to [0, \infty]$ *such that* $g(1) = 0$ *and* $a\mathbf{t}b = g^{-1}(g(0) \wedge (g(a) + g(b)))$ *for each* $a, b \in [0, 1]$. *Moreover,* **t** *is strict iff* $g(0) = \infty$.
(b) s *is an Archimedean t-conorm iff there exists a strictly increasing and continuous (additive) generator* h: $[0, 1] \to [0, \infty]$ *such that* $h(0) = 0$ *and* $a\mathbf{s}b = h^{-1}(h(1) \wedge (h(a) + h(b)))$ *for each* $a, b \in [0, 1]$. s is strict iff $h(1) = \infty$.

If $g(0) = 1$, g is called *normed generator*; h is said to be *normed* if $h(1) = 1$.

Theorem 3.2 (*Frank*). *A t-norm* **t** *and a t-conorm* s *do fulfil the condition*

$$a\mathbf{t}b + a\mathbf{s}b = a + b \quad \text{for each } a, b \in [0, 1]$$

iff the pair $(\mathbf{t}, \mathbf{s})$ *is of the form* $(\mathbf{t}_{F,\lambda}, \mathbf{s}_{F,\lambda})$ *with* $\lambda \in [0, \infty]$ *or* **t** *is the ordinal sum of a family* $\{([a_i, b_i], \mathbf{t}_{F,\lambda(i)})\}$, *whereas* s *is derived from* **t** *via the above equation.*

A *negation* is a nonincreasing function ν: $[0, 1] \to [0, 1]$ with $\nu(0) = 1$ and $\nu(1) = 0$. Strictly decreasing and continuous negations are called *strict negations*.

Involutive strict negations ($\nu(\nu(a)) = a$ for each a) are said to be *strong negations*. Any t-norm $\mathbf{t}$ and t-conorm $\mathbf{s}$ do generate negations defined by

$$\nu_{\mathbf{t}}(a) := \sup\{b \in [0,1]: a\,\mathbf{t}\,b = 0\} \text{ and } \nu_{\mathbf{s}}(a) := \inf\{b \in [0,1]: a\,\mathbf{s}\,b = 1\}.$$

These negations are strong if the generating t-operations are Archimedean and non-strict (see [8]). Let us define two new binary operations $\mathbf{t}^\circ$ and $\mathbf{s}^\circ$:

$$a\,\mathbf{t}^\circ\,b := \nu_{\mathbf{t}}(\nu_{\mathbf{t}}(a)\,\mathbf{t}\,\nu_{\mathbf{t}}(b)), \quad a\,\mathbf{s}^\circ\,b := \nu_{\mathbf{s}}(\nu_{\mathbf{s}}(a)\,\mathbf{s}\,\nu_{\mathbf{s}}(b)).$$

Theorem 3.3 (***Weber***). *If* $\mathbf{t}$ *and* $\mathbf{s}$ *are non-strict Archimedean t-operations, then*
(a) $\mathbf{t}^\circ$ *is a non-strict Archimedean t-conorm,*
(b) $\mathbf{s}^\circ$ *is a non-strict Archimedean t-norm,*
(c) $(\mathbf{t}^\circ)^\circ = \mathbf{t}$, $(\mathbf{s}^\circ)^\circ = \mathbf{s}$.

In the non-strict Archimedean case, $\mathbf{t}$ and $\mathbf{t}^\circ$ are called *complementary* t-operations (e.g. $\mathbf{t}_{S,p}$ and $\mathbf{s}_{Y,p}$).

Triangular operations and negations can be transferred to fuzzy sets via pointwise definitions. Namely, one defines the *sum* $A \cup_{\mathbf{s}} B$ of $A, B \in \mathrm{FFS}$ induced by a t-conorm $\mathbf{s}$ with $(A \cup_{\mathbf{s}} B)(x) := A(x)\,\mathbf{s}\,B(x)$, the *intersection* $A \cap_{\mathbf{t}} B$ and the *cartesian product* $A \times_{\mathbf{t}} B$ induced by a t-norm $\mathbf{t}$ with $(A \cap_{\mathbf{t}} B)(x) := A(x)\,\mathbf{t}\,B(x)$ and $(A \times_{\mathbf{t}} B)(x, y) := A(x)\,\mathbf{t}\,B(y)$, and the *complement* A^ν of A induced by a negation ν with $A^\nu(x) := \nu(A(x))$. Clearly, if $\mathbf{s} = \mathbf{s}_\vee$, $\mathbf{t} = \mathbf{t}_\wedge$ and $\nu(a) := 1 - a$, this notation collapses to the notation $A \cup B$, $A \cap B$ and A' from Section 2. Since $a\,\mathbf{s}\,0 = a$ for each a and $\mathbf{s}$, we get

$$A = \textstyle\bigcup^{\mathbf{s}}_{x \in \mathrm{supp}(A)} A(x)/x,$$

where $\bigcup^{\mathbf{s}}_{e \in \mathbf{J}} A_e$ denotes the sum (induced by $\mathbf{s}$) of a family $(A_e)_{e \in \mathbf{J}}$ of fuzzy sets.

Let us extend the generalized sigma counts characterized in Theorem 2.3 to fuzzy sets with operations induced by a t-norm $\mathbf{t}$ and a t-conorm $\mathbf{s}$. The underlying system of postulates is then (P1)-(P2) from Definition 2.1 together with

(P3') $\quad A \cap B = T \Rightarrow \sigma(A \cup_{\mathbf{s}} B) = \sigma(A) + \sigma(B).$

Clearly, the family of all possible scalar cardinalities σ is identical with that described in Theorem 2.3 for fuzzy sets with max and min operations because $A \cup_{\mathbf{s}} B = A \cup B$ whenever $A \cap B = T$. We see that the following important class of cardinality patterns must now be added to the list (A)-(G) from Section 2. By definition, normed generators of non-strict Archimedean t-conorms are cardinality patterns. For instance, the generators of $(\mathbf{t}_{W,\lambda})^\circ$ and $(\mathbf{t}_M)^\circ$, i.e. the functions $f_{7,\lambda}(a) := \ln(1 + \lambda a)/\ln(1 + \lambda)$ and $f_8(a) := 1 - \cos(\pi/2\, a)$, are cardinality patterns.

The use of any σ can be combined with the use of arbitrary t-operations leading to obtain, however, operational features which generally depend on the choice of t-operations. Although the finite additivity property

$$\sigma(\textstyle\bigcup^{\mathbf{s}}_{e \in \mathbf{J}} A_e) = \Sigma_{e \in \mathbf{J}}\, \sigma(A_e) \text{ if } A_e \cap A_{e'} = T \text{ for each } e \neq e'$$

holds true and, obviously, Theorem 2.2(b)-(e) is still valid, the valuation property, the finite subadditivity, the cartesian product rule, and the complementarity rule are not generally fulfilled. Let us formulate the following tasks (see [13]):

Find a cardinality pattern f, a t-norm **t** *and a t-conorm* **s** *such that*

(3.1) $$\forall A, B \in \text{FFS}: \ \sigma(A \cap_{\mathbf{t}} B) + \sigma(A \cup_{\mathbf{s}} B) = \sigma(A) + \sigma(B).$$

Find a cardinality pattern f and a t-conorm **s** *such that*

(3.2) $$\forall (A_e)_{e\in \mathbf{J}} \subset \text{FFS}: \ \sigma(\textstyle\bigcup^{\mathbf{s}}_{i\in \mathbf{J}} A_i) \le \Sigma_{i\in \mathbf{J}}\, \sigma(A_i).$$

Find a cardinality pattern f and a t-norm **t** *such that*

(3.3) $$\forall A, B \in \text{FFS}: \ \sigma(A \times_{\mathbf{t}} B) = \sigma(A) \cdot \sigma(B).$$

Find a cardinality pattern f and a negation ν such that (**M** *finite*)

(3.4) $$\forall A \in \text{FFS}: \ \sigma(A) + \sigma(A^{\nu}) = |\,\mathbf{M}\,|.$$

Theorem 3.4. *The valuation property* (3.1) *holds true iff*

(3.5) $$\forall a, b \in [0,1]: f(a\,\mathbf{t}\,b) + f(a\,\mathbf{s}\,b) = f(a) + f(b).$$

The finite subadditivity property (3.2) *is satisfied iff*

(3.6) $$\forall a, b \in [0,1]: f(a\,\mathbf{s}\,b) \le f(a) + f(b).$$

The cartesian product rule (3.3) *is preserved iff*

(3.7) $$\forall a, b \in [0,1]: f(a\,\mathbf{t}\,b) = f(a) \cdot f(b).$$

The complementarity rule (3.4) *is satisfied iff*

(3.8) $$\forall a \in [0,1]: f(a) + f(\nu(a)) = 1.$$

Proof. Since $\sigma(D) = \Sigma_{x\in \text{supp}(D)} f(D(x))$ for each D, the sufficiency of (3.5) for (3.1) is evident. On the other hand, if (3.5) does not hold, i.e. $f(a\,\mathbf{t}\,b) + f(a\,\mathbf{s}\,b) \ne f(a) + f(b)$ for some $a, b > 0$, then, putting $A := a/x$ and $B := b/x$ with arbitrary x, we get $\sigma(A \cap_{\mathbf{t}} B) + \sigma(A \cup_{\mathbf{s}} B) \ne \sigma(A) + \sigma(B)$. So, (3.5) is necessary for (3.1). The proofs of the equivalences (3.2)⇔(3.6), (3.3)⇔(3.7), and (3.4)⇔(3.8) are similar. □

Let us present a few examples of triplets (f, **t**, **s**) satisfying (3.5) and, thus, fulfilling the valuation property.

(a) If $\mathbf{t} = \mathbf{t}_{\wedge}$ and $\mathbf{s} = \mathbf{s}_{\vee}$, then (3.5) is satisfied by each f (cf. Theorem 2.2(f)).

(b) If $f = \text{id}$ (the identity function), Theorem 3.2 describes the family of all operations **t** and **s** satisfying (3.5). So, the valuation property is fulfilled e.g. by each $(\text{id}, \mathbf{t}_{F,\lambda}, \mathbf{s}_{F,\lambda})$ with $\lambda \in [0, \infty]$.

(c) If **s** is a non-strict Archimedean t-conorm with normed generator h, then $(h, \mathbf{s}^{\circ}, \mathbf{s})$ does satisfy (3.5). The valuation property is thus fulfilled e.g. by $(f_{3,p}, \mathbf{t}_{S,p}, \mathbf{s}_{Y,p})$, $(f_{7,\lambda}, \mathbf{t}_{W,\lambda}, (\mathbf{t}_{W,\lambda})^{\circ})$, and $(f_8, \mathbf{t}_M, (\mathbf{t}_M)^{\circ})$.

Obviously, if (f, **t**, **s**) does satisfy (3.1), then (3.2) is fulfilled by (f, **s**). Moreover, (3.6) is satisfied e.g. by $(\text{id}, \mathbf{s}_E)$.

The following are examples of pairs (f, **t**) satisfying (3.7).

(d) If $\mathbf{t} = \mathbf{t}_{\wedge}$, then (3.7) holds true iff f is equal to $f_{1,t}$ or $f_{2,t}$ (cf. Section 2).

(e) In consequence of Theorem 3.1, if **t** is strict with additive generator g, then

$g(a\,\mathbf{t}\,b) = g(a) + g(b)$ and, thus, $(e^{-g}, \mathbf{t})$ does fulfil (3.7). So, the cartesian product rule holds true, for instance, for (id, $\mathbf{t}_a$), $(f_9, \mathbf{t}_E)$ and $(f_{10,\lambda}, \mathbf{t}_{F,\lambda})$ with $1 \neq \lambda > 0$, where $f_9(a) := a/(2-a)$ and $f_{10,\lambda}(a) := ((\lambda^a - 1)/(\lambda - 1))^{1/\ln\lambda}$.

(f) If $\mathbf{t} = \mathbf{t}_a$, (3.7) collapses to the Cauchy functional equation. Its unique continuous solutions are the cardinality patterns $f = f_{3,p}$ with $p > 0$. Instances of discontinuous solutions are $f_{1,1}$ and $f_{2,0}$.

Finally, let us present some examples of pairs (f, ν) satisfying (3.8) and, thus, fulfilling the complementarity rule.

(g) If $\nu(a) = 1 - a$ for each $a \in [0, 1]$, then (3.8) holds true whenever (0.5, 0.5) is the symmetry point of the diagram of f. Examples of such cardinality patterns are $f_{4,p}$ and $f_{5,\lambda}$.

(h) If $\mathbf{s}$ is a non-strict Archimedean t-conorm with normed generator h, then $(h, \nu_{\mathbf{s}})$ does fulfil (3.8). So, (3.8) holds true e.g. for $f = f_{3,p}$ with $\nu(a) = (1 - a^p)^{1/p}$ $(\mathbf{s} = \mathbf{s}_{Y,p})$, $f(a) = 1 - \ln(1 + \lambda(1-a))/\ln(1+\lambda)$ with $\nu(a) = 1 - a/(1 + \lambda(1-a))$ $(\mathbf{s} = \mathbf{s}_{W,\lambda})$, and $f(a) = \sin(\pi/2\,a)$ with $\nu(a) = 2/\pi \arcsin(1 - \sin(\pi/2\,a))$ $(\mathbf{s} = \mathbf{s}_M)$.

In [13], a discussion about simultaneous fulfilment of two or more laws from among (3.1)-(3.4) is placed. (id, $\mathbf{t}_a$, $\mathbf{s}_a$, ν) with $\nu(a) = 1 - a$ seems to be a unique nontrivial system which guarantees simultaneous fulfilment of all of those laws. □

4. Other generalizations of sigma counts

In this section, we refer to the "fuzzy" approach to cardinality of a fuzzy set $A \in \mathrm{FFS}$ in which that cardinality is understood as some convex fuzzy set in $\mathbb{N}$. From the chronological viewpoint, the first well-defined type of such a cardinality is the FGCount of A (see [15]). More precisely, FGCount: $\mathrm{FFS} \to [0, 1]^{\mathbb{N}}$ and

$$\mathrm{FGCount}(A)(k) := [A]_k \text{ for each } k \in \mathbb{N},$$

where $[A]_k := \bigvee\{t\colon |A_t| \geq k\}$. So, $[A]_k = 1$ if $k \leq m$, $[A]_k = 0$ if $k > n$, and $[A]_k \in (0, 1)$ otherwise, where $m := |\mathrm{core}(A)|$ and $n := |\mathrm{supp}(A)|$. Each $[A]_k$ with $0 < k \leq n$ is the k-th element in the nonincreasing sequence of all positive values $A(x)$, including their possible repetitions. FGCount$(A)(k)$ expresses a degree to which A contains at least k elements.

The idea of FGCounts is suitable for fuzzy sets with max and min operations. Using fuzzy sets with t-operations, it should be redefined as follows (see [14]):

$$\mathrm{FGCount}_{\mathbf{t}}(A)(k) := [A]_1\,\mathbf{t}\,[A]_2\,\mathbf{t}\ldots\mathbf{t}\,[A]_k \text{ for each } k \in \mathbb{N},$$

where $\mathbf{t}$ denotes a t-norm and $[A]_1\,\mathbf{t}\,[A]_2\,\mathbf{t}\ldots\mathbf{t}\,[A]_k := 1$ for $k = 0$. Clearly, $\mathrm{FGCount}_{\wedge}(A) = \mathrm{FGCount}(A)$.

There exists an obvious connection between the sigma count sc_A of A and FGCount(A), namely sc_A can be viewed as a "summary" of FGCount(A), i.e. $sc_A = \Sigma_{k=1}^{n} \mathrm{FGCount}(A)(k)$. This suggests three other possible variants of a generalization of sc_A, namely

$$sc_{A,\mathbf{t}} := \Sigma_{k=1}^{n} [A]_1\,\mathbf{t}\,[A]_2\,\mathbf{t}\ldots\mathbf{t}\,[A]_k,$$

$$sc_{A,f,\mathbf{t}} := \Sigma_{k=1}^{n} f([A]_1 \,\mathbf{t}\, [A]_2 \,\mathbf{t}\, \ldots \,\mathbf{t}\, [A]_k),$$

and
$$sc_{A,\mathbf{t},f} := \Sigma_{k=1}^{n} f([A]_1) \,\mathbf{t}\, f([A]_2) \,\mathbf{t}\, \ldots \,\mathbf{t}\, f([A]_k)$$

with a cardinality pattern f. So, $sc_{A,\wedge} = sc_{A,\mathrm{id},\wedge} = sc_{A,\wedge,\mathrm{id}} = sc_A$. Conversely, the concept of the FGCount of A can be generalized in the following three ways:

$$\mathrm{FGCount}_f(A)(k) := f([A]_k),$$

$$\mathrm{FGCount}_{f,\mathbf{t}}(A)(k) := f([A]_1 \,\mathbf{t}\, [A]_2 \,\mathbf{t}\, \ldots \,\mathbf{t}\, [A]_k),$$

and
$$\mathrm{FGCount}_{\mathbf{t},f}(A)(k) := f([A]_1) \,\mathbf{t}\, f([A]_2) \,\mathbf{t}\, \ldots \,\mathbf{t}\, f([A]_k).$$

Each of these definitions generates convex fuzzy sets in $\mathbb{N}$ as cardinalities of fuzzy sets in $\mathbf{M}$, and we have $\mathrm{FGCount}_{\mathrm{id}}(A) = \mathrm{FGCount}_{\mathrm{id},\wedge}(A) = \mathrm{FGCount}_{\wedge,\mathrm{id}}(A) = \mathrm{FGCount}(A)$. If $A \in \mathrm{FCS}$, we obtain

$$sc_{A,\mathbf{t}} = sc_{A,f,\mathbf{t}} = sc_{A,\mathbf{t},f} = n$$

and

$$\mathrm{FGCount}_f(A) = \mathrm{FGCount}_{f,\mathbf{t}}(A) = \mathrm{FGCount}_{\mathbf{t},f}(A) = 1_{\{0,1,\ldots,n\}}$$

for each $\mathbf{t}$ and f. Each of the six proposed constructions is a nondecreasing function with respect to both A and the parameters f and $\mathbf{t}$, whenever they occur. However, the valuation property seems to be lost, unless $\mathbf{t} = \wedge$, $\mathbf{s} = \vee$ and (in the case of the generalized FGCounts) $f = \mathrm{id}$.

References

[1] D. Dubois and H. Prade. Fuzzy cardinality and the modeling of imprecise quantification. *Fuzzy Sets and Systems*, 16, 199-230, 1985.

[2] D. Dubois and H. Prade. Measuring properties of fuzzy sets: A general technique and its use in fuzzy query evaluation. *Fuzzy Sets and Systems*, 38, 137-152, 1990.

[3] S. Gottwald. A note on fuzzy cardinals. *Kybernetika*, 16, 156-158, 1980.

[4] A. Kaufmann. *Introduction à la Théorie des Sous-Ensembles Flous*, Vol. IV, Masson, Paris, 1977.

[5] A. de Luca and S. Termini. On the convergence of entropy measures of a fuzzy set. *Kybernetes*, 6, 219-227, 1977.

[6] A. de Luca and S. Termini. Entropy and energy measures of a fuzzy set. In M. M. Gupta, R. K. Ragade, R. R. Yager, Eds., *Advances in Fuzzy Set Theory and Applications*, North-Holland, Amsterdam, 321-338, 1979.

[7] H. T. Nguyen and E. A. Walker. *A First Course in Fuzzy Logic*, CRC Press, Boca Raton, 1997.

[8] S. Weber, A general concept of fuzzy connectives, nagations and implications based on t-norms and t-conorms. *Fuzzy Sets and Systems*, 11, 115-134, 1983.

[9] M. Wygralak. Fuzzy cardinals based on the generalized equality of fuzzy subsets. *Fuzzy Sets and Systems*, 18, 143-158, 1986.

[10] M. Wygralak. *Vaguely Defined Objects. Representations, Fuzzy Sets and Non-classical Cardinality Theory*, Kluwer Academic Publ., Dordrecht-Boston-London, 1996.

[11] M. Wygralak. On the best scalar approximation of cardinality of a fuzzy set. *Inter. Jour. of Uncertainty, Fuzziness and Knowledge-Based Systems*, 5, 681-687, 1997.

[12] M. Wygralak. Questions of cardinality of finite fuzzy sets. *Fuzzy Sets and Systems*, 102, 185-210, 1999.

[13] M. Wygralak, Triangular operations, negations, and scalar cardinality of a fuzzy set. In L. A. Zadeh, J. Kacprzyk, Eds., *Computing with Words in Information/Intelligent Systems*, Physica-Verlag, Heidelberg and New York, 1999, to appear.

[14] M. Wygralak and D. Pilarski. Triangular norm-based generalized cardinals for fuzzy sets, submitted.

[15] L. A. Zadeh. A computational approach to fuzzy quantifiers in natural languages. *Comput. and Math. with Appl.*, 9, 149-184, 1983.

[16] L. A. Zadeh, From computing with numbers to computing with words - From manipulation of measurements to manipulation of perceptions. In *Proc. EUROFUSE-SIC'99 Conf.*, Budapest, 1-2, 1999.

A Qualitative Approach for Processing Uncertainty

Hamid Seridi* **& Herman Akdag*, ****

* LERI, Université de Reims
Rue des Crayères, BP 1035
51687 Reims cedex 2, France
seridi@leri.univ-reims.fr

** LIP6, Univ. P. & M. Curie,
4, Place Jussieu, Boîte 169
75687 Paris Cedex 05 France
Herman.Akdag@lip6.fr

Abstract: In Bayesian networks as well as in knowledge-based systems, uncertainty in propositions can be represented by various degrees of belief encoded by qualitative values. In this paper, we present an approach of classical probability theory in the particular case where the set of probability degrees *[0,1]* is replaced by a totally ordered set of symbolic values. First, we define the four elementary operations (addition, subtraction, multiplication and division) allowing to manipulate these symbolic degrees of uncertainty, then we propose an axiomatic. The properties obtained from this axiomatic allow to show that our theory constitutes a qualitative approach for processing uncertain statements. The obtained results are usable in inferential processes as well as in Bayesian networks.

Keywords: Artificial intelligence, symbolic probability, qualitative uncertainty, knowledge representation, conditional probability, logic, multivalued logic, fuzzy logic, fuzzy reasoning.

1. Introduction

The aim of this paper is to present some new results obtained in the framework of ***Qualitative Uncertainty Theory***. The latter is situated in the problematic of the representation and the processing of uncertainty in the deductive process. Our approach consists in representing and exploiting the uncertainty by qualitative degrees, that can be interpreted as «symbolic» and «comparative» degrees of inaccuracy. The use of qualitative values is necessary in areas where the exact numerical values associated with a fact are unknown by experts. The experts can, in general, propose only intervals of values. Then, each interval can be translated as a symbolic value. These symbolic values can be compared with Zadeh's linguistic variables [16]. In this work, we manipulate these values with tools borrowed from the classical, multivalued and fuzzy logic, and therefore it may constitute a logico-symbolic approach.
The idea to link the logic and probabilities is not new. First, Polya emitted the idea of a « probabilistic logic » in the 60's. Since then many works in the field of Artificial Intelligence have been carried for instance by Nilsson [9] with his probabilistic logic (the most known of probabilistic logic), Shafer [13], etc. These studies lead to a kind of probabilistic logic, which allocates probabilities to logical propositions and to logical deductions. More precisely, the management of

knowledge is made by logical laws on logical propositions to which probabilities (numerical or symbolic) are associated. A quasi-opposite approach is the management of knowledge using a classical probability theory in which the numerical values and arithmetical operators are absent, so that calculations would be made by logic's tools (i.e. operators like implication, complementation, conjunction, etc...). We set our approach in this second framework as well as in the first. So, logic and probabilities are intimately linked, but the main concept is **to manipulate Qualitative Uncertainty Degrees with logico-symbolic tools**. Keynes [7], Koopmann [8] and others have been pioneers in proposing intuitive (or symbolic) probabilities. The work of Spohn [14] can also be quoted as precursory. Our approach presents some similarities with the theory of Aleliunas [3] and Darwiche & Ginsberg [5]. In their theory, the Qualitative Uncertainty Degrees are not always totally ordered and the logic model is not sufficiently expressive.

Following the works of Akdag and al. [1] on the representation of the uncertainty via the multivalued logic, the first step of our approach is the proposition of an intuitive axiomatic for *symbolic probability theory*. Akdag & Khoukhi [2] went further in the field of representation uncertainty and imprecision via the multivalued predicate logic. They proposed several solutions for defining each symbolic operator. Similarly, Pacholczyk & Pacholczyk [10] and Xiang and al. [15] proposed some versions of this theory based much more on the algebraic structure rather than the expressive aspect. In fact, their symbolic product leads the overall structure to incoherent results, called denominator-indifference and ambiguity-generation (i.e. the solution of the division is not unique). Another kind of this approach is presented by Dubois and al. [6] with the aim to remove this ambiguity. They also interpret the symbolic probability values as numerical subintervals of *[0,1]*. However, their investigation leads to partially uninformative results. So, our approach [11,12] consists of both a synthesis and a new proposition work based on well-chosen formulas dealing with statements of natural language.

We assume that the proposed qualitative uncertainty theory is situated between the classical probability theory and the possibility theory. Even though the problematic of our approach is close enough to that of Pacholczyk & Pacholczyk [10] and Xiang [15], we aim to remove the division-ambiguity and to preserve the expressive aspect in concordance with the intuition. However, as we will see in the third section, we make no approximation to construct our tables. Well-chosen formulas make easy translation of the four operations, by dealing with required properties. Adequate qualities of our tables are strengthened by results (theorems) of our Axiomatic. We also underline that all our tables (see section 3) are obtained using logical formulas which use the Lukasiewicz implication (because its properties preserve the expressive aspect of the natural inference), but it can be also translated into an addition and subtraction (of integer numbers), using the operators max and min.

2. On the qualitative uncertainty theory

The aforementioned works have in common the following points:

a) They use non-numerical degrees of uncertainty. Indeed, human expert often expresses his knowledge by using qualitative approximation of numerical values.

b) ***They are based on the association «probability degrees / logic»: i.e. laws of probabilities are constructed by logical operators which are associated to truth tables.***
c) ***They have both developed an axiomatic theory, which provides results either from axioms or from theorems.***

Darwiche & Ginsberg insisted on the need of having a partial ordering on symbolic values and defining a symbolic summation, a symbolic conditioning and disconditioning. Similarly, Akdag and al. [1] have argued in favor of a symbolic graduation from the ***Impossible to the Certain***, therefore a complete ordering. A scale of degrees is then introduced for representing the uncertainty. Our qualitative degrees of uncertainty belong to graduated scale $\mathbf{L_M}$ composed of **M** symbolic values which represent the measures of belief:

$L_M=\{\tau_\alpha, \alpha=0, M-1\}$ with the complete ordering relationship: $\tau_\alpha \leq \tau_\beta \Leftrightarrow \alpha \leq \beta$.

For the sake of simplicity, in this paper, all examples are in L_7. To each degree belonging to our scale, we can associate a linguistic value (see that our approach does not need a delicate definition of a man-machine interface):

$\tau_0 \Leftrightarrow$ **Impossible**		$\tau_4 \Leftrightarrow$ **Rather-possible**
$\tau_1 \Leftrightarrow$ **Nearly-impossible**	$\tau_3 \Leftrightarrow$ **Possible**	$\tau_5 \Leftrightarrow$ **Very-possible**
$\tau_2 \Leftrightarrow$ **Little-possible**		$\tau_6 \Leftrightarrow$ **Certain**

To be able to rewrite in symbolic the different axioms and theorems of the classical probability theory and especially to translate: $P(A)=1-P(A)$, $P(A\cup B)=P(A)+P(B)$ if $A\cap B=\varnothing$, $P(A\cup B)=P(A)+P(B)-P(A\cap B)$, $P(A\cap B)=P(B/A)*P(A)$, $P(\varnothing)=0$, $P(\Omega)=1$, $P(B/A)=P(A\cap B)/P(A)$, we use:

- the Lukasiewicz implication :

$\tau_\alpha \rightarrow_L \tau_\beta = \mathbf{min}(\tau_{M-1-\alpha+\beta}, \tau_{M-1})$, for simulating the four basic operators,

- the symbolic complementation :

$\neg\tau_\beta=\tau_{M-1-\beta}$ for translating the negation of a logical formula.

After having introduced the concept of total order in the scale of degrees, it is easy to see, as in [5], that it is necessary to define a symbolic addition, a symbolic multiplication and a symbolic division. We introduce a supplementary constraint: «***It is necessary that if C is the result of the division of A by B then B multiplying by C gives A***» (relationship between the qualitative multiplication and qualitative division). Then, we define a qualitative subtraction instead of using artificially the complementation operator. Thus, we are going to define a symbolic difference to translate the subtraction.

As follows, we define different symbolic operators. Then, we expose our axiomatic and study the first results, and as well as possible Bayesian networks extensions by dealing with conditional probabilities. Thereafter, we are going to be interested in the uncertainty of a logical implication and to the generalized modus ponens, very useful concepts for exploiting the knowledge-based systems.

3. New tables for qualitative uncertainty theory

3.1 Qualitative multiplication : As in most of the other above mentioned works, our operator has to verify some «intuitive» properties. Thus, we define a qualitative multiplication of two degrees τ_α and τ_β by the function MUL from $L_M \times L_M$ to L_M that verifies the following properties:

M1. $MUL(\tau_\alpha, \tau_0)=\tau_0$ — Absorbent element
M2. $MUL(\tau_\alpha, \tau_{M-1})=\tau_\alpha$ — Neutral element
M3. $MUL(\tau_\alpha, \tau_\beta)=MUL(\tau_\beta, \tau_\alpha)$ — Commutativity
M4. $MUL[\tau_\alpha, MUL(\tau_\beta, \tau_\gamma)]=MUL[MUL(\tau_\alpha, \tau_\beta), \tau_\gamma]$ — Associativity
M5. $MUL(\tau_\alpha, \tau_\beta)\leq MUL(\tau_\gamma, \tau_\delta)$ if $\tau_\alpha\leq\tau_\gamma$ and $\tau_\beta\leq\tau_\delta$ — Monotony
M6. $MUL(\tau_\alpha, \neg\tau_\alpha)=\tau_0$ — Complementarity

M2 to M5 are properties of a t-norm [4] to which we add the absorbent element and the complementarity.

Proposition 1 : The following function verifies the properties M1÷M6:

$$\mathbf{MUL_L}\ (\tau_\alpha, \tau_\beta) = \neg(\tau_\alpha \rightarrow_L \neg\tau_\beta) = \mathbf{max}(\tau_{\alpha+\beta-(M-1)}, \tau_0)$$

It corresponds in L_7 to the following table:

τ_β / τ_α	τ_0	τ_1	τ_2	τ_3	τ_4	τ_5	τ_6
τ_0	τ_0	τ_0	τ_0	τ_0	τ_0	τ_0	τ_0
τ_1	τ_0	τ_0	τ_0	τ_0	τ_0	τ_0	τ_1
τ_2	τ_0	τ_0	τ_0	τ_0	τ_0	τ_1	τ_2
τ_3	τ_0	τ_0	τ_0	τ_0	τ_1	τ_2	τ_3
τ_4	τ_0	τ_0	τ_0	τ_1	τ_2	τ_3	τ_4
τ_5	τ_0	τ_0	τ_1	τ_2	τ_3	τ_4	τ_5
τ_6	τ_0	τ_1	τ_2	τ_3	τ_4	τ_5	τ_6

Table 1. Qualitative multiplication in L_7

As the complementarity property is used to translate the negation of a logical formula, it imposes the occurrences of τ_0 in the diagonal of the above table. This property is very strong but it insures the *convergence* to τ_0 of two contradictory statements (i.e. a statement and its negation) emanating from a natural language, for example: *the temperature is certainly high and the temperature is not at all high.* Because of the complementarity, if two degrees of belief do not add up to certainty, they must multiply to falsehood, for example: $MUL_L(\tau_2, \tau_4)=\tau_0$. This is both normal and prudent given that we manipulate symbolic values which represent qualitative estimations of «intervals». So, the corresponding event of τ_0 could be considered either impossible or close enough to impossible.
The table 1 is not the unique choice to define the multiplication satisfying the above properties, but it is ***«the most expressive choice»*** [11].

3.2 Qualitative addition : Similarly, a qualitative addition of two degrees τ_α and τ_β is a function ADD from $L_M \times L_M$ to L_M that verifies the following properties:

A1. $ADD(\tau_\alpha, \tau_{M-1})=\tau_{M-1}$ — Absorbent Element

A2. $ADD(\tau_\alpha, \tau_0)=\tau_\alpha$ Neutral element
A3. $ADD(\tau_\alpha, \tau_\beta)=ADD(\tau_\beta, \tau_\alpha)$ Commutativity
A4. $ADD[\tau_\alpha, ADD(\tau_\beta, \tau_\gamma)]=ADD[ADD(\tau_\alpha, \tau_\beta), \tau_\gamma]$ Associativity
A5. $ADD(\tau_\alpha, \tau_\beta)\leq ADD(\tau_\gamma, \tau_\delta)$ if $\tau_\alpha\leq\tau_\gamma$ and $\tau_\beta\leq\tau_\delta$ Monotony
A6. $ADD(\tau_\alpha, \neg\tau_\alpha)=\tau_{M-1}$ Complementarity

A2 to A5 are properties of a t-conorm [4] to which we add the absorbent element and the complementarity properties. This second form of complementarity allows to have the sum of two complementary values equal to τ_{M-1}.

Proposition 2 : The following function verifies the properties A1÷A6:

$$\mathbf{ADD_L}(\tau_\alpha, \tau_\beta) = (\neg\tau_\alpha \rightarrow_L \tau_\beta) = \mathbf{min}(\tau_{\alpha+\beta}, \tau_{M-1})$$

It is the qualitative conorm associated to Lukasiewicz implication, also proposed by Pacholczyk & Pacholczyk [10].

3.3 Qualitative subtraction : We define a qualitative subtraction of two degrees τ_α and τ_β by the function SOUS from $L_M \times L_M$ to L_M that verifies the following properties:

S1. $SOUS(\tau_\alpha, \tau_0)=\tau_\alpha$ Neutral element
S2. $SOUS(\tau_\alpha, \tau_\gamma)\leq SOUS(\tau_\beta, \tau_\gamma)$ if $\tau_\alpha\leq\tau_\beta$
Increasing relatively to the first argument
S3. $SOUS(\tau_\alpha, \tau_\beta)\geq SOUS(\tau_\alpha, \tau_\gamma)$ if $\tau_\beta\leq\tau_\gamma$
Decreasing relatively to the second argument
S4. $SOUS(\tau_\alpha, \tau_\alpha)=\tau_0$

Proposition 3 : The following function verifies the properties S1÷S4:

$$\mathbf{SOUS_L}(\tau_\alpha, \tau_\beta) = \neg(\tau_\alpha\rightarrow_L \tau_\beta) = \mathbf{max}(\tau_{\alpha-\beta}, \tau_0)$$

It is the first time that a qualitative subtraction is introduced in this kind of theory. It allows us to define an important axiom linking probability of the union to the probability of the intersection (see **U6**). It corresponds in fact to the bounded difference of Zadeh, defined in the framework of the fuzzy logic [4].

3.4 Qualitative division : We define a qualitative division of two degrees τ_α and τ_β and such that $\tau_\alpha\leq\tau_\beta$ with $\tau_\beta\neq\tau_0$ by the function DIV from $L_M\times L_M$ to L_M that verifies the following properties:

D1. $DIV(\tau_0, \tau_\alpha)=\tau_0$ Absorbent element
D2. $DIV(\tau_\alpha, \tau_{M-1})=\tau_\alpha$ Neutral element
D3. $DIV(\tau_\alpha, \tau_\beta)\leq DIV(\tau_\gamma, \tau_\beta)$ if $\tau_\alpha\leq\tau_\gamma$ Increasing relatively to the first argument
D4. $DIV(\tau_\alpha, \tau_\beta)\geq DIV(\tau_\alpha, \tau_\gamma)$ if $\tau_\beta\leq\tau_\gamma$ Decreasing relatively to the second argument
D5. If $\tau_\alpha\neq\tau_0$ then $DIV(\tau_\alpha, \tau_\alpha)=\tau_{M-1}$ Boundary conditions.
D6. $DIV(\tau_0, \tau_0)$ is undetermined.

Proposition 4 : The following formula verifies the properties D1÷D5:

$$\mathbf{DIV_L(\tau_\alpha, \tau_\beta) = MUL_L(\tau_\alpha, \tau_\beta)} \qquad \mathbf{if\ \tau_\alpha=\tau_0\ and\ \tau_\beta\neq\tau_0}$$

$$\mathbf{DIV_L(\tau_\alpha, \tau_\beta) = ADD_L(\tau_\alpha, \neg\tau_\beta)} \qquad \mathbf{if\ \tau_\alpha\leq\tau_\beta\ and\ \tau_\beta\neq\tau_0}$$

It corresponds in L_7 to the following table:

τ_α / τ_β	τ_0	τ_1	τ_2	τ_3	τ_4	τ_5	τ_6
τ_0							
τ_1	τ_0	τ_6					
τ_2	τ_0	τ_5	τ_6				
τ_3	τ_0	τ_4	τ_5	τ_6			
τ_4	τ_0	τ_3	τ_4	τ_5	τ_6		
τ_5	τ_0	τ_2	τ_3	τ_4	τ_5	τ_6	
τ_6	τ_0	τ_1	τ_2	τ_3	τ_4	τ_5	τ_6

Table 2. Qualitative division in L_7

Compared to the table proposed in [10] and [15], we notice that denominator-indifference and ambiguity-generation are removed (i.e. the result of the division is a unique value), and that the link between the division and the multiplication effectively exists, in other words: **If** $\boldsymbol{\tau_x=DIV_L(\tau_\alpha, \tau_\beta)}$ **then** $\boldsymbol{\tau_\alpha=MUL_L(\tau_\beta, \tau_x)}$.

4. New axiomatic for qualitative uncertainty theory

Considering the qualitative uncertainty concept introduced by the aforementioned authors and based on the fact that natural language is composed of statements, we split up a statement **e** by an adverb α and a proposition **P** in such a way that α is the degree with which **e** satisfies **P**. So, for any statement supposed true, we can write (Tarski generalization): **e** is true $\Leftrightarrow$ **P** is α-true. Then, we propose a new axiomatic by using the ***predicate Inc*** of a multivalued logic. Thus, the logical formula «***P is*** τ_α ***-certain***» is translated into ***Inc(P)***$=\tau_\alpha$.

Definition 5 : We define the qualitative uncertainty for a logical formula **f** of some formal language **L**, by the function **Inc: L** $\rightarrow$ $\mathbf{L_M}$ that verify the following axiomatic:

U1. Inc(A)=τ_{M-1} i.e. if A is a tautology then A is certain.
U2. Inc(A)=τ_0 i.e. if A is a false then A is impossible.
U3. If Inc(A)=τ_0 then Inc($\neg$A)=$\neg\tau_0$ translate the negation of logical formula.
U4. If A≡B then Inc(A)=Inc(B) i.e. if A is equivalent to B then they have equal uncertainty.
U5. If Inc(A)=τ_α and Inc(B)=τ_β and Inc(A$\wedge$B)=τ_0 then Inc(A$\vee$B)=$ADD_L(\tau_\alpha, \tau_\beta)$.
i.e. if the logical formula (A$\wedge$B) is not satisfied (the associated events are mutually exclusive), then the uncertainty degree of the disjunction is equal to the sum of their degrees.
U6. If Inc(A)=τ_α and Inc(B)=τ_β then Inc(A$\wedge\neg$B)=$SOUS_L(\tau_\alpha, \tau_\beta)$.

i.e. if two logical formulas A and B are associated respectively to an event with a qualitative uncertainty degree, and we know nothing about Inc(A∧B), then the qualitative uncertainty degree of (A and not B) is equal to the difference of their degrees.

5. Formal consequences

In our case, we aim to obtain properties which are acceptable as a qualitative approach for processing uncertain statements of natural language.

C1. If Inc(A)=τ_α then Inc(A∧¬A)=τ_0 and Inc(A∨¬A)=τ_{M-1}.

Proof: Using U2 and U5, we get respectively Inc(A∧¬A)=τ_0 and Inc(A∨¬A)=τ_{M-1}.

C2. If Inc(A∧B)=τ_γ and Inc(A)=τ_α and Inc(B)=τ_β
then Inc[¬(A∧B)]=Inc(¬A∨¬B)=¬τ_γ.

Proof: Knowing that ¬(A∧B)=¬A∨¬B and using U4, we have:
Inc[¬(A∧B)] = Inc(¬A∨¬B).
From U3, we get: Inc[¬(A∧B)]=Inc(¬A∨¬B)=¬τ_γ.

C3. If Inc(A∨B)=τ_δ and Inc(A)=τ_α and Inc(B)=τ_β
then Inc[¬(A∨B)]=Inc(¬A∧¬B)=¬τ_δ.

Proof: Knowing that ¬(A∨B)= ¬A∧¬B and using U4, we have:
Inc(¬(A∨B)) = Inc(¬A∧¬B).
From U3, we obtain: Inc(¬(A∨B))=Inc(¬A∧¬B)=¬τ_δ.

C4. If Inc(A)=τ_α and Inc(B)=τ_β and Inc(A∧B)=τ_γ
then Inc(A∨B)=$ADD_L[SOUS_L(\tau_\alpha, \tau_\gamma), \tau_\beta]$.

Proof: Knowing that A∨B=A∨(B∧¬(A∧B)) and using U4, we have:
Inc(A∨B)=Inc(A∨(B∧¬(A∧B))). From U5, U6 and A3 we obtain:
Inc(A∨B)=$ADD_L[\tau_\alpha, SOUS_L(\tau_\beta, \tau_\gamma)]=ADD_L[SOUS_L(\tau_\beta, \tau_\gamma), \tau_\alpha]$.
Similarly if we consider A∨B=B∨(A∧¬(A∧B)), we get:
Inc(A∨B)=$ADD_L[\tau_\beta, SOUS_L(\tau_\alpha, \tau_\gamma)]=ADD_L[SOUS_L(\tau_\alpha, \tau_\gamma), \tau_\beta]$.

Remark : The reader must notice when he uses the property **C4**, that it is necessary first to undertake the subtraction, then the addition (the addition and subtraction do not follow commutativity because they are defined in a finite and discrete set). If we perform: $SOUS_L[ADD_L(\tau_\alpha, \tau_\beta), \tau_\gamma]$ and $ADD_L[\tau_\alpha, SOUS_L(\tau_\beta, \tau_\gamma)]$, we get: $SOUS_L[ADD_L(\tau_\alpha, \tau_\beta), \tau_\gamma] \neq ADD_L[\tau_\alpha, SOUS_L(\tau_\beta, \tau_\gamma)]$. For example: $SOUS_L[ADD_L(\tau_{M-1}, \tau_{M-1}), \tau_{M-1}] = \tau_0 \neq ADD_L[\tau_{M-1}, SOUS_L(\tau_{M-1}, \tau_{M-1})] = \tau_{M-1}$.
Indeed we have:

a) $SOUS_L[ADD_L(\tau_\alpha, \tau_\beta), \tau_\gamma] = \neg\tau_\gamma$.

Because if $\gamma\neq 0 \Rightarrow \tau_{\alpha+\beta} > \tau_{M-1} \Rightarrow \min(\tau_{\alpha+\beta}, \tau_{M-1})=\tau_{M-1} \Rightarrow \max(\tau_{M-1-\gamma}, \tau_0)=\neg\tau_\gamma$.

b) $ADD_L[\tau_\alpha, SOUS_L(\tau_\beta, \tau_\gamma)] = \tau_{\beta+\alpha-\gamma}$.

Because as $\gamma\leq\beta \Rightarrow \max(\tau_{\beta-\gamma}, \tau_0)=\tau_{\beta-\gamma} \Rightarrow \min(\tau_{\beta-\gamma+\alpha}, \tau_{M-1})=\tau_{\beta+\alpha-\gamma}$.
In other hand if $\gamma\neq 0 \Rightarrow \alpha+\beta>M-1 \Rightarrow \alpha+\beta-\gamma>M-1-\gamma \Rightarrow \tau_{\alpha+\beta-\gamma}>\neg\tau_\gamma$.
Hence: $ADD_L[\tau_\alpha, SOUS_L(\tau_\beta, \tau_\gamma)]>SOUS_L[ADD_L(\tau_\alpha, \tau_\beta), \tau_\gamma]$.

Definition 6 : The qualitative conditional uncertainty of B knowing A has occurred (i.e. $Inc(A) \neq \tau_0$) is equal to: $Inc(B/A)=DIV_L[Inc(A \wedge B), Inc(A)]$.

In the following definition, we introduce the notion of quasi-independence. We believe that, when precise informations are not available, a human expert can not assert that events are strictly independent.

Definition 7 : Two events A and B are quasi-independent if $Inc(B/A)=Inc(B)$.

Proposition 5 : If two events A and B are quasi-independent then $Inc(A \wedge B)=MUL_L[Inc(A), Inc(B)]$.

Proof: From definition 6 and 7, we have:
$Inc(B/A)=Inc(B)=DIV_L[Inc(A \wedge B), Inc(A)]$. Using the link between the division and multiplication (see section 3.4), we get: $DIV_L[Inc(A \wedge B), Inc(A)] = Inc(B) \Rightarrow Inc(A \wedge B) = MUL_L[Inc(A), Inc(B)]$.

C5. (Compound qualitative uncertainty formula) The qualitative uncertainty of $A \wedge B$ can also be computed as follows: $Inc(A \wedge B)=MUL_L[Inc(B/A), Inc(A)]$.

Proof: Using the definition 6 and the link between the division and multiplication (see section 3.4) we obtain: $Inc(A \wedge B)=MUL_L[Inc(B/A), Inc(A)]$.

C6. (Total qualitative uncertainty formula) Let A_i for i=1,2 be events such that their conjunction is the certitude and their disjunction is false. Moreover, if we know respectively the qualitativc uncertainty of each A_i and also of B given A_i, then we can compute the qualitative uncertainty of B as follow:

$$Inc(B)=ADD_L\{MUL_L[Inc(B/A_1), Inc(A_1)], MUL_L[Inc(B/A_2), Inc(A_2)]\}$$

Proof: According to C5 and U5, we have: $Inc(A_1 \wedge B)=MUL_L[Inc(B/A_1), Inc(A_1)]$ and $Inc(A_2 \wedge B)=MUL_L[Inc(B/A_2), Inc(A_2)]$. As $Inc(B)=Inc[(A_1 \wedge B) \vee (A_2 \wedge B)]$ with $(A_1 \wedge B) \wedge (A_2 \wedge B)=\varnothing$, then we have :
$Inc(B)=ADD_L\{MUL_L [Inc(B/A_1), Inc(A_1)], MUL_L [Inc(B/A_2), Inc(A_2)]\}$.

C7. (Generalization) We generalize the total qualitative uncertainty formula:
If $Inc(A_{k,})=\tau_{\alpha_k}$ with $k \in [1..n]$ for $n \geq 2$ and
$Inc(\vee_{k \in [1..n]} A_k)=\tau_{M-1}$ and $Inc(A_k \wedge A_l)=\tau_0$ $\forall k \neq l$ then for any event B such that:

$$Inc(B) = \tau_{\delta_n} = \begin{cases} ADD_L(\tau_{\gamma(n-1)}, \tau_{\gamma n}) & \text{if } n=2 \\ ADD_L(\tau_{\delta(n-1)}, \tau_{\gamma n}) & \text{if } n>2 \end{cases}$$

with $\tau_{\gamma k}=MUL_L [Inc(B/A_k), Inc(A_k)]$ for $k \in [1..n]$.

Proof: Let $B=\vee_{k \in [1..n]} (B \wedge A_k)$.

a) Consider the case n=2:
According to U4 and C6, we have:
$Inc(B)=ADD_L\{MUL_L[Inc(B/A_1), Inc(A_1)], MUL_L[Inc(B/A_2), Inc(A_2)]\}$.
As $\tau_{\gamma k}=MUL_L[Inc(B/A_k), Inc(A_k)]$ for k=1, 2 then $Inc(B)=ADD_L(\tau_{\gamma 1}, \tau_{\gamma 2})=\tau_{\delta 2}$.

b) Consider the case $n \geq 2$:

by recurrence on 'n', we have: $$\text{Inc}(B) = \tau_{\delta n} = \begin{cases} \text{ADD}_L(\tau_{\gamma(n-1)}, \tau_{\gamma n}) \text{if} & n = 2 \\ \text{ADD}_L(\tau_{\delta(n-1)}, \tau_{\gamma n}) \text{if} & n > 2 \end{cases}$$

with $\tau_{\gamma k}$=MUL$_L$[Inc(B/A$_k$), Inc(A$_k$)] for $k \in [1..n]$.

Preceding results allow us to propose a judicious alternative Bayes formula:

C8. (Qualitative Bayes formula)
If Inc(A$_k$)=$\tau_{\alpha k}$ with $k \in [1..n]$ for $n \geq 2$ and Inc($\vee_{k \in [1..n]}$ A$_k$) = τ_{M-1} and Inc(A$_k \wedge$A$_l$)=τ_0 $\forall k \neq l$ we have : Inc(A$_k$/B)=DIV$_L${MUL$_L$[Inc(A$_k$), Inc(B/A$_k$)], Inc(B)}

$$\text{with} \quad \text{Inc(B)} = \tau_{\delta n} = \begin{cases} \text{ADD}_L(\tau_{\gamma(n-1)}, \tau_{\gamma n}) & \text{if} \quad n = 2 \\ \text{ADD}_L(\tau_{\delta(n-1)}, \tau_{\gamma n}) & \text{if} \quad n > 2 \end{cases}$$

and $\tau_{\gamma k}$=MUL$_L$[Inc(B/A$_k$), Inc(A$_k$)] for $k \in [1..n]$.

Proof: The proof is given by using the definition 6, C5 and C7.

All previous results are coherent in accordance with the classical probabality theory. Now, we will propose some other results, very useful to manage uncertainty in knowledge-based systems. These results are not directly linked with the classical probability theory, but with fuzzy logic, possibility theory, etc.

Using the proposed tools, we find the result already given by [10].

C9. (Qualitative uncertainty of logical implication) If Inc(A)=τ_α and Inc(B)=τ_β and Inc(A$\wedge$B)=τ_γ then Inc(A$\supset$B)=Inc(A)$\rightarrow_L$Inc(A$\cap$B).

Proof: Let Inc(A)=τ_α, Inc(B)=τ_β and Inc(A$\wedge$B)=τ_γ with τ_γ=max($\tau_{\alpha+\beta-(M-1)}$, τ_0). Recall that A$\supset$B is equivalent to $\neg$A$\vee$B with $\neg$A$\vee$B=($\neg$A$\vee$A)$\wedge$($\neg$A$\vee$B)=$\neg$A$\vee$(A$\wedge$B). Using U4, we get: Inc(A$\supset$B)=Inc($\neg$A$\vee$(A$\wedge$B)). As $\neg$A and A$\wedge$B are incompatible, so Inc(A$\supset$B)=ADD$_L$($\neg\tau_\alpha$, τ_γ)=min($\tau_{M-1-\alpha+\gamma}$, τ_{M-1})=$\tau_\alpha \rightarrow_L \tau_\gamma$=Inc(A)$\rightarrow_L$Inc(A$\wedge$B) .

Proposition 6 : If (A$\wedge$B)$\neq\tau_0$, then Inc(A$\supset$B)=Inc(B/A).

Proof: Recall that Inc(B/A)=DIV$_L$ [Inc(A$\wedge$B), Inc(A)]. From the formula 4.2 of the proposition 4 we have: in the case $\gamma \neq 0$, Inc(B/A)=min($\tau_{M-1-\alpha+\gamma}$, τ_{M-1})=Inc(A$\supset$B).

Contrarily to the qualitative uncertainty of a logical implication, we propose for generalized qualitative modus ponens a different result of that in [10].

C10. (Generalized qualitative modus ponens) If Inc(A$\supset$B)=τ_λ and Inc(A)=τ_α then Inc(B)$\geq$max($\tau_{\alpha+\lambda-(M-1)}$, τ_0).

Proof: According to C9 we have: $Inc(A \supset B)=Inc(A) \rightarrow_L Inc(A \wedge B)=\min(\tau_{M-1-\alpha+\gamma}, \tau_{M-1})$. By virtue of increasing property of the Lukasiewicz implication as compared to its second argument we have: $\tau_\gamma \leq \tau_\beta \Rightarrow \tau_\alpha \rightarrow_L \tau_\gamma \leq \tau_\alpha \rightarrow_L \tau_\beta$.
By hypothesis we know that: $\tau_\alpha \rightarrow_L \tau_\gamma = \tau_\lambda$, so $\tau_\lambda \leq \tau_\alpha \rightarrow_L \tau_\beta$.
Consider the case $\tau_\alpha > \tau_\beta$, we have:

$$\tau_\lambda \leq \tau_{M-1-\alpha+\beta} \Rightarrow \lambda \leq M-1-\alpha+\beta \Rightarrow \beta \geq \alpha+\lambda-(M-1) \Rightarrow \tau_\beta \geq \tau_{\alpha+\lambda-(M-1)}.$$

Knowing that $\beta \in [0..M-1]$ then $\tau_\beta \geq \max(\tau_{\alpha+\lambda-(M-1)}, \tau_0)$.
For a good propagation of degrees, we choose: $\tau_\beta = \max(\tau_{\alpha+\lambda-(M-1)}, \tau_0)$.

6. An example

Let us consider an example of a gambler who proposes to a public to bet on three distinct cards in order to find a given card chosen beforehand. When someone wants to bet, he chooses a card among these three cards then with the help of rapid gestures, the gambler displaces the cards and put them face hidden on-line ahead of the bettor. If the player is not an accomplice, he found himself in front of two possibilities: either he avoids to follow the manipulations of the gambler in order not to be influenced or he paid attention to its gestures in order to follow the good card. Considering the three types of bettor (accomplice(B), avoiding to follow manipulations (C), following manipulations (D)), it's very difficult to deal with this problem numerically because there is no precise statistical available information about the repartition of the types of bettor in the given population. To avoid this kind of difficulty, we prefer to approach this problem qualitatively rather than quantitatively. Let us consider four propositions about the player: **A** (the player wins), **B** (the player is an accomplice), **C** (the player avoids to follow manipulations) and **D** (the player follows the gestures).
We assign uncertainty degrees to each proposition according to our belief:

- $Inc(B)=\tau_2$ because it is «**little possible**» that the player is an accomplice since in this example, the accomplice must rarely play; $Inc(A/B)=\tau_6$ because it is «**certain**» that the accomplice wins each time he plays.
- $Inc(C)=\tau_1$ because it is «**nearly impossible**» that a player does not follow manipulations; $Inc(A/C)=\tau_3$ because it is «**possible**» that a player who does not follows manipulations can win.
- $Inc(D)=\tau_4$ because it is «**rather possible**» that a player follows manipulations (usually people do so); $Inc(A/D)=\tau_3$ because it is «**possible**» for a player to win when he follows manipulations.

Let us compute:

a) The uncertainty degree that a given player wins :
$Inc(A)=Inc((A \wedge B) \vee (A \wedge C) \vee (A \vee D))$ because the propositions B, C and D are mutually exclusive and cover the players set. Using U5, we get : $Inc(A)=ADD_L[Inc(A \wedge B), ADD_L[Inc(A \wedge C), Inc(A \wedge D)]]$. Since A and B are not quasi-independent, we can not apply the proposition 5.
Therefore it is necessary to use C5. We obtain:
$Inc(A)=ADD_L[MUL_L(Inc(A/B),Inc(B)),ADD_L[MUL_L(Inc(A/C),Inc(C)), MUL_L(Inc(A/D),Inc(D))]]$.
So, $Inc(A)=ADD_L(MUL_L(\tau_6, \tau_2), ADD_L [MUL_L(\tau_3, \tau_1), MUL_L(\tau_3, \tau_4)])=\tau_3$. It shows that it is *possible* that a given person can win.

b) The uncertainty degree that a winner is an accomplice :
Using C8, we find :
$Inc(B/A)=DIV_L\{MUL_L[Prob(A/B), Prob(B)], Prob(A)\}=\tau_5$.
It means that it is *very possible* that a winner is an accomplice.
c) The uncertainty degree linking the winner to an accomplice :
Using C9, we have :
$Inc(A\supset B)=Inc(A)\rightarrow_L Inc(A\wedge B)$, and using C5 :
$Inc(A\wedge B)=MUL_L(Inc(A/B), Inc(B))=MUL_L(\tau_6, \tau_2)=\tau_2$.
So, $Inc(A\supset B)=\tau_3\rightarrow_L\tau_2=\tau_5$. It means that the degree of belief linking A to B is *very possible*.

7. Conclusion

This investigation is motivated by finding a model which simulates some activities of a cognitive agent, such as management of uncertain statements of natural language using a finite totally ordered set of symbolic values. Based on the classical probability theory and the M-valued predicate logic, we proposed a model analogue to that of [3]. Our axiomatic is similar to that of [10, 15]. The judicious choice of our operators enables us to remove the denominator-indifference and ambiguity-generation and to preserve the expressive aspect in concordance with the intuition. This investigation reveals that the overall structure provides an interesting aspect compared to that of classical probability, especially in the case when events are linked. In summary, we have presented in this theoretical framework a rigorous model for evaluating uncertainties in qualitative manner. Axioms and the derived consequences can be used in Bayesian networks as well as in knowledge-based systems, in the absence of quantitative estimations.

7. References

1. H. Akdag, M. De Glas & D. Pacholczyk «A Qualitative theory of Uncertainty», Fundamenta Informaticae, Vol 17, N° 4, 1992.
2. H. Akdag & F. Khoukhi «Une approche logico-symbolique pour le traitement des connaissances nuancées», Proceedings of the fifth IPMU, Paris, 1994.
3. R. Aleliunas «A Summary of New Normative Theory of Probabilistic Logic», Uncertainty in Artificial Intelligence 4, Elsevier Publication Science, North Holland, 1990.
4. B. Bouchon- Meunier «La logique floue et ses applications», Addison-Wesley, Paris, 1995.
5. Darwiche & M. Ginsberg «A Symbolic Generalization of Probability Theory», Proceedings of the American Association for Artificial Intelligence, San Jose, California, 1992.
6. D. Dubois, H. Prade, L. Godo and R. Lopez De Manteras «Qualitative Reasoning with Imprecise Probabilities», Journal of Intelligent Information Systems, 2, Kluwer Academic Publishers, Boston, p319-363, 1993.
7. J.M. Keynes «A Treatise on Probability», Macmillan, London, 1921.
8. B.O. Koopmann «The Axioms and Algebra of Intuitive Probabilities», Annals of Mathematics, Vol. 41, N° 2, 1940.

9. N. Nilsson «Probabilistic Logic», Artificial Intelligence, 28, 1986.
10. D. Pacholczyk & J. M. Pacholczyk «Traitement Symbolique des Informations Incertaines», Proceedings of RFIA, Nantes, 1996.
11. H. Seridi, F Bannay-Dupin, H. Akdag «Qualitative operators for dealing with uncertainty», Proceeding of Fuzzy-Neuro Systems'98, edited by C.Freksa, infix, p202-209, 1998.
12. H. Seridi, H. Akdag «Le traitement de l'incertain par une approche qualitative», Proceeding of IPMU'98, p1684-1690, Paris, 1998.
13. G. Shafer «The Art of Causal Conjecture», MIT Press, Cambridge, Massachusetts, 1996.
14. W. Spohn «A General Non-Probabilistic Theory of Inductive Reasoning», Uncertainty in Artificial Intelligence 4, Elsevier Publication Science, North Holland, 1990.
15. Y. Xiang, M.P. Beddoes and P. David «Can Uncertainty Management Be Realized In A Finite Totally Ordered Probability Algebra?», Uncertainty in Artificial Intelligence 5, edited by Elsevier science Publishers B.V. North-Holland, p41-57, 1990.
16. L. Zadeh «The concept of linguistic variable and its application in approximate reasoning». I, II, III, Information Sciences, vol. 8, 9. 1975.

A simple possibilistic modelisation of measurement uncertainty

V. Lasserre, G. Mauris, L. Foulloy

LAMII/CESALP, Université de Savoie, 41 Avenue de la Plaine, BP 806 F-74016 Annecy France
email : {lasserre, mauris, foulloy}@esia.univ-savoie.fr

Abstract: The measurement uncertainty in physical sensors is often represented by a probabilistic approach. But such a representation of measurements is not always adapted to the treatment of information, such as, for example, aggregation using symbolic methods. So a fuzzy subset representation based on the possibility theory is sometimes preferred. That is why we have proposed a truncated triangular probability-possibility transformation, which is an approximation of the optimal transformation, to be applied to the four most encountered symmetric probability distributions. In this paper, we propose an other way of defining a truncated triangular transformation: it can be considered as an approximation of the set of confidence intervals of the associated probability distribution. With this other point of view, we propose a new way of building the resulting possibility distribution. Then, we propose to extend the application of this transformation to any unimodal and symmetric probability distribution which can be assimilated to one of the four most encountered symmetric probability laws. Such possibility distributions are easy to build, easy to handle and suboptimal in terms of specificity.

1. Introduction

Many methods have been introduced to deal with measurement uncertainty: interval calculation, probability theory, possibility theory, all included in the Dempster-Shafer theory. In practice, in the case of physical sensors, statistics are generally available, and uncertainties are represented by a probability distribution. But though the probabilistic framework is well known, it sometimes leads to complex calculations to identify a law or when basic measurements are derived or combined. Moreover, this theory is not always adapted to advanced treatments such as aggregation, in particular when symbolic methods are used: a possibilistic representation is then preferred. Note that at the present time, a possibilistic representation of uncertainty is already adopted, for example when measurements are used in further treatments like fusion with other sensor measurements (see [1], [2]), or conversion into a symbolic format in order to supply reasoning systems (see [3], [4], [5]).

So a possibilistic modelisation is sometimes preferred instead of a probabilistic one, that is why several probability-possibility transformations have been proposed. Let us recall that, at the theoretical level, the transformation of a probability function into a possibility one have been completely studied by Dubois et al. [6], who define an optimum transformation. Unfortunately, this transformation is relatively complex to build and to handle. The other probability-possibility transformations that have been proposed are not satisfactory in terms of specificity. So we have proposed in [7] a truncated triangular transformation, which is an approximation of the optimal transformation, to be applied to the four most encountered symmetric probability laws: Gaussian, double-exponential, triangular and uniform laws.

In this paper, after having recalled the results given in [7], we propose an other way of understanding the truncated triangular transformation by considering the resulting truncated triangular possibility distribution (t.p.d.) from a statistical point of view: it can be considered as an approximation of the set of confidence intervals of the associated probability distribution. With this new point of view, we propose a new way of building the t.p.d.. Then, we propose to extend the application of the truncated triangular transformation to any unimodal and symmetric probability distribution which can be assimilated to one of the four most encountered probability laws.

2. Truncated triangular possibility distribution

The t.p.d. that we try to build is an approximation of the optimal possibility distribution proposed by Dubois et al. [6]. In this paragraph, it will be seen that two interpretations of the optimal possibility distribution are possible, so two interpretations of the t.p.d. are also possible, that is, two ways of building it.

2.1. Interpretation of the optimal transformation

2.1.1. Background: the optimal possibility distribution is seen as the result of the optimal transformation applied on the probability function

At the theoretical level, the transformation of a probability function into a possibility one has been completely studied by Dubois et al. [6], who define an optimum transformation as the transformation which loses as little information as possible. It is called the most specific transformation. Concretely, it gives the possibility distribution which has the smallest area, under the two following conditions (let X be a universe of discourse):

- the consistency principle: $P(A) \le \Pi(A), \forall A \subset X$
- the preference preservation:

$$p(a) < p(b) \Rightarrow \pi(a) < \pi(b)$$
$$p(a) = p(b) \Rightarrow \pi(a) = \pi(b), \forall a, b \in X$$

In the continuous case, the optimum transformation is defined like this: there is one solution for a unimodal continuous probability density function p with support $[a,b]$, such that p is increasing on $[a, x_0]$, and decreasing on $[x_0, b]$, where x_0 is the modal value of p. Defining a function $f: [a, x_0] \to [x_0, b]$, by:

$f(x) = max\{y / p(y) \ge p(x)\}$

then the optimal solution transforming p into a possibility distribution π is given by:

$$\pi_{optimal}(x) = \pi_{optimal}(f(x)) = \int_{-\infty}^{x} p(y)dy + \int_{f(x)}^{\infty} p(y)dy \qquad (1)$$

2.1.2. An other interpretation of the optimal possibility distribution: a set of confidence intervals of the associated probability distribution

Let us first recall the notion of confidence interval: let p be a probability distribution, and x_c be a "one point" estimation (for example the mean value of the probability distribution) of the "real" value. A confidence interval is defined around the "one point" estimation x_c, and the confidence corresponds to the probability for this interval to contain the "real" value. Such an interval is called a confidence interval, of confidence level $(1-\alpha)$ (95%, 99% for example). α is the risk level, that is, the probability for the real value to be outside the interval.

So, Dubois et al.[8] have suggested that $\pi_{optimal}(x)$ can be interpreted as the confidence degree associated to the interval $[x,f(x)]$. When $p(x)$ is symmetric, $f(x)$ is equal to $2x_0-x$ (with x_0, the modal value of $p(x)$), that is, the "one point" estimation x_c is taken equal to x_0.

Note that other transformations have been proposed (see [9], [10], [11], [12]), but they are either difficult to build -like the optimum transformation- or they are far from the optimal transformation in terms of specificity. That is why we have proposed in [7] a new transformation whose result is a t.p.d., and which can be considered as an approximation of the optimal transformation. The t.p.d. is easier to build than the optimal possibility distribution, and satisfies the consistency principle.

2.2. Truncated triangular transformation: the choice of its parameters

When the truncated triangular transformation is applied on symmetric probability functions, the general shape of the resulting possibility distribution is:

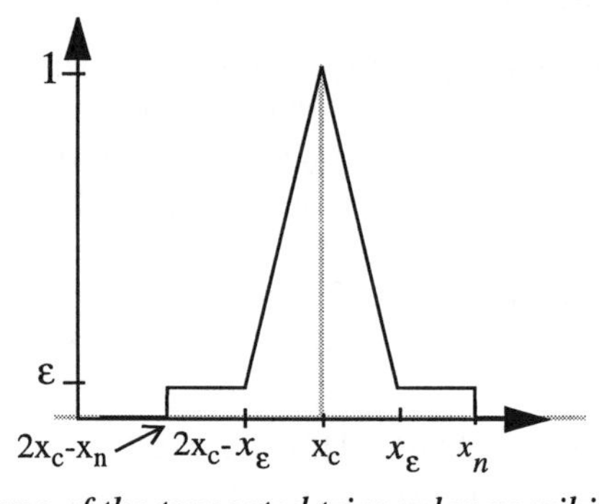

Figure 1 : General shape of the truncated triangular possibility distribution (t.p.d.)

The curve definition is thus (2):

$$\pi_{triang}(x) = \begin{cases} 1-\dfrac{(1-\varepsilon)}{(x_\varepsilon - x_c)}\cdot|x-x_c| & if \quad |x-x_c| \le (x_\varepsilon - x_c) \\ \varepsilon & if \ (x_\varepsilon - x_c) \le |x-x_c| \le (x_n - x_c) \\ 0 & if \quad |x-x_c| \ge (x_n - x_c) \end{cases} \qquad (2)$$

We propose to apply the truncated triangular transformation on the four most encountered unimodal and symmetric probability laws, of mean value x_m and standard deviation σ:

- *Gaussian law:* $p(x) = \frac{1}{\sigma\sqrt{2\pi}}e^{-\frac{(x-x_m)^2}{2\sigma^2}}$

- *Double-Exponential law:* $p(x) = \frac{1}{\sigma\sqrt{2}}e^{-\frac{\sqrt{2}|x-x_m|}{\sigma}}$

- *Triangular law:* $p(x) = \begin{cases} \frac{1}{\sigma\sqrt{6}} - \frac{|x-x_m|}{6\sigma^2} & \text{if } |x-x_m| < \sigma\sqrt{6} \\ 0 & \text{else} \end{cases}$

- *Uniform law:* $p(x) = \begin{cases} \frac{1}{2\sigma\sqrt{3}} & \text{if } |x-x_m| < \sigma\sqrt{3} \\ 0 & \text{else} \end{cases}$

Note that the uniform law is not unimodal, so the optimal possibility distribution corresponding to this law cannot be seen as the result of the application of the optimal transformation on the uniform law. Anyway, it can be seen as the set of confidence intervals of the uniform law, built around the mean value of the uniform law. So, the interest of the second interpretation of the optimal possibility distribution is already shown here.

If the truncated triangular transformation is applied on one of the four former probability laws, the resulting t.p.d. is completely determined when x_c, x_n, x_ε, ε are known. In the following, we show how to determine these parameters.

2.2.1. Choice of x_c

Three of these four probability laws are unimodal and symmetric, so for such probability distributions, their corresponding optimal possibility distributions can be seen as the results of the optimal transformation. In this case, the modal value x_0 of the probability law is chosen for x_c, in order to satisfy the preference preservation. For the uniform law, which is not unimodal, the resulting optimal possibility distribution can only be seen as the set of confidence intervals associated to the law. And for this law, x_c is chosen equal to the mean value of the uniform law. The choice of the mean value for x_c is justified by the fact that this value is the best estimation according to the maximum likelihood criterion. Note that for unimodal and symmetric probability laws, the mean, modal and median values are equal, so it can be said for each one of these four previous laws that the mean value is chosen for x_c.

2.2.2. Choice of x_n, x_ε and ε

We propose to make first the choice of x_n. Then x_ε is chosen such that a maximum of specificity is satisfied for the t.p.d.. Finally, ε is simply deduced in a single way from x_ε by (see [7]):

$$\varepsilon = \pi_{optimal}(x_\varepsilon) = 2\int_{x_\varepsilon}^{\infty} p(t)dt \qquad (3)$$

Note that it can be mathematically shown that the parameter ε does not depend on σ. So, the value of ε is the same for any σ of a given law.

The four probability laws on which we propose to apply the truncated triangular transformation can be classified in two groups:

- the group of bounded laws : triangular and uniform laws. For these laws, the most natural choice of x_n seems to be: $x_n = \{\max x \,/\, p(x) > 0\}$.

  In Table 1 are summarized the t.p.d. parameters of these two probability laws. Note already that the expressions of x_n and x_ε, for the t.p.d. of the four probability laws, are dependent on x_c -which is shown for the t.p.d. of the triangular law in Table 1-. It has been considered that for these four laws, $x_c = x_m$, so x_c is systematically replaced by x_m in Table 1, and in the next tables which give the results of the t.p.d. parameters of the two other laws.

Table 1: parameters of the t.p.d applied on the triangular and uniform laws

	t.p.d. for the triangular law	t.p.d. for the uniform law
x_c	x_m	x_m
x_n	$x_c + 2.45\sigma = x_m + 2.45\sigma$	$x_m + 1.73\sigma$
x_ε	$x_c + 1.63\sigma = x_m + 1.63\sigma$	$x_m + 1.73\sigma = x_n$
ε	0.11	0

- no-bounded laws which become : Gaussian law and exponential law. For these laws, an approximation is needed to choose x_n, and to do this approximation, several criteria can be applied. In the following will be described two of them which seem to be relevant. These criteria depend on the interpretation of the t.p.d. (see paragraph 2.1.): for the first criterion, the t.p.d. is simply seen as the result of a probability-possibility transformation, and for the second one, the t.p.d. is seen as an approximation of the set of confidence intervals associated to the studied probability law.

  - t.p.d. seen as the result of a probability-possibility transformation: the first possible choice is simply to see the t.p.d. as the result of a probability-possibility transformation, that is the equivalent possibilistic representation of a probabilistic one. In [7], we have adopted this point of view, and so, proposed to choose x_n such that $p(x_n)=10^{-3}$ (effectively, in the context of physical sensors, $p(x_n)<10^{-3}$ is seldom measured, so it can be approximated to 0). In Table 2 are summarized the t.p.d. parameters of these four probability laws, using this first criterion.

Table 2: parameters of the t.p.d. applied on the Gaussian and exponential laws, using the 1st criterion: $p(x_n)=10^{-3}$

	t.p.d. for the Gaussian law	t.p.d. for the exponential law
x_c	x_m	x_m
x_n	$x_m+3.5\sigma$	$x_m+4.7\sigma$
x_ε	$x_m+1.74\sigma$	$x_m+1.74\sigma$
ε	0.09	0.08

- t.p.d. seen as an approximation of the set of confidence intervals: the t.p.d. can also be seen as an approximation of the set of confidence intervals of the associated probability law, intervals which are built around x_c (for the symmetric probability laws that are considered here, it has been shown previously that x_c is chosen as the mean value x_m of the probability distribution). As it is difficult to obtain intervals which really correspond to confidence levels higher than 99%, we choose for the t.p.d. a largest confidence interval of confidence level equal to 0.99. That is, we propose to choose x_n such that $P[2x_m - x_n, x_n]=0.99$, with P, the probability measure associated to the considered probability density function.

So x_n is chosen such that:

$$\pi_{optimal}(x_n) = 1 - 0.99 = 0.01$$

In Table 3 are summarized the t.p.d. parameters of these two probability laws, using this second criterion.

Table 3: parameters of the t.p.d. applied on the Gaussian and double exponential laws, using the 2nd criterion: $P[2x_m - x_n, x_n]$=0.99

	t.p.d. for the Gaussian law	t.p.d. for the exponential law
x_c	x_m	x_m
x_n	$x_m + 2.58\sigma$	$x_m + 3.2\sigma$
x_ε	$x_m + 1.54\sigma$	$x_m + 1.46\sigma$
ε	0.12	0.13

2.3. Comparison of the t.p.d. with other probability-possibility transformations

In Table 4 are summarised the specificity degrees of the t.p.d. associated to the four previous probability laws, when the second criterion is used, in comparison with the specificity degrees of the possibility distributions obtained by applying the optimal transformation and the most used probability-possibility transformations (see [2], [13], [14] for examples using these transformations).

The expressions of these other transformations are:

- the inverse of the optimal transformation: $\pi(x) = \int_{-\infty}^{\infty} min(p(x), p(t))dt$
- the normalised transformation: $\pi(x) = \dfrac{p(x)}{p_m}$ with $p_m = sup_x p(x)$
- the Klir's transformation: $\pi(x) = \left(\dfrac{p(x)}{p_m}\right)^{\beta}$, with β satisfiying the conservation of uncertainty [11].

Note that the specificity degree of each resulting possibility distribution is obtained by computing the area under the distribution. It is shown that the possibility distributions obtained by these transformations are less specific than the t.p.d., except the optimal possibility distribution. So, the truncated triangular transformation is suboptimal in terms of specificity.

On figure 2, the t.p.d. of the Gaussian - centered and reduced - law is plotted, using the second criterion, in comparison with the possibility distributions obtained with the other most used probability-possibility transformations.

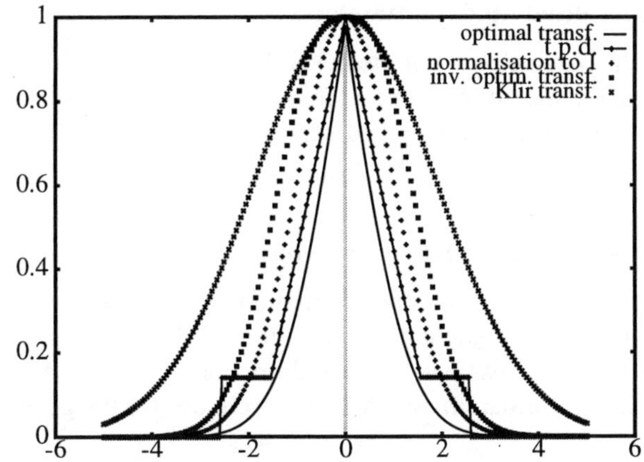

Figure 2 : comparison of the t.p.d. (using the second criterion) corresponding to the centered reduced gaussian law, with the other possibility transformations

Note that this second interpretation of the optimal transformation as the set of the confidence intervals (centered on the mean value) of the corresponding probability distribution shows the t.p.d. as an approximation of this set of confidence intervals. This approximation is quite good for confidence degrees between 0 and $1-\varepsilon$ (i.e. roughly 90% for the considered laws). Between $1-\varepsilon$ and 1, this approximation is worse. Note that if a higher approximation is needed for a slightly bigger confidence degree, x_ε can be slightly increased so that ε decreases; anyway some specificity will be lost. The confidence interval given for $x=x_n$ is exactly 99%. So, in the following, we will prefer this criterion.

3. Generalised truncated triangular transformation

To build a truncated triangular transformation which can be applied to any unimodal and symmetric probability distribution of a given mean value x_m and a given standard deviation σ, let us suppose first that any unimodal and symmetric probability distribution can be correctly modelised by one of the four previous probability laws. So, we will try to build a generalised t.p.d. which looks like the t.p.d. of the four most encountered probability laws as much as possible, under the consistency principle, i.e. an upper envelope of the four t.p.d.'s.

3.1. Value of the generalised t.p.d. parameter x_c

For the four symmetric probability laws, it has been shown that x_c is chosen as the mean value x_m of the probability law. So the same choice is made for the generalised t.p.d.:

$$x_c = x_m$$

3.2. Value of generalised t.p.d. parameter x_n

For the value of the parameter x_n of the generalised t.p.d., to build an upper envelope of the four t.p.d.'s, the maximum value is chosen among the ones defined for the four probability laws - of mean value x_m and standard deviation σ -, in order not to lose information (see Tables 1, 2 and 3): $x_n = x_m + 3.2\sigma$

3.3. Value of the generalised t.p.d. parameters x_ε and ε

On figure 3 are plotted the optimal transformations of the four centered reduced probability laws. Note that the optimal transformations of three laws (Gaussian, exponential, and triangular laws) cross one another almost on the same point: x=1.73. So, in order to lose as little information as possible, we choose for the generalised t.p.d.:

$$x_\varepsilon = x_m + 1.73\sigma .$$

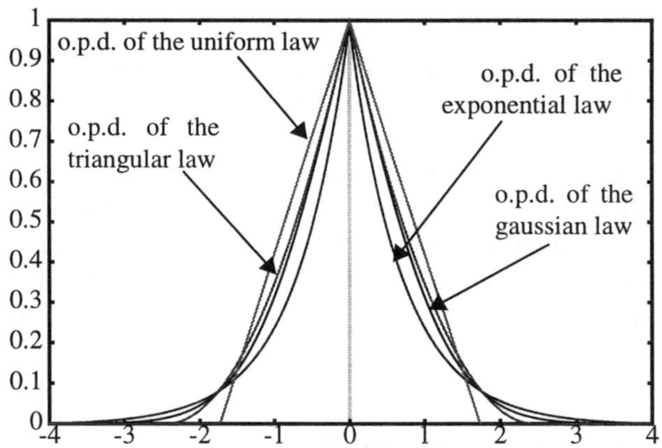

Figure 3 : the optimal possibility distributions (o.p.d.) corresponding to the four reduced centered probability laws

Then, the corresponding parameters ε for each law's t.p.d. are computed:

- Gaussian law: $\varepsilon = 0.081$,
- double exponential law: $\varepsilon = 0.086$,
- triangular law: $\varepsilon = 0.086$,
- uniform law: $\varepsilon = 0.0011$.

Then, we choose the maximum value of ε among the ones computed for each probability law, in order to satisfy the consistency principle: ε =0.086.

With this procedure, the value of x_ε is the same, but the value of ε is smaller. Some specificity is gained, but also a good approximation of the confidence intervals is obtained for confidence degrees smaller than 91.4%. The parameters of the generalised t.p.d. corresponding to a probability law assimilated to one of the four considered laws, of mean value x_m and standard deviation σ are defined as:

$$x_c = x_m, \quad x_\varepsilon = x_m + 1.73\sigma , \quad x_n = x_m + 3.2\sigma , \quad \varepsilon = 0.086 \tag{4}$$

If the generalised t.p.d. is compared with results given by the other most used transformations, applied on the four previous reduced probability laws, it can be noted that the generalised t.p.d. always gives the best results in terms of specificity (see table 4) (Let us recall that the specificity degree of each possibility distribution is obtained by computing the area under the distribution). In figure 4, the generalised t.p.d. of the centered reduced Gaussian law is plotted, in comparison with the possibility distributions obtained with the other most used probability-possibility transformations.

Table 4: Comparison of the different resulting possibility distributions, in terms of specificity

degrees of specificity	optimal transf.	t.p.d.	normal. transf.	inv. of the opt. transf.	Klir's transf.	generalised t.p.d.
Gaussian law	1.59	1.97	2.5	3.2	4.91	2.13
exponential law	1.4	2.1	1.4	2.8	7.05	2.13
triangular law	1.62	2.0	2.45	3.3	4.21	2.13
uniform law	1.73	1.73	3.45	3.45	3.5	2.13

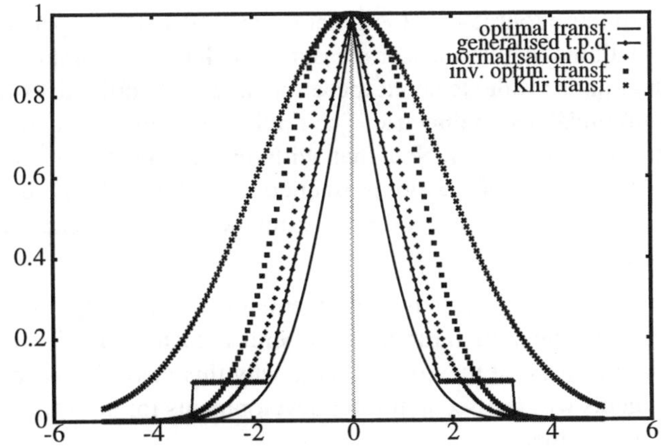

Figure 4 : comparison of the generalised t.p.d. corresponding to the centered reduced gaussian law, with the possibility distributions resulting from other transformations

3.4. Discussion

Let us suppose that any unimodal and symmetric probability distribution can be correctly modelised by one the four previous probability laws. Then, this unimodal and symmetric probability distribution can be transformed into a possibility distribution (a generalised t.p.d.) without previously modelising it into a probability law, which is known as being complex. So the procedure is simplified and the generalised t.p.d. is easy to build, and suboptimal in terms of specificity. Note that such a choice enables the generalised t.p.d. to give a good approximation of confidence intervals whose confidence levels are smaller than 91.4%.

Note finally that when enough primary measures are available to build a relevant histogram, the best way to lose as little information as possible under the consistency principle is to determine x_n by choosing the histogram limit. This choice will not influence the choice of x_ε which has been determined independently from x_n.

4. Conclusion

In this paper, we have proposed an other way of interpreting the truncated triangular transformation which is an approximation of the optimal transformation, and, which thus can be seen as an approximation of the set of confidence intervals associated to the considered probability distribution. Thanks to this point of view, we have proposed a new way of building the resulting possibility distribution (t.p.d.) when the truncated triangular transformation is applied on the four most encountered symmetric probability laws: for a sensor measurement modelisation, the "true value" is bound to be contained in the t.p.d. with 99% of confidence. This criterion seems interesting when it is known that, in the case of sensor measurements, it is difficult to obtain intervals which really correspond to confidence intervals larger than 99%.

Then we have proposed a generalised t.p.d. which can be applied to any of the four most encountered probability laws, and so, to any intermediate law which can be assimilated to one of these four laws. This generalised t.p.d. can be especially used when the standard deviation of a given sensor measurement has been computed a priori, and when no information is available about the associated probability distribution, except that the law is unimodal and symmetric. The t.p.d. is easy to build and to handle, and suboptimal in terms of specificity. Note that, with this new method of construction, the t.p.d. associated to each one of the four most encountered probability distributions and the generalised t.p.d. are giving good approximations of confidence levels roughly smaller than 90%.

An advantage to modelize sensors measurements by a possibility distribution is that the propagation of information in further treatments is easier to realise, and even more thanks to the simple shape of the t.p.d.. That is why this possibilistic modelisation of sensor measurements will be used in further developments for derivation and aggregation of sensor measurements.

References

[1] O. Strauss, "Filtering and fusing compass and gyrometer data using guess filter", *FUZZ'IEEE 97*, Barcelona, Spain, Vol. 3, pp. 1593-1599, 1997.

[2] M. Oussala, H. Maaref, C. Barret, "Kalman filter and possibility theory for the localisation of a mobile robot", *EUFIT'96*, Aachen, Germany, Vol. 3, pp. 1650-1655, 1996.

[3] Zadeh, "Quantitative fuzzy semantics", Information Sciences, Vol. 3, pp. 159-176, 1971.

[4] G. Mauris, E. Benoit, L. Foulloy, "Fuzzy symbolic sensors: from concepts to applications", Measurement, 12, pp. 357-384, 1994.

[5] W. Pedricz, E. Rowenta, "From fuzzy information processing to fuzzy communication channels", IEEE Instrumentation and Measurement Technical Conference IMTC'97, Ottawa, pp. 796-801, May 1997.

[6] D. Dubois, H. Prade, S. Sandri, "On Possibility/Probability transformations", *Fuzzy Logic*, R. Lowen and M. Roubens (eds.), Kluwer Academic Publishers, pp. 103-112, 1993.

[7] V. Lasserre, G. Mauris, L. Foulloy, "A simple probability-possibility transformation for measurement error representation: a truncated triangular transformation", *IFSA'97*, Prague, Vol. 3, pp. 476-481, 1997.

[8] D. Dubois, H. Prade, "Fuzzy sets, probability and measurement", *European Journal of Operational research,* 40, pp. 135-154, 1989.

[9] M.R. Civanlar, H.J. Trussell, "Constructing membership functions using statistical data", *Fuzzy Sets and Systems*, 18, pp. 1-13, 1986.

[10] S. Wonneberger, "Generalization of an invertible mapping between probability and possibility", *Fuzzy Sets and Systems,* 64, pp. 229-240, 1994.

[11] J.F. Geer and G.J. Klir, "A mathematical analysis of information-preserving transformations between probabilistic and possibilistic formulations of uncertainty", *Intern. J. of General Systems*, 20(2), pp. 143-176, 1992.

[12] Ree and Jager, "Control-data representation at knowledge level", *IEEE Intern. Conf. on Syst., Man and Cybernetics,* Le Touquet, France, Vol. 4, pp. 702-706, 1993.

[13] L. Roux, J. Desachy, "Information fusion for supervised classification in a satellite image", *FUZ'IEEE 95*, pp. 1119-1124, 1995.

[14] R. Palm, "Processing of signal distributions in control loops", *EUFIT'94,* Aachen, Germany, pp. 310-321, 1994.

Analogy as a Basis of Various Forms of Approximate Reasoning

B. Bouchon-Meunier, J. Delechamp*, C. Marsala, M. Rifqi
LIP6, UPMC, Case 169
4 place Jussieu
75252 Paris Cédex 05, France
* LCPC
58 boulevard Lefebvre
75015 Paris, France
{Bernadette.Bouchon-Meunier, Christophe.Marsala, Maria.Rifqi}@lip6.fr, delecham@lcpc.fr

Abstract

We present a general framework representing analogy, on the basis of a link between variables and measures of comparison between values of variables. This analogical scheme is proven to represent a common description of several forms of reasoning used in fuzzy control or in the management of knowledge-based systems, such as deductive reasoning, inductive reasoning or prototypical reasoning and interpolative reasoning.

1. Introduction

Analogy is a natural means of drawing a conclusion for human beings. Analogy can have several forms identified in psychology by Richard [14] : the first one corresponds to a heuristic method to formulate hypotheses by taking into account a link between two relations defined on two distinct universes and the knowledge concerning one of them to deduce an information concerning the other one. The second form consists in transferring a methodology used to deal with a class of situations, in order to deal with situations which are similar to those of this class but which do not belong to it. Some other forms of analogy can be identified, concerning the passage between linguistic terms or different domains. We focus on the two first forms because they have given rise to developments in Artificial Intelligence. Secretan identifies analogy in philosophy [17] as an oscillation between the resemblance which it means and the dissimilarity which it spans without reducing it. He notes that Platon and Aristote have already analyzed analogy and established the existence of a link or a relationship between elements taken into account in the analogy.

From these points of view, it appears that the two basic elements to define analogy are a *link* (or a transfer map) between two universes or domains and a *relation* (expressing a similarity or not) on each of the universes. Defined in the framework of psychology, link and relations are not rigid and, if we model them mathematically with the purpose to prepare an automatic analogy-based system, a convenient definition must be flexible and able to subsume the idea of resemblance.

Analogical reasoning has been formalized in a fuzzy set based approach in various directions [7][8][20], pointing out several ways of obtaining a conclusion by means of resemblances between cases. Approximate reasoning has been presented by L.A. Zadeh as a method of automatic reasoning as close as possible to human reasoning [23]. Then, it seems natural that there is some relationship between approximate reasoning and analogy, which is at the root of most human reasoning processes. Moreover, the fact that resemblance and dissimilarity are mentioned in philosophy leads to think about the concept of measure of comparison of objects [6], [15] which has been proven to be compatible with the contrast model introduced in psychology by Tversky [21], taking into account common features and distinctive features.

In this paper, we present a general view of analogy in a fuzzy setting, which allows to regard several approximate reasoning methods in a common framework. It will be proven that the scheme representing this general view can be regarded from several angles and we will show the differences in the figures corresponding to various methods in the sequel (bold symbols will represent the given information, normal symbols the obtained information).

Our purpose is to show that several kinds of analogy exist in many reasoning methods introduced in Artificial Intelligence, even though they are not identified in the field of analogical reasoning, specially in the case when a fuzzy framework is used in such a way that the imprecision preserved in the descriptions provides the conditions underlying the paradigm of analogy.

2. Definition of an Analogical Scheme

We study an analogy between two universes X and Y. Let us consider two variables V and W, which may be simple or compound, respectively defined on X and Y. We suppose that the characterizations of V and W are fuzzy, which means that precise values of V and W are considered as particular cases of more general types of values (imprecise, approximate, vague or linguistic) represented by fuzzy sets of the universes X and Y. We want to represent the fact that some knowledge regarding V can be used to exhibit knowledge regarding W. This means that there exists some relationship between the values of V and the values of W and, more particularly, that variations of V around a given value in X, either crisp or fuzzy, enable us to describe variations of W around a corresponding value in Y.

We consider $F(X)$ and $F(Y)$ defined from the sets $[0,1]^X$ and $[0,1]^Y$ of all fuzzy sets of X and Y. We consider their elements as references on which we base our reasoning to exhibit more information. The link between universes X and Y is represented by a given relation β on $[0,1]^X \times [0,1]^Y$.

We suppose, as it is usually the case in analogy, that variables V and W behave smoothly, which means that there is no gap in their behavior and, if V varies from a value A in $[0,1]^X$ to another one A' « similar to » or « not far from » A, then W varies from a value B such that $A\beta B$ to a value B' « similar to » or « not far from » B. It is clear that the analogy lies on the identification of the link β and a way to recognize that two descriptions are « similar ».

More precisely, we consider two relations R on $[0,1]^X \times [0,1]^X$ and S on $[0,1]^Y \times [0,1]^Y$ which represent the « similarity » or the « closeness » of fuzzy sets of X and Y respectively. We shall give later more details about their properties. We define an analogical scheme as follows :

Definition: For a given relation β on $[0,1]^X \times [0,1]^Y$ and two relations R on $[0,1]^X \times [0,1]^X$ and S on $[0,1]^Y \times [0,1]^Y$, an *analogical scheme* is a mapping $\mathfrak{R}_{\beta RS} : F(X) \times F(Y) \times [0,1]^X \to [0,1]^Y$ satisfying the following conditions $\forall A \in [0,1]^X$ and $\forall B \in [0,1]^Y$ such that $A\beta B$:

(i) $B = \mathfrak{R}_{\beta RS}(A, B, A)$

(ii) $\forall A' \in [0,1]^X$ such that ARA',

$B' = \mathfrak{R}_{\beta RS}(A, B, A')$ satisfies $A'\beta B'$ and BSB'.

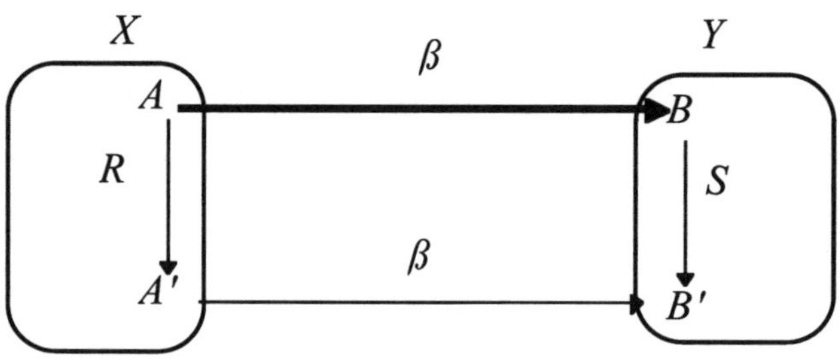

Figure 1. Analogical scheme

We can interprete this scheme as follows, as soon as β, R and S are defined properly : if A and B are known to be linked by β, and if the characterization A' of V is similar to A, we are able to find a characterization B' of W linked to A' through β and which is similar to B. We shall first study several types of reasoning which can be regarded as particular analogical schemes.

Figure 1 presents a representation of an analogical scheme, compatible with the classical approach of analogy in Artificial Intelligence [9].

3. Fuzzy deductive reasoning

In fuzzy logic, deductive reasoning is mainly based on a generalization of the modus ponens (m. p.) used in classical logic, through the so-called compositional rule of inference. Nevertheless, several other techniques have been proposed to avoid some of the drawbacks of the generalized modus ponens and we present the analogical schemes underlying some of them.

We consider a base of rules of the form :

(R_j) « if V is A_j, then W is B_j» $j \in J$,

where A_j and B_j are respectively normalized fuzzy sets of X and Y.

We introduce a link β between X and Y, such that $A\beta B$ if and only if one of the two conditions is satisfied :

(iii) there exists an object with value in X equal to A and value in Y equal to B,

(iv) there exists a rule R_j such that A is identical with A_j and B is identical with B_j.

3.1. Compositional rule of inference

We suppose that each rule R_j is associated with a fuzzy implication defined for any x in X and y in Y by $I_j(x,y)$ combining the membership functions of A_j and B_j.

The generalized m. p. works in such a way that, for any fuzzy value A' of V, any rule R_j enables us to exhibit a fuzzy value B' of W, which can be non specific if A' is too different from A. The membership function of B' is computed as a combination of the membership function of A' and the fuzzy implication I_j.

It can be proven [1] [2] [4] that, for the main forms of fuzzy implications, there exists a measure of comparison r on $[0,1]^X \times [0,1]^X$ and another one s on $[0,1]^Y \times [0,1]^Y$, with the same form as r, such that $s(B, B')$ is at least equal to a given threshold ρ as soon as $r(\mathrm{A}, A')$ is at least equal to ρ.

More precisely, in the case of conjunctive rules (for instance with the Mamdani or Larsen implication), the measures of comparison r and s are measures of similitude [6]. In the case of implicative rules, r and s are measures of satisfiability (particular cases of measures of similitude) [6] which differ, depending on the chosen fuzzy implication.

If we define a crisp relation R on $[0,1]^X \times [0,1]^X$ as follows :

$\forall A \in F(X)\ \ \forall A' \in [0,1]^X\ ARA' \Leftrightarrow r(A, A') \geq \rho$

and a crisp relation S in the same way on $[0,1]^Y \times [0,1]^Y$, then we can conclude that the compositional rule of inference is equivalent to an analogical scheme (see figure 2).

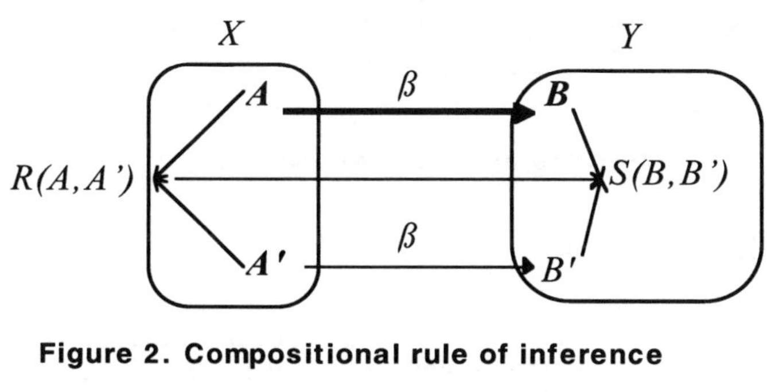

Figure 2. Compositional rule of inference

3.2. Magrez-Smets model

Magrez and Smets [12] [18] have suggested a different way of realizing an extended form of modus ponens, based on the concept of necessity. Evaluating the compatibility of A' with respect to A through the well-known conditional necessity $N(A \mid A')$, they assume that the compatibility of B' with respect to B, evaluated by means of $N(B \mid B')$ must have the same value. Consequently, they exhibit B' satisfying the following condition:

if $N(A \mid A')=\sigma$, then $N(B \mid B')= \sigma$.

If we define the two relations R on $[0,1]^X \times [0,1]^X$ and S on $[0,1]^Y \times [0,1]^Y$ in such a way that $R(A, A') = N(A \mid A')$ and $S(B, B') = N(B \mid B')$, we can conclude that the Magrez-Smets model is equivalent to an analogical scheme, as indicated on figure 3. In this case, the analogical scheme is the tool providing the solution B'.

3.3. Turksen model

In Turksen's works [18][19], a so-called similarity measure is used to compare A' to A, that we consider as the relation R on $[0,1]^X \times [0,1]^X$ and the value $R(A, A') = \rho$ is used as a parameter to define a modification function m_ρ, in such a way that the conclusion B' is obtained as $m_\rho(B)$. If we adopt the general definition of a relation S on $[0,1]^Y \times [0,1]^Y$ such that $S(B, B') = \rho$ if and only if $B' = m_\rho(B)$, then we see that this model is based on an analogical scheme identical to the form presented in section 3.2, which is again the tool providing itself the conclusion B' (see figure 3).

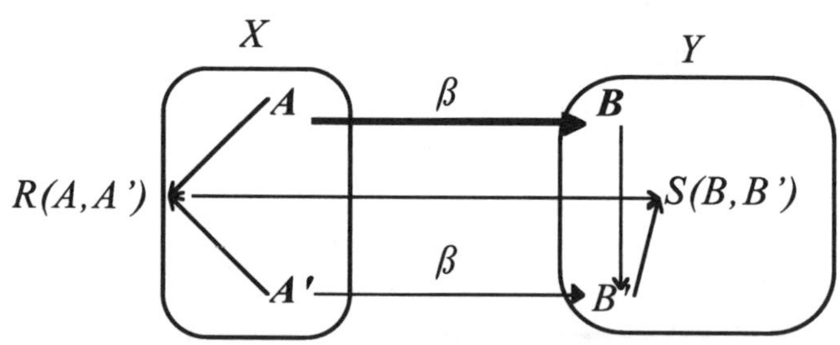

Figure 3. Magrez-Smets and Turksen models

4. Fuzzy inductive reasoning

On the one hand, inductive reasoning in mathematics has been presented by Goblot [10] as using analogy to construct hypotheses. On the other hand, analogy as a part of human reasoning is described in [11] as a « subtle, powerful inductive process ». There is clearly a relationship between inductive reasoning and analogy and we propose to regard inductive learning of rules as an analogical process.

We suppose given a population of objects E, characterized by values of a compound variable $V=(V_1, V_2, ..., V_m)$, where $V_1, V_2, ..., V_m$ are elementary attributes respectively defined on $X_1, X_2, ..., X_m$, and a class W, defined on a finite universe $Y=\{w_j, j \in J\}$. We suppose that, for a finite subset E_o of E, used as a training set, values of V and W are known. For other objects of E, the only value A of V is known and the value B of W is to be determined. We present hereunder the main methods available to enable us to determine this value.

4.1. Inductive methods constructing fuzzy rule bases

Several methods consist in two steps: the first one uses the training set E_o to construct the tool which will be the basis of the reasoning. The second step (classification step) corresponds to the utilization of this tool to deal with an object from E not belonging to E_o. More explanations can be found in [13] [15].

Let us focus on inductive learning methods (for instance based on a tree of attributes [5], prototypes [16]...) which provide a rule base during the first step, of the form:

(R_j) « if V_1 is A^1 and ... and V_i is A^i... then W is w_j», $j \in J$.

In figure 4, we represent the cartesian product of A^1,..., A^i... by the fuzzy set A of X, and $B=\{w_j\}$. In the case of decision trees, the selection of the most informative attribute through a measure of discrimination corresponds to the identification of a resemblance $H(A^1, ..., A^n)$ between the subsets of X describing the elements of E_o which will be attached to the vertex associated with the value w_j of the class.

Prototype-based reasoning uses E_o to identify the most typical values A^i on each component of V for objects in any class w_j of Y. A fuzzy prototype of w_j is a virtual object composed by these typical values for all attributes, based on resemblances and dissimilarities [15] [22].

We now study the second step of the reasoning. We consider the set $F(X)$ of fuzzy sets of X defined as the cartesian product of A^1,..., A^i,... where A^1, ... A^i, ... are the elements appearing in one of the rules R_j. The set $F(Y)$ is reduced to singletons of Y. A link β is defined as:

$(A^1, ... \ A^m) \ \beta \ w_j$ if and only if one of the two conditions is satisfied :

(v) there exists an object in E with value of V_i equal to A^i for $1 \leq i \leq m$ and value of W equal to w_j,

(vi) there exists a rule R_j of the form:

« if V_1 is A^1 and ... V_i is A^i and ... V_m is A^m then W is w_j».

We consider a measure of satisfiability r enabling us to compare fuzzy sets of X [6]. In the case where a class must be precisely identified, we define the relation R as follows:

$\forall A=(A_1, ... \ A_m) \in F(X) \ \forall A'=(A'^1, ... \ A'^m) \in [0,1]^X$

$ARA' \Leftrightarrow r(A, A') = max_{A''=(A''^1, ... \ A''^m) \in F(X)}(r(A'', A'))$

and the relation S is the identity :
$BSB' \Leftrightarrow B = B'$, with $A\beta B$ and $AR\,A'$.

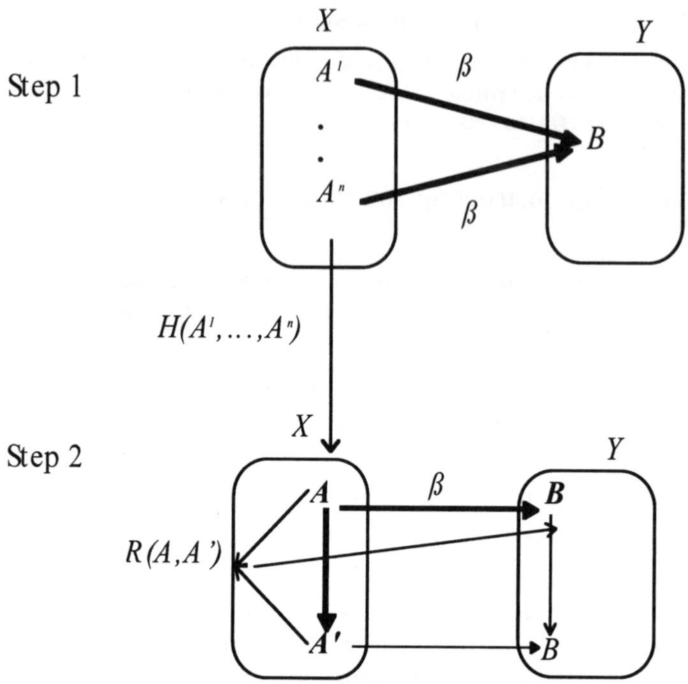

Figure 4. Inductive methods constructing fuzzy rule bases

With these notations, we see that the classification step (step 2) of this type of inductive learning is equivalent to an analogical scheme (see figure 4).

4.2. Case-based reasoning

In case-based reasoning, for a given element in E not belonging to E_o, $F(X)$ is the set of all n-tuples on $[0,1]^X$, $(A_1,\ldots,A_n)$, $n = 1, 2, \ldots$ and $F(Y)$ contains the values in Y for objects in E_o, the link β is such that $A\beta B$ if and only if there exists an object in E with value A in X and B in Y. A first phase consists in the selection of relevant n-tuples $(A_1,\ldots, A_n)$ characterizing elements of E_o, the selection being based on a measure of comparison R, for instance a distance. In a second phase, an adaptation process is used to determine B' from $(B_1,\ldots B_n)$ with $B_1 = \beta(A_1),\ldots, B_n = \beta(A_n)$. The relation S is a measure of comparison on Y. An analogical scheme $\Re_{\beta RS}$ is defined by means of the aggregation of $S(B_1, B'),\ldots, S(B_n, B')$ (see figure 5).

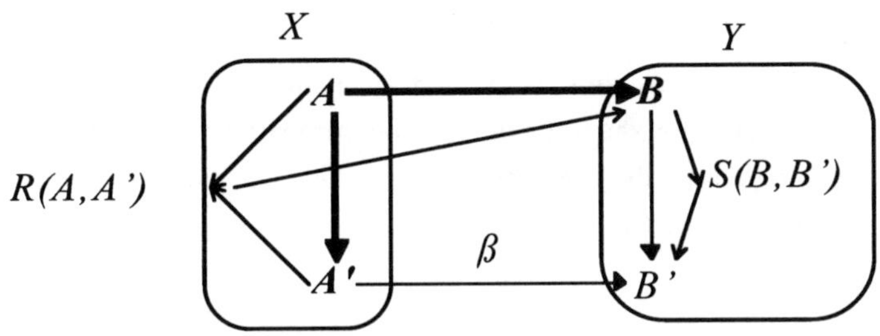

Figure 5. Case-based reasoning

Remark : We observe that the analogical scheme has not the same utility for inductive learning and for deductive reasoning by means of the compositional rule of inference. In the first case, the analogical scheme is the tool providing the result B' of the reasoning. In the second case, B' is given by the compositional rule of inference itself and we check afterwards that this result is compatible with the analogical scheme we have exhibited.

5. Interpolative reasoning

Interpolation has been studied in a fuzzy framework for many years. The authors have presented a model of interpolative reasoning [3] based on the ideas of graduality and analogy, which can be regarded as an analogical scheme.

We suppose that rules $(R_j), j \in J$, and a link β between X and Y, are given like in section 3. We further suppose that the knowledge is incomplete and this rule base is sparse, which means that there exist gaps between fuzzy sets A_j of X and a deductive method cannot be used efficiently.

We consider an order denoted by $\prec$ on fuzzy sets, for instance defined from their locations (the middles of their kernels). For a new description A' of variable V, we look for a description B of variable W and the method consists in determining the two rules, let us say R_1 and R_2, such that $A_1 \prec A' \prec A_2$. We compare A with A_1 and A_2 from two points of view : their locations and their shapes. We define concepts of :

- l-distinguishability of A' with regard to A_1 and to A_2 by $D_{lo}(A', A_1)$ and $D_{lo}(A', A_2)$, evaluating the differences of their locations,
- s-distinguishability of A' with regard to A_1 and to A_2, denoted by $D_{sh}(A', A_1)$ and $D_{sh}(A', A_2)$, evaluating the difference of their shapes.

We introduce analogous concepts on Y.

We define R on $[0,1]^X \times [0,1]^X$ and S on $[0,1]^Y \times [0,1]^Y$ by the aggregation of D_{lo} and D_{sh} and we consider $F(X) = [0,1]^X \times [0,1]^X$ and $F(Y) = [0,1]^Y \times [0,1]^Y$, in such a way that the pairs (A_1, A_2) and (B_1, B_2) are taken into account in the determination of B':

$B' = \Re_{\beta RS}\big((A_1, A_2), (B_1, B_2), A'\big)$

and B' is located between B_1 and B_2 in a way analogous to the way A' is located between A_1 and A_2, the shape of B' can be compared to the shapes of B_1 and B_2 in a way analogous to the way the shape of A' can be compared to the shapes of A_1 and A_2 (see figure 6).

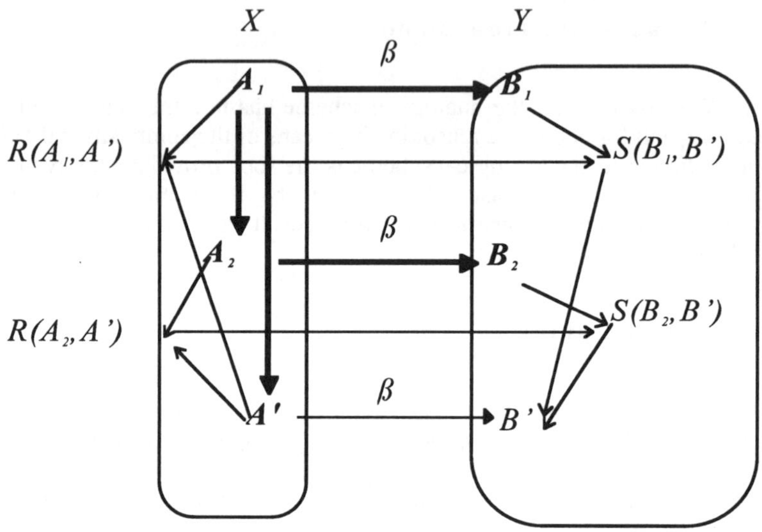

Figure 6. Interpolative reasoning

6. Conclusion

We have presented a general formalization of analogy by means of a mapping, depending on a link between variables and relations generally defined from measures of comparison of fuzzy values. One of the interests of such a formalization is to propose tools to define the resemblance between cases and methods to adapt the solution of a given case to a new situation. Another interest is to show that several reasoning methods, as different as inductive reasoning or deductive reasoning for instance, are particular cases of a general framework.

References

[1] B. Bouchon-Meunier, J. Delechamp, C. Marsala, M. Rifqi, Several Forms of Fuzzy Analogical Reasoning, *Proc. FUZZ-IEEE'97*, Barcelona, 1997.

[2] B. Bouchon-Meunier, J. Delechamp, C. Marsala, M. Rifqi. Analogy as a basis of various forms of reasoning, *Proc. ISCA 7th International Conference*, Melun, pp. 88-91, 1998.

[3] B. Bouchon-Meunier, J. Delechamp, C. Marsala, N. Mellouli, M. Rifqi. Analogy and fuzzy interpolation in the case of sparse rules, *Proc. EUROFUSE-SIC'99 Conference*, Budapest, pp. 132-136, 1999.

[4] B. Bouchon-Meunier, J. Delechamp, C. Marsala R. Mesiar, M. Rifqi. Fuzzy deductive reasoning and analogical scheme, *EUSFLAT-ESTYLF Joint Conference,* Palma de Mallorca, 1999

[5] B. Bouchon-Meunier, C. Marsala, M. Ramdani. Learning from imperfect data. in H. Prade, D. Dubois and R.R. Yager (eds), *Fuzzy Information Engineering: a Guided Tour of Applications*, pages 139-148, John Wileys and Sons, 1997.

[6] B. Bouchon-Meunier, M. Rifqi, S. Bothorel. Towards general measures of comparison of objects, *Fuzzy Sets and Systems* 84, 2, pp. 143-153, 1996.

[7] B. Bouchon-Meunier, L. Valverde. Analogical Reasoning and Fuzzy Resemblance, in *Uncertainty in Intelligent Systems* (B. Bouchon-Meunier, L. Valverde, R.Yager, eds.), Elsevier Science Pub., pp 247-255, 1993.

[8] B. Bouchon-Meunier, L. Valverde. A fuzzy approach to analogical reasoning, *Int. J. Soft Computing*, 1999, to appear.

[9] D. Coulon *et al.* Le raisonnement par analogie en intelligence artificielle, in *Actes 3e Journées Nationales PRC-GDR Intelligence Artificielle*, Hermès, pp. 45-88, 1990.

[10] E. Goblot. *Traité de logique*, Paris, 1947.

[11] J.H. Holland, K.J. Holyoak, R.E. Nisbett, P.R. Thagard. *Induction, processes of inference, learning and discovery*, The MIT Press, 1989

[12] P. Magrez, P. Smets. Fuzzy modus ponens : a new model suitable for applications in knowledge-based systems, *Int. J. Intelligent Systems* 4, 2, pp. 181-200, 1989.

[13] C. Marsala, Apprentissage inductif en présence de données imprécises: construction et utilisation d'arbres de décision flous, *Thèse de l'Université Paris VI*, also *Rapport LIP6* 98-14, 1998.

[14] J.-F. Richard. *Les activités mentales, comprendre, raisonner, trouver des solutions*, Armand Colin, 1995.

[15] M. Rifqi. Mesures de comparaison, typicalité et classification d'objets flous : théorie et pratique, *Thèse de l'Université Paris VI*, also *Rapport LAFORIA* TH96/15, 1996.

[16] M. Rifqi. Constructing prototypes from large databases, *Proc. International Conference IPMU'96*, Granada, 1996, pp. 301-306.

[17] P. Secretan. *L'analogie*, Que sais-je ? n°2165, Presses Universitaires de France, 1984.

[18] P. Smets, P. Magrez, Implication in fuzzy logic, *Int. J. Approximate Reasoning* 1, pp. 327-347, 1987.

[19] I. B. Turksen, C. Lucas. A pattern matching inference method and its comparison with known inference methods, *Proc. IFSA International Congress*, Bruxelles, 1991.

[20] I. B. Turksen, Zhao Zhong, An approximate analogical reasoning approach based on similarity measures, *IEEE Trans. Syst., Man and Cybern.* 18, 6, 1988.

[21] A. Tversky, Features of similarity, *Psychological Review* 84, 1977.

[22] L. A. Zadeh. A note on prototype theory and fuzzy sets. *Cognition*, 12:291-297, 1982.

Extension of totally coherent interval-valued probability assessments

Angelo Gilio
Dip. di Matematica
Viale Andrea Doria, 6
Università di Catania
95125 Catania (Italy)
gilio@dipmat.unict.it

Salvatore Ingrassia
Dip. di Economia Politica
Università della Calabria
87036 Arcavacata di Rende (Italy)
s.ingrassia@unical.it

Abstract: The concept of totally coherent set-valued probability assessments on a family of conditional events has been introduced in [15]. Here we examine the extendibility of interval-valued probability assessments and in this context some theoretical results are proved. These results are applied in the analysis of some well known inference rules of interest in the field of nonmonotonic reasoning.

1 Introduction

A suitable approach for managing uncertainty in situations of partial knowledge or vague information is based on imprecise probabilities, in particular interval-valued probability assessments, see e.g. [21]. This approach looks appealing because it allows to a pool of experts, having different knowledge and opinions, to establish a common basis in assessing probabilistic evaluations.

In many applications we are interested in making inferences only on a small number of conditional events. In this context the de Finetti's approach, based on the well known coherence principle, allows us to introduce in a flexible and gradual way consistent (precise or imprecise) probability assessments on arbitrary families of conditional events (see e.g. [3], [4], [5], [8], [11], [13], [17], [20] and bibliography therein). In these cases a crucial problem is the checking of the coherence of probability assessments on the given set of conditional events, which can be based on suitable algorithms making use of linear programming techniques (see [3], [6], [12]).

In the case of imprecise probabilities, a desiderable property concerns the coherence of every precise assessment which is consistent with the given imprecise probability assessment. This property has been been introduced in [15] as *total coherence*. Moreover, in the same paper some theoretical results have been obtained in the case of interval-valued assessments. In order to take the relevant decisions, if the total coherence of some interval-valued probability assessment is assured, the user would be free to choose his own precise assessments on the basis of the imprecise probabilistic judgements given by the experts. In [21] general results and principles are given in the context of lower and upper previsions of random quantities. We remark that the definitions adopted there are stronger than those introduced in [7] and [14]. In order to avoid possible ambiguities, in a subsequent paper [2] our generalized concept of coherence has been recalled *g-coherence.*

In this paper, we study the extension of totally coherent interval-valued probability assessments on an arbitrary finite family of conditional events. Based on a simple example, we show that in general a totally coherent imprecise assessment is not extendible and then we give some criterions of extendibility. Finally we apply our results in the context of nonmonotonic reasoning considering some well known inference rules.

The paper is organized as follows. In the next section we introduce the total coherence of an interval-valued probability assessment and summarize the related main results. In section 3 we formalize the problem studied in this paper; in Section 4 we give some necessary and sufficient conditions for the extension of a total coherent interval-valued probability assessment; in Section 5 we analyze some well known inference rules of interest in nonmonotonic reasoning. Finally in Section 6 we give some concluding remarks.

2 Totally coherent probability assessments

Let $\mathcal{F} = \{E_1|H_1, \ldots, E_n|H_n\}$ be a set of conditional events. We denote by $\mathcal{P} = (p_1, \ldots, p_n)$ a precise probability assessment on $\mathcal{F}$. Moreover, given two points $\alpha = (\alpha_1, \ldots, \alpha_n)$, $\beta = (\beta_1, \ldots, \beta_n) \in [0,1]^n$, with $\alpha_i \leq \beta_i$ for $i = 1, \ldots, n$, we denote by $\mathcal{P}_{\alpha,\beta}$ the interval-valued probability assessment on $\mathcal{F}$ such that

$$\alpha_i \leq p_i \leq \beta_i \,, \qquad\qquad i = 1, \ldots, n, \tag{1}$$

where $p_i = P(E_i|H_i)$. We write

$$\mathcal{P}_{\alpha,\beta} \;=\; \{[\alpha_1, \beta_1], \cdots, [\alpha_n, \beta_n]\} \,.$$

We remark that $\mathcal{P}_{\alpha,\beta}$ is associated with an interval contained in the unitary hypercube $[0,1]^n$. We denote by $\mathcal{P}_1, \ldots, \mathcal{P}_{2^n}$ the 2^n probability assessments relative to the vertices of this interval, that is $\mathcal{P}_i = (p_1, \ldots, p_n) \in \{\alpha_1, \beta_1\} \times \cdots \times \{\alpha_n, \beta_n\}$ for $i = 1, \ldots, 2^n$; these probability assessments will be referred to as the *vertices* of the interval-valued probability assessment $\mathcal{P}_{\alpha,\beta}$.

In the following we shall denote by $I_{\alpha,\beta}$ the interval associated with $\mathcal{P}_{\alpha,\beta}$, that is

$$I_{\alpha,\beta} \;=\; [\alpha_1, \beta_1] \times \cdots \times [\alpha_n, \beta_n] \,, \tag{2}$$

and by $V_{\alpha,\beta}$ the set of vertices of $I_{\alpha,\beta}$, that is

$$V_{\alpha,\beta} \;=\; \{\alpha_1, \beta_1\} \times \cdots \times \{\alpha_n, \beta_n\} \,. \tag{3}$$

In [15] we introduced the concept of ***totally coherent set-valued probability assessments***. In particular the following definition has been given in the case of interval-valued assessments.

Definition 1 An interval-valued probability assessment $\mathcal{P}_{\alpha,\beta}$ is *totally coherent* if every precise conditional probability assessment $\mathcal{P}_. = (p_1, \ldots, p_n)$ on $\mathcal{F}$, with

$$\alpha_i \leq p_i \leq \beta_i , \qquad\qquad i = 1, \ldots, n ,$$

is coherent.

The following theorem constitutes a basic result for checking the total coherence.

Theorem 2 An interval-valued assessment $\mathcal{P}_{\alpha,\beta}$ on $\mathcal{F}$ is totally coherent if and only if every precise assessment $\mathcal{P} = (x_1, \ldots, x_n)$ on $\mathcal{F}$, with

$$x_i \in \{\alpha_i, \beta_i\} , \qquad\qquad i = 1, \ldots, n,$$

is coherent.

Therefore the total coherence of $\mathcal{P}_{\alpha,\beta}$ amounts to the coherence of the 2^n vertices

$$(x_1, \ldots, x_n) \in \{\alpha_1, \beta_1\} \times \cdots \times \{\alpha_n, \beta_n\} .$$

In practical applications the total coherence of $\mathcal{P}_{\alpha,\beta}$ can be checked by means of a linear algorithm implemented with *Maple V*, see [2].

3 The problem of the extension

In this section we study the extension of a totally coherent interval-valued probability assessment $\mathcal{P}_{\alpha,\beta}$ defined on a family $\mathcal{F} = \{E_1|H_1, \ldots, E_n|H_n\}$ to a further conditional event $E_{n+1}|H_{n+1}$.

To begin with, let us give the following definition.

Definition 3 A totally coherent interval-valued assessment $\mathcal{P}_{\alpha,\beta} = \{[\alpha_1, \beta_1], \ldots, [\alpha_n, \beta_n]\}$ on a family $\mathcal{F} = \{E_1|H_1, \ldots, E_n|H_n\}$ is *extendible* to a conditional event $\{E_{n+1}|H_{n+1}\}$ if and only if there exists an interval $[\alpha_{n+1}, \beta_{n+1}]$ such that, for every $(p_1, \ldots, p_{n+1}) \in [\alpha_1, \beta_1] \times \cdots \times [\alpha_{n+1}, \beta_{n+1}]$, the precise probability assessment $(p_1, \ldots, p_n, p_{n+1})$ on $\mathcal{F} \cup \{E_{n+1}|H_{n+1}\}$ is coherent.

The extension of a totally coherent interval valued probability assessment in general is not possible, as the following counterexample shows.

A counterexample. To begin with, we recall that n events $E_1, E_2, \ldots, E_n$ are logically independent if each of the 2^n conjunctions $E_1 E_2 \cdots E_n$, $E_1 \cdots E_{n-1} E_n^c$, $\ldots$, $E_1^c E_2^c \cdots E_n^c$ is different from the impossible event $\emptyset$.

Let us consider the family $\mathcal{F} = \{A|H, B|AH\}$, where the events A, B and H are logically independent. It can be verified that for every pair of points

$$\alpha = (\alpha_1, \alpha_2) , \quad \beta = (\beta_1, \beta_2) ,$$

with

$$0 \leq \alpha_i \leq \beta_i \leq 1 , \quad i = 1, 2$$

the interval-valued assessment $\mathcal{P}_{\alpha,\beta}$ on $\mathcal{F}$ is totally coherent.

Now let us consider the extension of $\mathcal{P}_{\alpha,\beta}$ to the conditional event $AB|H$. It is well known that, for each $(x, y) \in [\alpha_1, \beta_1] \times [\alpha_2, \beta_2]$, the extension (x, y, z) of $\mathcal{P}$ to the family $\{A|H, B|AH, AB|H\}$ is coherent if and only if $z = xy$. Then, it does not exist any interval $[\alpha_3, \beta_3]$ such that the imprecise assessment $\{[\alpha_1, \beta_1], [\alpha_2, \beta_2], [\alpha_3, \beta_3]\}$ defined on $\{A|H, B|AH, AB|H\}$ is totally coherent. Therefore the (totally coherent) assessment $\mathcal{P}_{\alpha,\beta}$ on $\mathcal{F}$ is not extendible to $AB|H$.

This example can be generalized. As a matter of fact, the reason why $\mathcal{P}_{\alpha,\beta}$ is not extendible is that (x, y) univocally determines z. In general, a totally coherent interval-valued probability assessment

$$\mathcal{P}_{\alpha,\beta} = \{[\alpha_1, \beta_1], \ldots, [\alpha_n, \beta_n]\}$$

on a family $\mathcal{F} = \{E_1|H_1, \ldots, E_n|H_n\}$ cannot be extended to a further conditional event $E_{n+1}|H_{n+1}$ if the extension p_{n+1} of $(p_1, \ldots, p_n)$ to $E_{n+1}|H_{n+1}$ is univocally determined by the values $p_1, \ldots, p_n$, that is if there exists a map f such that

$$p_{n+1} = f(p_1, \ldots, p_n) .$$

In these cases, except some trivial cases like that one in which p_{n+1} is constant, $\mathcal{P}_{\alpha,\beta}$ is not extendible to $E_{n+1}|H_{n+1}$. For example, if $H_{n+1} \subseteq E_{n+1}$ then p_{n+1} is constant and in this case it is $p_{n+1} = 1$.

4 Conditions of extendibility

In this section we give some conditions for the extendibility of a totally coherent interval-valued probability assessment $\mathcal{P}_{\alpha,\beta} = \{[\alpha_1, \beta_1], \ldots, [\alpha_n, \beta_n]\}$ on a given a family $\mathcal{F} = \{E_1|H_1, \ldots, E_n|H_n\}$ to a further conditional event $E_{n+1}|H_{n+1}$. In other words, we give some conditions for the existence of an interval $[\alpha_{n+1}, \beta_{n+1}]$ such that the imprecise assessment

$$\mathcal{P}_{\alpha,\beta} = \{[\alpha_1, \beta_1], \ldots, [\alpha_n, \beta_n], [\alpha_{n+1}, \beta_{n+1}]\}$$

on $\mathcal{F} \cup E_{n+1}|H_{n+1}$ is totally coherent.

For any $\mathcal{P} = (p_1, \ldots, p_n) \in [\alpha_1, \beta_1] \times \cdots \times [\alpha_n, \beta_n]$ let $[p', p'']$ be the set of the coherent extensions of the assessment $\mathcal{P}$ on $\mathcal{F}$ to $E_{n+1}|H_{n+1}$. Then let p_* and p^* be the following quantities:

$$p_* = \sup_{\mathcal{P} \in I_{\alpha,\beta}} p' , \qquad p^* = \inf_{\mathcal{P} \in I_{\alpha,\beta}} p'' , \tag{4}$$

where $I_{\alpha,\beta}$ has been introduced in (2).

A general necessary and sufficient condition of extendibility of $\mathcal{P}_{\alpha,\beta}$ is given in the following theorem.

Theorem 4 Let $\mathcal{P}_{\alpha,\beta} = \{[\alpha_1, \beta_1], \ldots, [\alpha_n, \beta_n]\}$ a totally coherent interval-valued assessment on a family $\mathcal{F} = \{E_1|H_1, \ldots, E_n|H_n\}$ and let $E_{n+1}|H_{n+1}$ be a further conditional event. Then $\mathcal{P}_{\alpha,\beta}$ is extendible to $E_{n+1}|H_{n+1}$ if and only if $p_* \leq p^*$ and, in this case, every $[\alpha_{n+1}, \beta_{n+1}] \subseteq [p_*, p^*]$ is a coherent extension of $\mathcal{P}_{\alpha,\beta}$ to $E_{n+1}|H_{n+1}$.

Proof. The proof follows directly from Definition 3. In fact, if $p_* > p^*$ then it does not exist any value p_{n+1} such that $(p_1, \ldots, p_n, p_{n+1})$ is coherent for every $\mathcal{P} = (p_1, \ldots, p_n) \in I_{\alpha,\beta}$. On the contrary, if $p_* \leq p^*$, then for every $\mathcal{P} \in I_{\alpha,\beta}$ it is $[p_*, p^*] \subseteq [p', p'']$, where $[p', p'']$ is the set of the coherent extensions of $\mathcal{P}$ to $E_{n+1}|H_{n+1}$. Thus, for every

$$(p_1, \ldots, p_n, p_{n+1}) \in [\alpha_1, \beta_1] \times \cdots \times [\alpha_n, \beta_n] \times [p_*, p^*] ,$$

the assessment $(p_1, \ldots, p_n, p_{n+1})$ on $\{E_1|H_1, \ldots, E_n|H_n, E_{n+1}|H_{n+1}\}$ is coherent. Therefore, $\mathcal{P}_{\alpha,\beta}$ is extendible to $E_{n+1}|H_{n+1}$.
Moreover, for every $[\alpha_{n+1}, \beta_{n+1}] \subseteq [p_*, p^*]$, the interval-valued assessment $\{[\alpha_1, \beta_1], \cdots, [\alpha_n, \beta_n], [\alpha_{n+1}, \beta_{n+1}]\}$ on $\{E_1|H_1, \ldots, E_n|H_n, E_{n+1}|H_{n+1}\}$ is totally coherent, and then $[\alpha_{n+1}, \beta_{n+1}]$ is a coherent extension of $\mathcal{P}_{\alpha,\beta}$ to $E_{n+1}|H_{n+1}$. ∎

The above Theorem 4 is not directly applicable. We need a practical criterion for checking the extendibility of a given interval-valued assessment $\mathcal{P}_{\alpha,\beta}$. In analogy with (4), let us introduce the quantities

$$p_\circ = \sup_{(p_1,\ldots,p_n) \in V_{\alpha,\beta}} p' , \qquad p^\circ = \inf_{(p_1,\ldots,p_n) \in V_{\alpha,\beta}} p'' , \tag{5}$$

where $V_{\alpha,\beta}$ has been introduced in (3). Obviously, as $V_{\alpha,\beta} \subset I_{\alpha,\beta}$, we have

$$p_\circ \leq p_* , \qquad p^\circ \geq p^* . \tag{6}$$

Then, we obtain the following criterion for checking the extendibility of $\mathcal{P}_{\alpha,\beta}$.

Theorem 5 Let $\mathcal{P}_{\alpha,\beta} = \{[\alpha_1, \beta_1], \ldots, [\alpha_n, \beta_n]\}$ a totally coherent interval-valued assessment on a family $\mathcal{F} = \{E_1|H_1, \ldots, E_n|H_n\}$ and let $E_{n+1}|H_{n+1}$ be a further conditional event. Then $\mathcal{P}_{\alpha,\beta}$ is extendible to $E_{n+1}|H_{n+1}$ if and only if $p_\circ \leq p^\circ$. Moreover, it is $p_\circ = p_*$ and $p^\circ = p^*$.

Proof. We observe that, if $p_\circ > p^\circ$, then from (6) we obtain $p_* > p^*$ and based on Theorem 4 it follows that $\mathcal{P}_{\alpha,\beta}$ is not extendible to $E_{n+1}|H_{n+1}$.
On the contrary, if $p_\circ \leq p^\circ$, then for every $\mathcal{P} \in V_{\alpha,\beta}$ it is $[p_\circ, p^\circ] \subseteq [p', p'']$ so that both the probability assessments $(\mathcal{P}, p_\circ)$ and $(\mathcal{P}, p^\circ)$, defined on the family $\{E_1|H_1, \ldots, E_n|H_n, E_{n+1}|H_{n+1}\}$, are coherent. Then the interval-valued assessment $\{[\alpha_1, \beta_1], \cdots, [\alpha_n, \beta_n], [p_\circ, p^\circ]\}$ on $\{E_1|H_1, \ldots, E_n|H_n, E_{n+1}|H_{n+1}\}$ is totally coherent and $\mathcal{P}_{\alpha,\beta}$ is extendible to $E_{n+1}|H_{n+1}$. Therefore, $\mathcal{P}_{\alpha,\beta}$ is extendible to $E_{n+1}|H_{n+1}$ if and only if $p_\circ \leq p^\circ$. Moreover, if $p_\circ \leq p^\circ$, then for every $\mathcal{P} \in I_{\alpha,\beta}$ it is $[p_\circ, p^\circ] \subseteq [p', p'']$ and hence we have $[p_\circ, p^\circ] \subseteq [p_*, p^*]$. This yields $p_\circ = p_*$ and $p^\circ = p^*$. ∎

We point out that, as proved in the above theorem, the checking of the extendibility of $\mathcal{P}_{\alpha,\beta}$ can be greatly simplified, because it is sufficient for every assessment $\mathcal{P} \in V_{\alpha,\beta}$ to determine the values p', p''. In [2] the authors provide algorithms for checking the coherence of precise conditional probability assessments (see also references given therein). Then the computation of $p_\circ, p^\circ$ would require 2^n runs of such an algorithm.

5 Some applications

In this section we apply the above results for analyzing the extendibility of some totally coherent assessments defined on particular families of conditional events. The families here considered are relevant with respect to well known *inference rules*, which were studied in the context of a probabilistic approach to conditional logic in [1]; afterwards the same rules have been considered in nonmonotonic reasoning by several authors (see e.g. [9], [10], [16], [18] and [19]).

Example 6 (Disjunction rule) Let us consider the family $\{C|A, C|B, C|(A \vee B)\}$, where the events A, B and C are logically independent. It can be verified that for every $x \in \{0,1\}, y \in \{0,1\}$ the assessment (x, y) on $\{C|A, C|B\}$ is coherent. Thus the Theorem 2 implies that the interval-valued assessment $\{[\alpha_1, \beta_1], [\alpha_2, \beta_2]\}$ on $\{C|A, C|B\}$ is totally coherent for every pair of intervals $[\alpha_1, \beta_1], [\alpha_2, \beta_2]$, with

$$[\alpha_1, \beta_1] \subseteq [0, 1] \ , \ \ [\alpha_2, \beta_2] \subseteq [0, 1] \ .$$

In [12] it has been proved that the assessment (x, y) on $\{C|A, C|B\}$ can be extended coherently to the event $C|(A \vee B)$ if and only if the probability assessment z on $C|(A \vee B)$ verifies the relation $z \in [z', z'']$ with

$$z' = \frac{xy}{x + y - xy} \ , \qquad z'' = \frac{x + y - 2xy}{1 - xy} \ .$$

Moreover, as both z' and z'' increase as either x or y increase, the values

$$z_* = \sup_{(x,y) \in I_{\alpha,\beta}} z' \ , \qquad z^* = \inf_{(x,y) \in I_{\alpha,\beta}} z'' \ ,$$

where $I_{\alpha,\beta} = [\alpha_1, \beta_1] \times [\alpha_2, \beta_2]$, are attained respectively for $(x, y) = (\beta_1, \beta_2)$ and $(x, y) = (\alpha_1, \alpha_2)$. If we set

$$z_\circ = \sup_{(x,y)\in V_{\alpha,\beta}} z' , \qquad z^\circ = \inf_{(x,y)\in V_{\alpha,\beta}} z'' ,$$

where $V_{\alpha,\beta} = \{\alpha_1, \beta_1\} \times \{\alpha_2, \beta_2\}$, as proved in Theorem 5, we have

$$z_* = z_\circ \qquad \text{and} \qquad z^* = z^\circ .$$

On the basis of the Theorem 4 the interval-valued assessment $\{[\alpha_1, \beta_1], [\alpha_2, \beta_2]\}$ on $\{C|A, C|B\}$ is extendible to $C|(A \vee B)$ if and only if it results

$$\frac{\beta_1\beta_2}{\beta_1 + \beta_2 - \beta_1\beta_2} \leq \frac{\alpha_1 + \alpha_2 - 2\alpha_1\alpha_2}{1 - \alpha_1\alpha_2} .$$

In this case, the interval-valued assessment

$$\{[\alpha_1, \beta_1], [\alpha_2, \beta_2], [\alpha_3, \beta_3]\}$$

on the given family is totally coherent for every

$$[\alpha_3, \beta_3] \subseteq \left[\frac{\beta_1\beta_2}{\beta_1 + \beta_2 - \beta_1\beta_2}, \frac{\alpha_1 + \alpha_2 - 2\alpha_1\alpha_2}{1 - \alpha_1\alpha_2}\right] .$$

Example 7 (Triangularity rule) Given three logically independent events A, B, C, let us consider the family $\{C|A, B|A, C|AB\}$. It can be verified that the interval-valued assessment $\{[\alpha_1, \beta_1], [\alpha_2, \beta_2]\}$ on $\{C|A, B|A\}$ is totally coherent for every pair of intervals $[\alpha_1, \beta_1], [\alpha_2, \beta_2]$. In [12] it has been proved that the assessment (x, y) on $\{C|A, C|B\}$ can be extended coherently to the event $C|AB$ if and only if the probability assessment z on $C|AB$ verifies the relation $z \in [z', z'']$, with

$$z' = \begin{cases} \dfrac{x+y-1}{y} , & \text{if } \; x + y > 1 \\ 0 , & \text{if } \; x + y \leq 1 \end{cases} , \tag{7}$$

$$z'' = \begin{cases} \dfrac{x}{y} , & \text{if } \; x < y \\ 1 , & \text{if } \; x \geq y \end{cases} . \tag{8}$$

According to (7) and (8), the unitary square can be partitioned in the following four regions:

$$\begin{aligned} \mathcal{R}_1 &= \{(x, y) \in [0, 1]^2 \; : \; x + y > 1 \, , \, x < y\} \\ \mathcal{R}_2 &= \{(x, y) \in [0, 1]^2 \; : \; x + y > 1 \, , \, x \geq y\} \\ \mathcal{R}_3 &= \{(x, y) \in [0, 1]^2 \; : \; x + y \leq 1 \, , \, x < y\} \\ \mathcal{R}_3 &= \{(x, y) \in [0, 1]^2 \; : \; x + y \leq 1 \, , \, x \geq y\} . \end{aligned}$$

These regions are plotted in Figure 1. Moreover the *contour lines* of the

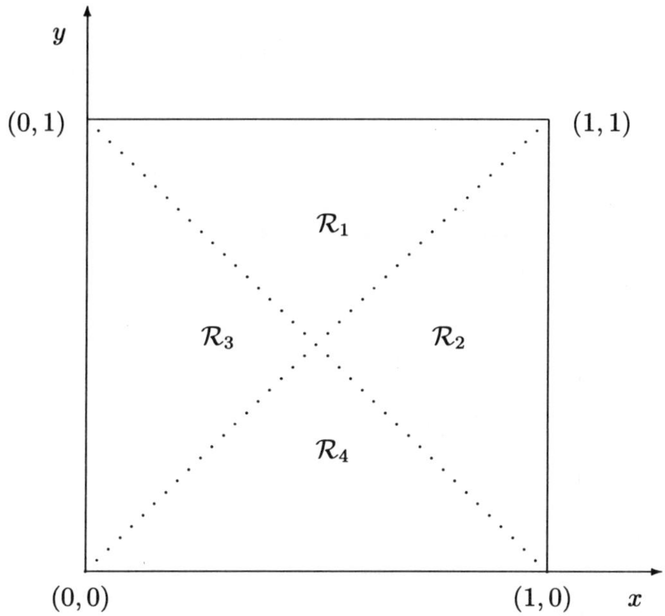

Figure 1: Partition of the unitary square according to the regions $\mathcal{R}_1, \ldots, \mathcal{R}_4$.

functions

$$f(x, y) = \frac{x + y - 1}{y}$$

and

$$g(x, y) = \frac{x}{y}$$

are *straight lines*, that is the values of $(x, y) \in I_{\alpha,\beta}$ such that

$$f(x, y) = \frac{x + y - 1}{y} = \lambda = \text{const.} \tag{9}$$

$$g(x, y) = \frac{x}{y} = \delta = \text{const.} \tag{10}$$

are straight lines. From (9), it results that the the point $(1, 0)$ belongs to the line having equation $x + y - 1 = \lambda y$, for every $\lambda \in (0, 1)$. Moreover the function $f(x, y)$ attains its maximum value, say $\lambda_{\max}$, in correspondence to the straight line through the point (β_1, β_2), see Figure 2. Then from (7) it follows

$$z_* = \begin{cases} \dfrac{\beta_1 + \beta_2 - 1}{\beta_2} & \text{if } (\beta_1, \beta_2) \in (\mathcal{R}_1 \cup \mathcal{R}_2) \\ 0 & \text{if } (\beta_1, \beta_2) \in (\mathcal{R}_3 \cup \mathcal{R}_4)\,. \end{cases} \tag{11}$$

Analogously from (10), it results that the point $(0, 0)$ belongs to the line having equation $x = \delta y$ for each $\delta \in (0, 1)$. Moreover the function $g(x, y)$ attains its

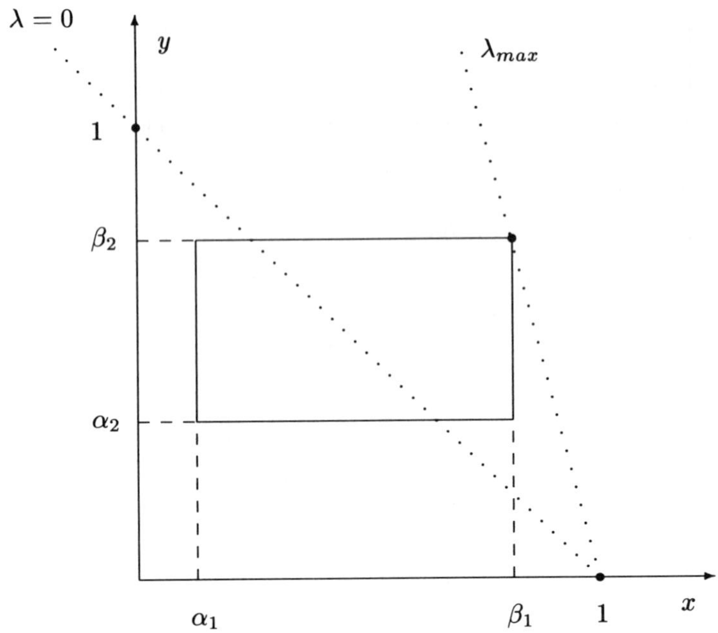

Figure 2: Plot of the function $f(x, y)$ for $\lambda = 0$ and λ_{max}.

minimum value, say $\delta_{\min}$, in correspondence of the straight line through the point (α_1, β_2), see Figure 3. Then it follows

$$z^* = \begin{cases} \dfrac{\alpha_1}{\beta_2} & \text{if } (\alpha_1, \beta_2) \in (\mathcal{R}_1 \cup \mathcal{R}_3) \\ 1 & \text{if } (\alpha_1, \beta_2) \in (\mathcal{R}_2 \cup \mathcal{R}_4) . \end{cases} \tag{12}$$

Then, in order to determine the interval $[z_*, z^*]$ we have to consider the position of the vertices $(\alpha_1, \beta_2), (\beta_1, \beta_2)$ with respect to the straight lines having equation

$$y = x \quad , \quad \text{and} \quad x + y = 1$$

that is the diagonals of the unitary square $[0, 1]^2$. According to (11) and (12), we have the following cases:

1. if $(\beta_1, \beta_2) \in \mathcal{R}_1 \cup \mathcal{R}_2$ and $(\alpha_1, \beta_2) \in \mathcal{R}_1 \cup \mathcal{R}_3$ then

$$z_* = \frac{\beta_1 + \beta_2 - 1}{\beta_2} \text{ and } z^* = \frac{\alpha_1}{\beta_2};$$

2. if $(\beta_1, \beta_2) \in \mathcal{R}_1 \cup \mathcal{R}_2$ and $(\alpha_1, \beta_2) \in \mathcal{R}_2 \cup \mathcal{R}_4$ then

$$z_* = \frac{\beta_1 + \beta_2 - 1}{\beta_2} \quad \text{and} \quad z^* = 1;$$

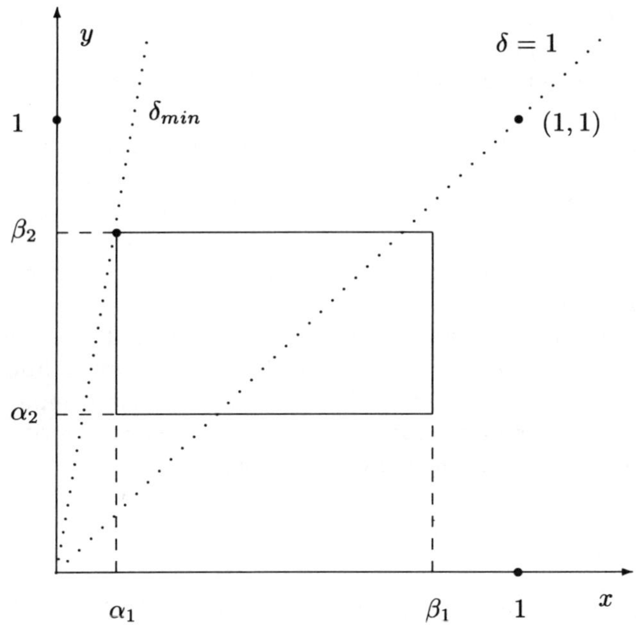

Figure 3: Plot of the function $g(x, y)$ for $\delta = 1$ and δ_{min}.

3. if $(\beta_1, \beta_2) \in \mathcal{R}_3 \cup \mathcal{R}_4$ and $(\alpha_1, \beta_2) \in \mathcal{R}_1 \cup \mathcal{R}_3$ then

$$z_* = 0 \quad \text{and} \quad z^* = \frac{\alpha_1}{\beta_2};$$

4. if $(\beta_1, \beta_2) \in \mathcal{R}_3 \cup \mathcal{R}_4$ and $(\alpha_1, \beta_2) \in \mathcal{R}_2 \cup \mathcal{R}_4$ then

$$z_* = 0 \text{ and } z^* = 1.$$

Then the interval-valued assessment $[\alpha_1, \beta_1], [\alpha_2, \beta_2]$ on $\{C|A, B|A\}$ is extendible if and only if $z^* \leq z^{**}$ and, in this case, for every $[\alpha_3, \beta_3] \subseteq [z^*, z^{**}]$, the interval-valued assessment

$$\{[\alpha_1, \beta_1], [\alpha_2, \beta_2], [\alpha_3, \beta_3]\}$$

on the family $\{C|A, B|A, C|AB\}$ is totally coherent.

6 Concluding remarks

In this paper the problem of the extendibility of a totally coherent interval-valued probability assessment $\mathcal{P}_{\alpha,\beta}$ on a family $\mathcal{F}$ of n conditional events has been studied. It has been shown that in general the assessment $\mathcal{P}_{\alpha,\beta}$ is not extendible to a further conditional event. Then some necessary and sufficient conditions for the extendibility of $\mathcal{P}_{\alpha,\beta}$ have been proved. In particular Theorem

5 leads to a useful criterion which can be implemented by suitable algorithms based on well known algebraic systems, e.g. *Maple V.*

This criterion can be applied making use of the algorithm proposed in [2] for determining the set $[p', p'']$ of the coherent extensions of a precise conditional probability assessment $\mathcal{P}$ on $\mathcal{F}$. In this case we remark that, in order to find the interval $[p_\circ, p^\circ]$, 2^n runs of this algorithm are required. In fact each run of the algorithm determines the interval $[p', p'']$ corresponding to the precise probability assessment associated to a given vertex. Then we need 2^n runs of the algorithm – equal to the number of vertices of $I_{\alpha,\beta}$ – for the computation of the interval $[p_\circ, p^\circ]$.

At present we are interested in finding some other criterion, less expensive from a computational point of view, for checking the extendibility of $\mathcal{P}_{\alpha,\beta}$. In fact, the analysis of some examples suggests that the computation of the interval $[p_\circ, p^\circ]$ would require only $n+1$ runs of the above algorithm. Working in progress concerns the deepening of this aspect.

References

[1] Adams E. W. (1975). *The Logic of Conditionals*, D. Reidel, Dordrecht.

[2] Biazzo V. and Gilio A. (1999). A generalization of the fundamental theorem of de Finetti for conditional events for imprecise conditional probability asssessments, in *Proceedings of the "1st Int. Symp. on Imprecise Probabilities and Their Applications"*, Ghent (Belgium), June 28 - July 2, 1999, 34-43.

[3] Coletti G. (1993), Numerical and qualitative judgements in probabilistic expert systems, in *Proceedings of the International Workshop on "Probabilitic Methods in Expert Systems"* R. Scozzafava (Ed.), SIS, Roma, 37-55.

[4] Coletti G., Gilio A. and Scozzafava R. (1993). Comparative probability for conditional events: a new look through coherence, *Theory and Decision*, **35**, 237-258.

[5] Coletti G. and Scozzafava R. (1995). Learning from data by coherent probabilistic reasoning, *Proceedings of ISUMA-NAFIPS '95*, College Park, September 17-20, 1995, 535-540.

[6] Coletti G. and Scozzafava R. (1996). Characterization of coherent conditional probabilities as a tool for their assessment and extension, *Journal of Uncertainty, Fuzziness and Knowledge-Based Systems*, **4**, n. 2, 103-127.

[7] Coletti G. and Scozzafava R. (1997). Exploiting zero probabilities, in *Proc. of EUFIT '97*, Aachen, Germany, ELITE Foundation, 1499-1503.

[8] Coletti, G. and Scozzafava, R. (1998). Null events and stochastic independence, *Kybernetika*, **34**, n. 1, 69-78.

[9] Dubois D. and Prade H. (1993). Probability in automated reasoning: from numerical to symbolic approaches, in "Probabilistic Methods in Expert Systems", Proc. of the International Workshop, R. Scozzafava (Ed.), SIS, Roma, 79-104.

[10] Dubois D. and Prade H. (1994), Conditional Objects as Nonmonotonic Consequence Relationships, *IEEE Transactions on Systems, Man, and Cybernetics*, **24** (12), 1724-1740.

[11] Gilio A. (1995). Probabilistic consistency of conditional probability bounds, in "Advances in Intelligent Computing - IPMU '94", Lecture Notes in Computer Science 945, B. Bouchon-Meunier, R. R. Yager, L. A. Zadeh (Eds.), Springer-Verlag, Berlin Heidelberg, 200-209.

[12] Gilio A. (1995). Algorithms for precise and imprecise conditional probability assessments, in *Mathematical Models for Handling Partial Knowledge in Artificial Intelligence*, G. Coletti, D. Dubois and R. Scozzafava (Eds.), Plenum Press, New York, 231-254.

[13] Gilio A. (1996) Algorithms for conditional probability assessments, in *Bayesian Analysis in Statistics and Econometrics*, in D.A. Berry, K.M. Chaloner and J.K. Geweke (Eds.), John Wiley, New York, 29-39.

[14] Gilio A. and Scozzafava R. (1994), Conditional events in probability assessments and revision, *IEEE Trans. on Systems, Man and Cybernetics*, **24**, n.12, 1741-1746.

[15] Gilio A. and Ingrassia S. (1998). Totally coherent set-valued probability assessments, *Kybernetika*, **34**, n. 1, 3-15.

[16] Kraus K., Lehmann D. and Magidor M. (1990). Nonmonotonic reasoning, preferential models and cumulative logics, *Artificial Intelligence*, **44**, 167-207.

[17] Lad F. (1995). Coherent prevision as a linear functional without an underlying measure space: the purely arithmetic structure of logical relations among conditional quantities, in *Mathematical Models for Handling Partial Knowledge in Artificial Intelligence*, G. Coletti, D. Dubois and R. Scozzafava (Eds.), Plenum Press, New York, 101-111.

[18] Lehmann D. and Magidor M. (1992). What does a conditional knowledge base entail?, *Artificial Intelligence*, **55**, 1-60.

[19] Pearl J. (1988). *Probabilistic Reasoning in Intelligent Systems: Networks of Plausible Inference*, Morgan and Kaufmann, San Mateo, CA.

[20] Scozzafava R. (1994). Subjective probability versus belief functions in artificial intelligence, *Int. J. General Systems*, **22**, 197-206.

[21] Walley P. (1991). *Statistical reasoning with imprecise probabilities*, Chapman and Hall, London.

Systems Modelling

Modelling, Simulation and Behavior Identification of Non-Linear Dynamical Systems with a New Fuzzy-Fractal-Genetic Approach

Oscar Castillo and Patricia Melin
Computer Science Department, Tijuana Institute of Technology
P.O. Box 4207, Chula Vista CA 91909, USA
ocastillo@tectijuana.mx

Abstract: We describe in this paper a new method for the simulation of non-linear dynamical systems. This method is based on a hybrid fuzzy-fractal-genetic approach to achieve, in an efficient way, automated simulation of a particular dynamical system given its mathematical model. The use of genetic algorithms is to achieve automated parameter selection for the mathematical models. The use of fuzzy logic is to simulate the process of expert behavior identification, by implementing the knowledge of identification by a set of fuzzy rules. We also use the concept of the fractal dimension of a time series to help make this identification more accurate. Experimental results for the case of robotic dynamic systems show the efficiency and accuracy of this new method for the simulation of complex non-linear dynamical systems.

1 Introduction

This paper describes the important problem of numerical simulation for non-linear dynamical systems and its solution by using Soft Computing (SC) methodologies. The numerical simulation of a particular dynamical system consists in the successive application of a map (difference equation) and the subsequent identification of the corresponding dynamic behaviors. The simulation of a given dynamical system consists in selecting the appropriate parameter values for the mathematical model and then applying the corresponding iterative method (map) to find the limiting behavior. In this paper, a new method for automated parameter selection based on the use of Genetic Algorithms (GA), is introduced. Also, a new method for dynamic behavior identification based on fuzzy logic, is introduced. The fuzzy-genetic approach for automated simulation consists in the integration of the method for automated parameter selection (based on GA) and the method for behavior identification (based on fuzzy logic).

In this paper, we describe briefly the problem of numerical simulation for non-linear dynamical systems and its solution using SC techniques. First, we present some basic concepts and the main goal of the field of numerical simulation. Then, we present some basic concepts about dynamical systems theory that we consider necessary to understand the methods that will be described later in the paper. Then, we describe the problem of automated simulation of dynamical systems. At the end, we describe a new method for automated simulation of non-linear dynamical systems using a hybrid fuzzy-fractal-genetic approach.

2 Numerical Simulation of Non-Linear Dynamical Systems

Real dynamical systems, can be represented by mathematical models expressed as non-linear differential equations of the following form:

$$dY/dt = f(Y, t, \theta) \quad (1)$$

where Y is a vector of dynamic variables, t is time, and θ is a vector of parameters, or as non-linear difference equations of the form:

$$Y_{t+1} = F(Y_t, Y_{t-1}, \ldots, \theta) \quad (2)$$

In the case of Equation (1) one says that the model is a continuous one. On the other hand, for Equation (2) the model is considered of the discrete type.

The simulation of the real dynamical system, in the first case, consists in the numerical solution of the non-linear differential equation along with the identification of all the possible corresponding dynamic behaviors of the system. For example, the numerical solution of the differential equation can be obtained by the well known second-order Runge-Kutta method (Nakamura, 1997):

$$\begin{aligned} Y_{n+1} &= Y_n + 1/2(k_1 + k_2) \\ k_1 &= h\,f(Y_n, t_n, \theta) \\ k_2 &= h\,f(Y_n, k_1, t_{n+1}, \theta) \end{aligned} \quad (3)$$

where h is the stepsize of the method. Equation (3) can be used for different parameter values of θ to obtain the different dynamic behaviors of the system described by the model of Equation (1). Of course, more advanced methods for the numerical solution of differential equations can be used if more accuracy is desired.

The simulation of the real dynamical system, in the second case, consists in the successive application of the map given by Equation (2) for different parameter values of θ and then identifying the different corresponding dynamic behaviors of the system.

In any case, the result of the numerical simulation of the real dynamical system (represented by Eq. (1) or Eq. (2)) is a time series of the following form:

$$Y_1, Y_2, Y_3, \ldots, Y_p \qquad \text{for } \theta = \theta^* \quad (4)$$

this time series represents the motion of the dynamical system for the specific parameter value $\theta = \theta^*$. It is well known in dynamical systems theory, that this time series can have many different types of dynamic behaviors ranging from very simple periodic fixed points to the very complicated "chaotic" behavior. Even more, for non-linear mathematical models it is possible to have all the range of dynamic behaviors for different parameter values of θ. For this reason, the numerical simulation of relative complex non-linear mathematical models requires a lot of exploration in order to find all of the possible dynamic behaviors for the real dynamical system.

There are theoretical results that can be used to establish the existence of chaotic trajectories or other dynamic behaviors for several dynamical systems (Devaney, 1989). However, in many cases it may be difficult or analytically impossible to detect a period-three cycle (required by Li/Yorke's Theorem) necessary to identify chaotic behavior, and for most differential equation systems there are no theoretical results at all. Experiments show that even for cycles of a relatively low period it may be impossible to distinguish regular time series from completely chaotic time series by simple visual inspection.

If a dynamical system is given whose behavior can not be investigated further by applying the standard geometric or analytical methods, numerical simulations are appropriate. The generated time series in such a simulation may exhibit simple patterns like monotonic convergencies or harmonic oscillations. However, the series may also appear to be random due either to:

- periodic behavior with a long period
- quasiperiodic behavior with many different frequencies
- deterministic chaos, or to
- noise generated by the use of specific algorithms during the simulation

The following numerical tools can be useful in deciding whether an actual time series generated by the simulation of a known dynamical system is regular, chaotic, or stochastic: spectral analysis, phase space embedding, correlation dimension, and Lyapunov exponents (Rasband, 1990).

3. Automated Simulation of Non-Linear Dynamical Systems

The problem of performing an efficient simulation for a particular dynamical system can be better understood if we consider a specific mathematical model. Let us consider the following model:

$$\begin{aligned} X' &= \sigma(Y-X) \\ Y' &= rX - Y - XZ \\ Z' &= XY - bZ \end{aligned} \tag{5}$$

where X, Y, Z, σ, r, b $\in$ R, and σ, r and b are three parameters which are normally taken, because of their physical origins, to be positive. The equations are often studied for different values of r in $0 < r < \infty$. This mathematical model has been studied by Rasband (1990), to some extent, however there are still many questions to be answer for this model with respect to its very complicated dynamics for some ranges of parameter values.

If we consider simulating Equation (5), for example, the problem is of selecting the appropriate parameter values for σ, r, b, so that the interesting dynamical behavior of the model can be extracted. The problem is not an easy one, since we need to consider a three-dimensional search space σ r b and there are many possible dynamical behaviors for this model. In this case, the model consisting of three simultaneous differential equations, the behaviors can range from simple periodic orbits to very complicated chaotic attractors. Once the parameter values are selected then the problem becomes a numerical one, since then we need to iterate an appropriate map to approximate the solutions numerically.

The problem of performing automated simulation for a particular dynamical system is then of finding the "best" set of parameter values for the mathematical model. Our general algorithm (Castillo & Melin, 1995) for selecting the "best" set of parameter values is shown in Figure 1.

The algorithm shown in Figure 1 can be explained as follows. First, the mathematical model is analyzed to "understand" it. Second, a set of admissible parameters is generated using the understanding of the model. Third, a specific genetic algorithm is used to select the best set of parameter values. Finally, the numerical simulations are performed and the dynamical behaviors are identified using fuzzy logic (Jang, Sun & Mizutani, 1997).

STEP 1	Read the mathematical model M.
STEP 2	Analyze the model M to "understand" its complexity.
STEP 3	Generate a set of admissible parameters using the understanding of the model.
STEP 4	Perform a selection of the "best" set of parameter values. This set is generated using a specific genetic algorithm.
STEP 5	Perform the simulations by solving numerically the equations of the mathematical model. At this time the different types of dynamical behaviors are identified using a fuzzy rule base.

Figure 1 New algorithm for selecting the best set of parameter values.

The implementation of the new method for Automated Simulation as a computer program was done using the MATLAB programming language. The choice of MATLAB is because of its symbolic manipulation features and also because it is an excellent language for developing prototypes (Nakamura, 1997). The knowledge base for simulation consists of two modules: Parameter Selection, and Dynamic Behavior Identification. In the following lines we will describe these two modules in more detail.

4. Method for Parameter Selection using Genetic Algorithms

The knowledge for simulation of the intelligent system consists in the application of a specific genetic algorithm (Goldberg, 1989) to select the best set of parameters of a particular dynamical system. Our genetic algorithm for parameter value selection (Castillo & Melin, 1998) can be defined as shown in Figure 2.

STEP 1	Initialize a population with randomly generated individuals (parameters) and evaluate the fitness value of each individual
STEP 2	(a) Select two members from the population with probabilities proportional to their fitness values (b) Apply crossover with a probability equal to the crossover rate (c) Apply mutation with a probability equal to the mutation rate (d) Repeat (a) to (d) until enough members are generated to form the next generation
STEP 3	Repeat steps 2 and 3 until the stopping criterion is met

Figure 2 Genetic algorithm for parameter value selection.

The fitness function should evaluate the dynamical information given by a particular set of parameter values, i.e. the fitness function should measure the power of the parameter set. Lets consider a three-dimensional model with 3 parameters θ, α, and γ, then assuming that we have only four possible dynamical behaviors:

B0: fixed point of period 1
B1: fixed point of period 2
B2: fixed point of period 4
B3: fixed point of period 8
B4: chaotic behavior

we will have that the parameter set $\pi = (\theta,\alpha,\gamma)$, where $\theta,\alpha,\gamma \in R$, can result in any of the five possible behaviors. In this case, we need to consider 5 individuals in the population and an initial population can be denoted as:

$$P_0 = (\pi_{01}, \pi_{02}, \pi_{03}\ \pi_{04}\ \pi_{05})$$

For an initial population there is a high probability that most of the π_i could give the B0 behavior, so there has to be evolution to obtain a better parameter set. The identification of the respective behaviors can be done by iteration of the dynamic systems or by other mathematical means, for example the fractal dimension or the Lyapunov exponents (Rasband, 1990). The fitness value of each individual in population P_i can by defined as follows (Castillo & Melin, 1998):

$F(\pi_{ij}) = 1$ for fixed point of period 1

$F(\pi_{ij}) = 2$ for fixed point of period 2

$F(\pi_{ij}) = 4$ for fixed point of period 4

$F(\pi_{ij}) = 8$ for fixed point of period 8

$F(\pi_{ij}) = 10$ for chaotic behavior

this is only one of the possible schemes that can be used for this case. In this case, we have assigned the fitness values proportional to the complexity of the dynamic behavior to guide the search of the genetic algorithm. However, the specific numeric values could be changed to suit the needs of particular applications. We need to remember here that the fitness function has to be designed for each specific application of a genetic algorithm.

A more general form for defining the fitness function for real dynamical systems can be establish by using the fractal dimension (Mandelbrot, 1987) d_f of the time series generated by the numerical simulation of the dynamical system. Mathematically, we can define the fitness function as:

$$F(\pi_{ij}) = e^{\,df(\pi ij)}, \qquad 0 \le d_f \le 3, \tag{6}$$

where $d_f(\pi_{ij})$ = fractal dimension of the time series for parameter set π_{ij}. The general idea of Equation (6) is to assign a bigger value to the fitness function when the complexity of the time series, generated by the simulation, is greater (which is true, of course, when d_f is of a higher value). Of course, here the use of the exponential function is only to spread the values of the fractal dimension but other functions could be used as well.

5 Method for Dynamic Behavior Identification using Fuzzy Logic

Once the parameter values have been found and the numerical simulations have been performed then the final step is to identify the possible dynamic behaviors of the system. The knowledge for behavior identification can be expressed as a fuzzy-rule base (Zadeh, 1973) that uses the information obtained in the numerical simulation to identify the different behaviors of the model. To give an idea of how this knowledge can be expressed as a fuzzy-rule base we show below two sample schemes that can be used for behavior identification.

5.1 Behavior identification based on the analytical properties of the model
We can build a set of fuzzy rules for dynamic behavior identification based on the analytical properties of the mathematical models and using the well known theorems of dynamical systems theory (Castillo & Melin, 1997). To give an idea of how this knowledge can be translated to fuzzy rules we show below some sample rules for several types of dynamical systems.

1) Single-link Robot Model: This mathematical model of a sinusoidally non-linear robot consists of two simultaneous differential equations:

$$q' = Q \qquad (7)$$
$$Q' = (K_t I - N\sin(q) - F_d Q) / M_q$$

where the parameters I, M_q, N, F_d and K_t are all positive. Lim, Hu and Dawson (1996) have presented an extensive gallery of periodic and a-periodic motions for this model. In this case the equilibria (q*,Q*) is stable if and only if the real parts of the eigenvalues are negative and this is equivalent to the rule:

IF $a > 0$ **THEN** Equilibria = stable

where a is defined by the characteristic equation:

$$\lambda^2 + a\lambda + b = 0$$

with a = - trJ, b = detJ. Where "trJ" is the trace and "detJ" is the determinant of the Jacobian Matrix.

2) Other Bi-dimensional Models: Similar bi-dimensional autonomous models can be written in the following manner:

$$X' = \alpha\, f(X,Y) \qquad (8)$$
$$Y' = \beta\, g(X,Y)$$

In this case, the Equilibria (X*,Y*) is stable if:

$$\alpha\, f_x + (g_y - \beta) < 0$$

where f_x and g_y are partial derivatives. In fuzzy logic language we have the following rule:

IF $[\alpha\, f_x + (g_y - \beta) < 0]$ **THEN** Equilibria = stable

Also we have the following rule for a Hopf Bifurcation:

IF $\alpha_0 = (\beta - g_y)/f_x$ **THEN** Hopf_Bifurcation

which gives us the condition for a Hopf bifurcation to occur.

3) Firth's Model of a single-mode laser: The basic equations of a single-mode (unidirectional) homogeneously broadened laser in a high-finesse cavity, tuned to resonance, may be written as a system of three differential equations (Abraham & Firth, 1984):

$$X' = \gamma_c\,(X + 2C_p)$$
$$P' = -\Gamma\,(P - XD) \qquad (9)$$
$$D' = -\gamma\,(D + XP - 1)$$

Here X is a scaled electric field (or Rabi frequency), γ_c is a constant describing the decay of the cavity field and C is the cooperativity parameter.

In this case, the Equilibria (X*,P*,D*) is stable if a, b, c > 0 and (ab - c) > 0, where a, b and c are defined by the characteristic equation for the system. We can also have more complicated rules for other types of dynamical behaviors.

4) Other three-dimensional Models: A three-dimensional system of differential equations can be written in the following form:

$$
\begin{aligned}
X' &= \alpha f(X,Y,Z) \\
Y' &= \beta g(X,Y,Z) \\
Z' &= \gamma h(X,Y,Z)
\end{aligned} \tag{10}
$$

In this case, the Equilibria (X*,Y*,Z*) is stable if a, b, c > 0 and (ab - c) > 0, where a, b and c are defined by the characteristic equation for the system:

$$\lambda^3 + a\,\lambda^2 + b\,\lambda + c = 0$$

In fuzzy logic language we have the rule:

IF a,b,c >0 **AND** (ab-c) >0 **THEN** Equilibria = stable

other rules follow in the same manner for all the types of dynamical behaviors possible for this class of mathematical models.

We have to note here that in this case the computer program for this method needs to obtain the symbolic derivatives for the functions in the conditions of the rules. This is critical for the problem of behavior identification, since we require these derivatives to obtain the values of the parameters in the rules. This will make this method time consuming because the time series from the simulations are not used at all.

5.2 Behavior identification based on the fractal dimension and the Lyapunov exponents

We can obtain a more efficient method of dynamic behavior identification, if we make use of the information contained in the time series that resulted from the simulation of the dynamical system. From the time series of the numerical simulations, we can calculate the Lyapunov exponents of the dynamical system and also the fractal dimension of the time series. With this dynamical information, we can easily identify the corresponding behaviors of the system.

For dissipative dynamical systems, we can use a set of fuzzy rules for behavior identification using the Lyapunov exponents. However, since the Lyapunov exponents can only identify between asymptotic stability, general limit cycles and chaos, we need to use the fractal dimension d_f to discriminate between the different periodic behaviors possible. Based on prior empirical work (Castillo & Melin, 1996), we have been able to use the fractal dimension to discriminate between different periodic behaviors. Then, if we combine the use of the Lyapunov exponents with the use of the fractal dimension, we can obtain a set of fuzzy rules that can identify in a one-to-one manner the different dynamic behaviors. The if-then rules have to be "fuzzy" because there is uncertainty associated with the numerical values of the Lyapunov exponents and also the classification scheme (for the limit cycles) using the fractal dimension is only approximated.

We show in Table 1 the knowledge base that we have developed for dynamic behavior identification for dynamical systems of up to three variables. The empty fields in Table 1 indicate no use of the fractal dimension for that case.

We can define membership functions for the numerical intervals of the fractal dimension, for the Lyapunov exponents and for the behavior identifications shown in Table 1. Once these membership functions are defined, the usual fuzzy reasoning methodology can be applied to implement this method of behavior identification. We show in the next section the implementation of this method in the fuzzy logic toolbox of MATLAB

6 Simulation Results for Robotic Dynamic Systems

Our new method for automated simulation of non-linear dynamical systems was implemented as a prototype intelligent system in the MATLAB programming language. We tested the prototype intelligent system with different data to validate the new method and also the implementation with very good results. In this section, we show some of the results obtained using the intelligent system for automated simulation, to give an idea of the performance of the system.

Table 1 Knowledge base for behavior identification using Lyapunov exponents and fractal dimension

IF		THEN
Lyapunov exponents	Fractal Dim	Behavior Identification
(-)		stable fixed point
(-, -)		stable fixed point
(0, -)	[1.1, 1.2)	limit cycle period 2
(0, -)	[1.2, 1.3)	limit cycle period 4
(0, -)	[1.3, 1.4)	limit cycle period 8
(0, -)	[1.4, 1.5)	limit cycle period 16
(-, -, -)		stable fixed point
(0, -, -)	[2.1, 2.2)	limit cycle period 2
(0, -, -)	[2.2, 2.4)	limit cycle period 4
(0, -, -)	[2.4, 2.6)	limit cycle period 8
(0, -, -)	[2.6, 2.8)	limit cycle period 16
(+, 0, -)	[2.8, 3.0)	chaos

To give an idea of the performance of our fuzzy-fractal-genetic approach for simulation, we show below simulation results obtained for several types of dynamical systems. First, we show in Figure 3 the fuzzy rule base for the prototype intelligent system developed in the fuzzy logic toolbox of the MATLAB programming language. In this figure we can see the implementation of the knowledge base for behavior identification described in Table 1 of this paper.

We show in Figure 4 the membership functions for the linguistic values of the behavior identification. The membership functions were defined in the membership function editor of the fuzzy logic toolbox.

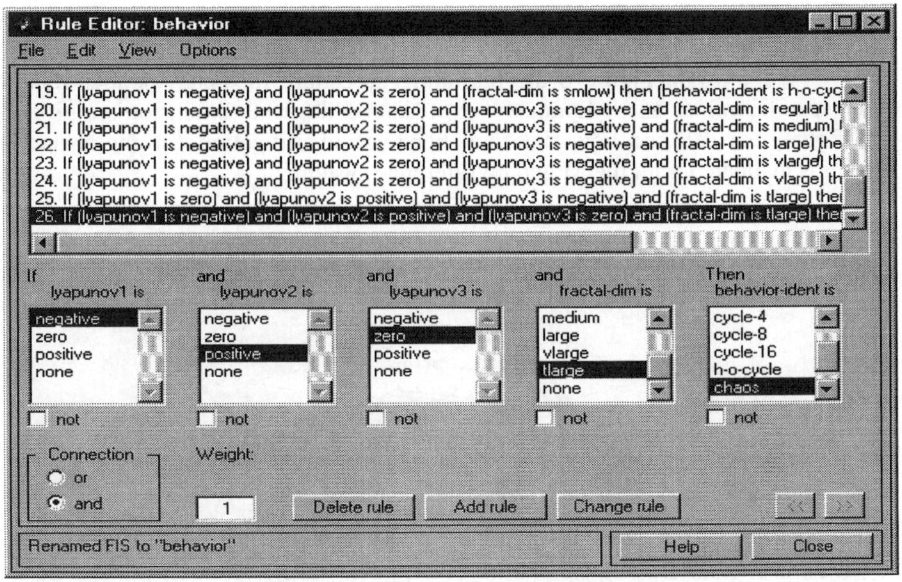

Figure 3 Fuzzy rule base in the rule editor of the fuzzy logic toolbox

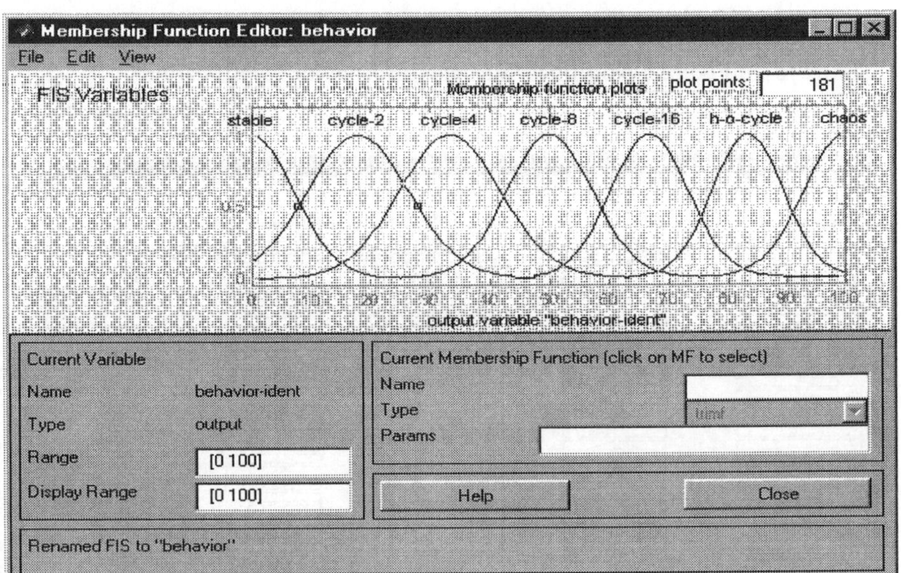

Figure 4 Membership function plots for the linguistic values of the behavior identification

We show in Figure 5 the non-linear surface for the problem of behavior identification using as input variables Lyapunov exponents and fractal dimension.

We show in Figure 6 the reasoning procedure for behavior identification when specific values of the Lyapunov exponents and fractal dimension are given. In this figure, we can see how the final behavior identification for the dynamical system is evaluated with the Mamdani inference system.

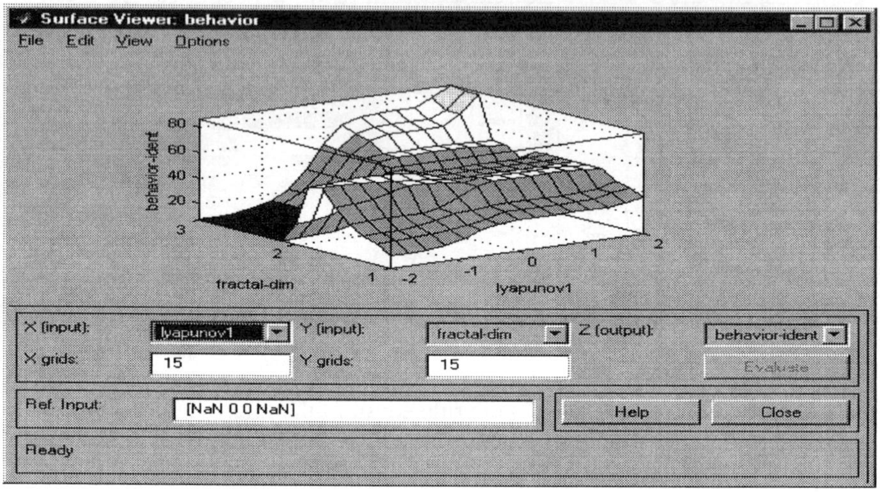

Figure 5 Non-linear surface for behavior identification

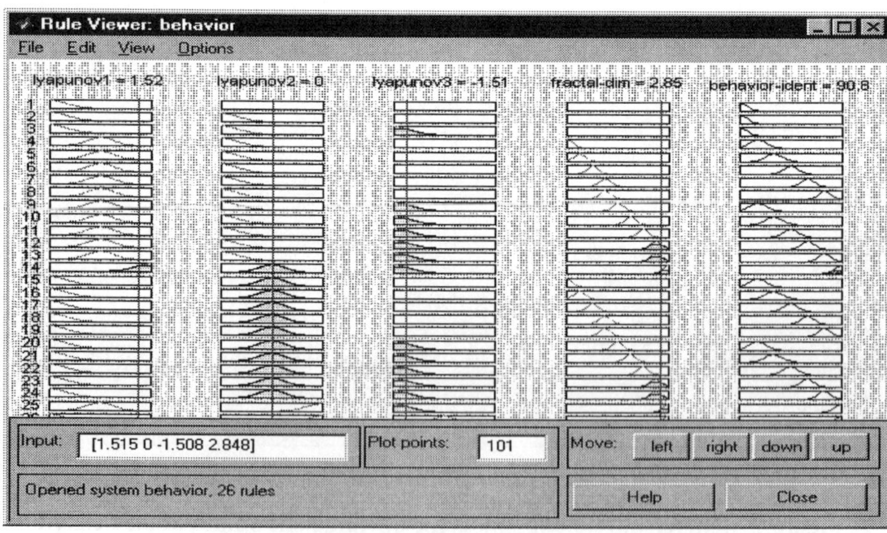

Figure 6 Behavior identification for specific values of Lyapunov exponents and fractal dimension

In Figure 7 we show the simulation results for a two-link robotic dynamic system with a mathematical model given by the two coupled second order differential equations:

$$q''_1 + a_1 q'_1 + b_1 \sin q_2 = c_1$$

$$q''_2 + a_2 q'_2 + b_2 \sin q_2 = c_2 \qquad (11)$$

where a_1, a_2, b_1, b_2, c_1 and c_2 are physical parameters of the robotic system. The simulation results shown in Figure 5 correspond to the parameter values:

$$a_1 = 212, \quad a_2 = 20, \quad b_1 = b_2 = 60, \quad c_1 = c_2 = 72$$

and to the initial conditions: $q_1(0) = 0.5$, $q'_1(0) = 5$, $q_2(0) = 5$, $q'_2(0) = 5$. The solution shown in Figure 7 is what is known as a "chaotic solution" because the orbit is oscillating (in an unstable manner) between an infinite number of periodic points. As a consequence of this fact the behavior identification in this case is of a "chaotic solution".

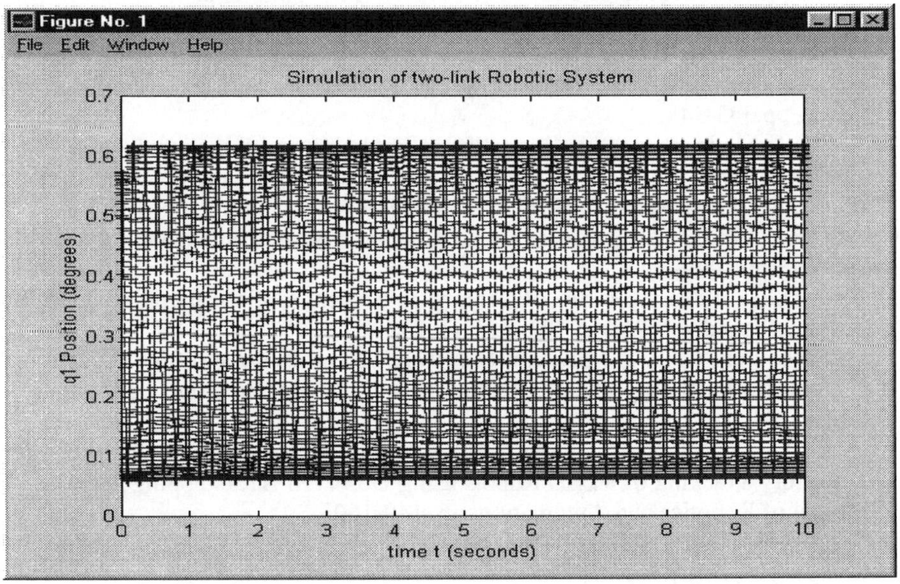

Figure 7 Simulation of two-link robot arm showing chaotic behavior for position q_1.

7 Conclusions

We have presented in this paper a new method for automated simulation of non-linear dynamical systems. This method is based on a hybrid fuzzy-fractal-genetic approach to achieve, in an efficient way, automated simulation for a particular dynamical system given its mathematical model. The use of genetic algorithms is to achieve automated parameter selection for the models. The use of fuzzy logic is to simulate the process of expert behavior identification by implementing the knowledge of identification by a set of fuzzy rules. We illustrated the application of this method for automated simulation for the case of robotic dynamic systems. The results show the efficiency of this new method for the simulation of complex non-linear dynamical systems. Still, more research work remains to be done in generalizing the method for other kinds of dynamical systems.

References

Abraham, E. & Firth, W. J. (1984). "Multiparameter Universal Route to Chaos in a Fabry-Perot Resonator", Optical Bistability, Vol. 2, pp. 119-126.

Castillo, O. & Melin, P. (1995). "An Intelligent System for the Simulation of Non-Linear Dynamical Economical Systems", Journal of Mathematical Modelling and Simulation in Systems Analysis, Edited by Achim Sydow, Gordon and Breach Publishers, Vol. 18-19, pp. 767-770.

Castillo, O. & Melin, P. (1996). "Automated Mathematical Modelling and Simulation of Dynamical Engineering Systems using Artificial Intelligence Techniques", Proceedings CESA'96, Gerf EC Lille, pp. 682-687.

Castillo, O. & Melin, P. (1997). "Mathematical Modelling and Simulation of Robotic Dynamic Systems using Fuzzy Logic Techniques and Fractal Theory", Proceedings of IMACS World Congress'97, Wissenschaft & Technik Verlag, Vol. 5, pp.343-348.

Castillo, O. & Melin, P. (1998). "Modelling, Simulation and Behavior Identification of Non-Linear Dynamical Systems with a New Fuzzy-Fractal-Genetic Approach", Proceedings of IPMU'98, EDK Publishers, Vol. 1, pp. 467-474.

Devaney, R. (1989). "An Introduction to Chaotic Dynamical Systems", Addison Wesley Publishing.

Goldberg, D.E. (1989). "Genetic Algorithms in Search, Optimization and Machine Learning", Addison Wesley Publishing.

Jang, J.-S. R., Sun, C.-T. & Mizutani, E. (1997). "Neurofuzzy and Soft Computing: A Computational Approach to Learning and Machine Intelligence", Prentice-Hall.

Lim, S.Y., Hu, J. & Dawson, D.M. (1996). "An Output Feedback Controller for Trajectory Tracking of RLED Robots using Observed Backstepping Approach", Journal of Robotics and Automation, pp. 149-160.

Mandelbrot, B. (1987). "The Fractal Geometry of Nature", W. H. Freeman and Company.

Nakamura, S. (1997). "Numerical Analysis and Graphic Visualization with MATLAB", Prentice Hall.

Rasband, S.N. (1990). "Chaotic Dynamics of Non-Linear Systems", Wiley Interscience.

Zadeh, L.A. (1973). "Outline of a New Approach to the Analysis of Complex Systems and Decision Processes", IEEE Transactions on Systems, Man and Cybernetics, Vol. 3, pp. 28-44.

Supervisory Fuzzy Controller

James J. Buckley
University of Alabama at Birmingham
Department of Mathematics
Birmingham, Alabama, 35294, USA
buckley@math.uab.edu

Thomas Feuring
University of Siegen
Department of Electrical Engineering and Computer Science
Hölderlinstr. 3, 57068 Siegen, Germany
feuring@informatik.uni-siegen.de

Abstract: In this paper we describe a supervisory fuzzy controller. This system can be used to advise, or train, people who are in control of a complex plant. The advantage of the supervisory fuzzy controller is that it is designed to interact with the human operators through accepting verbal evaluations and producing verbal suggestions. In order to find the verbal suggestions we propose the use of a trained neural network for the task of inverse linguistic approximation.

1 Introduction

Fuzzy controllers are designed for controlling machines so they act on crisp inputs and produce crisp outputs. In order to advise or train a human operator the use of crisp inputs and/or crisp outputs seems to be not appropriate. In this paper we are interested in modifying a fuzzy controller so that it can act on verbal inputs and verbal suggestions based on a predefined vocabulary. We will call these controllers supervisory fuzzy controllers (SFC). A diagram of the SFC is shown in Figure 1. We will discuss, in detail, all parts of this figure in the next section. In the third section an example of a SFC is presented. A brief summary is contained in the last section.

Let us now present the notation we will employ in this paper. We place a bar over a capital letter to denote a fuzzy subset of the real numbers. So $\overline{A}$, $\overline{B}$, ..., $\overline{L}$, etc. all represent fuzzy subsets of the real numbers. We write $\overline{A}(x)$, a number in $[0,1]$, for the membership function of $\overline{A}$ evaluated at x. A triangular fuzzy number $\overline{A}$ is defined by three numbers $a_1 < a_2 < a_3$ where the membership function is a triangle with base on the interval $[a_1, a_3]$ and vertex at $x = a_2$. We write triangular fuzzy number $\overline{A}$ as $(a_1/a_2/a_3)$.

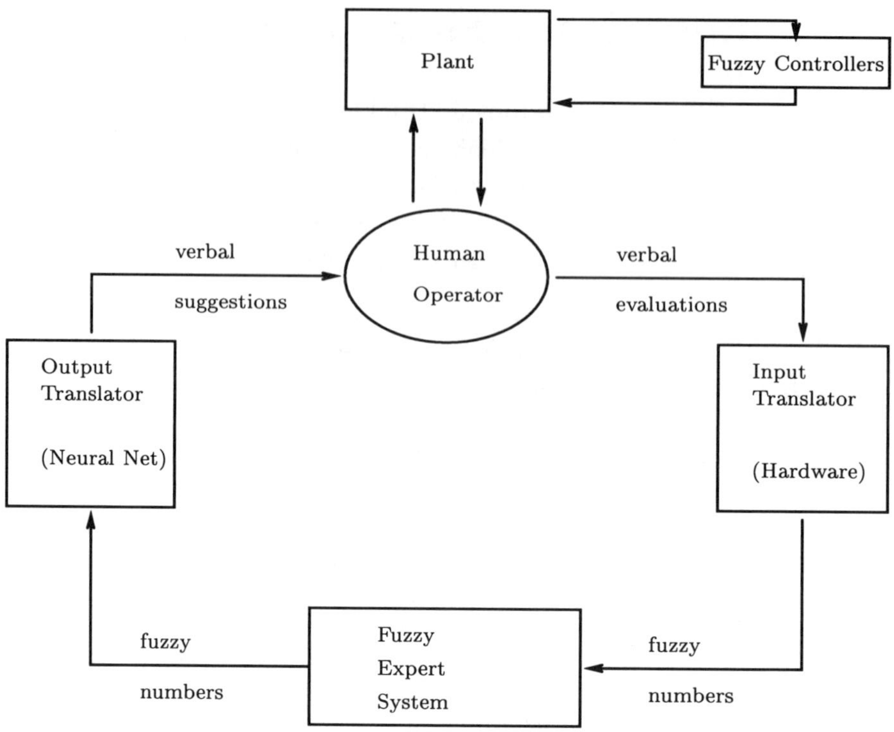

Figure 1: Supervisory Fuzzy Controller

We have to mention that in Figure 1 fuzzy controllers are presented together with the SFC. Let us now describe the interactions between the SFC and the fuzzy controller we will focus on.

In general, there are four possible situations to be considered: (1) no SFC; (2) no fuzzy controllers; (3) there are fuzzy controllers together with a SFC but they are "independent"; and (4) there is a SFC plus fuzzy controllers and they are "interactive". The first case is only about fuzzy controllers which we shall not discuss further in this paper. In the second case there is only a SFC which will operate very slowly. So, it can be used for processes which do not require fast turn around time (for example sailing a sail boat in open waters through a calm sea). Anyway, case 2 is essentially contained in the third case and we will not discuss it further. In case three by "independent" we mean that the fuzzy controllers are independent from the fuzzy rules in the SFC. That is, no input to a fuzzy controller is also an input to the SFC and vice versa, no input to the SFC is also an input to a fuzzy controller. In contrast to the "independent" case we have case 4, described in [1], where the two controller are "interactive". In the "interactive" case there is only one set of fuzzy rules for both the fuzzy controller and the SFC. That is, in case 4 the controller simultaneously processes error, change in error, and verbal evaluations to give defuzzified input to the plant and verbal suggestions to the human operators of the plant.

In this paper we will only discuss case 3. In case 3 the fuzzy controllers and the SFC are not completely independent but can interact in the following way. Suppose the SFC gives the verbal suggestion "close valve # C3". If a human operator closes this valve, then the plant's output will change, producing different inputs to the fuzzy controllers, which changes their output-input to the plant, etc., which in term changes the verbal evaluation of the plant.

2 Supervisory Fuzzy Controller

We will give the details on the various components of the supervisory fuzzy controller shown in Figure 1.

2.1 Verbal Evaluation

The human operators are allowed to use a very limited vocabulary to communicate with the SFC. Let us take as an example the variable pressure (P) and the human operators may communicate two things concerning pressure: its current value and how it is changing. With respect to how it is changing they can say: decreasing rapidly, decreasing, decreasing very slowly, no change, increasing very slowly, increasing, or increasing rapidly. For the value of pressure they may communicate: very low, low, slightly low, good, slightly high, high, or very high. All of these descriptions are defined by fuzzy numbers. Notice that hedges are built into the system since very high is separately defined as a fuzzy number and not constructed out of the fuzzy number for high. So let the fuzzy numbers for the change in pressure be $\overline{D}_1$ = decrease rapidly, ..., $\overline{D}_7$ =increase rapidly and for the value of pressure $\overline{P}_1$ =very low, ..., $\overline{P}_7$ =very high.

The method of communication to the SFC may take various forms. The human operators could use a special keyboard, use a mouse to click on the words, touch the words on a computer screen, or as in [1] draw the fuzzy numbers on the computer screen. Also there could be a voice recognition system trained to recognize certain words from a few of the human operators.

In fact, there could be uncertainty as to which word to use so we will allow multiple word inputs for each variable. That is, for change in pressure the input could be "decreasing or decreasing very slowly" and for the value of pressure "slightly high or high".

At certain times the input to the input translator will be words describing the value of a variable and possibly how it is changing. Suppose the variables are pressure (P) and temperature (T). When the human operators wish to consult the SFC they do not have to input words for all the variables. If they input observations only for change in pressure and change in temperature the system automatically takes the previous values for the other variables (value of pressure and value of temperature) to compute its suggestions.

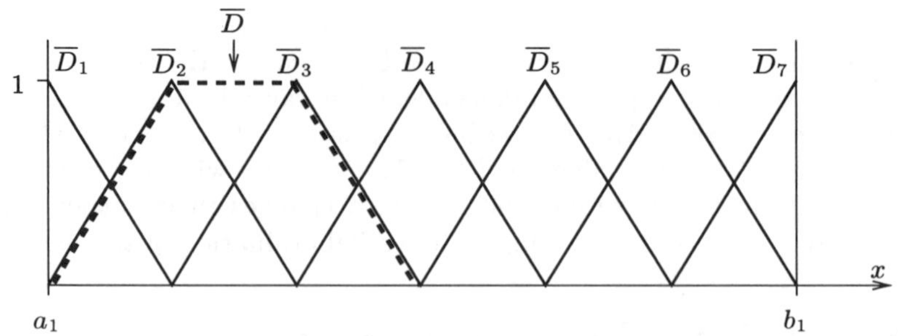

Figure 2: Fuzzy Numbers for Change in Pressure.

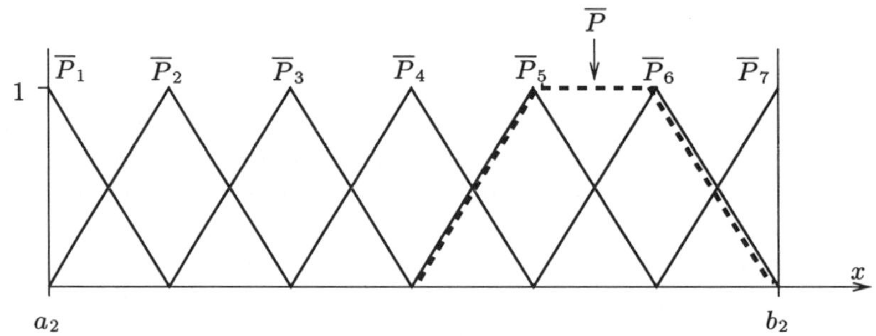

Figure 3: Fuzzy Numbers for Value of Pressure.

2.2 Input Translator

The job of the input translator is to translate the words into fuzzy numbers for input to the fuzzy expert system. Since the human operators use a very limited vocabulary, and all the words have been previously defined by fuzzy numbers, this translation is basically trivial and could be accomplished by a specially designed piece of hardware. The only problem is when an operator uses multiple words for a single variable. When multiple words are used for a variable we sort of take the union of the corresponding fuzzy numbers for input to the fuzzy expert system.

For example, consider the example discussed above in 2.1 where an operator said, pressure is "decreasing and decreasing slowly" and the value of the pressure is "slightly high and high". We usually use triangular fuzzy numbers for the $\overline{D}_i$ and $\overline{P}_j$ which are shown in Figures 2 and 3. Then the automatic translation of these verbal evaluations is $\overline{D}$ for the change in pressure and $\overline{P}$ for the value of pressure. Notice that $\overline{D}$ and $\overline{P}$ will be trapezoidal (fuzzy intervals) fuzzy numbers showing the uncertainty of the human observer. The input translator sends $\overline{D}$ and $\overline{P}$ to the fuzzy expert system.

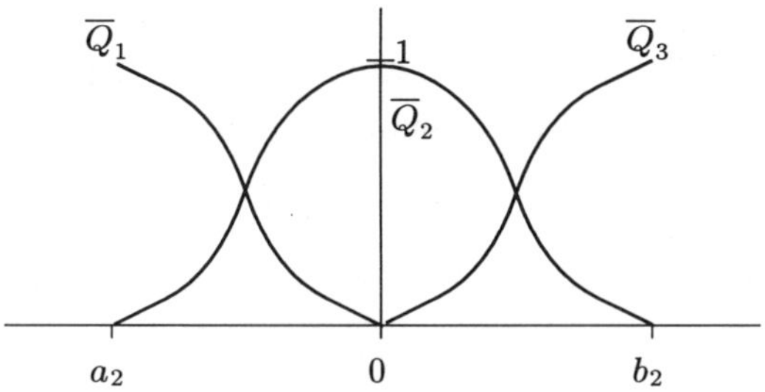

Figure 4: Fuzzy Sets for the Value of Pressure in the Fuzzy Expert System.

2.3 Fuzzy Expert System

The fuzzy expert system processes, through blocks of fuzzy rules, the fuzzy numbers it has received, for all the variables from the input translator, to produce discrete fuzzy sets for control actions. Suppose we have four input fuzzy sets two for pressure (change and value) and two for temperature (change and value). The fuzzy numbers are: (1) $\overline{D}$ for change in pressure; (2) $\overline{P}$ for pressure; (3) $\overline{C}$ for change in temperature; and (3) $\overline{T}$ for value of temperature. Of course, $\overline{D}$ can be one of the $\overline{D}_i$ in Figure 2 and $\overline{P}$ may be a $\overline{P}_j$ in Figure 3. There are M fuzzy rules of the type

$$R_s\text{: If } [\overline{D} = \overline{Q}_{1i}] \text{ and } [\overline{P} = \overline{Q}_{2j}] \text{ and } [\overline{C} = \overline{Q}_{3k}] \text{ and } [\overline{T} = \overline{Q}_{4l}]\text{, then } CA_1 = \overline{A}_n \text{ and } CA_2 = \overline{B}_p \ ,$$

where CA_1 = control action #1, CA_2 = control action #2 and the fuzzy numbers $\overline{Q}_{ij}$ are specially defined for each variable, $1 \leq s \leq M$. Also, the CA_i are discrete fuzzy sets

$$CA_1 = \left\{ \frac{\alpha_1}{\overline{A}_1}, \cdots, \frac{\alpha_N}{\overline{A}_N} \right\} \quad \text{and} \quad CA_2 = \left\{ \frac{\beta_1}{\overline{B}_1}, \cdots, \frac{\beta_P}{\overline{B}_P} \right\} \ , \tag{1}$$

where the α_i (β_j) are the membership values of the fuzzy sets $\overline{A}_i$ ($\overline{B}_j$) in CA_1 (CA_2). Given the inputs $\overline{D}$, $\overline{P}$, $\overline{C}$ and $\overline{T}$ the fuzzy expert system is to construct the discrete fuzzy sets CA_i, $i = 1, 2$.

First we need to specify the $\overline{Q}_{ij}$. Consider the $\overline{Q}_{2j}$ for the value of pressure. The $\overline{Q}_{2j}$ give a qualitative evaluation of pressure and possible definitions are shown in Figure 4. In Figure 4 linguistic translations of the $\overline{Q}_{2i}$ are: $\overline{Q}_{21}$ = danger, too low; $\overline{Q}_{22}$ = everything is OK; $\overline{Q}_{23}$ = danger, too high. These $\overline{Q}_{ij}$ are defined for all the input fuzzy sets. Here we only chose three fuzzy sets in order to reduce the set of possible rules.

Next we need to define the meaning of the $\overline{A}_n$ ($\overline{B}_p$) for the control actions. These fuzzy sets represent suggestions for the human operators. Let $I_{1i} = \overline{A}_i$, $1 \leq i \leq N$ and $I_{2i} = \overline{B}_i$, $1 \leq i \leq P$. For example, I_{12} could be "close valve V2" and I_{23} might be "empty contents of storage tank #2 into output tank".

Given the input fuzzy set $\overline{P}$, $\overline{D}$, $\overline{C}$ and $\overline{T}$ all the fuzzy rules are evaluated producing the discrete fuzzy sets CA_i, $1 = 1, 2$. Initially, all the α_i and β_j

values are set to zero. To evaluate rule R_s we need to compute the value of all the comparisons $[\overline{D} = \overline{Q}_{1i}]$, $[\overline{P} = \overline{Q}_{2j}]$, etc. Let E be some fuzzy equality relation defined on the set of fuzzy numbers. Then the value of $[\overline{D} = \overline{Q}_{1i}]$, say λ_i, is

$$\lambda_i = E(\overline{D}, \overline{Q}_{1i}) \ . \tag{2}$$

One might consider using the height of the intersection of $\overline{D}$ and $\overline{Q}_{1i}$, which is

$$\lambda_i = \sup_x(\min(\overline{D}(x), \overline{Q}_{1i}(x))) \ , \tag{3}$$

for E. So, we assume $E(\overline{P}, \overline{Q}_{2j}) = \lambda_j$, $E(\overline{C}, \overline{Q}_{3k}) = \lambda_k$, and $E(\overline{T}, \overline{Q}_{4l}) = \lambda_l$ have all been computed.

We next evaluate[1]

$$\gamma_s = T(\lambda_i, \lambda_j, \lambda_k, \lambda_l) \ , \tag{4}$$

for all rules, $1 \leq s \leq M$, for a t-norm T. The value for the antecedent of the rule R_s is γ_s. To obtain the α_i and β_j we have to aggregate the γ_s over the rules.

The memory update algorithm for the SFC now collects together all the rules that have the same $\overline{A}_n$, or the same $\overline{B}_p$, in their right hand side (consequence). Let Γ_n (Γ_p) be all s in $\{1, 2, \ldots, M\}$ whose consequence is $\overline{A}_n = CA_1$ ($\overline{B}_p = CA_2$) for $n = 1, 2, \ldots, N$ and $p = 1, 2, \ldots, P$. Then

$$\alpha_n = C\{\gamma_s \mid s \in \Gamma_n\} \quad \text{and} \quad \beta_p = C\{\gamma_s \mid s \in \Gamma_p\} \ , \tag{5}$$

$1 \leq n \leq N$, $1 \leq p \leq P$, for a t-conorm[2] C. In this way the fuzzy expert system constructs the discrete fuzzy sets CA_i, $i = 1, 2$.

We could use more general fuzzy rules than always having equality between fuzzy numbers. That is, a rule could have $[\overline{P} \leq \overline{Q}_{2j}]$ or $[\overline{C} \neq \overline{Q}_{3k}]$ or $[\overline{C} > \overline{Q}_{3k}]$, etc. The $\overline{Q}_{ij}$ could also be real numbers. All of these relations can be evaluated producing the γ_s numbers.

Where do these fuzzy rules come from? They come from the human observers who have been overseeing, and controlling, the complex process. For example, consider the control of a nuclear power plant. Many components of the plant can be individually controlled by controllers but the overall control is accomplished by human operators. The SFC acts as an advisor (back-up) for experienced human operators or as a training module for unexperienced operators.

The last thing to do, before we go to the output translator, is aggregate the $\overline{A}_n$ ($\overline{B}_p$) into one fuzzy set. We will employ the following method (like the center of gravity defuzzifier)

$$\overline{A}^* = \frac{\sum_{n=1}^{N} \alpha_n \overline{A}_n}{\sum_{n=1}^{N} \alpha_n} \quad \text{and} \quad \overline{B}^* = \frac{\sum_{p=1}^{P} \beta_p \overline{B}_p}{\sum_{p=1}^{P} \beta_p} \ . \tag{6}$$

The SFC sends $\overline{A}^*$ and $\overline{B}^*$ to the output translator.

[1] Any t-norm T is associative and may be extended to n arguments so that $T(x_1, \ldots, x_n)$ is defined.

[2] Any t-conorm C may be extended, though associativity, to n arguments so that $C(x_1, \ldots, x_n)$ is defined.

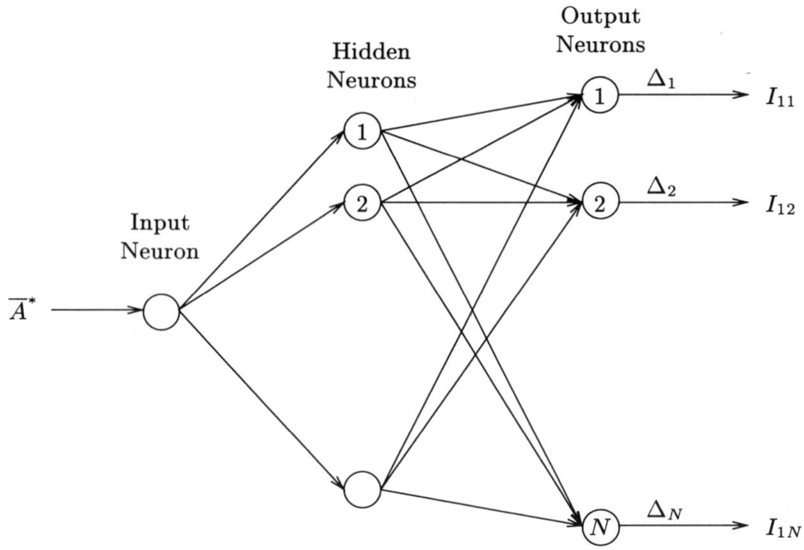

Figure 5: Output Translator for First Control Action.

2.4 Output Translator

The output translator translates the $\overline{A}^*$ ($\overline{B}^*$) into verbal suggestions (the I_{1i} and I_{2j}). This will be accomplished by a feedforward network. We require one neural net for each control action. The neural net for CA_1 is shown in Figure 5. This neural net is trained on the training set $(\overline{A}_i, I_{1i})$, $1 \leq i \leq N$. This means if we input $\overline{A}^* = \overline{A}_3$ then the output should be I_{i3}. Or, input $\overline{A}_3$, then $\Delta_3 \approx 1$, $\Delta_i \approx 0$, $1 \leq i \leq N$ with $i \neq 3$. The Δ_i are the strengths of the output signals at the i-th output neuron. Once trained, we can input $\overline{A}^*$ from the fuzzy expert system.

We have a similar neural net for $\overline{B}^*$ and the I_{2i}, $1 \leq i \leq P$. The output translator will not output all the I_{ij} but will perform thresholding first before sending its verbal suggestions to the human operators. Let $\tau \in [0,1)$, the thresholding constant. For CA_1, the output translator sends I_{1n} to the operators only if $\Delta_n \geq \tau$. Also, for CA_2 a I_{2p} is sent only when $\Delta_p \geq \tau$. So, for example, the operators could get only I_{12} for CA_1 but I_{23} and I_{24} for CA_2. The confidences (Δ_i) would also be given.

These verbal suggestions could be displayed on a computer screen or spoken through a voice box.

Why do we suggest a neural net for the output translator? The translation of an $\overline{A}^*$ back into I_{1n} is what has been called inverse linguistic approximation. Numerous papers have addressed the problem of inverse linguistic approximation ([2]-[4], [6] and its references, [7]). The procedure of inverse linguistic approximation is just non-linear interpolation and neural nets are perfect for this task. Hence, we propose a neural net, with fuzzy input and crisp output, for the output translator. In [6] the use of neural networks as output transla-

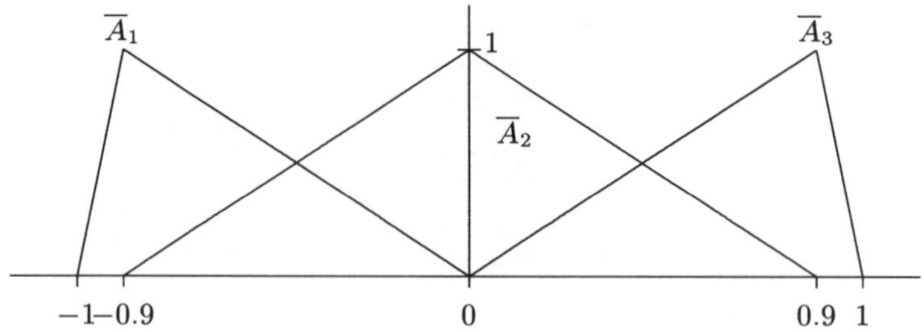

Figure 6: Fuzzy Sets for the Control Actions.

tors was also proposed. However, in that thesis another way of input coding was used. The neural net is described in more detail in the example in the next section.

3 Example

In this section we implement the ideas of the previous section and construct a small scale SFC. We will need to limit the number of variables and the fuzzy sets $\overline{Q}_{ij}$ (Figure 4) so that the fuzzy rule table is not too large.

Our basic variables are pressure (P) and temperature (T). The variables will be P, D =change in P, T, and C =change in T. As in subsection 2.2 there will be seven fuzzy numbers (see Figures 2 and 3) for P, D, T, and C. The descriptions of each of these fuzzy numbers is the same as given in 2.2 for P (T) and for D (C).

The fuzzy rules R_s ($1 \leq s \leq 81$) are given as in Subsection 2.3 (with parameters $i = j = k = l = 1, 2, 3$ and n, p in the set $\{1, 2, 3\}$).

We first define the fuzzy sets $\overline{Q}_{ij}$. We will assume that all the fuzzy numbers (also for the variables P, D, T, C) have been scaled so that they lie in $[-1, 1]$. We will also use the same $\overline{Q}$'s for all the variables. That is, $\overline{Q}_{ij} = \overline{Q}_j$, $i = 1, 2, 3, 4$ and $j = 1, 2, 3$. The $\overline{Q}_j$ are specified in Figure 4. For the membership functions for the $\overline{Q}_i$ we pieced together quadratic polynomials. Having only three $\overline{Q}$'s will greatly reduce the total number of fuzzy rules (now 81). There will be three fuzzy numbers for each control action as shown in Figure 6. For simplicity we have assumed that $\overline{A}_i = \overline{B}_i$, $i = 1, 2, 3$. Recall that the meaning of $\overline{A}_i$ is I_{1i} and the suggestions corresponding to $\overline{B}_i$ is I_{2i}, $i = 1, 2, 3$. The statements corresponding to these I_{ij} are as follows: (1) I_{11} = close valve V3; (2) I_{12} = no action required; (3) I_{13} = open valve V3; (4) I_{21} = increase fuel rate R2; (5) I_{22} = no action required; and (6) I_{23} = decrease fuel rate R2.

To evaluate the fuzzy rules we will use $T = \min$, $C = \max$, and the height of the intersection (equation 3) to compute the λ_i.

We need to present all 81 fuzzy rules. They will be given in nine 3×3 tables. One of the tables is given below and the other eight are omitted from the paper. Notice, that the values of the variables can interact in producing the consequences of a rule. For example, consider Table 1 where $\overline{P} = \overline{Q}_2$ and

		$\overline{D}$		
		$\overline{Q}_1$	$\overline{Q}_2$	$\overline{Q}_3$
	$\overline{Q}_1$	$\overline{A}_1, \overline{B}_2$	$\overline{A}_2, \overline{B}_2$	$\overline{A}_2, \overline{B}_2$
$\overline{P}$	$\overline{Q}_2$	$\overline{A}_2, \overline{B}_2$	$\overline{A}_3, \overline{B}_2$	$\overline{A}_3, \overline{B}_2$
	$\overline{Q}_3$	$\overline{A}_2, \overline{B}_2$	$\overline{A}_3, \overline{B}_2$	$\overline{A}_3, \overline{B}_2$

Table 1: Fuzzy Rule Table for $\overline{C} = \overline{Q}_3$ and $\overline{T} = \overline{Q}_1$.

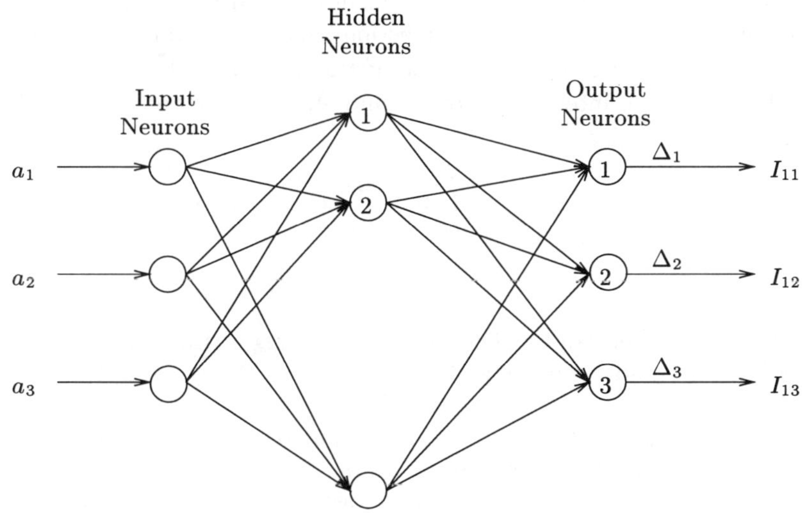

Figure 7: Output Neural Network in the Example.

$\overline{D} = \overline{Q}_2$. Normally, we would suggest $CA_1 = A_2$ but temperature is rising rapidly, so we would expect the pressure to be also increasing. We recommend $\overline{A}_3$ which opens the valve to decrease the pressure. This interaction of changes in temperature effecting pressure was incorporated in all the rule tables.

The interpretation of $\overline{Q}_1$ and $\overline{Q}_3$ on the change in pressure and the change in temperature must be further explained. $\overline{Q}_1$ for $\overline{D}$ ($\overline{C}$) means that pressure (temperature) is decreasing rapidly and $\overline{Q}_3$ for $\overline{D}$ ($\overline{C}$) is interpreted as pressure (temperature) is increasing rapidly.

The neural net used for the output translator is the heart of the SFC. The neural net will have fuzzy input (the $\overline{A}^*$ and $\overline{B}^*$ of Section 2.3) and crisp output (Figure 5). But since the $\overline{A}_i$ ($\overline{B}_i$) in Figure 6 are triangular fuzzy numbers the net can have crisp input (Figure 7). From Figure 6 we see that $\overline{A}_1 = \overline{B}_1 = (-1/-0.9/0)$, $\overline{A}_2 = \overline{B}_2 = (-0.9/0/0.9)$ and $\overline{A}_3 = \overline{B}_3 = (0/0.9/1)$. In Figure 7 $a_1 = -0.9$, $a_2 = 0$, $a_3 = 0.9$ for $\overline{A}_2$. Figure 7 shows the net for CA_1. The only changes for CA_2 would be at the output neurons where: (1) output neuron #1 has I_{21} with signal strength θ_1; (2) output neuron #2 has

I_{22} with θ_2; and (3) output neuron #3 has signal θ_3 and I_{23}. The training set for CA_1 is: (1) $(-1/0.9/0)$ and $\Delta_1 = 1$, $\Delta_2 = 0$, $\Delta_3 = 0$; (2) $(-0.9/0/0.9)$ and $\Delta_1 = 0$, $\Delta_2 = 1$, $\Delta_3 = 0$; and (3) $(0/0.9/1)$ and $\Delta_1 = 0$, $\Delta_2 = 0$, $\Delta_3 = 1$. The training set for CA_2 is the same so the net only has to be trained once.

In order to train the neural net a training set is needed. Of course, we already have a few training patterns given by $\overline{A}^* = \overline{A}_i, \Delta_i = 1.0, \Delta_j = 0.0\ j \neq i$ but we need a larger training set because we cannot expect that $\overline{A}^*$ equals $\overline{A}_i$ for one i. So, we randomly chose triangular fuzzy numbers in $[-1.0, 1.0]$. In order to evaluate the corresponding target values (Δ_j) a metric S is needed which computes the confidence value that the generated triangular fuzzy number equals $\overline{A}_i$. The method we used is inspired by Kerre's inequality relation [5] and computes the area of the intersection between $\overline{A}_i$ and $\overline{A}^*$. The resulting value is normed by the area of $\overline{A}_i$ so we get a value in $S(\overline{A}^*, \overline{A}_i) \in [0,1]$ where $S(\overline{A}^*, \overline{A}_i) = 0$ if the intersection of $\overline{A}^*$ and $\overline{A}_i$ is empty and $S(\overline{A}^*, \overline{A}_i) = 1$ if $\overline{A}^* = \overline{A}_i$. S is given by

$$S(\overline{A}^*, \overline{A}_i) = \frac{\int_{-\infty}^{\infty} \min(\overline{A}^*(x), \overline{A}_i(x))dx}{\int_{-\infty}^{\infty} \overline{A}_i(x)dx} . \tag{7}$$

Now, the training set can be generated by choosing a triangular fuzzy number $\overline{A} = (a_1/a_2/a_3)$ and computing the target values $\Delta_1 = S(\overline{A}, \overline{A}_1)$, ..., $\Delta_3 = S(\overline{A}, \overline{A}_3)$.

Let us now explain the details of the output translator training. The training set consisted of 300 input output pairs. A randomly chosen input fuzzy number only was taken into the training set if at least one confidence value was larger than 0.5. The net had three input neurons, seven hidden units and three output neurons standing for I_{11}, I_{12} and I_{13}. The learning rate was set to 0.001. After 91145 iterations the mean squared error on the training set was 0.000124.

We input an $\overline{A}^*$ $(\overline{B}^*)$ the same way because they are also triangular fuzzy numbers. From equation (6) we see that

$$\overline{A}^* = \sum_{n=1}^{3} \epsilon_n \overline{A}_n , \tag{8}$$

where

$$\epsilon_n = \frac{\alpha_n}{\sum_{i=1}^{3} \alpha_i} , \tag{9}$$

for $n = 1, 2, 3$. Therefore, $\epsilon_n \in [0,1]$ all n and $\sum_{n=1}^{3} \epsilon_n = 1$. If we set $\overline{A}_i = (a_{i1}/a_{i2}/a_{i3})$, $1 \leq i \leq 3$, then $\overline{A}^* = (\varphi_1/\varphi_2/\varphi_3)$ where

$$\varphi_i = \sum_{n=1}^{3} \epsilon_n a_{ni} , \tag{10}$$

for $i = 1, 2, 3$. So, given an $\overline{A}^*$, output from the fuzzy expert system, we input φ_i for a_i, $1 \leq i \leq 3$, into the net in Figure 7. Similarly, we find values for η_i

Verbal Evaluation	SFC Output
1. Pressure $= \overline{P}_6$	$\overline{A}^* = (-0.335/0.565/0.963)$
Change in Pressure $= \overline{D}_6$	$S(\overline{A}^*, \overline{A}_1) = 0.062$, $\Delta_1 = 0.098$
	$S(\overline{A}^*, \overline{A}_2) = 0.471$, $\Delta_2 = 0.495$
	$S(\overline{A}^*, \overline{A}_3) = 0.714$, $\Delta_3 = 0.751$
Temperature $= \overline{T}_4$	$\overline{B}^* = (-0.611/0.205/0.839)$
Change in Temperature $= \overline{C}_5$	$S(\overline{B}^*, \overline{B}_1) = 0.217$, $\theta_1 = 0.222$
	$S(\overline{B}^*, \overline{B}_2) = 0.731$, $\theta_2 = 0.741$
	$S(\overline{B}^*, \overline{B}_3) = 0.459$, $\theta_3 = 0.472$
2. Pressure $= \overline{P}_2$	$\overline{A}^* = (-0.450/0.450/0.950)$
Change in Pressure $= \overline{D}_6$ or $\overline{D}_7$	$S(\overline{A}^*, \overline{A}_1) = 0.113$, $\Delta_1 = 0.138$
	$S(\overline{A}^*, \overline{A}_2) = 0.563$, $\Delta_2 = 0.591$
	$S(\overline{A}^*, \overline{A}_3) = 0.645$ $\Delta_3 = 0.661$
Temperature $= \overline{T}_2$ or $\overline{T}_3$	$\overline{B}^* = (-0.633/0.000/0.633)$
Change in Temperature $= \overline{C}_3$	$S(\overline{B}^*, \overline{B}_1) = 0.262$, $\theta_1 = 0.259$
	$S(\overline{B}^*, \overline{B}_2) = 0.704$, $\theta_2 = 0.691$
	$S(\overline{B}^*, \overline{B}_3) = 0.262$, $\theta_3 = 0.249$

Table 2: Results in the Example.

in $\overline{B}^* = (\eta_1/\eta_2/\eta_3)$ which will be inputs to the output translator for CA_2. For the thresholding constant we will use $\tau = 0.5$ for both CA_1 and CA_2.

Now we are ready to actually run our small scale SFC on some input data. The operation of the SFC is straightforward. We input values for P, D, T and C. These will be triangular, or trapezoidal, fuzzy numbers. Then the λ values (equation (2)) are all computed. From these λ values we compute the γ_s (equation (4) with min $= T$) and the α_n, β_n (equation (5)) with $C =$ max). Then the α_n (β_n) are used to obtain the φ_i (η_i) as in equation (10). Finally, the φ_i (η_i) are inputted to the neural net to obtain the verbal suggestions for the operators. The results are in Table 2.

Consider the second experiment in Table 2. The inputs are: pressure is low; pressure is increasing or increasing rapidly; temperature is slightly low or low; and temperature is decreasing very slowly. The output translator states: (1) for control action #1 "no reaction required (0.591) or open valve V3 (0.661)"; and (2) for control action #2 "no action required (0.691)". In order to show that the neural net works quite well we also present the target confidence values of the SFC computed by $S(\overline{A}^*, \overline{A}_i)$ ($S(\overline{B}^*, \overline{B}_i)$) $i = 1, 2, 3$ (equation (7)) in Table 2.

4 Summary

This paper described the design of a supervisory fuzzy controller (Figure 1) for human operators of a complex plant (nuclear reactor). The human operators are allowed to verbally describe the status of various variables used to control the plant. These verbal descriptions come from a very limited vocabulary recognized by the input translator. The input translator translates these descriptions into fuzzy numbers for input to a fuzzy expert system. The fuzzy expert system processes these fuzzy numbers into fuzzy number output describing suggestions to the human operators. The output translator, which is a neural net, takes the fuzzy number output from the fuzzy expert system, and produces the verbal suggestions, of what to do, for the human operators. An example was presented, with four variables and 81 rules, showing the basic operation of a supervisory fuzzy controller.

A main contribution of this design was the use of a neural net as the output translator. The translation of fuzzy numbers into words is called inverse linguistic approximation. We believe a neural net is ideal for this job.

We also suggested two main applications of a supervisory fuzzy controller: (1) as an advisor (back-up) for experienced human operators; and (2) for training inexperienced human operators. We feel that a supervisory fuzzy controller could have great potential as a training module.

References

[1] J.J Buckley, Fuzzy I/O Controller, Fuzzy Sets and Systems 43, papges 127-137, 1991.

[2] R. Degani and G. Bortolan, The Problem of Linguistic Approximation in Clinical Decision Making, Int. J. Approximate Reasoning 2, pages 143-162, 1988.

[3] A. Dvorak, On Linguistic Approximation in the Frame of LFLC, In *Proceedings of Seventh IFSA'97*, volumne 1, pages 413-417, Prague, June 1997.

[4] F. Eshragh and E. H. Mamdani, A General Approach to Linguistic Approximation, Int. J. Man-Machine Studies 11, pages 501-519, 1979.

[5] E.E. Kerre, The use of fuzzy set theory in electrocardiological diagnostics, in: M.M. Gupta, E. Sanchez (eds.), Approximate Reasoning in Decision Analysis, pages 277-282, 1982.

[6] K. Lukas, Linguistic Approximation and Fuzzy Logic: Current Methods and a New Approach using Neural Networks, Johannes Kepler Univ., Austria, 1994.

[7] M. Sugeno and T. Yakusawa, A Fuzzy-Logic Based Approach to Qualitative Modeling, IEEE Trans. Fuzzy Systems 1, pages 7-31, 1993.

Hierarchical Fuzzy Logic Control

M. Mohammadian[1] and R. J. Stonier[2]
[1]School of Computing, University of Canberra, ACT Australia
[2]Faculty of Informatics and Communication
Central Queensland University, Queensland Australia
Masoud@ise.canberra.edu.au, r.stonier@cqu.edu.au

Abstract

In this paper a method for designing a three level, hierarchical, self-learning fuzzy logic control systems based on the integration of evolutionary algorithms and fuzzy logic is given to provide an integrated knowledge base for intelligent control of mobile robots for collision-avoidance in a common workspace. The robots are considered as point masses in the simulation study. Evolutionary algorithms are employed as the adaptive method for learning the fuzzy rules of the control systems as well as learning, the mapping, and interaction between fuzzy knowledge bases of different fuzzy logic systems.

1 Introduction

Fuzzy logic systems are increasingly being used in control applications as their ability to cope with uncertainty inherent in complex systems makes them an attractive method for solving complex, uncertain, and dynamic systems. Current fuzzy logic systems are developed usually for each individualistic system. These systems are unable to face the challenge of interaction that might be necessary between different fuzzy logic systems solving a complex problem. There is a need for a structured approach to design fuzzy logic systems for controlling complex systems that may have multiple fuzzy knowledge bases as a hierarchical structure.

In general a hierarchical fuzzy logic systems consists of several fuzzy logic systems each performing a specific task which are combined to form a system to solve a complex task. These controllers usually interact with each other to solve the problem at hand.

The division of individual fuzzy systems required to solve complex problems demands that those problems to be decomposed and distributed among different fuzzy logic systems. One of the main limitations in the application of hierarchical fuzzy logic systems in complex problem-solving domains is the lack of methods to structure the development of the hierarchical fuzzy logic systems for a well structured hierarchical fuzzy logic system can perform its tasks more efficiently.

In hierarchical fuzzy logic systems several fuzzy logic systems are developed each performing a specific task. These fuzzy logic systems are then combined to form a complete system. The output of each fuzzy logic controller in a hierarchical fuzzy logic systems has an effect on other fuzzy logic systems and consequently to the final output of the system.

In this paper a method for development of a complex three level hierarchical fuzzy logic systems is proposed with application to a simulated multi-robot system is considered. For the hierarchical fuzzy logic system first, a fuzzy logic system is developed to control the robot from any position to its target. The knowledge of how to control the robot is obtained by using evolutionary algorithms. Second a new fuzzy logic system is developed that learns to slow down the robots when arriving to their target. The second fuzzy logic's knowledge base works with the first fuzzy knowledge base. A mapping of the first knowledge base to the second one is learnt by the evolutionary algorithm. In this way the system adapts itself to the current knowledge available and uses this knowledge to improve the performance of the system by learning new concepts. In this case the available (or known) knowledge is how to control the robot to its target and the new concepts are the knowledge learnt about how to slow down the robot at the target. Third, a new fuzzy logic system is developed again using genetic learning to avoid collision of the robots working in the common workspace.

This paper is organised as follows: In Section 2 the learning of fuzzy rules of fuzzy logic systems using evolutionary algorithms is described. In Section 3 the application of this learning method to hierarchical fuzzy logic systems is considered and simulation results are presented. Conclusions are drawn and further research directions are given in Section 4.

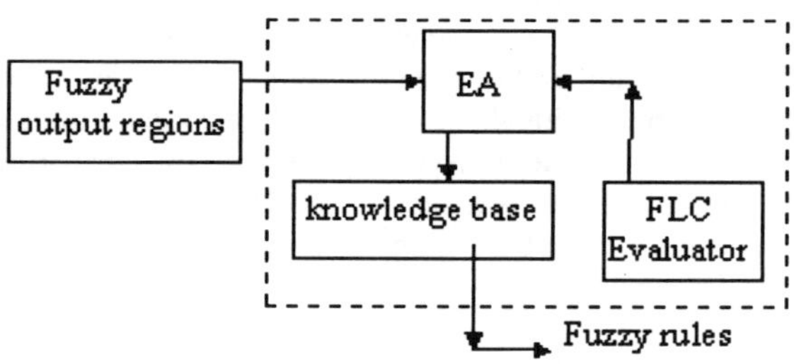

Figure 1: Fuzzy-GA rule generator architecture

2. Learning of Fuzzy Logic System using Evolutionary Algorithms

The design of the fuzzy knowledge base of a fuzzy logic system is based upon human experience and operator's knowledge of the system to be controlled [2], [3]. The fuzzy rules are usually formulated by a trial and error method which is not only time consuming but also does not guarantee 'optimal' fuzzy rules for the system. Incorporating evolutionary algorithms into the design of a fuzzy logic system can ensure automatic generation of fuzzy rules. We proposed earlier in [4], [5] an integrated architecture consisting of evolutionary algorithms and fuzzy logic for automatic rule generation of fuzzy logic systems. A block diagram of the Fuzzy-EA rule generation architecture is shown in Figure 1 .

As a simple illustration let us consider a fuzzy logic controller with two inputs (x and y) and a single output (z). As a first step to generating the fuzzy rules, the domain intervals of the input and output variables are divided into different regions, called fuzzy sets. The number of fuzzy sets is application dependent. Assume that x, y and z are all divided into five fuzzy regions each, with x and y denoted by the linguistic terms **VL, LO, MD, HI, VH** and z denoted by the linguistic terms **VS, SM, MD, HI, VH**.

A fuzzy membership function is assigned to each fuzzy set. Since x and y are divided into five fuzzy sets each, a maximum of twenty-five fuzzy rules can be written for the fuzzy logic system.
The consequent for each fuzzy rule can be determined by an evolutionary algorithm. In order to do so, the output fuzzy sets need to be encoded. (It is not necessary to encode the input fuzzy sets because they are static.) The fuzzy rules relating the input variables (x and y) to the output variable (z) have twenty-five possible combinations. The consequent of each fuzzy rule can be any one of the five output fuzzy sets. These output fuzzy sets are encoded by assigning a number for each fuzzy set, for example, 1 = **VS** (Very Small), 2 = **SM** (Small), 3 = **MD** (Medium), 4 = **HI** (High), and 5 = **VH** (Very High). We can therefore encode the fuzzy knowledge base as an individual string in an evolutionary algorithm as a linear array R of length 25 whose entry $R(j)$ is an integer lying between 1 and 5.

The population of size n consists of n such individual strings each representing a potential fuzzy knowledge base solution. The evolutionary algorithm randomly encodes an initial population. Each individual string is then decoded into the output linguistic terms. The set of fuzzy rules thus developed, is evaluated by the fuzzy logic controller based upon a fitness value which is specific to the system. At the end of each generation, copies of the best performing string from the parent generation are included in the next generation to ensure that the best performing strings are not lost. The population can now be evolved using processes of proportional selection, crossover and mutation. The latter two being described more specifically below for the robot application.

The algorithm progresses until a satisfactory fuzzy knowledge base is obtained, that is, the sting with the best fitness has fitness close to a desired value or a predetermined number of generation have been completed.

3. Hierarchical Fuzzy Logic Systems for a Multi-robot Control Problem

We use a Hierarchical Fuzzy Logic Control (HFLC) system [6], [7] for the multi-robot simulation.

The first level fuzzy knowledge base controls the basic direction of each robot from an initial position. The second level fuzzy knowledge base controls the speed of each robot on its way to its target, so that the speed of each robot is equal to zero at its entry to the target. The third level fuzzy knowledge base controls the robots so that there is no collision of robots in the workspace. Figure 2 shows the structure of the HFLC system.

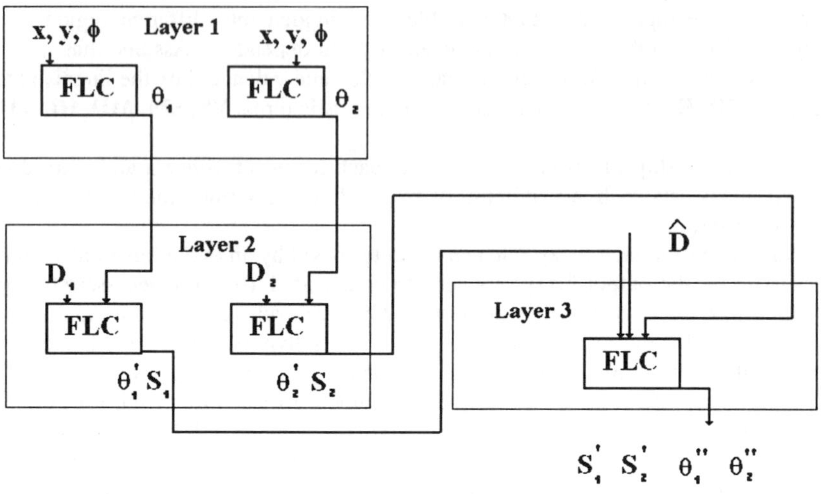

Figure 2: A hierarchical fuzzy logic system

First, we consider the genetic learning of the fuzzy knowledge base to control each robot to its target using constant speed (set at 0.5). For each robot there are now three inputs x, y, ϕ and single output θ. Here x, y are the cartesian coordinates in the plane, and ϕ is the heading angle relative to the x-axis, and θ is the control steering angle also measured relative to the x-axis, see [4].

We divide the domain regions for x, y, ϕ and θ into 5, 5, 7 and 7 regions respectively and assign appropriate linguistic variables. For each region a triangular fuzzy membership function is assigned; see Figure 3. The common workspace is shown in Figure 4. It is required that robot one reaches its target with heading angle 180° and for robot two 0°.

Instead of learning a fuzzy knowledge base from each configuration in a grid of initial configurations and then using a fuzzy amalgamation procedure (essentially an averaging of fuzzy rules across a number of strings depending on whether the rule is fired or not), to find a final fuzzy knowledge base that will effectively control each robot to its target, see [7], we start directly with a grid of 36 initial positions spread uniformly across the plane and with each point 6 heading directions -50°, 45°, 90°, 135°, and 240° (180 initial configurations)

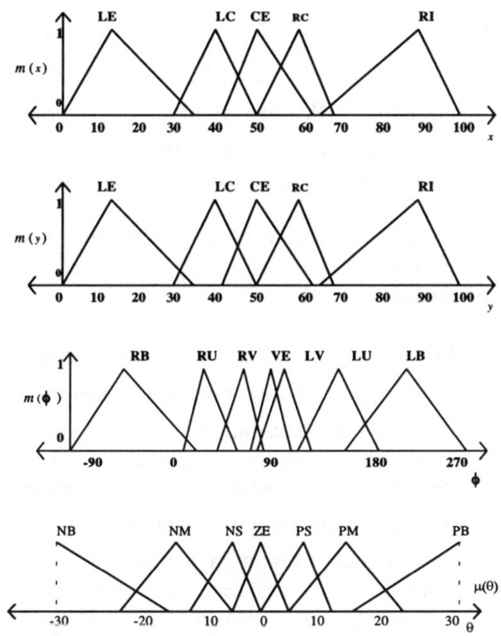

Figure 3: Fuzzy regions and membership functions of x, y, ϕ and θ

Modification is now made to the standard crossover procedure to provide a mechanism of local fuzzy amalgamation, and the way in which we evaluate the fitness of each string and determine the final "best fit" string, see details below.

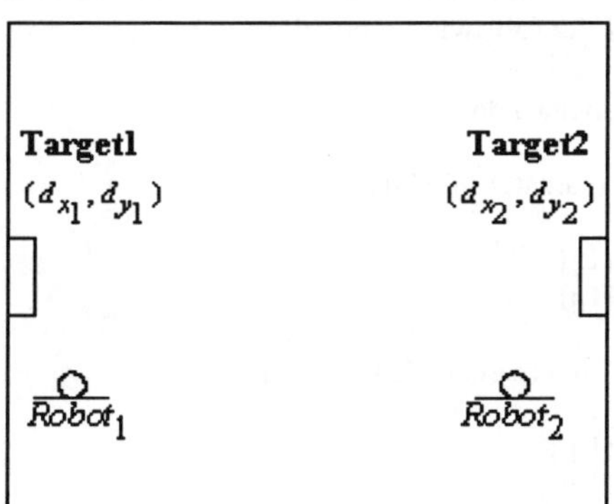

Figure 4: Workspace, robots and their targets.

In the first layer given an initial configuration, the primary objective function to be minimised for each robot is given by:

$$Obj_1 = b_1\sqrt{(x_r - x_t)^2 + (y_r - y_t)^2 + b_2\,(\phi_r - \phi_t)^2}$$

where x_r, y_r, ϕ_r and x_t, y_t, ϕ_t are the robot's final coordinates and heading angle and the target's coordinates respectively. Positive proportionality constants b_i are of our selection to enhance convergence. We determine the control simulation to be finished if the robots leave the workspace or a predetermined number of iterations (usually 1200) have been completed. Further to this objective function, constant penalties (10000) are added if the robot leaves the workspace other than via the target and a time penalty in included which is a function of the number of iterations completed. We may write the final objective function to be:

$$ObjFn_1 = a_1 Obj_1 + Penalties + a_2 TimePenalty$$

where the constants a_i are positive proportionality parameters of our selection. For each string an objective value is determined as an average of objective values determined from three initial configurations selected from the 180 as follows: One randomly selected from the 30 on line $x = 10$, the second randomly selected from the 30 on line $x = 90$, and the third randomly selected from within the full 180 configurations. This enabled more weight in learning to be put onto those initial configurations for which individually it was seen difficult to learn an appropriate set of rules. Then the fitness is set as $C - ObjFn_1$ for maximisation where C is a sufficiently large positive constant determined from experimentation with the algorithm, or taken as the maximum objective function in the current generation.

We now modify the linear array R defining each string so that each entry is a two dimensional array with first coordinate being the output linguistic variable θ, and second a coordinate which defines whether that rule is used or not in the evaluation of the fitness. It is set to 1 if the rule is used otherwise it is set to 0. Arithmetic crossover over is implemented by the following algorithm:

```
for j := 1 to length_of_individual do
 begin
  if((parent1[2,j]=0) and (parent2[2,j]=1)) then
  begin
    child1[1,j] := parent2[1,j];
    child2[1,j] := parent2[1,j];
  end
  else if ((parent1[2,j]=1) and (parent2[2,j]=0)) then
  begin
    child1[1,j] := parent1[1,j];
    child2[1,j] := parent1[1,j];
  end
  else
 begin
 child1[1,j] := round(alpha*parent1[1,j] + (1-alpha)*parent2[1,j]);
 child2[1,j] := round((1- alpha)*parent1[1,j] + alpha*parent2[1,j]);
  end;
 end;
end;
```

This algorithm says that if a given rule (j) in parent1 is not used and the corresponding rule in parent2 is used, then both children inherit the rule that is used. Likewise, the reverse holds. If both rules are used or not used, we perform the traditional type of arithmetic crossover defined by a constant α, with $\alpha \in (0,1)$, except that rounding is used to ensure that integer entries are maintained. (Alpha was set at 0.7.) The purpose of the crossover algorithm is to ensure that information within the rule structure is passed to the children. In essence it is performing in some sense, fuzzy amalgamation, on 'the fly' at a local level.

With mutation probability $p = 0.001$, the mutation operator was modified to: If the output θ lies between 1 and 7 it is mutated up or down by one with equal probability, if 1 it is mutated to 2, and if 7 it is mutated to 6.

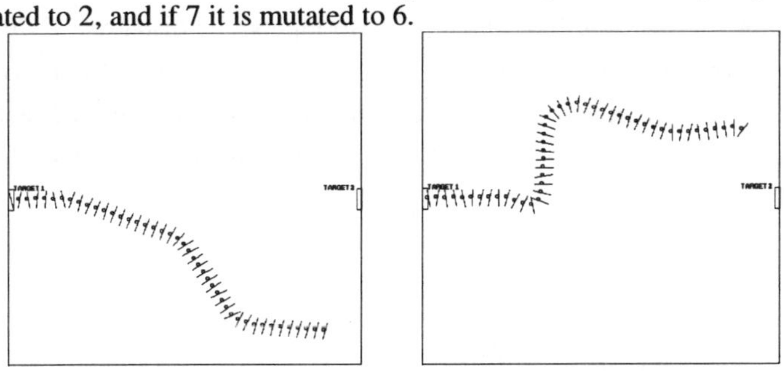

(a) (b)

Figure 5: Robot trajectory of $robot_1$ from initial configurations:
(a) (90, 10, 135°) and (b) (90, 70, 135°)

A population of 600 was used and the algorithm was found to converge to an acceptable set of fuzzy rules within 10000 generations. The final fuzzy rule base accepted was found by averaging the best 20 in the final population in the same manner as fuzzy amalgamation.

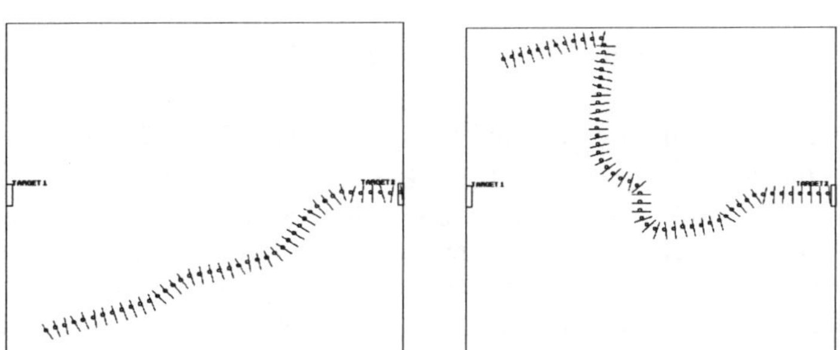

(a) (b)

Figure 6: Robot trajectory of $robot_2$ from initial configurations:
(a) (90, 10, 135°) and (b) (70, 70, 135°)

For these calculations typical values of the proportionality constants were $b_1 = 1$, $b_2 = 10$, $a_1 = 1$, $a_2 = 0.1$. Illustrations of how well the two final fuzzy knowledge bases control the robots to their targets are given in Figure 5, and Figure 6. Good trajectories were obtained from all initial configurations, see Figures 5 and 6. The two individual fuzzy rule bases, one for each robot constitute the entire fuzzy knowledge base in layer 1. In all 175 rules were learnt for the control of each robot to its target.

Having learnt an appropriate fundamental knowledge base for steering control of each robot to its target, we wish to control the speed of each robot to zero as it reaches its target. The objective here in the second layer knowledge bases is to determine corrections to steering angles and speed S_i of each robot while approaching its target. For each robot's knowledge base, there are two inputs, the distances D_i between the robot and its target and the current steering angle of each robot θ_i, and two outputs, θ_i', S_i, i =1..2, the correction to the steering angle, and the speed of each robot for the next iteration. Figure 7 shows the fuzzy sets and fuzzy membership functions of D_i.

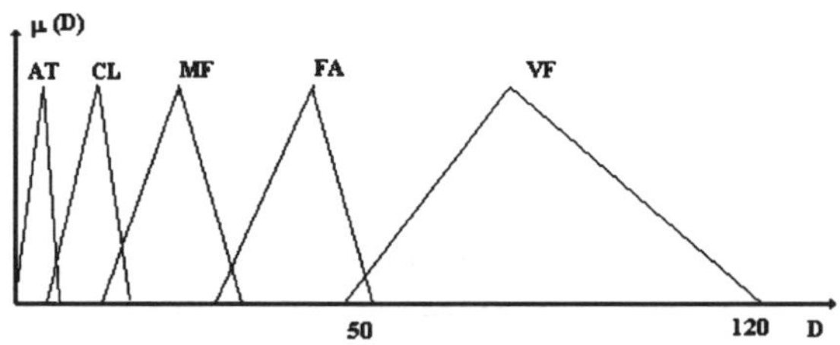

Figure 7: The fuzzy sets and membership of D_i

There are thirty-five fuzzy rules to be learnt for each robot. An example of a fuzzy rule may be:

If D_1 = **AT** and θ_1 = **NS** then S_1 = **VS** also θ_1' = **PB**

In determining the output we take for θ_i' support values, **PB** = 5.0, **PM** = 3.5, **PS** = 1.25, **ZE** = 0.4, **NS** = -0.4, **NM** = -0.125, **NB** = -0.35, and for S support values, **VF** = 0.45, **FA** = 0.35, **MF** = 0.25, **SL** = 0.18, and **VS** = 0.08. Each robot's fuzzy knowledge base at layer two can be formed as a 5 by 7 table with cells now storing a three dimensional array of length 35 that holds the two outputs for the corresponding actions that must be taken given the conditions corresponding to D_i and θ_i are satisfied, as well as a third coordinate which determines whether the rule has been fired or not. Ammendments to crossover and mutation operators follow in a logical manner. Again the same grid of 180 configurations is chosen on the plane.

The objective function for each string is defined as:

$$ObjFn_2 = ObjFn_1 + a_3 S_f^2$$

where a_3 is a positive proportionality constant and S_f^2 is the final speed of the robot when the simulation is terminated. When an initial configuration is given, the first knowledge base is accessed to determine the appropriate steering angles. The genetic learning then proceeds as in the first layer. It was found that with the previous parameters, setting $a_3 = 100$ produced satisfactory results in that speed was reduced to near zero for each robot as it entered the target. For mutation probability $p = 0.001$, $\alpha = 0.6$, and a small population of around 50, the evolutionary algorithms converged to a satisfactory knowledge base for each robot within 30000 generations.

Illustrations of how well these second layer, fuzzy knowledge bases control the robots to their target are shown in Figure 8 and 9. We note the decreased step in the iterations along the trajectory to the target indicating speed reduction.

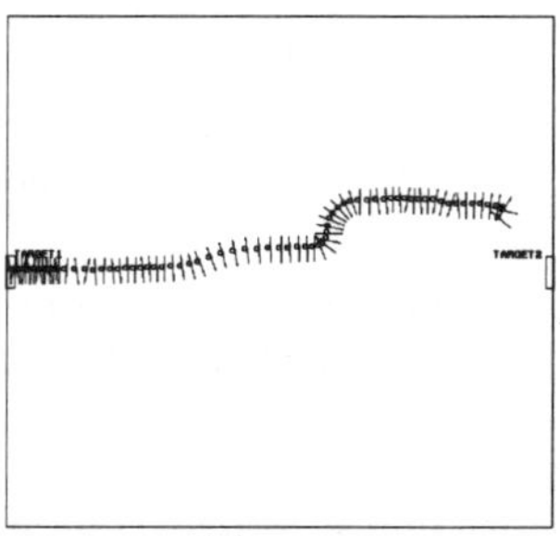

(a)

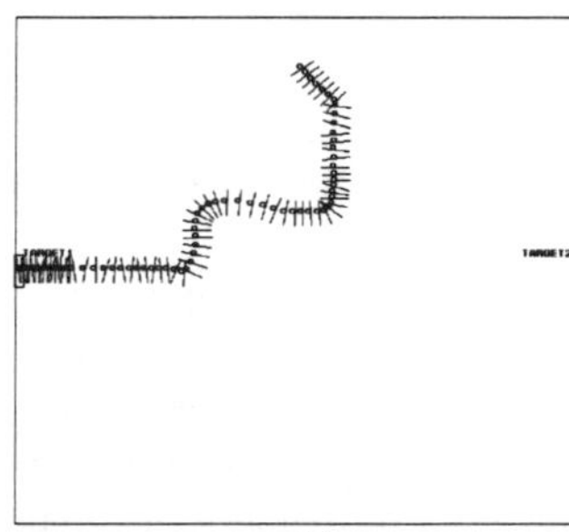

(b)

Figure 8: Robot trajectory of $robot_1$ from: (a) (90, 60, 45°) and (b) (90, 10, -50°)

Having learnt the fundamental rule bases at layers one and two for steering control and speed of each robot to its target, the objective now is to develop a single third layer fuzzy knowledge base to determine corrections θ_i'' to steering angles for each robot to avoid collision with the other whilst approaching their target. In this layer there are three inputs $\hat{D}$, θ_1 and θ_2, with outputs θ_1'' and θ_2'', and S'_1 and S'_2 the new speeds for each robot. Here $\hat{D}$ is the current physical distance between robots, θ_1'' and θ_2'', are corrections to the steering angle of each robot and S'_1 and S'_2 are the new current speeds of each robot, see Figure 2.

For $\hat{D}$ we use the same fuzzy regions and membership as for D, and supports for θ_i'' and S'_i are the same as given for the second layer. In the analysis for the third layer we first determined using the already obtained knowledge bases that for the combined two robot system, there were 1152 initial configurations for which two robots collided on there way to their respective targets. Collision being defined when $\hat{D} < 20$. As in the first two layers we constructed an evolutionary algorithm to determine a set of fuzzy rules to best control each robot to their targets without collision. The fitness of each string in this scenario consisted of the same components as previously, adding together the components for each robot, and inclusion of a 200 penalty if the robots collided. The initial configuration data set consisted of those 1152 initial configurations at which collision was known to occur.

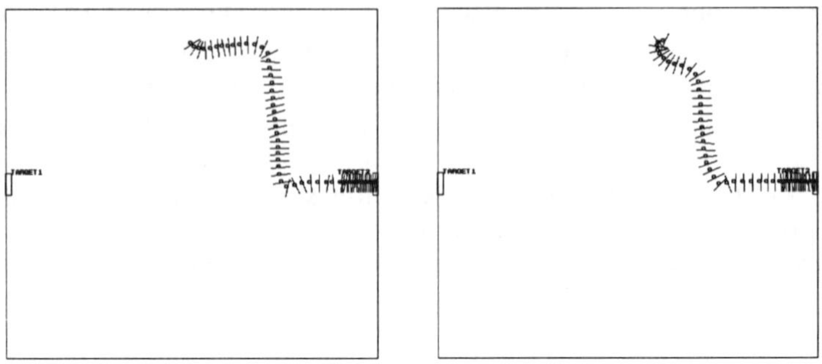

(a) (b)

Figure 9: Robot trajectory of $robot_2$ from: (a) (50, 90, -50°), and (b) (60, 90, 90°)

Setting a population of 500 individuals, values of mutation and crossover probability basically the same as before, and this time just using simple random mutation and one-point crossover, we found that in 2500 generations the fuzzy rule base learnt by the algorithm reduced the number of crashes to 575. The results from the analysis of learning in this layer have not been completed at the time of writing. Further extension to this evolutionary algorithm is continuing with operators of mutation and crossover as defined in the two previous layers.

Figure 10 shows the robot trajectories using the HFLC determined for the three layers. The robots are controlled to their target whilst avoiding collision and each has its speed reduced as the desired target is reached.

5. Conclusion

We have proposed a HFLC for a multi-robot control problem simulated by two point-mass mobile robots in a common workspace. This was achieved by dividing the problem into smaller manageable parts. In the first layer, ignoring the possibility of collision, steering angles for the control of each robot to their associated target were determined by evolutionary algorithms. In the second layer evolutionary algorithms were used to determine adjustments to steering angle and speed of each robot to control the robot to its target with near zero speed. Finally a third layer was developed to adjust the speed and steering angle of the robots to avoid collision of the robots as they were controlled to their targets.

By using the hierarchical structure the number of control laws has been significantly reduced. If only one fuzzy logic system was used to solve this problem with the inputs x, y, ϕ, D for each robot and separation distance $\hat{D}$, each with the same fuzzy sets described in this paper then there would be 3828125 fuzzy rules needed for its fuzzy knowledge base. Using the given hierarchical system we have had only to learn a total number of 1645 fuzzy rules.

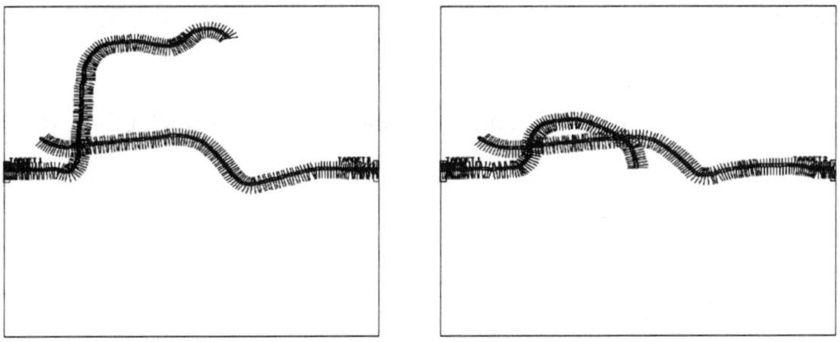

(a) (b)

Figure 10: Robot trajectories at initial configuration:
(a) $robot_1$ = (50,50,45°), $robot_2$ = (10,60,-50°)
(b) $robot_1$ = (60,50,90°), $robot_2$ = (10,60,-50°)

In learning these rules we have implemented a variation of arithmetic crossover which incorporates where a certain rule has been fired or not. This operator has substantially reduced the number of generations required to obtain a satisfactory knowledge base which will achieve the desired objectives from a broad range of initial configurations not just those as specified in the initial configuration data set. As mentioned, research into removing all crash scenarios at the third level is continuing.

References

[1] D. Goldberg. Genetic Algorithms in search, optimisation and machine learning. *Addison Wesley*, 1989.

[2] C. C. Lee. Fuzzy logic in control systems : fuzzy logic controller-part 2. *IEEE Transaction on Systems, Man and Cybernetics*, 20(2), pages 419-435, 1990.

[3] C. C. Lee. Fuzzy logic in control systems : fuzzy logic controller- part 1. *IEEE Transaction on Systems, Man and Cybernetics*, 20(2), pages 404-418, 1990.

[4] M. Mohammadian and R. J. Stonier. Generating Fuzzy Rules by Genetic Algorithms. *Proceedings of 3rd IEEE International Workshop on Robot and Human Communication*, pages 362-367, Nagoya, 1994.

[5] M. Mohammadian, M. Kingham, and M. Hassan.. Adaptive Holding Policies for IP over ATM Networks using Fuzzy Logic and Genetic Algorithms. *IEEE International Conference on Communication System,* Singapore, pages 25-29, Westin Stamford,November 1996.

[6] G.V.S. Raju and J. Zhou. Adaptive Hierarchical Fuzzy Controller. *IEEE Transactions on Systems, Man and Cybernetics*, pages 973-980, 1993.

[7] R. J. Stonier and M. Mohammadian. Intelligent Hierarchical Control for Obstacle-Avoidance. *Computational Techniques and Applications: CTAC95*, Melbourne, Australia, July, 1995.

[8] L. Wang. A course in fuzzy systems and control. *Prentice Hall*, USA, 1997.

Learning and Optimization

A machine learning technique for helping the knowledge acquisition process

J.L. Castro, J.J. Castro-Schez*, J.M. Zurita

Dpto. Ciencias de la Computación e I.A.
E.T.S.I. Informática. Universidad de Granada
Avenida de Andalucía, 38, 18071 Granada
castro@decsai.ugr.es zurita@decsai.ugr.es

*Dpto. Informática
Escuela Universitaria de Informática.
Universidad de Castilla la Mancha
Ronda de Calatrava, 5, 13071 Ciudad Real
jjcastro@jur-to.uclm.es

Abstract

Knowledge acquisition is one of the key activities faced by knowledge engineers during the expert systems development process. There are problems such as the expert's inaccessibility, difficulties for transmitting the expert's knowledge and wrong translations from acquired knowledge to operational forms that complicate the knowledge acquisition stage. Machine learning is presented as a mechanism that resolves some of those problems. However, any machine learning technique acquires some knowledge but not enough knowledge for building expert systems. This paper presents a new approach to knowledge acquisition which makes use of a machine learning technique. This technique generates a set of fuzzy rules that identify the evident knowledge. The maximal structure of a rule and the evident rules will be found using this algorithm.

1 Introduction

In everyday life, an obvious way to acquire knowledge is through learning by observation, that is from examples. If not, let's ask the following questions: How do apprentices become masters? As the apprentices watches the master, he or she observes examples of commonly occurring problems, as well as "hard cases" and notes the master's responses in each case. While the master may not directly instruct the apprentice in all of the heuristics applied during the problem-solving activities, the apprentice begins to learn by *induction.*

Also we can mention that experts are scarce commodities in all organisations, because his/her time is highly protected. Organisations only permit little interruptions of its experts. Nevertheless, organisations are always ready to provide the knowledge engineer with a set of the expert's past actions, which shows the way the expert reasons. The knowledge engineer analyses the set of past actions and attains general conclusions from specific examples. After this, the knowledge engineer will be familiar with the domain and will perform more interesting interviews.

Moreover, there are cases in which the expert is not able to totally explain his or her way of performing, that is, the processes or heuristic which leads to solving the problem. Experts have a natural tendency to provide examples of problems and sample solutions. Knowledge engineers must acquire knowledge from this data.

Induction, that is to say, the process for inferring "laws" or developing theories by observing and analysing events or cases in which that law is applied allows the knowledge engineer to solve some of the problems mentioned earlier (such as the expert's inaccessibility). Since knowledge acquisition from examples is employed by knowledge engineer, it seems to us that knowledge acquisition tools must have a machine learning module.

Knowledge Acquisition (KA) is closely related to research in the machine learning field. Induction-based knowledge acquisition requires the domain expert to provide the examples and critical information by entering them in a computer program which builds an induction table for data analysis.

Several researchers have examined the problem of learning classification rules from examples. Applications such as Iterative Dichotomizer 3 (ID3) and C4[10] and their cousins have been employed for obtaining knowledge bases that are used for expert systems whose task is classification. Sometimes, the rules obtained for those inductive learning methods [3],[4],[5],[6],[9] are more useful than the rules provided by a domain expert. The rules obtained in this manner are only guaranteed to be valid for the examples from which the induction is made. Thus, as we mentioned before machine learning techniques are useful in knowledge acquisition but they cannot be applied exclusively. Theories inferred from examples do not guarantee the acquisition of high quality knowledge.

Machine learning techniques can be employed for avoiding some of the difficulties mentioned before which might be present in the knowledge acquisition process. Moreover with the application of machine learning techniques we can take advantage of some benefits such as extracting and translating evident expert knowledge or heuristics, which are present in the set of examples, one tool for treating an expert's or and organisation's tendency to provide examples about the way of reasoning for its experts.

In this paper we describe a new machine-learning technique which must be applied as one module of a knowledge acquisition tool designed for building expert systems. Our idea is to develop a technique that obtains a set of rules which we can use for designing questions that to ask the expert. The rules generated (maximal rules) must be general, that is to say, they must have have less components in the antecedent part of the rule and identifying simultaneously the largest number of examples in the given set of input-output data. The algorithm must generate a minimal set of maximal rules to identify the knowledge inherent to the set of examples.

2 Background

Since, the rules will be employed for designing questions to ask the expert, these must be totally understood by the expert and be formed by concepts belonging to the expert's conceptual structure.

Most of the tools developed for automating the knowledge acquisition process make use of binary logic as mechanism of representation. Many times with the latter, the expressions learnt are hardly natural and don't show totally the expert's knowledge. There are in all experts and generalising in all human beings a vagueness and uncertainty when they assign values between absolute truth and falsehood. Thus, the concept of fuzzy set and fuzzy logic is shown in the expert system as a natural method for representing the way the expert reasons.

The success of knowledge acquisition efforts depends in part on being able to conceptualise the domain. The process of conceptualisation involves evoking and abstracting concepts, that is to say discovering their primary concepts, attributes and values.

When a knowledge engineer begins to acquire knowledge, the first problem he faces is to provide a domain for familiarisation. One of the primary tasks is to work with a domain expert to identify his or her conceptual structure. To do so, we propose a Repertory Grid technique which obtains concepts, attributes and values employed by the expert and a primary model of the expert's world. The origin of this technique can be traced to a psychologist named George Kelly[8] who developed the personal constructs theory.

To develop a grid, we must first elicit a set of elements which will be decisions, classes, alternative events, states or entities that the expert can use. Next, we must stimulate the domain expert to provide a set of constructs (characteristics, dimensions of similarity and difference between elements). Once constructs and elements have been identified, we ask the domain expert to value each element according to the constructs that have been provided.

After each element has been valued according to each construct, the results may be analysed using a variety of techniques. Whatever technique is used, the purpose of the analysis is to measure similarities and distances among objects. When we find elements that are very similar or near, we increase their distance by means of introducing a new construct which takes different values for each element or modification of the value that the construct takes.

Thus, we obtain the concepts, attributes and domains which are employed by the expert. Moreover, we obtain a set of rules that model the way the expert reasons. These rules can also be employed to plan future interviews. We do not aim to describe how we employ the repertory grid technique, or in which manner we modify this technique for our propose of knowledge acquisition. This will be the subject for futurepapers. A very simple example of repertory grid is shown in Table 1.

	Iris-Setosa	**Iris-Versicolor**	**Iris-Virginica**
Petal width	HN, MN	SN,Z,SP	SP,HP,MP
Petal length	-	Not HP	Not SP

Table 1. Example of a Grid.

The expert gives us the set of elements, {Iris-Setosa, Iris-Versicolor, Iris-Virginica} and a construct, Petal width. The expert values this construct for each element. However, there are two elements very near Iris-Versicolor and Iris-Virginica depending on the Petal width construct. This makes the expert introduce a new construct Petal length, which discriminates between those elements. Then, we detect a new conflict, what happens when Petal width is SP and Petal length is HN or MN or SN or Z or MP, the expert must introduce a new construct.

The rules that we can elicit from this grid are:

R_0: If Petal width is HN,MN then Iris-Setosa.
R_1: If Petal width is SN,Z,SP and Petal length is not HP then Iris-Versicolor.
R_2: If Petal width is SP,HP,MP and Petal length is not HP then Iris-Virginica.

After this we have the set of elements which are employed by the expert, its attributes and domains and some general rules.

According to Zadeh we make use of fuzzy logic for modelling human behaviour. The expert is described by means of a set of If-Then rules with vague predicates. Fuzzy clustering[13], neuronal networks[2][11], utilisation of an ATMS[4], definition and use of activation hyperboxes over the domain variables[1] have been employed for extracting a set of fuzzy rules from a set of examples.

Since our propose is find a set of rules that allows us to plan interviews, we are going to develop an inductive learning method that generates a minimal set of fuzzy rules capable of modelling the expert knowledge present in a set of examples.

We start out from a set of examples that shows the way the expert reasons:

$\theta=\{e_1,\dots,e_m\}$ — *m* is the number of reasoning examples
$e_i=((x_{i1},\dots,x_{in}),y_j)$ — *n* is the number of variables used in the reasoning process and *j* is the number of output values.

where $x_{i1},\dots,x_{in}$ are the values of the variables used in the reasoning process (input variables) and y_j is the value of the expert's response (output variable). We recall that these input and output variables have been obtained by means of a repertory grid.

The θ set is a subset of the set product of the inputs and outputs ($X^n \times Y$). Our first objective will be to approximate the function: $\Omega: X^n \rightarrow Y$, that completely models the way the expert reasons.

We shall approximate that function by means of a set of fuzzy rules. This work presents an algorithm which constructs a set of fuzzy rules with the greater generality from the set of examples, after we suggest the use of a genetic algorithm for obtaining the minimal set of fuzzy IF-THEN rules which identify the evident knowledge present in the set of examples that show the way the expert reasons.

The form of our fuzzy rules will be the following:

R_j: **IF** *X* is *E* **THEN** *Y* is y_j

where *X* is the set of variables used to reason, *E* is a set of subsets of fuzzy labels and *Y* is the expert's response. Another way to write the rule is:

IF X_0 is E_0 and X_1 is E_1 and ... and X_n is E_n **THEN** Y is y_j

where *X* is *E,* is a contraction of the expression X_0 is E_0 and X_1 is E_1 and ... and X_n is E_n, with *X* being the set $(X_0, X_1, \ldots, X_n)$ of input variables and *E* the set $(E_0, E_1, \ldots, E_n)$ of sets of labels.

We shall assume that the fuzzy sets E_i (values of X_i in the rule) are taken from the set of labels L_i, with L_i being $\{L_1, \ldots, L_k\}$ where *k* indicates the number of labels. Therefore $E_i \in P(L_i)$, with P being the function of parts of a set.

The set of rules with the greater generality will be obtained from the set of training examples, making use of the algorithm proposed by *Castro et al.*[5]. Let's remind ourselves about the ideas in that algorithm.

3 Learning maximal structure rules in fuzzy logic

The algorithm suggested in [5] basically is composed of two stages. In the first stage a set of very particular rules is constructed from a set of examples. After this, in the second stage those particular rules are generalised yielding a set of maximal rules. To do so, the algorithm performs in the following manner:

The algorithm divides the domains of the input variables into fuzzy regions (each region will have assigned a fuzzy membership function μ_i) and encode the output. For constructing the set of particular rules, the values of the input variables in each example will be represented by means of the label which presents the maximum degree (according to $L = \max\{\mu_j(x_i)\}$), and the output is encoded.

Example 3.1. The example ((*3.5,2.0,7.5,1.1*),*z*) is one example of the training set, where *3.5,2.0,7.5* and *1.1* are concrete values of the input variables and *z* is the value of the output variable. In order to construct a particular rule from this example, the algorithm first determines the degrees of *3.5,2.0,7.5* and *1.1* in different regions.

Secondly it assigns a given *3.5,2.0,7.5* and *1.1* to the region with the maximum degree. This example will be translated into the rule:

IF X_0 is $\{L_1\}$ and X_1 is $\{L_3\}$ and X_2 is $\{L_2\}$ and X_3 is $\{L_1\}$ **THEN** Y is y_i

where L_1, L_2 and L_3 are the labels which present the maximum degree and y_i represents the output.

The set of particular rules identifies completely the way the expert reasons according to the set of training examples. Now, we generalise each particular rule for obtaining general rules. To do so, it takes each initial rule and checks whether that rule subsumes in some rule of the set of general rules.

Definition 3.1. The rule R_i $((E_{i1},E_{i2},...,E_{in}),y_j)$ subsumes in the rule R_k $((E_{k1},E_{k2},...,E_{kn}),y_x)$, that will be noted as **subsume(R_i,R_k)** if $E_{i1} \subseteq E_{k1}$, $E_{i2} \subseteq E_{k2}$,...,$E_{in} \subseteq E_{kn}$ and $y_j=y_x$.

Example 3.2: The rule ((SN,HP,HN,HN),y_1) subsumes in the rule: IF X_3 is {HN,MN} THEN Y is y_1. Since the input variables X_0, X_1 and X_2 don't appear in the rule, they can take any value of the set of the labels in this variable. If the set of the labels is the same for X_0, X_1, X_2 and X_3 and it is $\mathcal{L}$= {HN,MN,SN,Z,SP,MP,HP} The rule ((SN,HP,HN,HN),y_1) subsumes in the rule (($\mathcal{L}$,$\mathcal{L}$,$\mathcal{L}$,{HN,MN}),y_1), obviously SN$\subseteq\mathcal{L}$, HP$\subseteq\mathcal{L}$, HN$\subseteq\mathcal{L}$, {HN}$\subseteq${HN,MN} and $y_1=y_1$.

When the particular rule subsumes in some general rule, then it is ignored, since that rule is already generalised, and we take a new rule from the set of particular rules.

If the rule does not subsume in any definitive rule, the algorithm attempts to generalise it. To do so, it applies a process of amplification. In an abridged manner, the process of amplification performs as follows:

The input data for the process will be the rule to generalise, $((E_1,E_2,...,E_n),y_j)$, the process consists of performing amplifications in each variable. That is, it amplifies each E_i, for i=1,...,n with the labels of its domain that have still not been considered for it.

When we try to carry out an amplification, it checks whether it is possible.

Definition 3.2. An amplification from R_i to $R_{i'}$ (with $R_{i'}$ being the rule: IF X is $E_{i'}$ THEN y_p), is *possible* if there is no rule R_j (with R_j being the rule: IF X is E_j THEN y_q) in the set of particular rules that verifies that $E_j \subseteq E_{i'}$ and do not subsume $(R_j,R_{i'})$, that is, there is no rule R_j which verifies that $E_j \subseteq E_{i'}$ and $y_p \neq y_q$.

If an amplification from R_i to $R_{i'}$ is not possible then it carries on working with R_j. When it is possible the process amplification continues working with $R_{i'}$.

Example 3.3: If we have three input variables, and their domains have been divided into three fuzzy regions which have been named with the fuzzy labels N (Negative),

Z (Zero) and P (Positive), that is $\mathcal{L}$={N,Z,P}=$\mathcal{L}_1$=$\mathcal{L}_2$=$\mathcal{L}_3$ and we have the particular rule ((N,Z,P),y_3). The amplifications are carried out in the following way:

((N,Z,P),3) → (({N,Z},Z,P),3) → (($\mathcal{L}_1$,Z,P),3) → (($\mathcal{L}_1$,{Z,N},P),3) → (($\mathcal{L}_1$,$\mathcal{L}_2$,P),3) → (($\mathcal{L}_1$,$\mathcal{L}_2$,{P,N}),3) → (($\mathcal{L}_1$,$\mathcal{L}_2$,$\mathcal{L}_3$),3).

If there is one particular rule ((N,N,Z),y_2) in the set of particular rules, an amplification from (($\mathcal{L}_1$, $\mathcal{L}_2$,{P,N}),3) to (($\mathcal{L}_1$, $\mathcal{L}_2$, $\mathcal{L}_3$),3) is not possible, since N$\subseteq\mathcal{L}_1$, N$\subseteq\mathcal{L}_2$, Z$\subseteq\mathcal{L}_3$ and $y_2 \neq y_3$.

3.1 One improvement to this algorithm

Since our objective will be to obtain a set of general rules about the expert's domain which can help us to plan interviews with the expert for acquiring more knowledge, we suggest removing the existing noise from the training set. The algorithm will lose precision in the learning of the set mentioned above but it will obtain a set of more general rules with a smaller number of rules.

Let's us see what this improvement consists of:

We calculate, for each example in the set of training examples, two measures which point out the distance with respect to the examples of the same type and with the examples of the different types. These measures will be the following:

$$P^+(R_i)= \sum_j e^{-\alpha\, d(Ri,Rj)}$$

where Rj are examples of the same type.

$$P^-(R_i)= \sum_j e^{-\alpha\, d(Ri,Rj)}$$

where Rj are examples of the different types.

With *d* being a function which calculates the distance between two examples, for example, the *quadratic distance*:

$$d(R_i,R_j)=\sqrt{(e_i^1 - e_j^1)^2 + \ldots + (e_i^n - e_j^n)^2}$$

where $R_k=(e_k^1, \ldots e_k^n)$

This improvement helps to ensure that the knowledge acquired will be more general knowledge.

4 Using a genetic algorithm for obtaining the best general rules

The set of general rules obtained with the algorithm proposed in [5] may have a large size. Since, we want a minimal set of general rules that permits us to plan interviews, we present the idea of evolution as a mechanism for obtaining it. That is to say, permitting the evolution of this set of general rules until obtaining a set of maximal or definitive rules which contain the more evident knowledge in the sense mentioned above.

This evolutionary process can be carried out by means of a genetic algorithm, with some supplementary information (to manage some restrictions).

4.1 Genetic algorithm input specifications

The individuals in our population will have a chain of elements which belong to the alphabet A={0,1,#} as the structure in their chromosomes. The length of the chain depends on the number of fuzzy sets which are used to divide the domain for each input variable and the length of the code used for encoding the output.

$$Length(chain) = \sum_{i=o}^{n} |L_i| + \begin{cases} Length(Output\ code) \\ |L_s| \end{cases}$$

with $|L_i|$ being the cardinal number of the set of fuzzy sets into which we have divided the domain of the variable X_i, with $|L_s|$ being the same number but making reference to the output variable and *Length(Output code)* is the length of the code used to encode the output value.

Our chromosomes have two clearly distinguishable parts: a *kernel* that comprises information about the individual's features and a *head* which processes information about the species to which it belongs.

The reproduction will be performed as it occurs in an ecosystem, that is between elements of the same species. The head is useful to satisfy this restriction. The reproduction will be possible between elements which have the same head (same species).

The reproduction between individuals has to be carried out bearing in mind the characteristics that we want to be present in the final set of general rules. That is, to obtain rules which have a maximal structure in the sense of both having less components in the antecedent part of the rule and simultaneously identifying the largest number of examples in the given set of input-output data.

The initial population will be obtained making use of the algorithm [5]. The data produced by this algorithm will be encoded as coded bit strings. Let's us have a look at all these ideas by means of an example (Example 4.1).

Example 4.1: If we have three input variables and their domains are divided into the following fuzzy sets:

$X_0 \rightarrow \ell_0$={N,Z,P}
$X_1 \rightarrow \ell_1$={HN,MN,SN,Z,SP,MP,HP}
$X_2 \rightarrow \ell_2$={HN,SN,Z,SP,HP}

and the output is encoded with a code of a length equal to one.

The length of the chain (chromosomes) will be the following:

$$\text{Length(chain)} = 3+7+5+1 = 16$$

If the general rule: If X_0 is Z and X_1 is MP and X_2 is HN THEN Y is Iris-Virginica have been obtained by the algorithm [5], it will be encoded as coded bit strings shown in Figure 1.

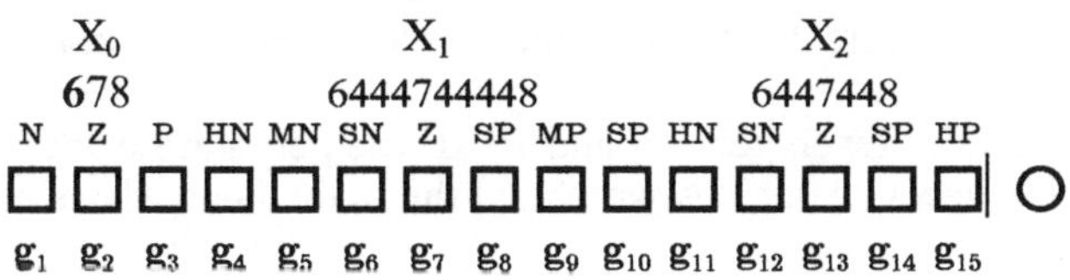

Figure 1. Chromosome of the example.

The rest of the values will be placed in # (☐), to indicate that at the beginning it can take some value (0 ☑or 1 ■).

One species is distinguished from another by means of the values in the kernel genes. If we permit the mutation in the genes that decide to which species an individual belongs, we cause confusion about which are the features of that species.

Hence, the mutation of one species into another will be impossible, that is to say the mutations in the genes which distinguish between the species (head) will occur with a probability equal to zero. This is another restriction in our problem.

The idea mentioned above is not senseless, there are some research articles which show that mutations rarely occur, and that it depends on the species and genes. Moreover, these research articles have shown that all the genes do not change with the same frequency. The genes that change with relative facility are the unstable genes, while those genes that change very rarely are called stable genes.

We shall determine the stable genes in the chromosomes of the individuals from the initial population before performing the evolutionary process. The process calculates the genes in which it is not convenient for mutations to be carried out.

Let's look at how to find the stable genes:

When two chromosomes from different species only have two different genes in the kernel, one being 1 and the other # in the first chromosome and # and 1 in the second chromosome, then these non specified genes are converted into genes 0 (☑) on which mutations may never be carried out.

Example 4.2: In the same environment in example 4.1, we have in the set of general rules the following rules:

- IF X_0 is Z and X_1 is MP and X_2 is HN THEN Y is Iris-Virginica.
- IF X_0 is Z and X_1 is HP and X_2 is HN THEN Y is Iris-Versicolor.

which correspond to the following individuals in the initial population, see Figure 2.

Figure 2: Chromosomes in the initial population

These individuals differ in genes 9 and 10. These genes are marked as stable genes or non mutable genes. After this we obtain the individuals whose chromosomes are shown in Figure 3.

Figure 3: Chromosomes after making non mutable genes

The genetic algorithm will be applied to each class separately. Thus, reproduction will only be possible between elements with the same head (individual from the same species).

4.2 Applying a genetic algorithm for generalising the set of particular rules

Once we have a set of rules from which we aim to obtain the minimal set of general or maximal rules, the idea of evolution comes into play.

We make use of a genetic algorithm for modifying the population of individuals in successive steps. We designate the population in the state *t* as $\alpha(t)$. N is the number of fuzzy rules obtained by means of the algorithm[5], it is the size of population of one species and it will be kept constant.

We are interested in reproducing those individuals that are best adapted to the environment (that is to say, the set of training examples). The fitness function indicates how one individual is adapted to the environment. Since, we want to obtain the minimal set of more general or maximal rules our fitness function should reward the rules that classify the largest number of examples incurring the lowest number of errors. That is, a function $f(e_p,e_n)$ which will be increasing with respect to the number of correctly classified examples (e_p) and decreasing with respect to the number of erroneously classified examples (e_n).

The fitness function should also reward those more general rules, that is those with the largest number of specified genes (genes with values 0 or 1). Thus, we take the less complex rules. One possible fitness function will be the following:

$$f(e)=\frac{e_p - e_n}{e_t} \times \lambda + \frac{g_d}{g_t} \times (1-\lambda)$$

with e_p being the number of examples in the training set (environment), which are correctly classified by the rule *e*, with e_n being the number of examples which are erroneously classified by the rule *e*, and e_t being the total number of examples in the training set, with g_d being the number of specified genes in the rule *e* and g_t being the total number of genes for the chromosome.

We have proven the algorithm with different values for λ. When λ value is near to the value 1 we obtain a set of rules that is a little less general or maximal but that identifies the largest number of examples in the given set of input-output data. We have used λ=0.9.

Let's see how we determine whether a example is correctly or erroneously classified by one rule.

Definition 4.1. The individual e_i ($e_{i1}e_{i2}...e_{in}Y$) is correctly classified by the rule R_j ($r_{j1}r_{j2}...r_{jn}X$) if the specified kernel genes of the e_i (genes 0 and 1), verify that $e_{ik}=r_{jk}$ ($k\in\{1,...,n\}$) and both belong to the same species, that is Y=X.

Definition 4.2. The individual e_i ($e_{i1}e_{i2}...e_{in}Y$) is erroneously classified by the rule R_j ($r_{j1}r_{j2}...r_{jn}X$) if the specified kernel genes of the e_i (genes 0 and 1) verify that $e_{ik}=r_{jk}$ ($k\in\{1,...,n\}$) and they belong to different species, that is $Y\neq X$.

Example 4.3: We have the following individuals in the population $e_{1,}$ 1#######1#1####3 and $e_{2,}$ ##1#####1#1####2 and the rule R_y for which the chromosome is 101####1101111#3. We can verify that the example e_1 is correctly classified by the rule R_y, since $1(e_{11})=1(R_{y1})$, $1(e_{19})=1(R_{y9})$, $1(e_{111})=1(R_{y11})$ and both belong to the same species (same heads) 3=3. However the example e_2 is erroneously classified by the rule R_y, since $1(e_{23})=1(R_{y3})$, $1(e_{29})=1(R_{y9})$, $1(e_{211})=1(R_{y11})$ and their heads are different $3\neq2$.

The steps in the genetic algorithm are the following:

Step 1: Initialisation

$\alpha(t)$ will be the initial population, which was obtained as was explained earlier.

Step 2: Selection

For all i verifying that $1 \le i \le N$, to reproduce the individuals in $\alpha(t)$ at one new population $\beta(t)$. The chromosome $A_i \in \alpha(t)$ appears in $\beta(t)$ with a probability equal to:

$$p(A_i)=\frac{\mu(A_i)}{\sum_{k=1}^{N}\mu(A_k)}$$

μ is the fitness function.

Step 3: Modification

Modifying the chromosomes in $\beta(t)$ using the genetic operators to produce the new population $\alpha(t+1)$.

Step 4: Evolution

If we haven't obtained the desired degree of evolution. Do t=t+1 and go to Step 2.

Step 5: End

We don't attempt "to waver" in complicated spaces to search for optimal solutions. We are interested in consolidating a set of initial rules, thus we shall obtain the best rules or most evident rules present in the set of training examples. Fue to the aforementioned cause, we restrict the mutations and reproductions.

The genetic operator that will be employed are crossover and mutation operators. Let's look at how these operators are defined:

Definition 4.3. The most important operator in a genetic algorithm is the *crossover operator*. This operator will allow us to unite information about each species. This operator combines the features of two individuals over a new individual. The proposed crossover operator (∇) is that shown in Table 2.

∇	**0**	**1**	**#**
0	0	0	0
1	0	1	1
#	0	1	#

Table 2: The crossover operator

The reproduction of two individuals from the same species, $e_{i1}e_{i2}...e_{in}$ and $e_{j1}e_{j2}...e_{jn}$, will produce a new individual for which the chromosome will be $e_{i1}\nabla e_{j1}...e_{in}\nabla e_{jn}$.

We do not permit all reproductions. We only permit those reproductions in which the breeding at least adapts itself to the environment equal to the worst of his or her parent, that is

$$f(\text{breeding}) \ge \text{minimum}(f(\text{father}), f(\text{mother}))$$

When this does not happen the reproduction is not permitted.

We shall calculate the fitness function of pairs which will be discarded, those which involve a high computational cost. This is the principal criticism that could be made to our restriction mentioned above. However, this cost is not too large because the reproduction will only be carried out between individuals of the same species and according to the proposed fitness function most of the time the breeding improves on the parent (according to the definition of the proposed crossover operator). This calculation will only make sense in the first selections to avoid the reproduction of individuals who introduce noise. In this manner, we avoid noise being propagated.

Definition 4.4. The mutation will only be possible in those genes that are not specified (genes #), the rest of the values are considered sto betable genes. The mutation in the head genes will no be permitted because this could cause a change in the features of the species (species with the same features).

We make the same restriction with respect to mutation for an individual, not all mutations will be permitted. We shall only permit those mutations that improve the fitness function of the original individual (that is produced from the mutation).

We say that a mutation is malignant when the fitness function of the new individual deteriorates the value of the fitness function of the original individual. A mutation will be possible providing that it verifies that f(new individual)$\geq f$(original individual).

At this point, we can make the same remark about the computational cost, we calculate the fitness function of mutated individuals which will be rejected. If we permit all the mutations we introduce noise (malignant mutations) in the population. It does destabilise the population, and extra time will be necessary to get back to stability. Malignant mutations don't affect the problem of the search for a solution in a search space, and they can be presented as well since they can lead to new search spaces. However, malignant mutations affect our problem, they increase the learning time because they interrupt stability. Hence this computational cost is compensated.

4.3 A set of successive steps which lead to acquire a set of general rules.

We have developed an algorithm that obtains the variables and their domains which are used by the expert in his or her reasoning process, which takes a set of training examples as input and returns a minimal set of maximal or general rules. The basic idea of the algorithm is to acquire the evident rules from the set of examples that show the way the expert reasons. The rules obtained will be employed for planning interviews with the expert.

This algorithm can be described in the following way:

Step 1: To obtain the input variables and their domains.

We make use of a repertory grid based technique for obtaining the expert's conceptual structure, that is the concepts and their domains that he or she has about the domain.

Step 2: To remove the existing noise from the training set.

We remove those examples that are "sufficiently" far away from the remainder of the examples in the same class.

Step 3: To obtain a set of general rules.

To do so, we suggest the algorithm proposed by *Castro et al.* in [5]

Step 4: To apply the genetic algorithm to individuals in each species.

If the number of rules generated for one species is sufficient (bigger than *M*), then apply the genetic algorithm.

Step 5: To reduce the number of rules obtained.

We remove those rules included in other more general rules.

Step 6: End

The algorithm should produce a set of general rules which hold the knowledge present in the set of examples provided by the expert or the organisation to which he or she belongs. This set of general rules will be useful for planning future interviews with the expert during the knowledge acquisition process.

5 Experiments

We have worked with *Iris Plants Database*, which was created by *Fisher*[7]. The data set contains 3 classes (Iris-setosa, Iris-versicolor, Iris-virginica) with 50 instances each. An example is made up of 4 numeric-predictive attributes and the class.

The attributes are the following, X_0 is the sepal length, X_1 is the sepal width, X_2 is the petal length and X_3 is the petal width. All the attributes are measured in centimetres. There are 150 instances that do not contain missing (i.e. unavailable) attribute values. We have used 120 instances (80%) for learning and 30 instances (20%) for proving the rules that have been learnt.

The Table 3 shows how this algorithm reduces the number of rules obtained, achieving similar results (that is, the percentage of instances that have been correctly classified) to those obtained by *Castro*[5].

The knowledge that this algorithm acquires will be more evident knowledge present in the set of training examples. The rules produced by this algorithm also will be more useful for our purpose of knowledge acquisition. If not, let us look at the rules obtained by each algorithm:

Test	Without reduction (Castro[5])	With reduction
1	100/15	100/5
2	96.6/13	96.6/5
3	96.6/13	100/3
4	96.6/12	96.6/5
5	96.6/13	96.6/5
6	96.6/14	100/5
7	93.3/11	90/3
8	93.3/11	90/3
9	96.6/13	96.6/5
10	100/15	100/5

Table 3. Percentage of success/number of rules

The algorithm proposed by *Castro*[5] obtains the following set of rules:

R_0: IF X_3 is {HN,MN} THEN Y is Iris Setosa
R_1: IF X_2 is NOT {MP} and X_3 is {Z,SN} THEN Y is Iris Versicolor
R_2: IF X_1 is NOT {HN,MN} and X_2 is NOT {MP,HP} and X_3 is NOT {MN,HN,MP} THEN Y is Iris Versicolor
R_3: IF X_0 is Z and X_1 is HN and X_2 is SP and X_3 is SP THEN Y is Iris Versicolor
R_4: IF X_1 is NOT {SN,MN} and X_2 is NOT {MP,HP} and X_3 is NOT {MN,HN,SP} THEN Y is Iris Versicolor
R_5: IF X_0 is NOT HN and X_1 is NOT HN and X_2 is NOT {MP,HP} and X_3 is NOT {MP,MN,HN} THEN Y is Iris Versicolor
R_6: IF X_1 is NOT SN and X_2 is NOT SP and X_3 is {SP,SN} THEN Y is Iris Versicolor
R_7: IF X_3 is HP THEN Y is Iris Virginica
R_8: IF X_2 is NOT SP and X_3 is {MP,HP} THEN Y is Iris Virginica
R_9: IF X_0 is NOT Z and X_1 is NOT {SN,Z} and X_3 is {SP,MP,HP} THEN Y is Iris Virginica
R_{10}: IF X_0 is Z and X_1 is HN and X_2 is SP and X_3 is SP THEN Y is Iris Virginica
R_{11}: IF X_1 is NOT Z and X_3 is {MP,HP} THEN Y is Iris Virginica
R_{12}: IF X_2 is NOT {SP,MP} and X_3 is {SP,MP,HP} THEN Y is Iris Virginica
R_{13}: IF X_1 is NOT MN and X_2 is NOT SP and X_3 is {SP,MP,HP} THEN Y is Iris Virginica
R_{14}: IF X_2 is NOT {Z,SP} and X_3 is {Z,MP,HP} THEN Y is Iris Virginica

If we apply the proposed algorithm to the same set of training examples we obtain the following set of rules:

R_0: IF X_3 is {HN,MN} THEN Y is Iris Setosa
R_1: IF X_3 is {SN,Z} THEN Y is Iris Versicolor
R_2: IF X_2 is NOT HP and X_3 is {SN,Z,SP} THEN Y is Iris Versicolor
R_3: IF X_3 is {MP,HP} THEN Y is Iris Virginica

R_4: IF X_2 is NOT SP and X_3 is {SP,MP,HP} THEN Y is Iris Virginica

As we can observe the final set is more appropriate for the propose of planning interviews with the expert, this set is easier to understand.

We have also been working with the *Pima Indians Diabetes Database*. This database was created by Vincent Sigillito fromthe Johns Hopkins University. The data set contains 2 classes, Diabetes and No-Diabetes with 500 instances for No-Diabetes class and 268 for Diabetes class. An example consists of 8 attributes and the class.

All attributes are numerically valued: Number of times pregnant, Plasma glucose concentration at 2 hours in an oral glucose tolerance test, Diastolic blood pressure, Triceps skin fold thickness, 2 Hour serum insulin, Body mass index, Diabetes pedigree function and Age. There are 768 instances (the total) that do not contain missing (i.e. unavailable) attribute values. We have used 576 instances (75%) for learning and 192 instances (25%) for proving the rules that have been learnt. Most of the attributes values in the examples from the training set appear very closely grouped together. This fact complicates the database. The Pima Indians Diabetes Database has been used in [11].

Table 4 shows the results obtained for the algorithm proposed when we apply it to this database.

Test	Without reduction Castro[5]	With reduction
1	70.3/129	65.1/15
2	66.2/127	65.1/21

Table 4. Reduction of fuzzy rules

The suggested algorithm reduces the number of rules obtained without acting on the percentage of instances from the set of tests that have been correctly classified. Moreover, the rules obtained will be those that hold the evident knowledge from the set of examples that show the way the expert reasons.

6 Conclusions

We have studied how we can use a machine learning technique in the process for knowledge acquisition. We have developed a machine learning technique that can be useful as a mechanism for planning interviews with the expert. The algorithm makes use of a repertory grid based technique for obtaining the expert's concepts, attributes and domains, an inductive learning algorithm for obtaining a set of general rules and a genetic algorithm for obtaining the minimal set of more general rules. The mechanism for representation employed has been fuzzy logic sincethis the closest one to the way the expert reasons.

This algorithm is interesting for obtaining the evident rules that experts are not able to express. The set of rules obtained will be useful for planning future interviews with the expert for achieving our propose of knowledge acquisition. Some aspects of this algorithm will be studied in future works, such as, how we employ the rules obtained for carrying out interviews, developing a repertory grid based technique that will obtain the expert's conceptual structure, etc...

References

[1] Abe, S. and M. Lan (1995). A method for fuzzy rules extraction directly from numerical data and its application to pattern classification. *IEEE Transactions on Fuzzy Systems,*Vol 3, 1:18-28.

[2] Benitez, J., A. Blanco and I. Requena (1995). An empirical procedure to obtain fuzzy rules using neural network. *Proceedings of the 6th IFSA Congress.*

[3] Castro, J., M. Delgado and F. Herrera (1993). A learning method of fuzzy reasoning by genetic algorithms. *Proceedings of the 11th European Congress of Fuzzy and Intelligent Technologies.*

[4] Castro, J. and J. Zurita (1996). An inductive learning algorithm in fuzzy systems. *Fuzzy Sets and Systems*, 89:193-203.

[5] Castro, J., J. Castro-Schez and J. Zurita (1999). Learning maximal structure rules in fuzzy logic for knowledge acquisition in expert systems. *Fuzzy Sets and Systems*, 101:331-342.

[6] Delgado, M. and A. Gonzalez (1993). An inductive learning procedure to identify fuzzy systems. *Fuzzy Sets and Systems*, 55:121-132.

[7] Fisher, R. (1936). The use of multiple measurements in taxonomic problems. *Annual Eugenics*, 7(2):179:188.

[8] Kelly, G. (1975) The Psychology of Personal Constructs. New York:Norton.

[9] Michalski, R. A theory and methodology of inductive reasoning. In *Machine Learning: An Artificial Intelligence Approach,* Vol. I, 83-134. Morgan Kaufman, Los Altos,CA.

[10] Quilan, J., P. Compton, K. Horn and L. Lazarus (1986). Inductive knowledge acquisition: A case study. *Proceedings Second Australian Conference on Applications of Expert Systems.* In J.R. Quilan (De.) Applications of Expert Systems. Maidenhead: Academic Press (in press).

[11] Sestito, S. and T. Dillon (1993). Knowledge acquisition of conjunctive rules using multilayered neural network. *International Journal of Intelligent Systems*, 8,:779-805.

[12] Smith, J., J. Everhart, W. Dickson, W. Knowler and R. Johannes (1988). Using the ADAP learning algorithm to forecast the onset of diabetes mellitus. *Proceedings of the Symposium on Computer Applications and Medical Care.* IEEE Computer Society Press, 261-265.

[13] Wang, L. and J. Mendel (1992). Generating fuzzy rules by learning from examples. *IEEE Transactions on Systems, Man, and Cybernetics*, Vol 22, 6:1414-1427.

[14] _____, Repertory Grid Technique (1987). Concise Encyclopaedia of Psychology, R. Cornisi, Ed. New York:Wiley-Interscience.

Use of Attribute Selection Criteria in Decision Trees in Uncertain Domains

B. Crémilleux[1], C. Robert[2]

[1]GREYC, CNRS - UPRESA 6072
Université de Caen
F-14032 Caen Cédex France
cremilleux@info.unicaen.fr
[2]Institut de Recherche en Mathématiques Appliquées
Université Joseph Fourier
F-38041 Grenoble Cédex France
Claudine.Robert@imag.fr

Abstract

There are many attribute selection criteria involved in the induction of decision trees. We present criteria derived from an impurity measure in a unified framework and we use the same background to describe ORT criterion [12]. We compare the theoretical backgrounds of C.M. criteria with those of the ORT criterion and we illustrate their differences. We set lazy decision trees with regards to these families of criteria, and we debate their use with uncertain data sets. Finally, we clarify the choice of these approaches and we separate their domains of application.

1 Introduction

Decision trees have been used successfully for many different decision making and classifications tasks in many domains like medicine. Broadly speaking, a decision tree is built from a set of training data having attribute values and a class name. The result of the process is represented as a tree in which nodes specify attributes and branches specify attribute values. Leaves of the tree correspond to sets of examples with the same class or to elements in which no more attributes are available. Construction of decision trees is described, among others, by Breiman et al. (1984) [3] who present an important and well-known monograph on classification trees. A number of standard techniques have been developed, for example like the basic algorithms ID3 [19], CART [3] and the questionnaire theory [16]. A survey of different methods of decision tree classifiers and the various existing issues are presented in Safavian and Landgrebe (1991) [22].

In induction of decision trees various attribute selection criteria are used to estimate the quality of attributes in order to select the best one to split on. Section 2 briefly sets out two main paradigms to generate decision trees: the C.M. criteria which are stemmed from an impurity measure [3][5] and the ORT criterion [12] which is based on a canonical scalar product. We present C.M. criteria in an unified framework [9] to better confront these paradigms and we compare the theoretical backgrounds of C.M. criteria with those of the ORT criterion. We connect the question of the advantages and disadvantages of each of these families of criteria with the presence or not of uncertainty in the used data and the necessity to prune or not the tree to avoid over-specified information. Section 3 briefly illustrates differences which may happen in practical situations between C.M. and ORT criteria. In Section 4, we set lazy decision trees with regards to these families of criteria and we debate their use in uncertain domains. To conclude, we will see that the choice of a paradigm, according to us, depends whether the used data sets embed uncertainty or not, whether the phenomenon under study admits deterministic causes, and what level of intelligibility is required.

2 C.M. and ORT criteria

2.1 C.M. criteria

Many possible attribute selection criteria for building decision trees exist, but we know at a theoretical level that criteria derived from an impurity measure perform comparably [3][5][9]. We used here the term of impurity because it is the more usual in the machine learning community [3][12]. We called such criteria C.M. criteria (concave-maximum criteria) because an impurity measure, among other characteristics, is defined by a concave function. The most commonly used criteria which are the Shannon entropy (in the family of C4.5 software [20]) and the Gini criterion (in CART algorithms [3]), are C.M. criteria. We present criteria derived from an impurity measure in an unified framework [9] in order to better understand C.M. and ORT criteria.

To compare these families of criteria, it is necessary now to recall the basic constraints of the problem [3][9]. Let us call D the class of the examples of a data set, with values $d_1, \ldots, d_k$, Ω a node and Y any attribute defined on Ω, with values $y_1, \ldots, y_m$. Let us consider an attribute selection criterion denoted Ψ (see Fig. 1).

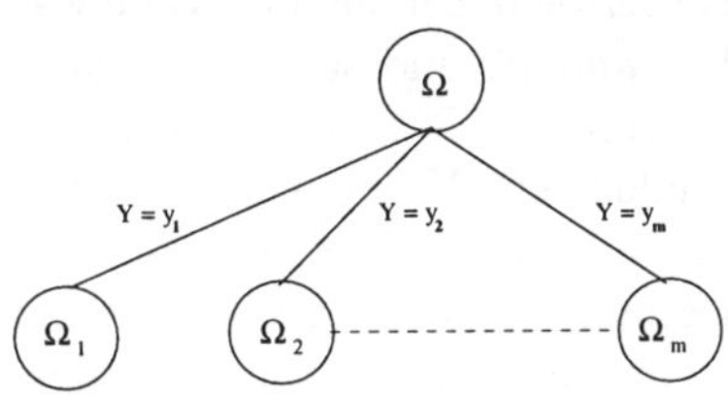

Figure 1: Splitting of a node Ω using an attribute Y.

i. The minimum value of Ψ is reached if and only if the sub-nodes induced by Y are pure with respect to D, that is if and only if two examples with the same value of Y imply that they have the same value of D.

ii. Let P (respectively $P_i, i = 1, \ldots, m$) be the frequency distribution of D in Ω (respectively on the set $Y = y_i, i = 1, \ldots, m$). Ψ has its maximum value if and only if $P_1 = \ldots = P_m$ (which implies that $P = P_i$ for all i).

iii. $\Psi(Y)$ can be viewed as a combined measure of impurity of the sub-nodes induced by Y. If we want Ψ to take into account the respective sizes of the sub-nodes Ω_i, the simplest form for Ψ is: $\Psi(Y) = \sum_i^m \alpha_i \varphi(\Omega_i)$ where $\Omega_1, \ldots, \Omega_m$ are the sub-nodes yielded by Y, α_i is the rate of Ω_i in Ω, and φ is a function that quantifies the impurity of D in the node Ω_i.

Thus we are led to address the question of defining an impurity measure. A minimal set of constraints is:

1. The impurity of D in Ω depends only on the frequency distribution $P = (p_1, \ldots, p_k)$ of D in Ω. Thus a measure of impurity is a function φ defined on the set of $k - uples$ with positive coordinates, the sum of which is 1. We will note either $\varphi(P)$ or $\varphi(\Omega)$ the impurity of a node Ω.

2. φ doesn't depend on the way we code D. Thus φ has to be equal over all permutations of the components of P. The mathematical term for this is: φ is a symmetric function.

3. φ reaches its minimum value minφ if and only if D is a constant function on Ω.

4. φ reaches its maximum value maxφ if all values of D are equally frequent.

5. Combining groups tends to increase the impurity. For example, when we combine r groups Ω_i, D might be constant on each of them, while D might not be constant on the whole group; from i) $\varphi(\Omega_i) = \min \varphi$ and $\varphi(\Omega) \geq \min \varphi$ with $\Omega = \Omega_1 \cup \ldots \cup \Omega_r$.

One can then show [9], that if φ is strictly concave and is symmetric, then it satisfies constraints (1) to (5) and any element of the set $\mathcal{C}$ of symmetric strictly concave functions is a proper function to define an impurity measure. So, from this set of constraints, we have a whole set of possible criteria, which will be called concave minimum criteria (for example, the information gain and the Gini criterion are C.M. criteria). The value of the criterion in a node reflects how appropriately the chosen attribute divides the data. With impurity measures, the smaller the value of Ψ, the better the split. Let us recall that, from iii), $\Psi(Y)$ can be viewed as a combined measure of impurity of the sub-nodes induced by Y: we will see that this point is of great interest to explain differences between ORT and C.M. criteria.

Many domains are uncertain and in such areas, like medicine, we are sure a priori that it is impossible to build a tree that correctly classifies all the examples. In such situations, decision tree algorithms tend to divide nodes having few examples and a main drawback appears (see [3][18][6][23]): the resulting trees tend to be very large and overspecified. Some branches, especially towards the bottom, are due to sample variability and are statistically meaningless (one can also say that they are present due to noise in the sample). Such branches must either not be built or be pruned. If we do not want to build them, we have to set out rules to stop the building of the tree.

We know it is better to generate the entire tree and then to prune it (see for example [3][14]).

With C.M. criteria, one can define a straightforward pruning method (which is called C.M. pruning because it goes with using a C.M. criterion to build the tree) perfectly coherent with the building of the tree [8]. We will see below that C.M. pruning is not tied to the use of the pruned tree as a classifier and it is suitable in uncertain domains. C.M. pruning builds a new attribute binding the root of a tree with its leaves, the attribute's values corresponding to the branches leading to a leaf. It permits computation of the global quality of a tree. It corresponds to the difference between the impurity of the root of the tree and the mean impurity of its leaves, this difference being normalized to a value in [0, 1]. The global quality of a tree is equal to 1 if and only if all its leaves are pure and it is equal to 0 if and only if the frequency distributions of D in its root and in all its leaves are identical. The best sub-tree for pruning is the one that yields the highest quality pruned tree. C.M. pruning produces a family of nested trees spreading from the initial large tree to the tree restricted to its root. The curve of the global quality index as a function of the number of pruned tree gives a pragmatic method to stop the pruning process [8]. The computational cost of C.M. pruning is particularly low and it is tractable even with large databases.

The principal methods for pruning decision trees are examined in Mingers and others [17][11]. Most of these pruning methods are based on minimizing a classification error rate when each element of the same node is classified in the most frequent class in this node. These pruning methods are inferred from situations where the built tree will be used as a classifier and they systematically discard a sub-tree which doesn't improve the used classification error rate. The resulting pruned tree is different from that produced when one uses C.M. pruning. For example C.M. pruning doesn't systematically discard a sub-tree, the classification error rate of which is equal to the rate of the root. In Figure 2, D is bivalued and in each node the first (resp. second) value indicates the number of examples having the first (resp. second) value of D. This sub-tree doesn't lessen the error rate, which is 10% both in its root or in its leaves; nevertheless the sub-tree is of interest since it points out a specific population with a constant value of D while in the remaining population it's impossible to predict a value for D. The global quality index of this sub-tree is 0.55, which means that it explains 55% of the initial impurity.

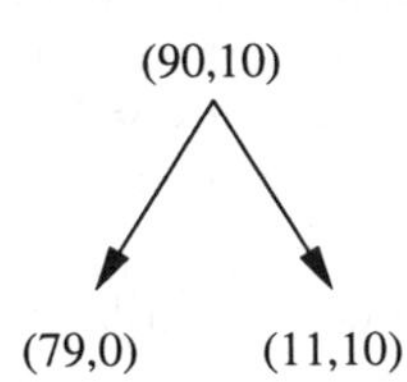

Figure 2: A tree which could be interesting although it doesn't decrease the number of errors.

2.2 The ORT criterion

In order to better confront C.M. and ORT criteria, we present now ORT criterion from the set of constraints previously cited.

Let us come back to conditions i), ii), and iii). Condition i) states that Ψ reaches its minimum value exclusively when Y induces pure sub-nodes. However, purity of all leaves is an ideal situation which is unheard-of in uncertain domains. So we can replace condition i) by another one, favouring attributes that simply separate the different values of D (the class). Thus we consider the following condition:
iv) $\Psi(Y)$ is minimum if and only if $Y(\omega) \neq Y(\omega')$ implies $D(\omega) \neq D(\omega')$.

If D has two values, Y three values and $P_1 = (1,0), P_2 = (1,0), P_3 = (0,1)$, all leaves induced by Y are pure while iv) implies $\Psi(Y) > \min \varphi$, which is not sensible. This drawback disappears if we consider attributes Y with fewer values than D. Fayyad and Irani [12] claim that grouping values of attributes and building binary trees yield better trees; we agree with them for many situations, but nevertheless, for example in medical areas, physicians do not always agree to group values since it yields meaningless trees and thus non-binary trees must not be definitively discarded. However, in this section, in order that condition iv) implies that $\Psi(Y)$ is minimum as soon as all sub-nodes are pure, we consider attributes Y with two values (this doesn't hold true for D which can still have more than two values).

There are also situations where taking into account the respective sizes of the sub-nodes is not necessary. For example, let us suppose that we try to clear up strategies for therapy in the case of a well diagnosed disease and that the choice of therapy relies on p dichotomous attributes; we can consider two methods:

1. We collect a sample of real cases where D codes the prescribed therapy and then scrutinize the tree built with this data set.

2. We consider the 2^p possible values of $(Y_1, \ldots, Y_p)$; we ask an expert to write down for each of the 2^p situations the therapy he recommends. This method yields trees which are useful tools in building expert systems or in consensus conferences.

In method 1), it is essential to take into account the respective sizes of the sub-nodes and thus to retain condition iii). In method 2), there is no reason to do so. Therefore we discard condition iii) in this section and we consider criteria satisfying ii) and iv). As frequency distributions are also elements of R^k (where k is the number of values of D), the cosine of (P_1,P_2) is the simplest function to consider. Let us note $P_1.P_2$ the canonical scalar product: $P_1.P_2 = \sum_{j=1}^{k} p_{1j}p_{2j}$ with $P_1 = (p_{11}, \ldots, p_{1k})$ and $P_2 = (p_{21}, \ldots, p_{2k})$ being the frequency distributions of D in the sub-nodes induced by Y. A selection attribute criterion is defined by the function Ψ, the minimum of which will define the best attribute to select:

$$\Psi(Y) = \cos(P_1, P_2) = \frac{P_1.P_2}{||P_1||||P_2||}$$

with $||P_i||^2 = \sum_{j=1}^{k} p_{ij}^2 \quad i = 1, 2$

This criterion is, up to a sign $-$, the ORT criterion [12] (in the ORT criterion one has to maximize $1 - \Psi(Y)$).

3 ORT versus C.M. criteria

To show the differences between C.M. and ORT criteria, let us consider the data set given in the appendix and the trees induced from this data depicted in Figure 3: a tree built with a C.M. criterion is represented at the left and the tree built with the ORT criterion at the right. ORT rapidly comes out with the pure leaf $Y_2 = y_{21}$ while C.M. criterion splits it and arrives later at the split leaves. We give here just a simple example, but some others both in artificial and real world domains are detailed in [10]: they show that ORT criterion produces more often than C.M. criteria trees with small leaves at their top. We will also see in [10] that overspecified leaves with C.M. criteria tend to be small and at the bottom of the tree (thus easy to prune) while leaves at the bottom of ORT trees can be large. Thus, in the example of therapy strategies, ORT criterion may perform better in method 2) while C.M. criteria are to be used in method 1).

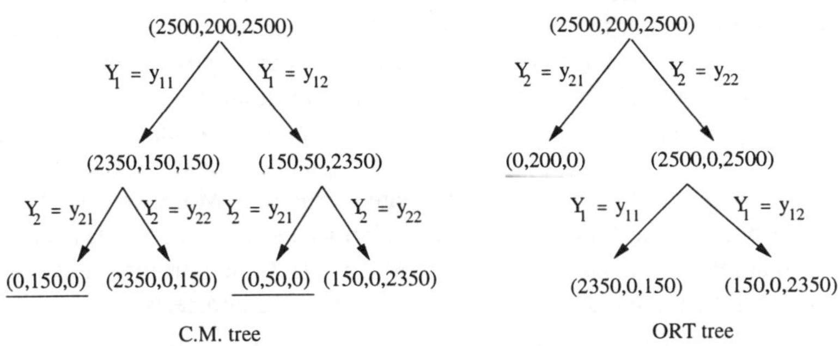

Figure 3: An example of C.M. and ORT trees.

The issue of taking into account the number of examples covered by a rule is debated in Clark and Boswell [7]. They claim rules established from few examples are unreliable in domains with uncertainty. Let d_1 and d_2 be two values of the class. They prefer for instance a rule $(R1)$ covering 1000 examples having the value d_1 and 1 example of d_2 to a rule $(R2)$ covering 5 examples having the value d_1 and 0 example of d_2. They upgrade their CN2 system in order to avoid producing highly specific rules by using the Laplacian error estimate. The accuracy of the Laplace estimate for predicting the value of D is 99.8% for R1 and 85.7% for R2. Experimental comparison on twelve real world domains shows this strategy significantly improves CN2 accuracy.

So, ORT favours attributes that simply separate the different classes without taking into account the number of examples of nodes so that ORT produces trees with small pure (or nearly pure) leaves at their top more often than C.M. criteria. Nevertheless, in uncertain domains, such leaves may be irrelevant and it is difficult to prune them without destroying the tree. However pruning is perhaps useless in the domains where the ORT criterion is preferred.

4 Lazy decision trees

4.1 Motivations

A single decision tree built from a training set is the best (according to the used attribute selection criterion) *on average* on all examples. But, there may be better attributes choices for classifying specific instances.

Let us consider the following example. Suppose a data set of patients which we would like to classify as *sick* or *healthy*. Let us assume that this data set includes a boolean attribute Human Immuno-deficiency Virus (called HIV). In this situation, if a patient has the value *true* for HIV, his class is likely to be *sick*. That means that, for this patient, the HIV attribute is highly informative for the classification task. But, even if we suppose that all instances having HIV positive are classified as *sick*, if the proportion of patients having HIV positive is small, it is likely that a C.M. tree doesn't choose this attribute at the top of the tree and the HIV-positive instances will be fragmented throughout the nodes. Using ORT criterion, we may hope that HIV attribute will be chosen at the top of the tree, which seems sensible in this situation, since this attribute gives prominence to a deterministic situation.

Nevertheless, let us note that we have to choose here between perfectly classifying few patients with a single attribute or to start explaining the class of many patients but with the cost of building a more complicated structure. Moreover, what happens if several attributes - like HIV - are highly informative each one to classify few instances? If a single tree is built, it is necessary to select one attribute at the root and the final tree will be unable to take advantage of special characteristics of an instance that may give rise to an extremely short explanation to classify it.

Lazy trees [13] have been introduced - among other things - to solve this question. The main idea of this strategy is to highlight the "best" path in a virtual decision tree for each instance to classify. A key point is to use all the available information for *each instance*. If we come back to our previous example, we know that HIV attribute seems to be a good choice at the root of the tree for patients having HIV positive. For an other instance, we will see in the next section that lazy approach may lead to select another attribute to get again a short path specific to this instance to classify it. If an instance has no value for an attribute, lazy approach will construct the best tree with remainder attributes. Thus, we will see below that it is a natural mean to handle missing values.

Next sections outline lazy trees and compare the advantages and disadvantages of this approach to those of usual decision trees built with C.M. and ORT criteria.

4.2 Overview of the method

In lazy approach, the first part of the induction process (i.e., building a classifier) is non-existent: all the work is done during the classification step.

The basic algorithm has in input a training set of labelled instances (i.e., class is known) and a new instance to classify (i.e., a test instance). It predicts in output the class value of the test instance. Aside from stop conditions, the core of the process is to select an attribute and apply it recursively on the sub-problem containing data with the same outcome of the attribute as the test instance. The overall effect is that of tracing a path in an virtual tree made specifically for the test instance.

Such an approach has been described by White [25] in order to deal with noisy data. The latter adds conditional probabilities (probabilities which are conditional on the full set of attributes) in order to relax assumptions between attributes. The process of classifying a new case proceeds by following a path through the tree from its root down to its leaf where the estimated probabilities of class membership are located. The combinatorial explosion inherent in generating large classification trees is circumvented by only building the particular path required at each stage. White estimates that this approach is suitable for all domains where there is some level of uncertainty as intrinsic to the nature of the problem.

In a more recent work, Friedman et al. [13] set lazy trees approach in relation to ordinary trees. They present a new lazy algorithm - LAZYDT - that conceptually constructs the "best" decision tree for each test instance. In practice, only a path is generated, and a caching scheme makes the algorithm fast.

The heart of the algorithm is the selection of an attribute at each recursive call. Unlike ordinary decision trees, the input of lazy approach has an extra information, the test instance, and one would like to use that information to choose the appropriate attribute. LAZYDT uses, as attribute selection criterion, a normalization of the difference between the entropies for the current node and for the node where the test instance would be branched to. This normalization avoids negative gain and allows to take into account the actual class values and not only the frequencies. By re-weighting the instances at every node, normalization leads to have equal weight for each value of the class. Furthermore, to avoid fragmentation of data, LAZYDT chooses a binary split on a single value (for attributes with more than two values, only splits on any value that is not equal to the test instance's value are allowed). According to us, normalization and binary split, which concur the aim of these stated by the ORT framework, are the cornerstone of the process which highlights quickly a deterministic situation appropriate to the test instance, even if few instances are affected.

4.3 Discussion

Unlike C.M. and ORT frameworks, which generate a single tree from a data set, lazy decision trees are able to produce the "best" tree appropriate to each instance to classify. The criterion used in LAZYDT is able to produce short paths giving prominence to deterministic situations, even with few instances. In this sense, this criterion is quite similar to ORT. But, as the criterion used in lazy trees relies on the node where the test instance will be sent, generated paths depend on the specific values of the test instance and we can hope to build the "best" path for *each* test instance: here is a difference with ORT.

In uncertain domains, missing values and noise are unavoidable and a great interest of lazy approach is its flexibility. Lazy trees use the available information so that missing values are naturally handled by considering only splits on attributes values that are known in the test instance. So, Friedman et al. [13] claim that this approach is robust with respect to missing values and doesn't need to resort to the complicated methods usually seen in induction trees (e.g., sending portions of instances down different branches like in C4.5 [20] or using surrogate attributes like in CART [3]). This method has been explicitly proposed by Brunet in [4]. Nevertheless, Ragel notes that this approach doesn't solve missing values in the training set (with LAZYDT, instances with unknown values are excluded when their values are missing for an attribute in a path). Ragel [21] proposes a pre-processing method to deal with missing values which temporarily ignored them, without deleting data. This one is based on a search of relevant associations within data to predict missing values. The core of the used algorithm stems from associations rules [1] (we will come back briefly to this method in conclusion).

But, with lazy trees, the user has to cope with multi-paths and not with a single decision tree. The latter is a graphical structured summary of a data set. Experience in induction tasks shows that this result is a key point of the success of decision trees. It is the foundations of a fruitful iterative process of discovery: building a tree brings a new light on the studied phenomenon which suggests the construction of a new tree, and so on. By this mean, the user may reach a goal that he didn't suspect. With lazy decision trees, we miss the point and its lack of intelligibility is a clear drawback. Let us note that the use of a tree as a classifier is highlighted in the artificial intelligence field. We claim that its use as an efficient data-mining description tool, oriented by an *a* priori classification of its elements, is as important as its use as a classifier.

There is also not a simple analogy between pruning in lazy decision trees and pruning in ordinary ones. According to Friedman [13], it is the weakest point of LAZYDT. Experiments on the usual data sets used in the community (U. C. Irvine repository) show that the lack of pruning of lazy trees is a clear drawback with corrupted data [13]. As we have seen in Section 2.1, pruning is a fundamental point in uncertain domains. Until this question of pruning in lazy approach is not be clarified and resolved, it is obvious that it will slow down the use of lazy decision trees in such domains.

5 Conclusion

The C.M. attribute selection criteria and the C.M. pruning can be performed consistently within the same theoretical framework. It is a general framework since on the one hand there are no specific conditions on the attributes and on the other hand it doesn't rely on any specific use of the pruned tree. We have seen that C.M. pruning is suitable in uncertain domains because it allows to keep sub-trees with leaves yielding the determination of relevant decision rules, even when keeping the sub-trees doesn't increase the classification efficiency.

We can say that both ORT and C.M. criteria favour keeping in the same subset elements with the same value of the class. The C.M. criteria, taking into account the size of the nodes, favour trees with big leaves at the top and small leaves (easy to prune without destroying the tree) at the bottom. ORT might track a statistical random effect at the top of the tree rather than a characteristic of the phenomenon under study. Conversely if we know a priori that the phenomenon under study admits deterministic causes in some rare situations, the ORT criterion may find the description of these situations while C.M. criteria do not. Thus these criteria have different fields of applications. Let us remark that if we do not specialize in binary trees then C.M. criteria always work while the generalization of ORT criterion is not a simple task [15].

If classification is the main focus of the induction work, by constructing a path which takes into account characteristics of each instance, lazy decision trees is a very attractive approach. It is a suitable mean to highlight rare but interesting situations which imply few cases. In this sense, lazy decision trees are powerful than ORT criterion. But the latter, as well as the C.M. criteria framework, by offering a single decision tree, allows the user to understand the phenomenon embedded in data and has the advantage of the intelligibility. Furthermore, in uncertain domains, we know that situations with few cases may be due to random effects and that pruning is a key point: this step is not clarified in lazy decision trees yet.

To conclude, we can point out that lazy decision trees is a more sophisticated approach than ordinary decision trees: the search is dedicated for each example and not on average on all the data. This concept can be further developed: for example, association rules method [1] is a recent and efficient approach to extract all the associations of large databases. With this approach, classification task comes down to a search dedicated to each value. The counterpart to this exhaustive search is the huge amount of rules that are produced. If it is not a drawback for an automatic process, on the other hand the user has some difficulties to interpret the rules and to understand the phenomenon. Hence, there are some works on generalization of association rules [24] in order to summarize them. When such a synthesis of association rules will be available, it may be a new mean to run more effective data summaries as decision trees, and the question of the used attribute selection criterion would be obsolete.

References

[1] R. Agrawal, H. Mannila, R. Srikant, H. Toivonen, and A. I. Verkamo. *Fast discovery of association rules*, chapter 12. Advances in Knowledge Discovery and Data Mining. AAAI/MIT Press, 1996.

[2] L. Breiman. Some properties of splitting criteria. *Machine Learning 21*, pages 41–47, 1996.

[3] L. Breiman, J. H. Friedman, R. A. Olshen, and C. J. Stone. *Classification and regression trees.* Statistics probability series. Wadsworth, Belmont, 1984.

[4] T. Brunet. Le problème de la résistance aux valeurs inconnues dans l'induction: une forêt de branches. In *proceedings des 8eme journées francophones sur l'apprentissage*, Saint-Raphaël (France), 1993.

[5] W. Buntine and T. Niblett. A further comparison of splitting rules for decision-tree induction. *Machine Learning 8*, pages 75–85, 1992.

[6] J. Catlett. Overpruning large decision trees. In *proceedings of the Twelfth International Joint Conference on Artificial Intelligence IJCAI 91*, pages 764–769, Sydney, Australia, 1991.

[7] P. Clark and R. Boswell. Rule induction with CN2: some recent improvements. In Y. Kodratoff, editor, *proceedings of European Working Sessions on Learning EWSL 91*, Lecture notes in artificial intelligence. N° 482, pages 151–163, Porto (Portugal), 1991. Springer-Verlag.

[8] B. Crémilleux and C. Robert. A pruning method for decision trees in uncertain domains: Applications in medicine. In *proceedings of the workshop Intelligent*

Data Analysis in Medicine and Pharmacology, ECAI 96, pages 15–20, Budapest, Hungary, 1996.

[9] B. Crémilleux and C. Robert. A theoretical framework for decision trees in uncertain domains: Application to medical data sets. In E. Keravnou, C. Garbay, R. Baud, and J. Wyatt, editors, *6th Conference on Artificial Intelligence In Medicine Europe (AIME 97)*, Lecture notes in artificial intelligence. N° 1211, pages 145–156, Grenoble (France), 1997. Springer-Verlag.

[10] B. Crémilleux, C. Robert, and M. Gaio. Uncertain domains and decision trees: Ort versus c.m. criteria. In *7th Conference on Information Processing and Management of Uncertainty in Knowledge-based Systems*, pages 540–546, Paris (France), 1998. EDK.

[11] F. Esposito, D. Malerba, and G. Semeraro. Decision tree pruning as search in the state space. In P. B. Brazdil, editor, *proceedings of European Conference on Machine Learning ECML 93*, Lecture notes in artificial intelligence. N° 667, pages 165–184, Vienna (Austria), 1993. Springer-Verlag.

[12] U. M. Fayyad and K. B. Irani. The attribute selection problem in decision tree generation. In *proceedings of Tenth National Conference on Artificial Intelligence*, pages 104–110, Cambridge, 1992. MA: AAAI Press/MIT Press.

[13] J. H. Friedman, R. Kohavi, and Y. Yun. Lazzy decision trees. In *proceedings of the thirteenth National Conference on Artificial Intelligence AAAI 96*, pages 717–724, Portland (Oregon), 1996.

[14] S. B. Gelfand, C. S. Ravishankar, and E. J. Delp. An iterative growing and pruning algorithm for classification tree design. *IEEE Transactions on Pattern Analysis and Machine Intelligence 13(2)*, pages 163–174, 1991.

[15] G. H. John. *Enhancements to the data mining process*. PhD thesis, Stanford University, 1997.

[16] J. Lorigny. Questionnaire theory applied to wording recognition. In *proceedings of the IEEE Conference on Information Theory*, volume 29, pages 67–82, Les Arcs (France), 1982. CNRS.

[17] J. Mingers. An empirical comparison of pruning methods for decision-tree induction. *Machine Learning 4*, pages 227–243, 1989.

[18] T. Niblett. Constructing decision trees in noisy domains. In *proceedings of 2nd European Working Sessions on Learning EWSL 87*, pages 67–78, Bled (Yugoslavia), 1987. Sigma Press.

[19] J. R. Quinlan. Induction of decision trees. *Machine Learning 1*, pages 81–106, 1986.

[20] J.R Quinlan. *C4.5 Programs for machine learning*. Morgan Kaufmann, San Mateo, Californie, 1993.

[21] A. Ragel. Preprocessing of missing values using robust associations rules. In J. M. Zytkow and M. Quafafou, editors, *proceedings of the 2nd European Symposium on Principles of Data Mining and Knowledge Discovery PKDD 98*, Lecture notes in artificial intelligence. N° 1510, pages 414–422, Nantes (France), 1998. Springer-Verlag.

[22] S. R. Safavian and D. Landgrebe. A survey of decision tree classifier methodology. *IEEE Transactions on Systems, Man, and Cybernetics 21(3)*, pages 660–674, 1991.

[23] C. Schaffer. Overfitting avoidance as bias. *Machine Learning 10*, pages 153–178, 1993.

[24] R. Srikant and R. Agrawal. Mining generalized association rules. In *proceedings of the 21st International Conference on Very Large Data Bases VLDB 95*, pages 407–419, 1995.

[25] A. P. White. Probabilistic induction by dynamic path generation in virtual trees. In M. A Bramer, editor, *proceedings of the 6th conference Expert Systems ES 86*, pages 35–46, Brighton (Great Britain), 1987. Cambridge University Press.

Appendix

We give here the data file used to build trees for Figure 3. Let us recall that D denotes the class that we want to explain, and $Y_1, \ldots, Y_p$ are the attributes.

	D	Y_1	Y_2
1	d_1	y_{11}	y_{22}
...	...	...	...
2350	d_1	y_{11}	y_{22}
2351	d_1	y_{12}	y_{22}
...	...	...	...
2500	d_1	y_{12}	y_{22}
2501	d_2	y_{11}	y_{21}
...	...	...	...
2650	d_2	y_{11}	y_{21}
2651	d_2	y_{12}	y_{21}
...	...	...	...
2700	d_2	y_{12}	y_{21}
2701	d_3	y_{11}	y_{22}
...	...	...	...
2850	d_3	y_{11}	y_{22}
2851	d_3	y_{12}	y_{22}
...	...	...	...
5200	d_3	y_{12}	y_{22}

Table 1: Data file used to induce decision trees of Figure 3.

Mass Assignment Based Induction of Linguistic Decision Trees

J.F.Baldwin, J.Lawry and T.P.Martin

A.I. Group,
Department of Engineering Mathematics,
University of Bristol, Bristol BS8 1TR,
United Kingdom
{jim.baldwin, j.lawry, trevor.martin}
@bristol.ac.uk

Abstract : A mass assignment based ID3 algorithm (MA-ID3) for the induction of decision trees on words is described. Such decision trees encode sets of qualified conditional rules on linguistic variables. The potential of this algorithm is illustrated by means of several examples relating to both real world and model classification and prediction problems.

1 Introduction

The ID3 and C4.5 algorithms (see [9] and [11]) have been successfully applied to a wide variety of machine learning problems. It is well known, however, that such approaches have some limitations. For instance, ID3 is inappropriate for databases containing significant noise since the generated rules will fit the noise that may lead to a high error rate when classifying unseen cases. Furthermore, often in practice classification problems have continuous attribute values associated with them necessitating the partitioning of relevant universes if ID3 type algorithms are to be applied. The use of crisp partitions in this context (i.e. as in C4.5) can be problematic since sudden and inappropriate changes to the assigned class may result from small changes in attribute values. This property also means that these algorithms cannot be applied to prediction and function approximation problems.

The use of fuzzy sets to partition universes can have significant advantages over more traditional approaches and their use in machine learning methods can help overcome many of the above difficulties. For example, fuzzy decision rules tend to be more robust and less sensitive to small changes in attribute values near partition boundaries. Also, such rules tend to have greater generalisation capabilities than their crisp counterparts. The concept of fuzzy partition allows us to incorporate both overlapping classification and attribute classes into our model in a coherent way and the inherent interpolation properties of smooth fuzzy sets enables function approximation and prediction problems to be considered.

In addition, to the issues discussed above the increasing availability of large and complex databases poses a new challenge to the field of machine learning. The potential utility of such information can only be fully realised if it can be summarised by coherent general models where the emphasis is on the fact that these models should be comprehensible to anyone given a moderate amount of training. Clearly, from this perspective, knowledge representation becomes much more important to the whole area. To address some of these issues we introduce, in the sequel, an induction algorithm based on mass assignment theory (MA-ID3) for learning probabilistic decision trees on linguistic variables. Such decision trees encode sets of qualified linguistic conditional rules.

The concept of a linguistic variable was first introduced by Zadeh (see [14]) as a model of how words or labels can represent vague concepts in natural language. A linguistic variable is essentially a variable taking as its values a (finite) set of words or labels. More formally;

Definition 1.1 (Linguistic Variable)
A linguistic variable is a quadruple $\langle L, T(L), U, M \rangle$[1] in which L is the name of the variable, $T(L)$ is a finite term set of labels or words (i.e. the linguistic values), U is a universe of discourse and M is a semantic rule.

The semantic rule M then is defined as a function that associates a normalised fuzzy set with each word in $T(L)$. In other words the fuzzy set $M(w)$ can be viewed as encoding the meaning of w so that for $u \in U$ the membership value $\chi_{M(w)}(u)$ quantifies the suitability or applicability of the word w as a label for the value u.

In order to coherently describe the MA-ID3 algorithm it is necessary to briefly introduce the mass assignment framework for manipulating linguistic variables. A mass assignment for a fuzzy concept [3] can be interpreted as a probability distribution over possible definitions of the concept. These varying definitions might be provided by a population of voters where each voter is asked to give his or her crisp definition of the concept.

Definition 1.2 (Mass Assignment)
Let f be a fuzzy subset of a finite universe Ω such that the range of the membership function of f, χ_f, is $\{y_1, \ldots, y_n\}$ where $y_i > y_{i+1} > 0$. Then the mass assignment of f, denoted $\boldsymbol{m}_f$, is a probability distribution on 2^{Ω} satisfying

$$\boldsymbol{m}_f(F_i) = y_i - y_{i+1} \text{ where } F_i = \{x \in \Omega | \chi_f(x) \geq y_i\} \text{ for } i = 1, \ldots, n$$

$\{F_i\}_{i=1}^{n}$ are referred to as the focal elements(sets) of $\boldsymbol{m}_f$.

[1] Zadeh originally defined a linguistic variable as a quintuple by including a syntactic rule according to which new terms (i.e. linguistic values) could be formed by applying quantifiers and hedges to existing words. In this context, however, we shall assume that the term set is predefined and finite.

2 A Mass Assignment Theory of Linguistic Descriptions

Given the above interpretation we can regard the semantic function M as being determined by a group voting model (see [2], [6] and [8]) across a population of voters as follows; each voter is asked to provide the subset of words from the finite set $T(L)$ which are appropriate as labels for the value u. The membership value $\chi_{M(w)}(u)$ is then taken to be the proportion of voters who include w in their set of labels.

Example 2.1
Consider the set of words {*small, medium, large*} as labels of a linguistic variable *SIZE* with values in U=[0,100]. Given a set of 10 voters a possible voting pattern for the value 25 is

voter 1	voter 2	voter 3	voter 4	voter 5	voter 6	voter 7	voter 8	voter 9	voter 10
small *medium*	*small* *medium*	*small* *medium*	*small* *medium*	*small* *medium*	*small*	*small*	*small*	*small*	*small*

This gives $\chi_{M(small)}(25) = 1$ and $\chi_{M(medium)}(25) = 0.5$

Now this voting pattern can be represented by a mass assignment on the power set of {*small, medium, large*}, {*small, medium*}:0.5,{*small*}:0.5, which in turn represents a fuzzy set on the set of words, namely *small*/1+*medium*/0.5.

This fuzzy set can be viewed as a linguistic description of the value 25 in terms of the words *small, medium* and *large* and is denoted by $des_{SIZE}(25)$. Notice that the linguistic description of 25 can be expressed in terms of the semantic function M in the following manner;

$$small / \chi_{M(small)}(25) + medium / \chi_{M(medium)}(25)$$

Hence, in practice we need only define the fuzzy sets *M*(*small*), *M*(*medium*) and *M*(*large*) from which we can determine any linguistic description. More, formally a linguistic description of a value is defined by;

Definition 2.2 (Linguistic Description of a Value)
Let $u \in U$ then the linguistic description of u relative to the set of words $T(L)$ is a fuzzy subset of $T(L)$

$$des_L(u) = \sum_{w \in T(L)} w / \chi_{M(w)}(u)$$

In cases when the linguistic variable is fixed we drop the subscript L and write $des(u)$.

In example 2.1 each voter was permitted to select a set of labels for the value 25. Suppose we now insist that they select only one label. Assuming that for each voters all the labels in their original set of labels are equally likely then we obtain a probability distribution on labels. This distribution is equivalent to the least prejudiced distribution of the linguistic description of 25 (see [3] and [4]).

$$lp_{des(25)} = small : 0.75, medium : 0.25$$

When forced to choose 75% of the voting population pick *small* as a label for 25 and 25% pick *medium*.

Definition 2.3 (Least Prejudiced Distribution)
For g a fuzzy subset of a finite universe Ω such that g is normalised then the least prejudiced distribution of g is a probability distribution on Ω given by

$$\forall x \in \Omega \ \boldsymbol{lp}_g(x) = \sum_{G_i : x \in G_i} \frac{\boldsymbol{m}_g(G_i)}{|G_i|}$$

where $\boldsymbol{m}_g$ is the mass assignment of g and $\{G_i\}_i$ is the corresponding set of focal elements.

3 Probabilistic Decision Trees on Linguistic Variables.

Linguistic conditional rules have been applied successfully in the area of fuzzy control. Such rules might take the form:

"IF temperature is *hot* AND pressure is *high* THEN quantity of coolant is *small*" where *hot*, *high* and *small* are words describing the appropriate attributes.

We propose to use an ID3 type algorithm to automatically generate sets of qualified linguistic conditionals e.g.

"It is *highly likely* that IF number of times pregnant is *high* AND insulin level is *low* THEN diabetes."
where *high* and *low* are words and *highly likely* is modelled by a real number between 0 and 1 quantifying the degree of belief in the conditional.
We represent such rules as conditional probabilities i.e.

$$\boldsymbol{Pr}\ (\text{diabetes} \mid \text{no. times pregnant is } high \text{ and insulin level is } low) = 0.9$$

More specifically then our objective is to develop an inductive learning algorithm that will;

(1) Partition attribute universes into fuzzy sets representing the meaning of a set of words. Each of these sets of fuzzy sets is a linguistic covering of the relevant universe in the sense that for every element there exists a fuzzy set in the partition in which the element has membership one.
(2) Generate decision trees where the attributes are restricted to linguistic values from the set of words and where at the end of each branch B every classification C is given a probability $\boldsymbol{Pr}\ (C|B)$

The trees are generated according to the same expected entropy criterion for selecting the most discriminating feature as is used in standard ID3 [9]. Nodes are terminated if the maximum of the class probabilities is greater than some pre-specified threshold. However, since the partitions of attribute space are fuzzy any one data object may belong to a number of branches. This means that some new method must be developed in order to determine the conditional probabilities required for the entropy calculation.

Suppose we have a database D of tuples of values of a set of attributes $A_1, \cdots, A_n$ together with a classification label $Class$. How do we determine the probability of a particular combination of words, say $\langle w_{A_1}, \cdots, w_{A_n}, c \rangle$, being applicable to a data object selected at random from D? Clearly this value is given by the sum over the objects $o \in D$ of the probability that o is selected times the probability that $\langle w_{A_1}, \cdots, w_{A_n}, c \rangle$ is applicable as a label for o. Assuming that all objects are equally likely this can be expressed by

$$\frac{1}{|D|} \sum_{o \in D} \boldsymbol{Pr}\left(\langle w_{A_1}, \cdots, w_{A_n}, c \rangle \text{ is suitable as a label for } o \right)$$

Now assuming the voting model interpretation of linguistic descriptions introduced in section 2 then the probability that $\langle w_{A_1}, \cdots, w_{A_n}, c \rangle$ is suitable as a label for o is given by the proportion of voters from some population voting for this combination of labels when they are forced to choose exactly one label for each attribute. Now if we further assume that for each voter his or her choice of label for attribute A_i is independent of his or her choice of label for A_j where $i \neq j$ then we obtain the following result;

$$\boldsymbol{Pr}\left(\langle w_{A_1}, \cdots, w_{A_n}, c \rangle \text{ is suitable as a label for } o \right)$$
$$= \left(\prod_{i=1}^{n} \boldsymbol{lp}_{des(o_{A_i})}\left(w_{A_i}\right) \right) \boldsymbol{lp}_{des(o_{Class})}(c)$$

where $o = \langle o_{A_1}, \cdots, o_{A_n}, o_{Class} \rangle$

A probabilistic decision tree can be represented as a set of branches each augmented by a probability distribution over the classes i.e.

$$T = \left\{ B_1 : \boldsymbol{Pr}(LClass|B_1), \cdots, B_m : \boldsymbol{Pr}(LClass|B_m) \right\}$$

where B_i is a branch defined by the conjunction

$$\left(LA_{i_1} = w_{A_{i_1}} \right) \wedge \cdots \wedge \left(LA_{i_k} = w_{A_{ik_i}} \right)$$

such that $\{i_1, \cdots i_{k_i}\} \in \{1, \cdots, n\}$ and LA_i is a linguistic variable representing the label of A_i. Then for the linguistic variable $LClass$ representing the label of $Class$ and for word $c \in T(LClass)$ we have that

$$\boldsymbol{Pr}(LClass = c|B_i) = \frac{\sum_{0 \in D_{B_i}} \boldsymbol{lp}_{des(o_{Class})}(c) \prod_{j=1}^{k_i} \boldsymbol{lp}_{des\left(o_{A_{ij}}\right)}\left(w_{A_{ij}}\right)}{\sum_{c \in T(LClass)} \sum_{0 \in D_{B_i}} \boldsymbol{lp}_{des(o_{Class})}(c) \prod_{j=1}^{k_i} \boldsymbol{lp}_{des\left(o_{A_{ij}}\right)}\left(w_{A_{ij}}\right)}$$

where D_{B_i} is the set of data objects from D with non zero membership in $M_{w_{A_{i1}}} \times \cdots \times M_{w_{A_{ik_i}}}$. Now $\{B_1, \cdots, B_m\}$ forms a mutually exclusive and exhaustive set of events over the sample space $2^{T(LA_1)} \times \cdots \times 2^{T(LA_n)}$. Hence, given an unknown data object Jeffrey's rule [7] can be used to obtain the distribution of $LClass$ for that object so that

$$\boldsymbol{Pr}(LClass|o) = \sum_{i=1}^{m} \boldsymbol{Pr}(B_i|o)\,\boldsymbol{Pr}(LClass|B_i)$$

Now each branch specifies a set of labels for attributes and $\boldsymbol{Pr}(B_i|o)$ is simply the probability that this particular set of words would be selected to label o. Therefore,

$$\boldsymbol{Pr}(B_i|o) = \prod_{j=1}^{k} \boldsymbol{lp}_{des\left(o_{A_{ij}}\right)}\left(w_{A_{ij}}\right)$$

4 The Application of Mass Assignment ID3 to Machine Learning

In this section we shall attempt to illustrate the potential of MA-ID3 when applied to a number of test and real word problems from the fields of machine learning and data mining. Examples of both classification and prediction problems will be considered. As default the algorithm generates uniform linguistic partitions of trapezoidal fuzzy sets for which the degree of overlap can be specified. The first problem is a toy problem intended to illustrate the benefit of using fuzzy partitions over standard crisp partitions both in terms of the simplicity and the generalisation capabilities of the decision trees obtained.

Example 4.1
Consider a problem where we want to learn the concept of profit from the concepts of income and outgoing. Suppose then that we have a database of 256 regularly spaced triples <*INCOME*, *OUTGOING* , *CLASS*> where *CLASS* has values in {*profit*, *loss*} and both *INCOME* and *OUTGOING* have been scaled so that they lie between 0 and 1. Now we know that the concept of profit is captured by the single rule

$$(CLASS = profit) \text{ IFF } INCOME \geq OUTGOING$$

How well would a decision tree based on uniform crisp partitions learn the notion of profit? For 2 crisp sets partitioning the universes the best that any crisp decision tree can do is to give 50% correct. This is because the decision tree divides the attribute into four regions, one of which it correctly classifies as profit, one of which it correctly classifies as loss and two of which it is unable to classify! (see figure 1)

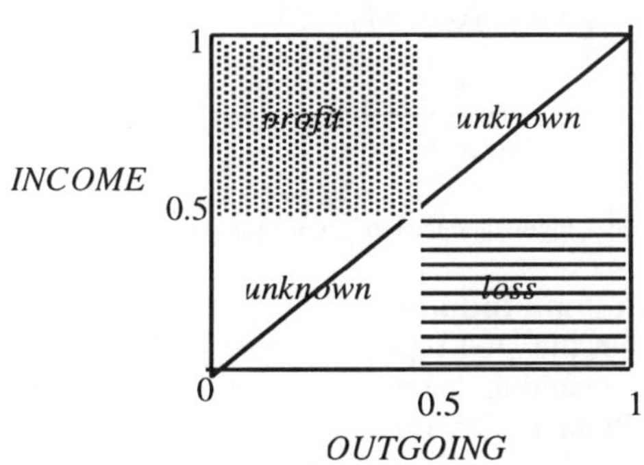

Figure 1: Decision surface generated by a crisp decision tree.

Of course we can improve on this results by using a denser partition. For example, using 3 partition sets we obtain an accuracy of 66.67%. In general using n evenly spaced partition sets we obtain an accuracy of $(n\text{-}1/n)$x100 %.

Using MA-ID3 with two totally overlapping fuzzy sets on each attribute universe we can obtain an accuracy of 94.14%. To obtain this same level of accuracy with crisp decision trees partitions of 16 sets are required. The linguistic variables are defined such that $T(LOUTGOING) = T(LINCOME) = \{small, large\}$ where $M(small) = [0:1, 0.5:1, 1:0]$ and $M(large) = [0:0, 0.5:1, 1:1]$. Note that here we are using the Fril notation for piecewise linear functions (see [1]). The decision surface generated by this tree is shown in figure 2 and the linguistic decision tree is shown in figure 3.

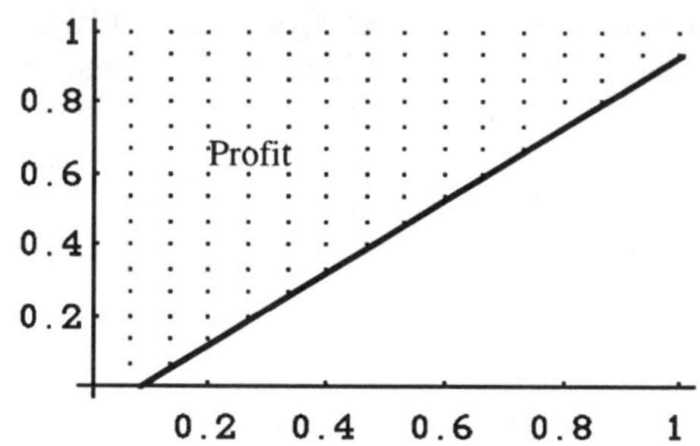

Figure 2: Decision surface generated by a mass assignment decision tree.

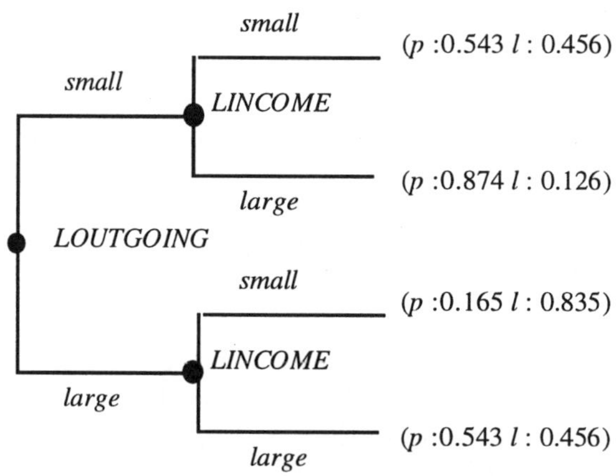

Figure 3: Linguistic decision tree for the profit example.

Example 4.2 (Diabetes in Pima Indians)
This database is taken from the UCI repository (see [13]) and is a fairly well know bench mark problem in machine learning. The problem relates to incidents of diabetes mellitus in the Pima Indian population living near Phoenix Arizona. The diagnostic, binary-valued variable investigated is whether the patient shows signs of diabetes according to World Health Organisation criteria. The database contains

details of 768 females all of which are older than 21. This was split into a training and test set each containing 384 instances. There are 8 attributes:

1 Number of times pregnant
2 Plasma glucose concentration
3 Diastolic blood pressure
4 Triceps skin fold thickness
5 2-Hour serum insulin
6 Body mass index
7 Diabetes pedigree function
8 Age

Each attribute space was partitioned by a uniform linguistic partition of 5 fuzzy sets with a 65% overlap. These could be viewed as corresponding to the meanings of labels *very small*, *small*, *medium*, *large* and *very large* for each attribute. Clearly, since the attribute universes are distinct the semantic function M will differ between attributes. The decision tree was generated to a maximum depth of 4 given a tree of 161 branches. This gave an accuracy of 81.25% on the training set and 79.9% on the test set. These results compare favourably with those of Quinlan's C4.5 algorithm [11] as well as with neural network approaches such as [12].

The following example illustrates how MA-ID3 can be applied to prediction problems as well as classification problems. Since we can generate linguistic partitions of output universes this essentially enables us to treat classification and prediction problems identically with regard to induction of the decision tree. Clearly, however, in order to obtain a predicted output value given an input we must utilise some form of defuzzification method. We shall adopt a straight forward linear combination method for defuzzification whereby the predicted value given an input I is taken to be a weighted sum of the average of the peak values of $M(w_i)$ where $T(LClass) = \{w_1, \cdots, w_k\}$ such that the weights are proportional to the probabilities $\boldsymbol{Pr}(LClass = w_i | I)$. More formally, if $M(w_i)$ has average peak value t_i and $\boldsymbol{Pr}(LClass = w_i | I) = \alpha_i$ for $i = 1, \cdots, k$ we take our predicted value to be $\sum_{i=1}^{k} \alpha_i t_i$

Example 4.3 (Modelling sinxy)
In this example we consider a function approximation problem involving a complex continuous function. Here the database consists of 528 triples $\langle X, Y, \boldsymbol{sin}\, XY \rangle$ where the pairs $\langle X, Y \rangle$ form a regular grid on $[0,3]^2$. Due to the complexity of the function on this occasion 10 equally spaced trapezoidal fuzzy sets with 50% overlap are used to partition the independent variable domain $[0,3]$.

To automatically form a partition of the output universe we use an algorithm originally developed for the Fril Data Browser (see [3] and [5] for details) based on the heuristic that the dependent attribute values generated by the data set should be evenly distributed across the partition sets. The MA-ID3 algorithm was used to generate a decision tree with 100 branches. The percentage error (relative to the output universe) on a regular test database of 1024 points was 4.22% and the control surface is given in figure 4.

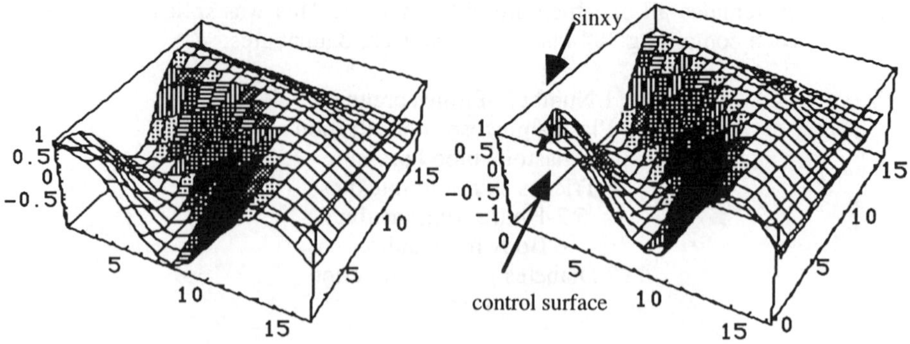

Figure 4: The left hand side plot shows the control surface generated by the decision tree. The right hand side plots shows the same control surface together with sinxy.

5 Pruning Probabilistic Decision Trees

For many real world modelling problems large numbers of attributes are required and also some areas of the attribute space require high levels of information granularity (e.g. for regions near complex non-linear decision boundaries). This can lead to decision trees with large numbers of branches. For instance, the decision tree for the diabetes problem discussed in example 4.2 has 161 branches and although this is considerably less than the maximum of $5^4 = 625$ branches possible for trees of depth 4 and granularity 5 it is desirable to obtain trees of much lower complexity.

In the following we shall discuss a forward pruning algorithm involving the grouping of words to form compound expressions such as *low or medium*. For many classification and prediction problems different regions of the attribute space require different levels of information granularity [15], [16]. Hence, given that we are taking uniform partitions of the attribute space there are likely to be areas where the level of granularity is unnecessarily high. The idea is essentially to detect such regions and lower the level of granularity by grouping words. Words describing continuous variables naturally form a total ordering, for instance *small* $\leq$ *medium* $\leq$*large*. This can be formalised as follows:

Definition 5.1 (An Ordering on Words)
Let *L* be a linguistic variable describing values in a totally ordered universe *U*. Then for words $w_1, w_2 \in T(L)$ we have that $w_1 \leq w_2$ if and only if $\forall x, y \in U$ such that $x \leq y$ $\chi_{M(w_1)}(y) \leq \chi_{M(w_1)}(x)$ and $\chi_{M(w_2)}(x) \leq \chi_{M(w_2)}(y)$

Now assuming that all attributes with ordered universes are partition by ordered linguistic partitions in the sense of definition 5.1 we propose the following forward pruning algorithm. Evaluating a linguistic variable at any leaf node of a sub-tree generates a set of classification probabilities for each word. Use the expected entropy measure to select the most discriminating feature. If this feature has an ordered universe then apply the following word grouping algorithm:

1. Divide into leaf and branch nodes according to the stopping criterion
2. For leaf nodes group words with 'similar' distributions

3. For branch nodes group adjacent words with similar distributions of 'low' entropy

If the attribute is not ordered then the above algorithm is applied treating all nodes as leaf nodes. The similarity of distributions and the level of entropy are determined according to the following measures respectively

$$S(\boldsymbol{Pr}_1, \boldsymbol{Pr}_2) = 1 - \underset{c \in T(LClass)}{\boldsymbol{Max}} \left| \boldsymbol{Pr}_1(c) - \boldsymbol{Pr}_2(c) \right|$$

$$RH(\boldsymbol{Pr}) = \frac{H(\boldsymbol{Pr})}{\boldsymbol{log}_2(|T(LClass)|)}$$

Thus, for two adjacent branch nodes S must be greater than a predefined threshold and RH must be less than another threshold for both distributions in order for grouping to occur. For grouped words the decision tree probabilities are calculated as before but where the probability of $w_1 \vee \cdots \vee w_k$ being selected as a label for a value u is taken to be the sum of the probabilities that each of the individual words are selected i.e.

$$\sum_{i=1}^{k} \boldsymbol{lp}_{des(u)}(w_i)$$

Example 5.2 (figure Eight)
In this problem a figure eight shape was generated according to the parametric equation $x = 2^{-0.5}(\boldsymbol{sin}\, 2t - \boldsymbol{sin}\, t)$, $y = 2^{-0.5}(\boldsymbol{sin}\, 2t + \boldsymbol{sin}\, t)$ where $t \in [0, 2\pi]$. Points in $[-1.6, 1.6]^2$ are classified as legal if they lie within the figure and illegal if they lie outside (see figure 5). The database consisted of 961 points $\langle X, Y, CLASS \rangle$ from a regular grid on $[-1.6, 1.6]^2$.

The X any Y universes where partitioned into a linguistic partition of 10 words. For MA-ID3 without pruning a tree of 100 branches was generated giving an accuracy of 97.5%. If the forward pruning algorithm is applied then the resulting tree has 19 branches (see figure 6) giving an accuracy of 96.67%. A plot of those points classified as legal according to the pruned tree is given below in figure 5.

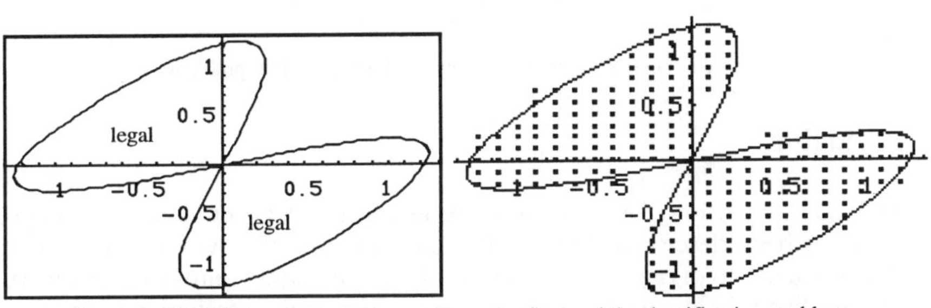

Figure 5: The left hand side diagram shows the figure eight classification problem. The right hand side is a scatter plot of points classified as legal according to the decision tree.

Returning now to the diabetes problem discussed earlier if we apply the forward pruning algorithm the tree complexity is halved to 80 branches. This reduced tree now gives an accuracy of 80.46% on the training set and 78.38% on the test set. The above forward pruning method can be applied in conjunction with other post pruning algorithms such as those described in [10]. For example, the standard error approach based on Laplace's law applied to the forward pruned tree from the diabetes database reduces the complexity to 28 branches. The accuracy then obtained with this tree is 78.125% on the training set and 78.9% on the test set.

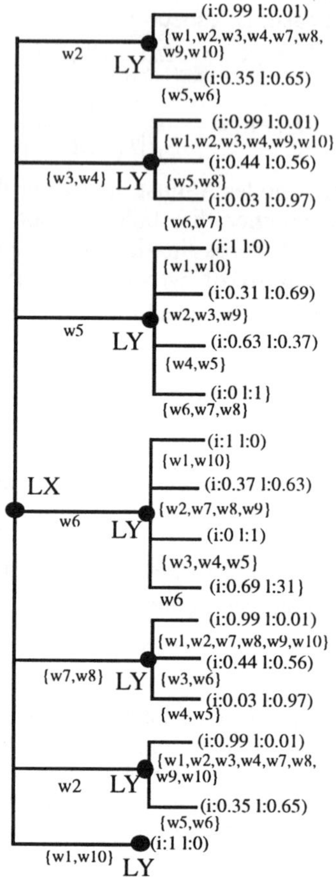

Figure 6: Forward pruned decision tree for figure eight problem.

6 Conclusion

The MA-ID3 algorithm for generating probabilistic decision trees on linguistic variables has been described. Such trees constitute an effective way of modelling complex systems involving continuous attributes in terms simple linguistic rules. The use of fuzzy-linguistic partitions together with mass assignment theory can overcome many of the difficulties associated with traditional machine learning techniques. Furthermore, the possibility of using fuzzy classification classes means that the scope of this method is greater than many standard machine learning methods. Finally, the automatic generation of linguistic rules is likely to become increasingly important in the field of data mining where so called 'glass box' models are essential.

Acknowledgements

This research was supported by an E.P.S.R.C grant.

References

[1] J.F. Baldwin, T.P. Martin, B.W. Pilsworth, *FRIL Manual (Version 4.0)*, FRIL Systems Ltd, Bristol Business Centre, Maggs House, Queens Road, Bristol BS8 1QX, UK, (1988).
[2] J.F. Baldwin , 'Computational Models of Uncertain Reasoning in Expert Systems', *Computer s Math. Applic.* 19 No. 11 (1990) pp105-119
[3] J.F. Baldwin, T.P. Martin, B.W. Pilsworth, *FRIL -Fuzzy and Evidential Reasoning in A.I*, Research Studies Press, John Wiley, (1995).
[4] J.F. Baldwin, J. Lawry, T.P. Martin, 'A Mass Assignment Theory of the Probability of Fuzzy Events', *Fuzzy Sets and Systems* 83 (1996) pp353-367
[5] J.F. Baldwin, T.P. Martin, 'A Fuzzy Data Browser in Fril', *Fuzzy Logic* (Ed J.F. Baldwin), John Wiley & Sons Ltd, (1996).
[6] B.R. Gaines 'Fuzzy and Probability Uncertainty Logics' *Journal of Information and Control* 38 (1978) pp154-169
[7] R.C.Jeffrey, *The Logic of Decision*, Gordon & Breach Inc., New York, (1965).
[8] J. Lawry, 'A Voting Mechanism for Fuzzy Logic' *The International Journal of Approximate Reasoning* 19 (1998), pp315-333.
[9] J.R.Quinlan, 'Induction of Decision Trees', *Machine Learning* 1 pp81-106, (1986).
[10] J.R. Quinlan, 'Simplifying Decision Trees', *International Journal of Man-Machine Studies*, 27 (1987) pp221-234
[11] J.R.Quinlan, *C4.5: Programs for Machine Learning*, San Mateo: Morgan Kaufmann, (1993).
[12] J.W. Smith, J.E. Everhart, W.C. Dickson, W.C. Knowler, R.S. Johannes, 'Using the ADAP Learning Algorithm to Forecast the Onset of Diabetes Mellitus', *Proceedings on the Symposium on Computer Applications and Medical Care*, (1988) pp261-265
[13] WWW,UCI Machine Learning repository, *http://www.ics.uci.edu/~mlearn/MLRepository.html*
[14] L.A. Zadeh, 'The concept of a linguistic variable and its applications to approximate reasoning', Part I: *Information Sciences* 8 (1975) pp199-249 ; Part II: *Information Sciences* 8 (1975) pp301-357; Part III: *Information Sciences* 9 (1976) pp 43-80
[15] L.A. Zadeh, 'Fuzzy Sets and Information Granularity', in: M. Gupta, R. Ragade, R. Yager, (Eds), *Advances in Fuzzy Set Theory and Applications*, North-Holland, Amsterdam (1979) pp3-18.
[16] L.A. Zadeh, 'Towards a Theory of Fuzzy Information Granularity and its Centrality in Human Reasoning and Fuzzy Logic', *Fuzzy Sets and Systems* 90 (1997) pp111-127

Using Maximum Entropy to Estimate Missing Information in Tree-like Causal Networks

Gerald R Garside Dawn E Holmes Paul C Rhodes
Dept of Computing, University of Bradford, Bradford, BD7 1DP, UK
g.r.garside@bradford.ac.uk, d.e.holmes@bradford.ac.uk,
p.c.rhodes@bradford.ac.uk

Abstract

Causal trees and causal inverted trees are specific types of causal network for which minimally prejudiced estimates for missing conditional probability values can be correctly and efficiently obtained using the Maximum Entropy principle. The fact that almost all the independence relationships can be omitted from the Maximum Entropy model enables this efficiency to be achieved. Such estimates enable existing methods for updating information to be used in these tree-like causal networks when not all of the causal information is available. Previous and current work carried out by the authors is described. An example of the theoretical work and an example of an algorithm are given.

1. Introduction

Efficient methods for updating information in causal networks have been described by Pearl [13] and Lauritzen and Spiegelhalter [10]. For these methods to be applicable it is necessary that all the values of the conditional probabilities implied by the network are available. This means that the probabilities of a particular outcome of an event, conditioned by the outcomes of those events which affect it must be known for every possible combination of the outcomes of those events. In practical situations some of these values may not be available and it is then impossible to apply the abovementioned methods.

The situation can be remedied, however, by using the Maximum Entropy principle to provide estimates for any missing values. The estimates thus obtained are minimally prejudiced and consistent with all the available information. The use of Maximum Entropy in the area of probabilistic reasoning has been discussed by Rhodes and Garside [14]. Maung and Paris [11] have shown that the general problem of finding the Maximum Entropy solution in probabilistic systems is NP-complete and so, if we are to apply the methodology to causal networks, we must show that estimates for missing information can be found efficiently, ie. in polynominal time.

The authors began their investigations with causal trees, the simplest type of causal network to analyse, first solving the problem for causal binary trees and then causal multiway trees. More complicated types of networks, namely causal inverted trees, were tackled next and the efficient computation of estimates for missing information using the Maximum Entropy principle were proved, first for causal inverted binary trees and then the more general causal inverted multiway trees. Finally the results for causal trees and causal inverted trees have been amalgamated to solve the problem for causal polytrees, the most general form of tree-like causal networks.

Section 2 defines a causal network and outlines the Maximum Entropy model that can be used for describing the probability distribution of the network. Section 3 outlines the work undertaken in tree-like causal networks. The flavour of the theoretical and algorithmic aspects of the work is given in Sections 4 and 5 by examples of an independence proof and an algorithm to calculate estimates for missing probability values. Section 6 draws conclusions and indicates the further work that is required to complete the investigations.

2. Causal Networks and Maximum Entropy

Let **G** be a directed acyclic graph consisting of a set of n nodes (or vertices), **V**, and a set of directed edges, **B**, between members of **V**. **V** represents the set of events in some system and an edge $< v, w > \varepsilon\, \mathbf{B}$, $v, w \varepsilon \mathbf{V}$, represents a cause-effect relationship between v and w, ie. v influences w. v is a *parent* of w and w is a *child* of v. Let M_v be the set of parents of v.

Each event represented by $v \varepsilon \mathbf{V}$ has a finite set of possible outcomes $\{E_v^{\,j} \mid j = 1..n_v\}$. Let e_v be a variable that can take any one of these outcomes.

A general state of the system can be represented by $\mathbf{e} = e_1 e_2 .. e_n = \bigwedge_{i=1}^{n} e_i$ and there will be $N = \prod_{i=1}^{n} n_i$ such states.

Let **P** be a probability distribution over the states of the system which is determined by the following constraints, **C**.

(C1) $\sum_{\mathbf{e}} P(\mathbf{e}) = 1$ (known as the 'sum to unity').

(C2) $P(e_v \mid \bigwedge_{u \varepsilon M_v} e_u)$ are conditional probabilities with known values for all $v \varepsilon \mathbf{V}$, all e_v and all $\bigwedge_{i=1}^{n} e_i$ (known as the causal information).

(C3) Those independence relationships implied by $d-separation$ in **G**.

Verma and Pearl [17] have shown that all the independence relationships in a causal network are those implied by d-separation. For a definition of d-separation, see Neapolitan [12].

There are a great number of independence relationships in (C3) above, far more than are required to completely determine **P**. However, all are consistent with **P** and so we consider (C3) to be any 'sufficient set' of these relationships which will, together with (C1) and (C2), determine **P**.

Then $\mathbf{N} = < \mathbf{G}, \mathbf{P}, \mathbf{C} >$ is a causal network.

Once **G** is known the independence relationships of (C3) are completely determined, as are all the required conditional probabilities of (C2). Thus, in any particular practical situation, it is only the quantitative causal information in (C2) that can be unknown due to lack of knowledge concerning that practical system.

The algorithms devised by Pearl and by Lauritzen and Spiegelhalter for updating information in **N** explicitly (ie. for calculating probabilities of the type $P(e_i | \bigwedge_{j \varepsilon J} E_j^{x_j})$ given that each event $j \varepsilon J$ has been instantiated to some $E_j^{x_j}$) use only the conditional probability information (C2) in the constraints **C** above and generally run in time which is proportional to the size of this information, ie. in linear time.

The number of independence relationships (C3) belonging to a 'sufficient set' is always proportional to N, the number of states in the system, ie. exponential in size. If the Maximum Entropy model requires all, or an exponentially large subset of, these independence relationships to be included in an algorithm, then obtaining estimates for any missing causal information will require exponential time and thus be computationally infeasible for all but small problems. It is therefore essential to determine whether this is the case. If it is not, we can attempt to derive efficient algorithms for obtaining the Maximum Entropy estimates for the missing causal information.

Consider now a situation in which some of the conditional probability constraints in (C2) of **C** above that are implied by **G** have unknown values. The set of constraints consisting of (i) the sum to unity of (C1), (ii) those members of (C2) for which quantitative information is available and (iii) a 'sufficient set' of independence relationships in (C3) will not completely determine **P**. Of the infinite set of probability distributions which will satisfy these constraints, we wish to choose that which maximises entropy, ie. maximises the function

$$H = -\sum_{\mathbf{e}} P(\mathbf{e}) \log(P(\mathbf{e})) \tag{1}$$

subject to the set of constraints **C**. Applying the theory of Lagrange multipliers transforms this into the problem of maximising

$$F = -\sum_{\mathbf{e}} P(\mathbf{e}) \log(P(\mathbf{e})) - \sum_{j=0}^{M} \lambda_j C_j \tag{2}$$

where each C_j is a constraint from (C1), (C2) or (C3) in the form $C_j = 0$, λ_j is the Lagrange multiplier associated with the jth constraint and there is a total of $M+1$ constraints. The required probability distribution has the form

$$P(\mathbf{e}) = \prod_{j=0}^{M} e^{-\lambda_j \frac{\partial C_j}{\partial P(\mathbf{e})}} \tag{3}$$

and the authors of this paper are trying to develop solutions to this model which can be computed in linear time.

3. Causal Trees and Inverted Trees

The work has been started by investigating the potential of the Maximum Entropy approach in causal networks for which **G** is a tree. One type of tree, called a *causal tree*, is such that a node has no more than one parent but can have any number of children. For the two-valued event version it has been shown (Garside [1] and [2]) that if no independence relationships are included in the Maximum Entropy model of Equation (3), the resulting solution for $P(\mathbf{e})$ satisfies all independence relationships in a particular sufficient set and is thus the required solution. Linear time algorithms have been developed for finding the minimally prejudiced estimates of missing probability values (Garside and Rhodes [15] and [5]). Holmes and Rhodes [7] have extended this to cases with multivalued events. Each algorithm involves a single traversal of the tree.

A second type of network in which **G** is a tree is the *causal inverted tree*. Here a node may have any number of parents but only one child (see Figure 1 for a small example). It has been shown (Rhodes and Garside [16], Garside, Rhodes and Holmes [6] and Holmes, Rhodes and Garside [9]) that only independence between parents need be included in Equation (3) in order to obtain the probability distribution which satisfies all independence constraints. Linear time algorithms have been developed which involve iterative traversals of the tree and whose convergence to the Maximum Entropy solution has been proved (Garside [3] and [4]).

Holmes [8] has shown that the results from causal trees and causal inverted trees can be brought together to efficiently obtain estimates for missing information in causal polytrees, which are the most general form of tree-like causal networks.

In order to give a flavour of the theoretical work undertaken we include an example of an independence proof for a causal tree (Section 4) and as an example of the algorithms developed we give one for finding estimates of missing information in a causal inverted binary tree (Section 5).

4. An Independence Proof

To avoid over-complex notation in this example we shall restrict ourselves to causal multiway trees in which events have only two possible outcomes (true and false). E_i will denote that event i is true and $\bar{E}_i$ that it is false. The variable e_i can take either E_i or $\bar{E}_i$. A conjunction of variables, $\bigwedge_{i \varepsilon X} e_i$ will be denoted by $\mathbf{e}_X$.

Garside [1] has shown that a particular sufficient set of independence relationships (see below) are satisfied by the probability distribution obtained by solving the model implied by Equation (3) when *all* independence relationships are ignored. This set is included in a larger one which consists of the following members:-

For each node $a \varepsilon \mathbf{V}$:

(*I*1) $$P(\mathbf{e}_X | E_a \mathbf{e}_Y) = P(\mathbf{e}_X | E_a) \tag{4}$$

where $X \subseteq U$, U being the set of non-descendants of a and $Y \subseteq D$, D being the set of descendants of a. Note that here node a d-separates X and Y (by the "head to tail" criterion, see Neoplitan [12]).

(*I*2) $$P(\mathbf{e}_{X_1} \mathbf{e}_{X_2} .. \mathbf{e}_{X_r} | E_a) = \prod_{i=1}^{r} P(\mathbf{e}_{X_i} | E_a) \tag{5}$$

where $X_i \subseteq B_{i,}$ $i = 1..r$, the B_i being sets of vertices in any selection of subtrees with children of a as the roots and such that $r > 1$. Here node a d-separates any two disjoint collections of the X_i (by the "tail to tail" criterion, see Neapolitan [12]) and so the relationship in Equation (5) expresses independence between subsets of vertices in different collections of subtrees immediately below node a.

We will give a proof of the relation in Equation (4) here which is an extension of that given by Garside [2]. Equation (5) can be proved in a similar fashion.

In this case M in Equation (3) is simply the number of required conditional probability values in (C2). In a causal tree, the conditional probabilities required on each edge $< a, b >$ are

$$P(E_b | E_a) = \beta \text{ and } P(E_b | \bar{E}_a) = \bar{\beta} \tag{6}$$

The only other value needed for (C2) is that of $P(E_s)$ where s is the root of the tree. Garside and Rhodes [5] have shown that, when all independence relationships are ignored, Equation (3) reduces to

$$P(\mathbf{e}) = \prod_{j=0}^{M} e^{-\lambda_j \sigma_j(\mathbf{e})} \tag{7}$$

where $\sigma_j(\mathbf{e})$ is a constant which is β, $1-\beta$, $\bar{\beta}$ or $1-\bar{\beta}$ depending on whether $\mathbf{e}$ contains $E_b E_a$, $\bar{E}_b E_a$, $E_b \bar{E}_a$ or $\bar{E}_b \bar{E}_a$ respectively when the constraint in Equation (6) is the jth constraint. The 'sum to unity', ie. (C1), is considered to be the zeroth constraint and for this $\sigma_0(\mathbf{e}) = 1$.

Let $\mu(E_b | E_a) = e^{-\lambda_j(1-\beta)}$ and $\mu(\bar{E}_b | E_a) = e^{-\lambda_j(-\beta)}$ with $\mu(E_b | \bar{E}_a)$ and $\mu(\bar{E}_b | \bar{E}_a)$ similarly defined. Let $U' = U - X$, $D' = D - Y$ and let $\mathbf{e}_X$ be a particular assignment to the outcomes of the events in X. Denote the parent of node i by $\hat{\imath}$. Then for any state $\mathbf{e} = \mathbf{e}_X \mathbf{e}_{U'} E_a \mathbf{e}_Y \mathbf{e}_{D'}$ of the system, Equation (7) becomes

$$P(\mathbf{e}_X \mathbf{e}_{U'} E_a \mathbf{e}_Y \mathbf{e}_{D'}) = \mu_0 \left\{ \prod_{i \varepsilon U} \mu(e_i | e_{\hat{\imath}}) \right\}_{\mathbf{e}_X} \{\mu(E_a | e_{\hat{a}}\}_{e_{\hat{a}}} \left\{ \prod_{j \varepsilon D} \mu(e_j | e_{\hat{\jmath}}) \right\}_{E_a, \mathbf{e}_Y} \tag{8}$$

where μ_0 denotes $e^{-\lambda_0}$ and the subscripts outside the curly brackets remind us that, where applicable, any event contained within such brackets takes the value indicated in the subscript. Summing over all possible $\mathbf{e}_{U'}$, $\mathbf{e}_{D'}$ gives

$$P(\mathbf{e}_X E_a \mathbf{e}_Y) = \sum_{\mathbf{e}_{U'},\mathbf{e}_{D'}} P(\mathbf{e}_X \mathbf{e}_{U'} E_a \mathbf{e}_Y \mathbf{e}_{D'}) \tag{9}$$

$$= \mu_0 \sum_{\mathbf{e}_{U'}} \left[\left\{ \prod_{i\varepsilon U} \mu(e_i|e_{\hat{i}}) \right\}_{\mathbf{e}_X} \{\mu(E_a|e_{\hat{a}})\}_{e_{\hat{a}}} \right] \sum_{\mathbf{e}_{D'}} \left[\left\{ \prod_{j\varepsilon D} \mu(e_j|e_{\hat{j}}) \right\}_{E_a,\mathbf{e}_Y} \right]$$

This decomposition into two separate summations is crucial in being able to prove the result, as will be seen.

Now consider another particular assignment, $\mathbf{e}'_X$, to the outcomes of the events in X. An expression similar to Equation (9) can be obtained in which $\mathbf{e}_Y$ is identical to that in Equation (9). Dividing one into the other leads to

$$\frac{P(\mathbf{e}_X E_a \mathbf{e}_Y)}{P(\mathbf{e}'_X E_a \mathbf{e}_Y)} = \frac{\sum_{\mathbf{e}_{U'}} \left[\left\{ \prod_{i\varepsilon U} \mu(e_i|e_{\hat{i}}) \right\}_{\mathbf{e}_X} \{\mu(E_a|e_{\hat{a}})\}_{e_{\hat{a}}} \right]}{\sum_{\mathbf{e}_{U'}} \left[\left\{ \prod_{i\varepsilon U} \mu(e_i|e_{\hat{i}}) \right\}_{\mathbf{e}'_X} \{\mu(E_a|e_{\hat{a}})\}_{e_{\hat{a}}} \right]} \tag{10}$$

since the sums over $\mathbf{e}_{D'}$ cancel. Equation (10) is true for all $\mathbf{e}_Y$ and the right hand side is independent of $\mathbf{e}_Y$. Thus

$$\frac{P(\mathbf{e}_X E_a)}{P(\mathbf{e}'_X E_a)} = \frac{\sum_{\mathbf{e}_Y} P(\mathbf{e}_X E_a \mathbf{e}_Y)}{\sum_{\mathbf{e}_Y} P(\mathbf{e}'_X E_a \mathbf{e}_Y)} = \frac{P(\mathbf{e}_X E_a \mathbf{e}_Y)}{P(\mathbf{e}'_X E_a \mathbf{e}_Y)} \tag{11}$$

Rearranging Equation (11) to

$$\frac{P(\mathbf{e}'_X E_a \mathbf{e}_Y)}{P(\mathbf{e}_X E_a \mathbf{e}_Y)} P(\mathbf{e}_X E_a) = P(\mathbf{e}'_X E_a) \tag{12}$$

and summing both sides over all $\mathbf{e}'_X$ gives

$$\frac{P(E_a \mathbf{e}_Y)}{P(\mathbf{e}_X E_a \mathbf{e}_Y)} P(\mathbf{e}_X E_a) = P(E_a) \tag{13}$$

which leads to Equation (4).

5. An Algorithmic Example

For this example we turn to causal inverted binary trees. Rhodes and Garside [16] have shown that, in addition to the constraints (C1) and C2), the Maximum Entropy model requires only independence between parents of each node $w\varepsilon\mathbf{V}$, q and r say, to be explicitly stated. In this case q and r are d-separated by the "head to head" criterion described by Neapolitan [12]. The number of such independence relationships is directly proportional to the number of nodes in the tree. By considering algebraically the ratios of carefully chosen pairs of state probabilities, it is possible to derive estimates for the Lagrange multipliers for the conditional probability constraints with unknown values and hence to estimate these unknown values. The constraints concerning w, q and r are

$$P(E_w|E_qE_r) = \beta_{wqr}, P(E_w|E_q\bar{E}_r) = \beta_{wq\bar{r}}, \tag{14}$$

$$P(E_w|\bar{E}_qE_r) = \beta_{w\bar{q}r}, P(E_w|\bar{E}_q\bar{E}_r) = \beta_{w\bar{q}\bar{r}}$$

with associated Lagrange multipliers λ_{wqr}, $\lambda_{wq\bar{r}}$, $\lambda_{w\bar{q}r}$ and $\lambda_{w\bar{q}\bar{r}}$. The independence constraint involving q and r is

$$P(E_qE_r) = P(E_q)P(E_r) \tag{15}$$

Suppose β_{wqr} is not known. Its Maximum Entropy estimate is shown to be (Rhodes and Garside [16])

$$_{mp}\beta_{wqr} = \frac{\left(\frac{B_{y\bar{w}x}}{B_{ywx}}\right)^{-\alpha_x}\left(\frac{B_{yw\bar{x}}}{B_{y\bar{w}\bar{x}}}\right)^{1-\alpha_x}}{\left\{1+\left(\frac{B_{y\bar{w}x}}{B_{ywx}}\right)^{-\alpha_x}\left(\frac{B_{yw\bar{x}}}{B_{y\bar{w}\bar{x}}}\right)^{1-\alpha_x}\right\}} \tag{16}$$

where y and x are the child and co-parent of w respectively, $\alpha_x = P(E_x)$, $B_{ywx} = e^{-\lambda_{ywx}(1-\beta_{ywx})}/\beta_{ywx}$ with $B_{yw\bar{x}}$, $B_{y\bar{w}x}$ and $B_{y\bar{w}\bar{x}}$ similarly defined. This indicates that $_{mp}\beta_{ywx}$ can be found using only local information and a tree traversal will find all estimates.

However, α_x may depend on other estimates and so an iterative process consisting of several tree traversals is necessary to obtain the correct estimates. Garside [3] has shown that the objective function of Equation (2) for this case has a unique maximum and that the algorithm described in Rhodes and Garside [16] converges to this maximum.

Consider the small five-node example of Figure 1 in which the missing values are indicated by " ? ". Let α' and β' denote approximations to the minimally prejudiced estimates $_{mp}\alpha$ and $_{mp}\beta$ when α and β are not known. The algorithm consists of three phases: initialisation, propagation and iterative tree traversal. Propagation obtains initial estimates, α'_i, for $P(E_i)$ where i is a node with parents (see Equation 17). Tree traversal involves passing a Φ-message from child to parent and then updating values of α', β', λ and B when proceeding forwards and updating values of α' for vertices with parents when backtracking. When applied to the tree in Figure 1 the algorithm proceeds as follows:

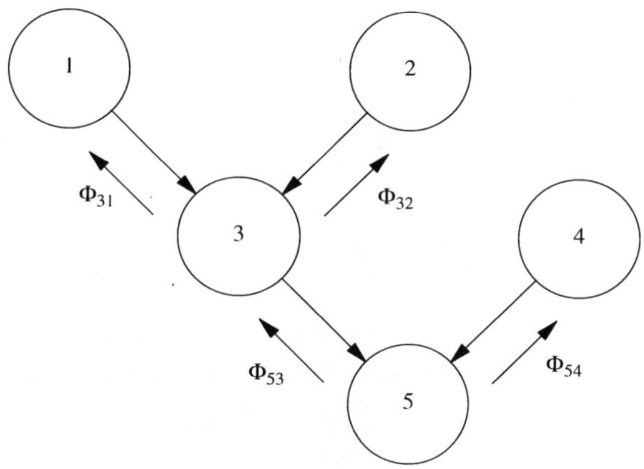

$P(E_1) = \alpha_1$

$P(E_2) = ?$	$P(E_4) = ?$
$P(E_3 \mid E_1 E_2) = \beta_{312}$	$P(E_5 \mid E_3 E_4) = \beta_{534}$
$P(E_3 \mid E_1 \bar{E}_2) = ?$	$P(E_5 \mid E_3 \bar{E}_4) = \beta_{53\bar{4}}$
$P(E_3 \mid \bar{E}_1 E_2) = ?$	$P(E_5 \mid \bar{E}_3 E_4) = \beta_{5\bar{3}4}$
$P(E_3 \mid \bar{E}_1 \bar{E}_2) = \beta_{3\bar{1}\bar{2}}$	$P(E_5 \mid \bar{E}_3 \bar{E}_4) = ?$

Figure 1: A simple causal inverted tree

(**A1**) {*Initialisation*}

$$\alpha'_2 = \alpha'_4 = 0.5; \quad \beta'_{31\bar{2}} = \beta'_{3\bar{1}2} = 0.5; \quad {}_{mp}\beta_{5\bar{3}\bar{4}} = 0.5; \quad e^{-\lambda_{5\bar{3}\bar{4}}} = 1; \quad B_{5\bar{3}\bar{4}} = 2;$$

$$e^{-\lambda_{5ij}} = \beta_{5ij}/(1-\beta_{5ij}); \quad B_{5ij} = e^{-\lambda_{5ij}(1-\beta_{5ij})}/\beta_{5ij} \quad \text{for } ij = 34, 3\bar{4}, \bar{3}4;$$

Note: The estimate of 0.5 for ${}_{mp}\beta_{5\bar{3}\bar{4}}$ is correct and all other values involving node 5 will never alter.

(**A2**) {*Propagation*}

$$\alpha'_3 = \alpha_1\alpha'_2\beta_{312} + \alpha_1(1-\alpha'_2)\beta'_{31\bar{2}} + (1-\alpha_1)\alpha'_2\beta'_{3\bar{1}2} + (1-\alpha_1)(1-\alpha'_2)\beta_{3\bar{1}\bar{2}} \quad (17)$$

Note: α_5 is never used so α'_5 need not be calculated.

(**A3**) {*Tree Traversal*}

(**A3. 1**) {*Node* 5}

A Φ_{53}-message is passed up to node 3 as $\Phi_{53} = \left(\frac{B_{5\bar{3}4}}{B_{534}}\right)^{-\alpha'_4}\left(\frac{B_{53\bar{4}}}{B_{5\bar{3}\bar{4}}}\right)^{1-\alpha'_4}$

(**A3.2**) $\{Node\ 3\}$

Calculate approximations

$$\beta'_{31\bar{2}} = \beta'_{3\bar{1}2} = \Phi_{53}/(1+\Phi_{53}); \quad B_{31\bar{2}} = B_{3\bar{1}2} = (1+\Phi_{53})/\Phi_{53};$$

Calculate

$$e^{-\lambda_{3ij}} = \Phi_{53}\beta_{3ij}/(1-\beta_{3ij}) \quad \text{and then} \quad B_{3ij} = e^{-\lambda_{3ij}(1-\beta_{3ij})}/\beta_{3ij} \quad \text{for } ij = 12, \bar{1}\bar{2};$$

Since α_1 at node 1 is known, there is no updating to be done. Consequently passing a Φ_{31}-message would be spurious. However, α_2 is missing at node 2, so a Φ_{32}-message is passed up to node 2 as $\Phi_{32} = \left(\frac{B_{31\bar{2}}}{B_{312}}\right)^{-\alpha_1}\left(\frac{B_{3\bar{1}2}}{B_{3\bar{1}\bar{2}}}\right)^{1-\alpha_1}$;

(**A3.3**) $\{Node\ 2\}$

Calculate $\alpha'_2 = \Phi_{32}/(1+\Phi_{32});$

(**A3.4**) $\{Backtrack\ to\ node\ 3\}$

Calculate α'_3 using Equation (17);

(**A3.5**) $\{Backtrack\ to\ node\ 5\}$

Φ_{54}-message is passed up to node 4 as $\Phi_{54} = \left(\frac{B_{53\bar{4}}}{B_{534}}\right)^{-\alpha'_3}\left(\frac{B_{5\bar{3}4}}{B_{5\bar{3}\bar{4}}}\right)^{1-\alpha'_3}$;

(**A3.6**) $\{Node\ 4\}$

Calculate $\alpha'_4 = \Phi_{54}/(1+\Phi_{54});$

Repeat steps (A3.1) to (A3.6) until the desired accuracy in the estimates for ${}_{mp}\alpha$ and ${}_{mp}\beta$ is achieved.

6. Conclusions and Further Work

Work completed by the authors has shown that correct and efficient algorithms exist for calculating minimally prejudiced estimates for missing conditional probabilities in all forms of tree-like causal networks.

This efficiency is achieved because the independence relationships implied by "tail to tail" and "head to tail" d-separation can be excluded from the Maximum Entropy model. Those implied by "head to head" d-separation must be included but this does not increase the order of the model.

The similaries found in both the analysis and the algorithms for causal trees and causal inverted trees give rise to optimism that the general causal network can be successfully completed using similar techniques.

The authors are currently investigating the general causal network defined in Section 2 with a view to providing an efficient algorithm which can be incorporated into a 'front end' to be used in conjunction with existing methods of updating information in causal networks when some of the required conditional probability values are not known.

7. References

[1] G. R. Garside. Independence relationships in causal multiway trees. *Internal Research Report*, RS-96/CS/RUU/04, Dept of Computing, Univ. of Bradford, UK, 1996.

[2] G. R. Garside. Conditional independence in causal multiway trees. *Internal Research Report*, RS-96/CS/RUU/05, Dept of Computing, Univ. of Bradford, UK, 1996.

[3] G. R. Garside. Some results supporting the use of maximum entropy in causal inverted binary trees. *Internal Research Report*, RS- 96/CS/RUU/03, Dept of Computing, Univ. of Bradford, UK, 1996.

[4] G. R. Garside. Some results supporting the use of maximum entropy in causal inverted multiway trees. *Internal Research Report*, RS-98/CS/RUU/01, Department of Computing, Univ. of Bradford, UK, 1998.

[5] G. R. Garside and P. C. Rhodes. Computing marginal probabilities in causal multiway trees given incomplete information. *Knowledge – Based Systems*, 9, pp 315-327, 1996.

[6] G. R. Garside, P. C. Rhodes and D. E. Holmes. The efficient estimation of missing information in causal inverted multiway trees. To be published in *Knowledge – Based Systems*.

[7] D. E. Holmes and P. C. Rhodes. Reasoning with incomplete information in a multivalued multiway causal tree using the maximum entropy formalism. *Intern. J. Intel. Syst.* , 13(9), pp 841-858, Sept 1998.

[8] D. E. Holmes. Efficient estimation of missing information in multivalued singly connected networks using maximum entropy. Presented at the MAX-ENT '98 Conference, Munich, July 1998.

[9] D. E. Holmes, P. C. Rhodes and G. R. Garside. Efficient computation of marginal probabilities in multivalued causal inverted multiway trees given incomplete information. *Intern. J. Intel. Syst.* , 14(6), pp 535-558, June 1999.

[10] S. L. Lauritzen and D. J. Spiegelhalter. Local computations with probabilities on graphical structures and their applications to expert systems. *J. Roy. Statist. Soc. Ser. B*, 50(2), pp 157-224, 1988.

[11] I. Maung and J. B. Paris. A note on the infeasibility of some inference processes. *Intern. J. Intel. Syst.*, 5, pp 595-603, 1990.

[12] R. E. Neapolitan. Probabilistic reasoning in expert systems: theory and algorithms, Chapter 6, Wiley, New York, 1990.

[13] J. Pearl. Probabilistic reasoning in intelligent systems: networks of plausible inference, Morgan-Kaufmann, San Mateo, California, 1988.

[14] P. C. Rhodes and G. R. Garside. The use of maximum entropy as a methodology for probabilistic reasoning. *Knowledge – Based Systems*, 8(5), pp 249-258, 1995.

[15] P. C. Rhodes and G. R. Garside. Using maximum entropy to compute marginal probabilities in a causal binary tree need not take exponential time. In *Proceedings of the European Conference on Symbolic and Quantitative Approaches to Reasoning and Uncertainty,* pp 352-363, Springer Lecture Notes in Computer Science, Berlin, 1995.

[16] P. C. Rhodes and G. R. Garside. Computing marginal probabilities in causal inverted binary trees given incomplete information. *Knowledge – Based Systems*, 10, pp 213-224, 1998.

[17] T. Verma and J. Pearl. Causal networks: semantics and expressiveness. In *Proceedings of the Fourth AAAI Workshop on Uncertainty in AI,* Univ. of Minnesota, Minneapolis, Minnesota, 1988.

Why leximin FCSPs are so hard for local search

João Moura Pires, Fernando Moura Pires, Rita Almeida Ribeiro
Departamento de Informática - FCT
Universidade Nova de Lisboa
2825 Monte Caparica, Portugal
{jmp, fmp, rr}@di.fct.unl.pt

Abstract: In this paper we investigate why solving leximin fuzzy constraint satisfaction problems (FCSP) with non-enumerative algorithms, such as hill-climbing, simulated annealing and genetic algorithms, provide disappointing results. Specifically, we analyse the structure and properties of the leximin FCSPs and its influence on the search strategy of non-enumerative algorithms.

1. Introduction

This paper suggests that the use of non-enumerative optimisation algorithms, without including further information to guide the search, is not a good approach to solve leximin-optimal Fuzzy constraint satisfaction problems (FCSP). Due to the nature and shape of the leximin it is not easy to find a good solution without adding more information so as to locate areas containing "good" solutions and in order to guide the search

Fuzzy constraint satisfaction problems are an extension of constraint satisfaction problems (CSP). The crisp constraints are replaced by fuzzy constraints [1] to express the gradual violation of elastic constraints. In a FCSP a constraint is satisfied to a degree (rather than just satisfied or not satisfied), hence the acceptability of a potential solution also becomes a gradual notion. FCSPs are applied in many different areas such as structural design [16] and scheduling problems [9]

Solving a FCSP amounts, generally, to find an instantiation for its variables that maximizes the satisfaction level of the least satisfied constraint. Indeed, the approach aggregates the constraints by means of the min operator. It has been shown that due to the idempotence of the min operation, most CSP computation techniques easily extend to the fuzzy setting [3], [4]. Since min-optimal solutions to a FCSP may be numerous, two refinements of the ranking of solutions have been proposed, namely those referred to as the **discrimin** and **leximin** orderings [5]. These refinements do not only take into account the least satisfied constraint, but also compare other satisfaction levels. In this paper, we focus on the **leximin FCSP** because a leximin-optimal solution is also a discrimin-optimal solution.

Non-enumerative algorithms can be classified into three main categories: population-based, multi-point and single-point. The search process of non-enumerative algorithms requires two *à priori* definitions: selection of the number of points to be used simultaneously, and selection of the starting points. Some algorithms use single starting points, as for instance Hill Climbing (HC), Tabu Search (TS) [14][15] and Simulated Annealing (SA) [2]. Other algorithms are based in a population of points, as for instance Genetic Algorithms (GA) [13]. Further, single-point algorithms can also be used as multi-run versions. In these multi-run versions, the starting points

may be randomly chosen or constructed with heuristics, when available. The perspective here is not to discuss the algorithms, per se, but to address their suitability to solve leximin FCSP.
The use of non-enumerative algorithms to solve CSP has proven to be rather successful [12]. Hence, the use of non-enumerative optimisation algorithms to solve FCSP should also be a valuable tool (some attempts along these lines already exist in the literature [20]).
The paper is organized as follows. Section 2 provides the background of FCSP's. Section 3 discusses the structure and properties of the leximin FCSP. Section 4 suggests some hints on how to improve the search process of non-enumerative algorithms in order to solve leximin FCSP. Section 5 presents future research topics.

2. Background on FCSP's

Crisp constraint-satisfaction-based models offer a general framework for interpretation design and decision problems [20], [18]. A constraint satisfaction problem is defined by a set of variables on finite domains and a set of constraints related to these variables. A CSP solution is an instantiation of the problem variables that satisfy all the constraints. When such solution exist the CSP it is said to be consistent, otherwise it is called inconsistent.
When faced with CSP's that have too many equally satisfying solutions, these problems can be solved with an extension of the CSP, called **fuzzy constraint satisfaction problems** [3]. The extension is achieved by replacing crisp constraints with fuzzy constraints [1], where the idea of satisfying a constraint is replaced by a satisfaction level (degree) for the constraints.
Formally, a FCSP is defined by a set of decision variables $\boldsymbol{X} = \{X_1, \ldots, X_N\}$, a set of domains $\boldsymbol{D} = \{D_1, \ldots, D_N\}$ where D_i is the domain of X_i, and is supposed to be finite (with cardinality $|D_i| = d_i$) and a set of fuzzy constraints $\boldsymbol{C} = \{C_1, \ldots, C_K\}$ where C_k is a fuzzy relation defined over the Cartesian product of the domains of the variables included in C_k. Thus, a membership value is associated to each tuple of values of the variables related by C_k. The membership degree express preferences among solutions by ranking the instantiations which are more or less acceptable with respect to the satisfaction of the flexible constraint C_k. In this paper we are dealing with FCSP's where no natural order exists for the variable domains.
In the sequel, wc consider fuzzy sets defined by a finite linearly-ordered valuation set, where only the ordering between grades is meaningful as, for instance {0, 1, 2, 3, 4, 5, 6, 7, 8, 9, 10}. With such a valuation set, fuzzy-set intersection, union and complementation can only be defined by min, max and the order-reversing operation of the valuation set. The valuation set is denoted $\boldsymbol{L}$, with $L + 1$ elements, where 0 and L denote the bottom and top elements, respectively
A solution to a FCSP is denoted by $\boldsymbol{x}$ and is a vector of values in $\boldsymbol{X} = D_1 \text{ x} \ldots \text{ x } D_N$. The level of satisfaction for the constraints, denoted $Sat(\boldsymbol{x})$, is defined, as proposed by Bellman and Zadeh [1], as follows:

$$Sat(\boldsymbol{x}) = \min_k \mu_{C_k}(\boldsymbol{x}), \tag{1}$$

and the optimal solution, $\boldsymbol{x}^*$, so called "min optimal" is:

$$Sat(\boldsymbol{x}^*) = \max_x \min_k \mu_{C_k}(\boldsymbol{x}). \quad (2)$$

In a fuzzy framework, solving a FCSP problem amounts to find at least one solution that is maximal for $>_{min}$. Hence, finding a solution for a FCSP is an optimization problem.

The satisfaction level of a min-optimal solution for a FCSP is said to be:

- **inconsistent**, if it does not satisfy at least one constraint.
- **fully consistent,** if it completely satisfies all constraints.
- **partially consistent,** if there is at least one constraint - not fully satisfied - and the satisfaction levels of all constraints are positive.

For the min-based FCSP's, the solutions can be discriminated by (at most) L levels of consistency. In each equivalence class, all solutions share the same satisfaction level, which is the one of the least satisfied constraint(s). Two solutions in the same equivalence class are not discriminated, even if they could be distinguished by considering other levels of satisfaction for the remaining constraints.

In addition, it is well known that CSP problems are NP-complete [17]. The main tools for solving CSP's are backtracking-based search algorithms and constraint-propagation techniques. Finding a min-optimal solution is a NP-hard problem, which can be solved using a branch and bound-based algorithm, [3], [4]. The use of the min-operator allows for a direct generalization to the FCSP of the constraint propagation algorithms used in the classical CSP framework (for example, the AC3 by Mackworth [17]). The levels of satisfaction are propagated by extensions of existing algorithms (see, for example, [3], [4]). This is essentially due to the idempotence of the min-operator.

2.1. Refinements of the min-ordering

There are two main refinements for the min- ordering in a FCSP framework: the **discrimin,** proposed by Fargier *et al.* [10], and the leximin (see Moulin, [19]). A detailed study of these refinements, with different equivalent formulations, can be found in [5],

In general, for each $\boldsymbol{x}$ in $\boldsymbol{X}$ we can define a fuzzy set over the set of constraints $\boldsymbol{C}$ which represents the constraints satisfied by $\boldsymbol{x}$. Here, such a fuzzy set is denoted by $\mathcal{S}(\boldsymbol{x})$, defined as $\{C_k / \mu_{C_k}(\boldsymbol{x})\}$.

Let $\boldsymbol{x}$ and $\boldsymbol{y}$ be two solutions and let $\mathcal{S}(\boldsymbol{x})$ and $\mathcal{S}(\boldsymbol{y})$ be the corresponding fuzzy sets, respectively. With the **discrimin** ordering, we compare the least satisfied discriminating constraint, i.e., we look for the lowest-satisfied constraint among the constraints that are not equally satisfied. Let us denote by $\Delta(\boldsymbol{x}, \boldsymbol{y})$, the subset of constraints that are not equally satisfied, by $\boldsymbol{x}$ and $\boldsymbol{y}$, i.e., the constraints C_k for which $\mu_{C_k}(\boldsymbol{x}) \neq \mu_{C_k}(\boldsymbol{y})$. Formally $\boldsymbol{x} >_{\text{discrimin}} \boldsymbol{y}$ iff:

$$\min_{C_k \in \Delta(\boldsymbol{u},\boldsymbol{v})} \mu_{C_k}(\boldsymbol{x}) > \min_{C_k \in \Delta(\boldsymbol{u},\boldsymbol{v})} \mu_{C_k}(\boldsymbol{y}) \quad (3)$$

Whenever the least satisfied discriminating constraints are equally satisfied by $\boldsymbol{x}$ and $\boldsymbol{y}$, neither $\boldsymbol{x} >_{\text{discrimin}} \boldsymbol{y}$ nor $\boldsymbol{x} <_{\text{discrimin}} \boldsymbol{y}$ and $\boldsymbol{x}$ and $\boldsymbol{y}$ are said to be *indifferent.*

The **leximin** ordering refines the discrimin ordering. A solution $\boldsymbol{x}$ is preferred to a solution $\boldsymbol{y}$, in a *leximin* order, if there is a threshold α such that for all $\beta < \alpha$, the

number of constraints satisfied by $\boldsymbol{x}$ (at level at least β) is equal to the number of constraints satisfied by $\boldsymbol{y}$, and it satisfies more constraints than $\boldsymbol{y}$ at level α. This is equivalent to comparing the cardinalities at increasing level cuts.
Let $\boldsymbol{u}(\boldsymbol{x})$ denote the ranking vector corresponding to $\mathcal{S}(\boldsymbol{x})$ where the elements of $\boldsymbol{u}(\boldsymbol{x})$ are in an increasing order, i.e., in such way that $u(\boldsymbol{x})_k < u(\boldsymbol{x})_{k+1}$ for all k from 1 to K - 1. Then, formally, $\boldsymbol{x} >_{\text{leximin}} \boldsymbol{y}$ iff $\exists$ j < K , such that $\forall\ i < j,\ u(\boldsymbol{x})_i = u(\boldsymbol{y})_j$ and $u(\boldsymbol{x})_j > u(\boldsymbol{y})_j$. and furthermore, $\boldsymbol{x} =_{\text{leximin}} \boldsymbol{y}$ iff $\boldsymbol{u}(\boldsymbol{x}) = \boldsymbol{u}(\boldsymbol{y})$. Fargier, [8], has shown that a leximin optimal solution is a solution that violates the smallest number of fuzzy constraints, in the sense of fuzzy cardinality.
These different orderings (min, discrimin and leximin) correspond to an increasing refinement. Non-distinguishable solutions for one order may be distinguished by the next one.
Dubois *et al* [7], discussed how to compute discrimin-optimal and leximin-optimal solutions for special classes of FCSP's, and they present algorithms for some specific problems such as, for instance, scheduling problems with flexible constraints, as well as flexible assignment problems. The underlying idea is to find a min-optimal solution and then, by saturating the least satisfied constraint(s), to generate a new sub-problem, whose min-optimal solutions has been improved (in the sense of discrimin or leximin) with respect to the first solution found. This process is repeated until no more sub-problems can be generated; and a leximin or discrimin optimal solution is reached. However, for a general FCSP the generation of the sub-problems requires an NP-complete algorithm.
In the next section we will discuss the structure and properties of leximin FCSP's. Since, a *leximin* optimal solution is also a *discrimin* optimal one, the *discrimin* solution is not further discussed in this paper

3. Leximin Structure and Properties

Let $\mathcal{L}_{K,L}$ be the set of lexi-vectors for K constraints and a satisfaction scale with L + 1 levels, as defined in the previous section. In the following we show how to calculate the cardinality of $\mathcal{L}_{K,L}$ and discuss various mappings from $\mathcal{L}_{K,L}$ to [0, 1].

3.1. $\mathcal{L}_{K,L}$ Cardinality

For a problem with K constraints and by using a satisfaction scale with L + 1 degrees, the number of possible different leximin vectors grow exponentially with both K and L. Let *lexi-levels*(K, L) be a function that calculates the cardinality $|\mathcal{L}_{K,L}|$, defined by (see appendix for details):

$$lexi-levels(K,L) = \begin{cases} 1 & L = 0 \\ L+1 & K = 1 \\ \sum_{i=0}^{L} lexi-levels(K-1, L-i) & \end{cases}$$

Note that, for implementation purposes, the above can be efficiently calculated by the following expression *lexi-levels*(K, L) = *lexi-levels*(K - 1, L) + *lexi-levels*(K, L - 1) (see appendix).

To find a min-optimal solution of a FCSP corresponds to an optimization problem with an optimization function that can have $L + 1$ different values. The corresponding leximin-optimal problem may use a very large number of different values. Figure 1, shows how many lexi-vectors are needed for a problem characterized by $L = 4$ (with a satisfaction scale of $\{0, 1, 2, 3, 4\}$) and for a number of constraints varying from 2 to 10.

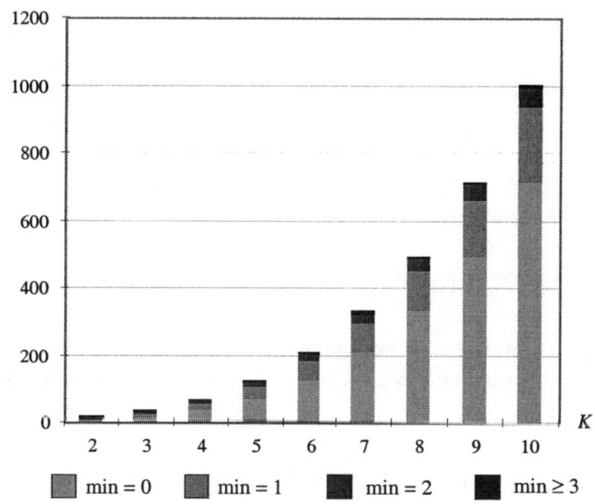

Figure 1. Lexi-vectors for L = 4 and K in {1, ..., 10}.

The leximin order is a refinement of the min order. Figure 1 shows how each min-level is refined in terms of how many lexi-vectors correspond to each min-level. Specifically, the number of lexi-vectors indicating inconsistency (when at least one of the constraints is not satisfied) is *lexi-level*$(K - 1, L)$.
Even when leximin ordering is a total order, it is important to note that each lexi-vector corresponds to a set of possible satisfaction levels on the constraints, i.e., all the possible permutations of the satisfaction levels used in that lexi-vector. The leximin is also a refinement of discrimin-order and some discrimin incomparable solutions can be discriminated by the leximin. Let's denote by $Inc_{\text{ordering}}(\mathcal{S})$ the set of fuzzy sets that are incomparable to or equal to $\mathcal{S}$ by one specific ordering. For instance, for $L = 2$ and $K = 3$, a solution that fully satisfies constraint C_2, and does not satisfies C_1 and C_3, is the fuzzy set $\mathcal{S} = \{C_1/0, C_2/2, C_3/0\}$. The discrimin considers this solution incomparable with the following, $Inc_{\text{discrimin}}((0\ 2\ 0)) = \{(0\ 0\ 1), (0\ 0\ 2), (1\ 0\ 0), (1\ 0\ 1), (1\ 0\ 2), (2\ 0\ 0), (2\ 0\ 1)\ (2\ 0\ 2)\}$. With the leximin we are able to discriminate (0 2 0) from all the cases in $Inc_{\text{discrimin}}$, except (0 0 2) and (2 0 0).

3.2 Optimisation Function

The choice of the mapping to be used in the optimization function is relevant for those algorithms that use the reward value, i.e., the difference in the objective function between a point and a neighbor. This includes the simulated-annealing (SA), tabu-search (TS), and genetic-algorithms (GA), when the later use roulette

wheel or integral selection for instance. In such choices, one important factor is the sensibility variation along the lexi-vectors.
We will consider any mapping T: $\mathcal{L}_{K,L} \rightarrow [0, 1]$ such that:

- $T((0 \ldots 0)) = 0$;
- $T((L \ldots L)) = 1$;
- T is strictly increasing with respect to the leximin order.

Let $\boldsymbol{u}$ denote a lexi-vector and $Pos(\boldsymbol{u})$ is its ranking in the leximin-ordering, such that $Pos((0 \ldots 0)) = 1$ and $Pos((L \ldots L)) = |\mathcal{L}_{K,L}|$ (see appendix for details). In this paper, we will consider four types of mappings: linear, logarithmic, OWA (ordered weighted average), and logarithmic-OWA. Figure 2 shows these mappings, for a problem with $K = 3$ and $L = 4$.
A linear mapping from the lexi-vectors, ranked by leximin ordering, to [0, 1], is denoted by T_{linear} and defined:

$$T_{\text{linear}}(\boldsymbol{u}) = (Pos(\boldsymbol{u}) - 1) / (|\mathcal{L}_{K,L}| - 1)$$

Note that with T_{linear} the distance between two consecutive lexi-vectors is always the same no matter which consecutive ones are considered. With the mapping denoted by $T_{\text{loglinear}}$ defined as:

$$T_{\text{loglinear}}(\boldsymbol{u}) = \log_{|\mathcal{L}_{K,L}|}(Pos(\boldsymbol{u})),$$

the distance between two consecutive lexi-vectors decreases towards the top lexi-vector, and therefore the scale sensitivity is greater at lower lexi-vectors (which represent more inconsistency)
The leximin can be expressed as an OWA [22], as shown by [6]:

$$OWA_{\lambda}(\boldsymbol{u}) = \sum_{i=1}^{K} u_i . \lambda^{K-i},$$

where λ is a parameter that should be greater than L in order to guarantee that this additive version ranks the lexi-vectors, as the leximin ordering do. Hence:

$$T_{\text{OWA}(\lambda)}(\boldsymbol{u}) = \text{OWA}_{\lambda}(\boldsymbol{u}) / \text{OWA}_{\lambda}((L \ldots L))$$

With T_{OWA} the greater distances occur at each modification of the min, i.e., when the lexi-vectors as $(\alpha - 1, \alpha, \ldots, \alpha)$ and $(\alpha, \ldots, \alpha)$ for $\alpha = 1$ to L. But this mapping shows a better sensibility on top lexi-vectors than on lower lexi-vectors.
Therefore, we can define $T_{\text{LogOWA}(\lambda)}$ as

$$T_{LogOWA(\lambda)}(\boldsymbol{u}) = \log_{OWA_{\lambda}((L,\ldots,L)+1)}(OWA_{\lambda}(\boldsymbol{u}) + 1),$$

(see also Figure 2.) which runs a better sensibility on lower lexi-vectors than the $\text{OWA}_{(\lambda)}$.

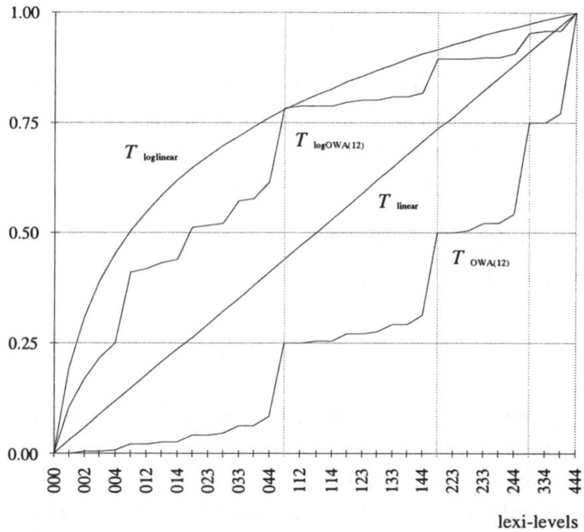

Figure 2. Examples of leximin optimisation functions for $K = 3$ and $L= 4$.

Figure 3 shows for $T_{\text{loglinear}}$, $T_{\text{OWA}(12)}$ and $T_{\text{LogOWA}(12)}$, for each lexi-vector the incremental change from the previous one. As expected, $\Delta T_{\text{loglinear}}$ continuously decreases; $\Delta T_{\text{LogOWA}(12)}$ and $\Delta T_{\text{OWA}(12)}$ show a peak at each min transition, but the former increase the peak amplitude as we go to the top lexi-vectors while the second decreases them. Furthermore, in the inconsistency region (min = 0), only $\Delta T_{\text{LogOWA}(12)}$ shows a good variation.

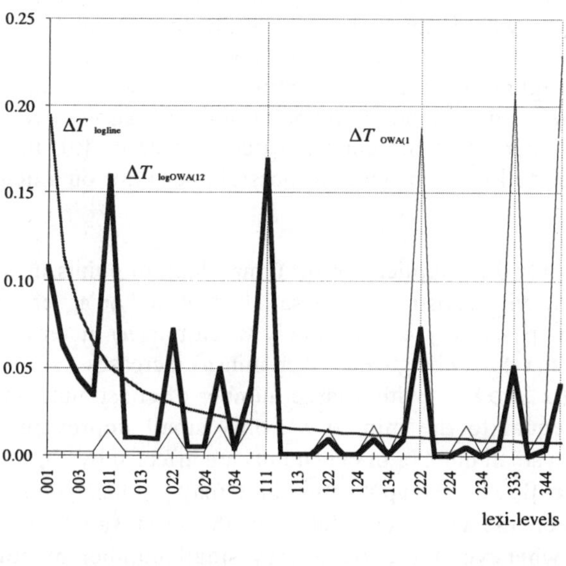

Figure 3. Sensibility examples of leximin optimisation functions for K = 3 and L= 4.

3.3. *T* on a Neighbourhood of *x*

The guidance of single point optimization algorithms is based on the variation of the value of the optimization function on the current point and a set of points that are accessible from the current point (it's neighbours). When this variation is "big" all over the solution space, this kind of algorithm faces more difficulty and can be compared to a random search search.
Consider an FCSP, *P*. The leximin version of *P* can be stated as the following optimization problem: find a $\boldsymbol{x}^* \in X$ such that

$$\boldsymbol{x}^* = \max_{x \in X} T(\boldsymbol{u}(\boldsymbol{x})),$$

where $\boldsymbol{u}: X \rightarrow \mathcal{L}_{K,L}$ encodes the FCSP (as defined above) and $T: \mathcal{L}_{K,L} \rightarrow [0, 1]$. We can say that $\boldsymbol{u}$ sets the *structural* aspects of the function to be optimized and *T* its *intensity* (without changing its structural aspects).
The intensity (*T*) is only relevant for the optimization algorithms whose search depends on the values of $T(\boldsymbol{u}(\boldsymbol{x})) - T(\boldsymbol{u}(\boldsymbol{x}'))$. But all the optimization algorithms will be influenced by the structural aspects.
We will show that leximin FCSP as formulated above has globally an "irregular shape".
Given a point $\boldsymbol{x}$ in the search space, the single-point algorithms consider a neighborhood of $\boldsymbol{x}$, denoted as $N_\Upsilon(\boldsymbol{x})$, as the set of points $\boldsymbol{x}'$ reachable from $\boldsymbol{x}$ by means of the operator Υ, which is a transformation on some components of $\boldsymbol{x}$. On of the most common used operators is changing the value of one component, i. e., $\Upsilon(x_1, \ldots, x_i, \ldots, x_N) = (x_1, \ldots, x_i', \ldots, x_N)$, where $x_i' \in D_i - \{x_i\}$.
At each application of operator Υ, at least one constraint is involved and, therefore, at least one constraint may becomes completely unsatisfied; which correspond to saying that no matter what is the lexi-vector of the current point of the search (in the consistency region), the quality of the solution may drop (in its neighbourhood) to the inconsistency region. In terms of the optimization function this means that it may exist "holes" in the neighborhood of any point in the consistency region. The drop, if exists, may be greater when the current value is near to 1.0. In general, we can identify at least the following patterns of possible behavior on a neighborhood of $\boldsymbol{x}$, where $\boldsymbol{u} = \boldsymbol{u}(\boldsymbol{x})$:

- when $\min(\boldsymbol{u}) > 0$ an application of Υ may lead to points in the inconsistency region, i. e., with constraints not satisfied at all, or at least with $\min(\boldsymbol{u}') < \min(\boldsymbol{u})$. This possibility is more likely when $\min(\boldsymbol{u})$ increases. The difference $T(\boldsymbol{u}(\boldsymbol{x})) - T(\boldsymbol{u}(\boldsymbol{x}))$ may be greater when $\min(\boldsymbol{u})$ increases
- when $\boldsymbol{u} = (\alpha \ldots \alpha)$ (or with a large number of constraints whose satisfaction degree is equal to the min of $\boldsymbol{u}$), only small improvements are allowed (supposing a small number of constraints are affected by Υ);
- when $\boldsymbol{u} = (\alpha\ \beta \ldots \beta)$, the application of Υ may produce good improvements (if Υ focused on the variables related by the least satisfied constraint); more generally, whenever there are a very small number of constraints whose satisfaction degrees are equal to min(u) the search of good improvements should be done by focusing Υ on the variables related by those constraints;

- a leximin optimal solution may be near (in terms of operator ϒ) to points with very small quality and in general "good" points can have neighbours with "poor" quality.

It should be noted that whenever the variable domains are linearly ordered and the fuzzy relations take that domain order into account, this local perturbation on the optimization function will be smoothed in realistic problems.
Let's consider an additive version of a FCSP P, denoted as P_Σ and stated as follows: find a $\boldsymbol{x}^* \in \boldsymbol{X}$ such that

$$\boldsymbol{x}^* = \max_{x \in X} \Sigma_{k=1,K}\ \mu_{C_k}(\boldsymbol{x}).$$

P_Σ is not equivalent to the min or leximin version of P, in the sense that the order of solution is not the same. Meanwhile, we refer to it only for comparison purposes in terms of optimization function defined in the same space. P_Σ does not have the local perturbation observed in the leximin version of P.

4. Influence on Optimisation Problems of the Leximin Shape

The main theoretical conclusion arrived in the previous sections is that the leximin optimization function, for FCSP's with non- ordered variable domains, usually displays very irregular "shapes" on the neighborhood of many points of the solution space. This property affects the quality of results obtained with non-enumerative algorithms (such as SA, HC, GA) when applied without further information to guide the search with special codification. Some preliminary experimental evidences are available, but are not explicitly presented in this paper, and they are as follows.
For a set of binary FCSP's, randomly generated with the parameters $N = 10$, $|D_i| = 10$ for $i = 1$ to N, K = 27 and L = 10) [21] the SA and GA fail to find good quality solutions. The same occurs with a multi-run version of HC. In both cases, the starting points used to run the problems were generated randomly.
Conversely, when the same problems were tested with starting points generated with many diferent heuristics on a multi-run HC, the results obtained were quite good [20].
Considering the leximin structural problems and the preliminary results obtained, we clearly see that further information is needed to enable non-enumerative algorithms to perform well. The main information that can be included in the algorithms to improve the search process is:

- use of problem information to generate good starting points [20] (or a starting population for GA);
- a dynamic selection of the operator ϒ by using problem information and the pattern quality of the current solution;
- choosing more suitable mappings, T for the optimisation function.

5. Future research

In this paper, we discussed the complex structure and properties of the leximin FCSP. Due to that complex structure, solving these problems with non-enumerative algorithms is not a suitable tool, without including further information to guide the search.

In order to fully support our claim we need further research on the topics:

- **Shape**: Study the variability on the leximin rank at the neighbourhood of a solution. For randomly chosen points calculate the average, standard deviation, percentiles etc. to extract information about that might be included in the optimisation function.
- **T influence**: Systematic study of the influence of the optimisation function upon the solution performance (quality, number of iterations, CPU time). This study should be done for SA, TS, and GA using the same set of benchmarks problems.

Other aspects that we also think worthwhile considering are:

- Testing the use of different optimisation functions at different stages of the search (depending on, for instance, the quality of current solution, pattern of $\boldsymbol{u}$ in the current solution, number of current iteration).
- Tuning of the algorithm control parameters depending on the pattern of $\boldsymbol{u}$ in the current solution. (see [11]).

6. References

[1] Bellman R.E, and L. A. Zadeh. (1970). "Decision-making in a fuzzy environment" *Management Science*, 17, 141-164.

[2] Connoly, D. (1992). "General Purpose Simulated Annealing",. *Journal of the Operational Research Society*, 43(5), 495-505.

[3] Dubois, D., H. Fargier, and H. Prade (1994) "Propagation and satisfaction of flexible constraints". In R. Yager and L. Zadeh (eds.) , *Fuzzy Sets, Neural Networks and Soft Computing*., Kluwer Academic Publ., Dordrecht, 266-187

[4] Dubois, D., Fargier, H. and H. Prade, (1996a) "Possibility Theory in Constraint Satisfaction Problems: Handling Priority. Preference and Uncertainty", *Applied Intelligence,* **6** pp. 287-307.

[5] Dubois, D., Fargier, H. and H. Prade, (1996b) "Refinements of the maximin approach to decision making in a fuzzy environment", *Fuzzy Sets and Systems*, Vol. 81, pp. 103-122.

[6] Dubois D., H. Fargier, and H. Prade (1996). "Ordered weighted operations, "discri-min" and leximin in multicriteria decision" *Soft Computing with Industrial Applications* (Proc. of the 2nd World Automation Congress ,WAC'96), Montpellier, France, May 27-30, 1996. (M. Jamshidi, M. Fathi, F. Pierrot, (eds.), TSI Press Series, Albuquerque, NM, 167-172.

[7] Dubois, D. and Fortemps, P. (1997). "Improved solutions to fuzzy constraint satisfaction problems", *Proc. of the 5th Europ. Congress on Intelligent Techniques and Soft Computing (EUFIT'97),* Aachen, Germany, 1997, pp. 967-969.

[8] Fargier, H. (1994). "Problèmes de satisfaction de constraintes flexibles: application à l'ordonnancement de production". Ph. D. Thesis., Université Paul Sabatier, Toulouse.

[9] Fargier, H. (1997). "Fuzzy scheduling: principles and experiments", in: Fuzzy Information Engineering: A Guided Tour of Applications (D. Dubois et al., eds.), Wiley, New York, 1997, pp. 655-668.

[10] Fargier, H., J. Lang, and T. Schiex (1993). "Selecting preferred solutions in fuzzy constraint satisfaction problems". *Proc. of the 1st Europ. Congress on Fuzzy and Intelligent Technologies (EUFIT'93)*, Aachen, Germany, Sept. 7-10, 1128-1134.

[11] Fortemps, P., Moura-Pires, J. and Prade, H. (1997). "Towards expressing heuristics with fuzzy logic", submited.

[12] Freuder, E. C., and Wallace, R. J. (1992). Partial constraint satisfaction. AI - 58, 21-70

[13] Goldberg, D. E. (1989). *Genetic Algorithms in Search, Optimization & Machine Learning*. Addison Wesley.

[14] Glover, F. (1989) "Tabu Search - Part 1", *ORSA Journal on Computing* 1(3), pp. 190-206.

[15] Glover, F. (1990) "Tabu Search - Part 2", *ORSA Journal on Computing* 2(1), pp.4-32.

[16] Guan, Q. and Friedrich, G. (1992). "Extending constraint satisfaction problem solving in structural design", *Proc. of the 5th Inter. Conf. IEA/AIE*, Paderborn, Germany, June, 1992, pp. 341-350.

[17] Mackworth, A. (1977). "Consistency in networks of relations". *Artificial Intelligence* , 8, 99-121.

[18] Montanari, H. (1974). "Networks of constraints: Fundamental properties and applications to picture processing". *Information Sciences* 7, 95-142.

[19] Moulin H. (1988). *Axioms of Cooperative Decision Making*. Cambridge University Press, Cambridge, UK.

[20] Moura-Pires, J. (1997) "Starting points in optimization algorithms for solving discrimin and leximin Fuzzy-CSP", *Actes de la 3ème Conf. Nationale de Résolution Pratique de Problèmes NP-Complets* (JNPC'97), Rennes, France, 1997, pp. 95-101.

[21] Moura-pires, J. (1997) "Random generation of binary CSPs and FCSPs". Internal report DI-97, Departamento de Informática, Universidade Nova de Lisboa.

[22] Yager, R. R. (1988) "On Ordered Weighted Averaging Aggregation Operators in Multicriteria Decision Making". *IEEE Transactions on Systems, Man, and Cybernetics*. 18, 183-190.

Appendix: Combinatorial aspects of leximin

For K constraints and a satisfaction scale with $L + 1$ levels we can calculate the number of lexi-vectors between (including the limits):

- $(0 \ldots 0)$ and $(L \ldots L)$ by

$$lexid(K, L, 0, L) = \sum_{i=0}^{L} \text{lexi-levels}(K-1, L-i)$$

- $(j \ldots j)$ and $(L \ldots L)$ by

$$lexid(K, L, j, L) = \sum_{i=j}^{L} lexi-levels(K-1, L-i)$$

- $(j \ldots j)$ and $(l\, L \ldots L)$ by

$$lexid(K, L, j, L) = \sum_{i=j}^{l} lexi-levels(K-1, L-i)$$

Therefore the number of lexi-vectors such that the least satisfied constraint is α, i. e., the number of lexi-vectors that refines a min level of α is calculated by

$$lexid(K, L, \alpha, \alpha)$$

Further more the function *lexi-level* verify the following equations:

- $lexi\text{-}levels(K, L) = lexi\text{-}levels(K - 1, L) + lexi\text{-}levels(K, L - 1)$
- $lexi\text{-}levels(K, L) = lexi\text{-}level(L, K)$

Given a lexi-vector $\boldsymbol{u} = (u_1, \ldots, u_k, \ldots u_K)$, where $u_k \leq u_{k+1}$, is easy to calculate its position, denoted by Pos($\boldsymbol{u}$), in the leximin ordering, such that $Pos((0 \ldots 0)) = 1$ and $Pos((L \ldots L)) = |\mathcal{L}_{K,L}|$, by:

$$lexid(K, L, 0, u_1 - 1) + \sum_{i=2}^{K} lexid(i, L, u_{k-i}, u_{k-i+1} - 1),$$

supposing that $u_0 \neq 0$. If its not the case the leading zeros must be stripped and the K lowered by the same number of stripped zeros.

Neural Relevance Feedback for Information Retrieval

Fabio Crestani*

International Computer Science Institute
1947 Center Street, Suite 600
Berkeley, CA 94704, USA
fabioc@icsi.berkeley.edu

Abstract. Relevance feedback is a technique used in interactive Information Retrieval (IR) systems to enable a user to provide additional information to help the system identify more relevant documents. The additional information is provided in the form of relevance judgements on retrieved documents. One of the most advanced relevance feedback technique in operative IR system is based on a probabilistic function. Recent results show that it is possible to implement relevance feedback also using neural networks. This paper presents the results of an experimental investigation into the use of the Back Propagation learning algorithm for implementing relevance feedback. The investigation compares the performance of the proposed neural relevance feedback technique against to and in combination with probabilistic relevance feedback. The results obtained seem to indicate that, while probabilistic relevance feedback often outperforms neural relevance feedback, the combination of the two techniques is more effective than both techniques taken separately.

1 Introduction

In the last 50 years much effort has been devoted to improve the performance of Information Retrieval (IR) systems. In recent years research has explored many different directions trying to use results achieved in other areas, like artificial intelligence, neural networks, and expert systems [9].

Previous research shows that, though giving encouraging results, neural networks (NN) cannot be effectively used in IR at the current state of the technology (see [21, 8] for extensive reviews of the work done in this area). The scale of real IR applications, where hundreds of thousands of documents are used, makes it impossible to use NN in an effective way, unless we use poor document and query representations. However, recent results [15, 5] show that it may be still possible to use NN in IR for very specific tasks where the number of patterns involved (and therefore the training) is reduced to a manageable size.

In this paper we therefore investigate the possibility of using NN in IR and in particular we focus on their use in the process called "relevance feedback". Relevance feedback is not always present in operative IR systems, but it has been widely recognised to improve retrieval performance [14, 13, 10]. The purpose of this research is to

* Most of the work reported in this paper was done while the author was at the Department of Computing Science of the University of Glasgow, Scotland.

investigate the possibility of using NN to implement relevance feedback. We study the effectiveness of this "neural relevance feedback" both against to and in combination with classical relevance feedback techniques. The results reported here show that the use of NN for relevance feedback is not as effective as traditional relevance feedback techniques. However, the combination of neural and probabilistic relevance feedback techniques seems to achieve higher levels of effectiveness than both techniques taken separately.

The paper is structured as follows. Section 2 briefly describes the background of the study, that is the information retrieval problem and solutions. Section 3 describes in general what the relevance feedback technique is and how it works. Sections 4 and 5 describe in details the two relevance feedback technique used in this study: the probabilistic and the neural relevance feedback techniques. Section 6 presents the experimental settings and evaluation, and gives an analysis of the results. Section 7 concludes the paper summarising the work presented and indicating directions of future work.

2 Information Retrieval

Information Retrieval is the branch of computing science that aims at storing and allowing fast access to a large amount of multimedia information [19, 23, 11]. An *Information Retrieval System* is a computing tool that enables a user to access information by its semantic content using advanced statistical/probabilistic techniques. The information processed by the IR system is usually unstructured, as opposed to structured information as dealt by a database management systems (DBMS). Most present IR systems store and enable the retrieval of textual information or documents, with collections of very large size, often containing millions of documents.

Modern IR systems work in the following way. A user submits a query to the IR system using a query language (e.g., a boolean expression) or using natural language. The task of the IR system is to identify and retrieve all documents in the document collection that "satisfy" or are "relevant" the query.

Both documents and natural language queries are subject to a preliminary phase called "indexing". During indexing documents and queries are passed through a query and a document processors that decomposes them into their constituents words. Non-content-bearing words ("the", "but", "and", etc.) are discarded, and suffixes are removed, so that what remains to represent queries and documents are lists of terms. Terms are then weighted according to some weighting formula in order to quantify their importance in the context of the document or the query. Document indexing is performed off-line because, given the size of the document collections, the process may require several hours. Query indexing is instead performed at run-time when the user submits the query.

Document and query representations are compared using a matching algorithms. IR systems can be broadly grouped in two classes: those performing *exact matching* between document and query and those performing *partial matching* [12]. IR systems based on exact matching show to the user the documents that match exactly the query representation (usually a boolean expression). Partial matching IR systems typically rank the matched documents so that those most likely to be relevant (those with the highest similarity to the query) are presented to the user first. In this paper we will concentrate on partial matching IR systems. An example of a partial matching IR system is depicted in Figure 1.

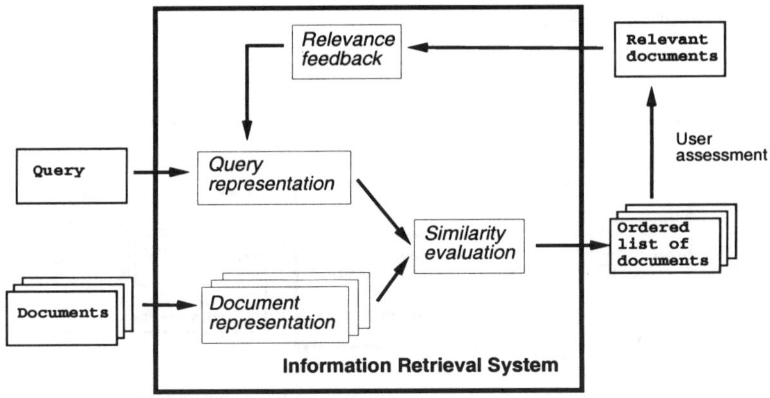

Fig. 1. Schematic view of an Information Retrieval System.

Some retrieved documents will be relevant to the user need expressed in the query and some will instead be irrelevant. In some advanced IR system, the user can appraise the documents that he considers relevant and feed them back to the IR system to perform another retrieval run. The process by which this information is fed back to the IR system is called *relevance feedback* (RF). The component of an IR system that performs RF is called RF device. The IR system takes the output of the RF device and use it as a new query to produce a new ranking of documents. If the IR system is interactive this feedback process will go on until the user is happy with the resulting list of retrieved relevant documents.

3 Relevance Feedback and Query Modification

RF is a technique that allows a user to interactively express his information requirement by modifying his original query formulation with further information. This additional information is often provided by indicating some relevant documents among the documents retrieved by the system. When a document is marked as relevant the RF device analyses the text of the document, picking out terms that are statistically significant, and adds these terms to the query. RF is a good technique for specifying an information need, because it releases the user from the burden of having to think up lots of terms for the query. Instead the user deals with the ideas and concepts contained in the documents. It also fits in well with the known human trait of "I don't know what I want, but I'll know it when I see it".

Obviously the user cannot mark documents as relevant until some are retrieved, so the first search has to be initiated by a query and the initial query specification has to be good enough to pick out some relevant documents from the collection. It is enough that at least one document in the list of retrieved documents matches, or come close to match, the user's interest, to initiate the RF process. The user can mark the document(s) as relevant and starts the RF process. If RF performs well the next list should be closer to the user's requirement and contain more relevant documents. A schematic view of a RF device is depicted in Figure 2.

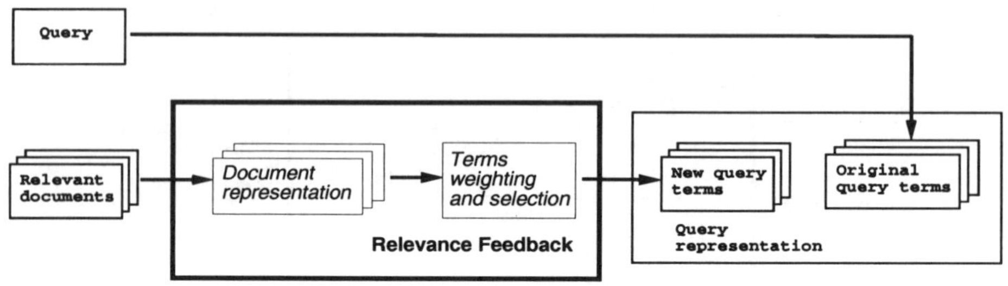

Fig. 2. Schematic view of Relevance Feedback device.

The above description refers to the classical way of considering RF [13]. There is, however, a different way of viewing RF. RF can be seen as a filter that receives as input a query and a set of relevant documents and that gives as output a modified or adapted query. This process of query adaptation is supposed to alter the original user formulated query to take into consideration the information provided by features of relevant documents. Basically, RF performs the following function:

$$RF: \ (q_i, d_1^i, d_2^i, d_3^i, \ldots d_l^i) \longmapsto q_i'$$

where q_i is the original representation of the query i, d_j^i is the representation of a document relevant to the query q_i, and q_i' is the new query resulting from the RF process.

The set is composed of only a subset (l documents) of all the documents (k documents, with $k > l$) that are relevant to that particular query. The aim of the RF is to retrieve the other $(l - k)$ relevant documents. This is achieved by moving these additional relevant documents to the top of the ranked list from there previous position, so that the user can see and assess them.

In IR there are different RF techniques [13]. The particular RF technique used by an IR system depends on the underlying retrieval model. In the following section we will illustrate a technique called probabilistic RF, which is based on the probabilistic IR model [7].

4 Probabilistic Relevance Feedback

Probabilistic relevance feedback (PRF) is one of the most advanced RF technique of operational IR systems [11]. Briefly, this technique consists of adding new terms to the original query. The terms added are chosen by taking the first m terms in a list where all the terms present in relevant documents are ranked according to the following weighting function [17]:

$$w_i = \log \frac{r_i \, (N - n_i - R + r_i)}{(R - r_i) \, (n_i - r_i)}$$

where: N is the number of documents in the collection, n_i is the number of documents with an occurrence of term i, R is the number of relevant documents pointed out by the user, and r_i is the number of relevant documents pointed out by the user with an occurrence of term i.

Essentially, PRF compares the frequency of occurrence of a term in the documents marked as relevant with its frequency of occurrence in the whole document collection. If a term occurs more frequently in the documents marked as relevant than in the whole document collection it is assigned a higher weight. There are two ways of choosing the terms to add to the query: (1) adding terms whose weight is over a predefined threshold, or (2) adding a fix number of terms, the k terms with the highest weight. In the experiments reported in this paper we used the second technique. After a few tests, the number of terms added to the original query was set to 10. This number has been proved experimentally to be quite effective, without modifying the extending the scope of the query too much [20].

5 Neural Relevance Feedback

In [4] an adaptive IR system using NN was presented. We refer back to that paper for the architecture, the algorithm, and the learning performance of the system. The way the system can be used to implement a new RF technique, called *neural relevance feedback* (NRF), has been explained in detail in [5]. Here we briefly describe the way NRF works and we suggest the interested reader to look at the cited paper for the implementation details, which are not necessary for the discussion reported here.

NRF is a way of performing RF using NN. A RF device based on NRF learns from training examples to associate new terms to the original query formulation. The NRF device acts in a way similar to the classical RF. The main difference is that the weights used to order and select the terms are obtained from the output of a 3–layer feedforward NN trained using the Back Propagation (BP) learning algorithm [18, 1]. Each node in the NN input layer represents a query term and each node in the output layer represent a document term. The BP learning algorithm was chosen because of its definition itself, as back propagation of errors. In fact, BP propagates backward in the layers of the NN the difference between the desired output (the representation of a relevant document) and the actual output (the representation of a irrelevant document). The BP learning algorithm aims at reducing this difference to the smallest value.

Figure 3 shows how NRF acts. A NRF device works in two phases. In the *training phase* the input and the output layer of the NN are set to represent a training example composed of a query representation q_i and a relevant document representation d^i_j. The BP algorithm is used for learning, and is repeated for every relevant document d^i_j, in the training set. The learning is monitored by the NN control structure and when some predetermined condition is met (such as, for example, a mean error below a certain threshold) the training phase is halted. What follows is the *spreading phase*. In this phase the activation produced on the input nodes by the query spreads from the input layer to the output layer using the weight matrices produced during the training phase. A new query is produced by adding to the terms already present in the query the first m (here $m = 10$) higher activated terms (nodes) on the output layer.

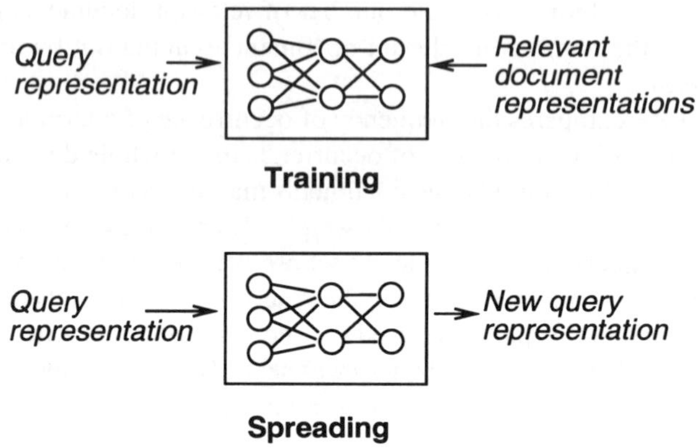

Fig. 3. The phases of a Neural Relevance Feedback device.

6 Experimental Analysis

We decided to compare the two RF techniques to see if one was better than the other from an experimental IR point of view. The motivation behind this analysis lies in the results of a previous investigation into a comparison of the results of the two previously described RF techniques [3]. In that study we discovered, given the best possible parameters settings, PRF performed as well as PRF, but retrieved different sets of documents. The experimentation reported in this paper is more accurate, uses larger data sets, and aims at testing the possibility of combining the two techniques.

We chosed to perform our analysis following the classical IR experimental methodology as described in [23], using IR effectiveness measures and IR test collections. The main retrieval effectiveness measures used in IR are recall and precision.

Recall (R) is the proportion of all documents in the collections that are relevant to a query and that are actually retrieved:

$$Recall = \frac{\mid relevant\ and\ retrieved\ documents \mid}{\mid relevant\ documents \mid}$$

Precision (P) is the proportion of the retrieved set of documents that is also relevant to the query:

$$Precision = \frac{\mid relevant\ and\ retrieved\ documents \mid}{\mid retrieved\ documents \mid}$$

The results reported in the following sections are presented using recall and precision graphs (P/R graphs). These graphs are obtained by depicting the precision figures at standard levels of recall.

6.1 Experimental and Evaluation Settings

The document collections chosen for the investigation are the *ASLIB Cranfield 1400*, the *CACM*, and the *NPL* test collections. The main characteristics of these three test collections are summarised in Table 1. These are classical IR test collections used by many researchers in the field and described in a large number of references (see for example [2, 22])

Data	*Cranfield*	*CACM*	*NPL*
documents	1400	3204	11429
queries	225	52	93
terms in doc.	5000	7121	7492
terms in query	274	356	337
avg. doc. length	53.61	24.26	19.96
avg. query length	8.95	11.5	7.15
avg. rel. doc.	7.28	15.31	22.41

Table 1. Test collections data

We are aware of the fact that the collections used in our experiments can be considered small from the IR point of view, however, at the current stage, our research was not concerned with efficiency issues, and we decided that size was not so important. There are still many open issues in the application of NN to IR, and the problem of scaling the results is one of the major ones.

PRF was implemented on top a classical probabilistic IR system with code from [11], while NRF was implemented on top of a NN simulator called PlaNet [16] using a 3–layer feedforward NN with BP learning. The number of input nodes was set to 195, the number of hidden nodes to 100, and the number of output nodes to 1142. The numbers of input and output nodes correspond, respectively, to the number of terms used in all queries and to the number of terms used by all documents of the test collection. These settings are the results of previous investigations and will not be explained here for reasons of space. The interested reader can find all the details in [5].

6.2 Comparing Probabilistic and Neural Relevance Feedback

Since our first comparative look at PRF and NRF we noticed that the set of terms added to the initial query was very often different. In other words, taking the same initial query and feeding back the same documents to the PRF and NRF we obtained different sets of terms (and different weights for the same terms) to be added to the query. In a test over 30 queries randomly chosen from the set of queries of our CACM experimental collection we found that the difference between the two sets of m ($m = 10$) terms to be added to the query was on average 32%, i.e., at least 3 terms where different. The difference in weights between the same term present in both sets was on average 96%. Analogous differences were found using the other test collections. Was this difference sufficient to cause different retrieval performance?

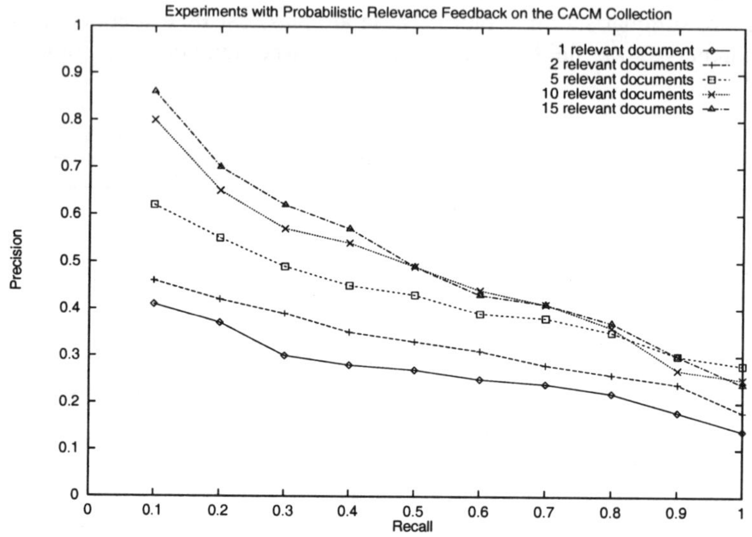

Fig. 4. Performance of Probabilistic Relevance Feedback.

We compared the performance of PRF and NRF using training sets of different sizes. Figures 4 and 5 show graphically how the performance of NRF and PRF increases when the RF device is given an increasing number of relevant documents. The results reported in the tables refers to the CACM collection, similar results were obtained using the Cranfield and the NPL collections, with the largest differences being recorded for the Cranfield collection. This shows what we expected: both PRF and NRF act like pattern recognition devices and the more information they receive the more they can discriminate between patterns of relevant and not relevant documents. The performance has been evaluated averaging over all queries in the relevance assessment at different values of the number of relevant documents given as feedback (the training sets). The graphs show that the NRF increases more rapidly in performance than the PRF. This is due to the better characteristics of non linear discrimination of NRF, that enables it to separate better the two sets of relevant and irrelevant documents (the two patterns). This concept is depicted in Figure 6. In fact, PRF performs a linear regression on the data provided by the training set. This is equivalent to determining a hyper-plane that divides in the best possible way the relevant and the irrelevant documents. NRF, on the other hand, performs a nonlinear regression, determining a more complex surface that

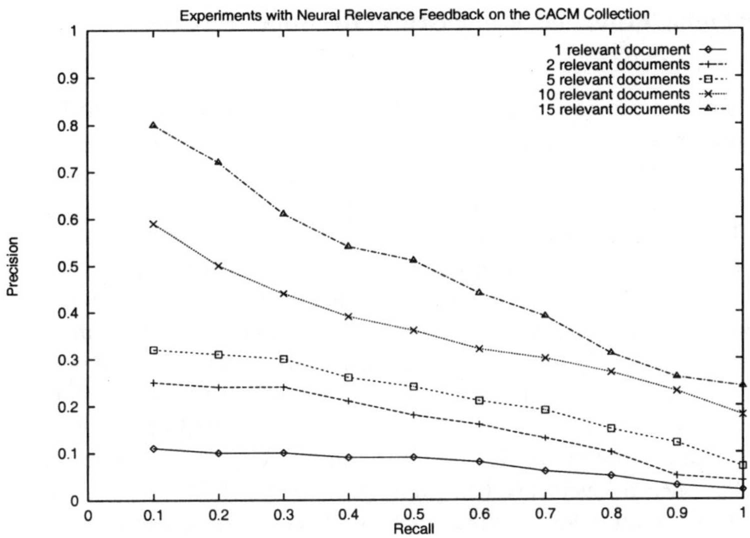

Fig. 5. Performance of Neural Relevance Feedback.

divides the relevant and the irrelevant documents. This explains why for higher levels of training NRF performs better that PRF.

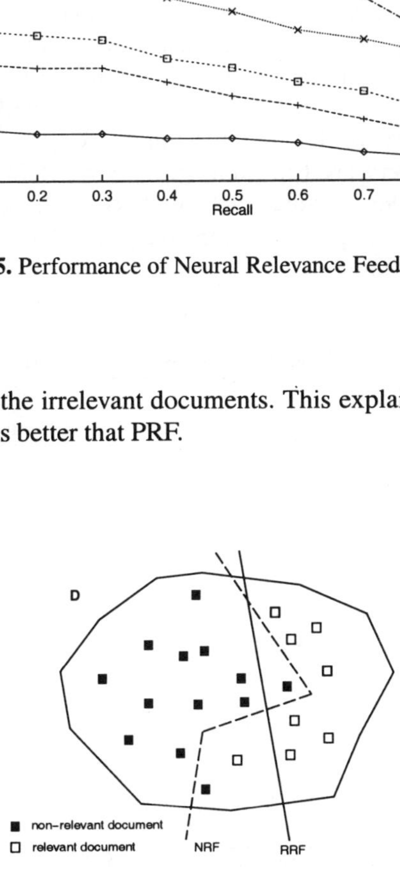

Fig. 6. A comparison of Neural and Probabilistic Relevance Feedback

From the IR point of view, however, the performance of PRF are better than those of NRF. PRF is more effective at lower levels of training. This makes PRF more useful in applications where the percentage of relevant documents versus the total number of document used in the relevance feedback is usually low.

6.3 Combining Probabilistic and Neural Relevance Feedback

The results of the previous section together with the observation that PRF and NRF identify different sets of terms to add to those present in the original query formulation, prompted us to try to combine these two RF techniques and see if the combination was more effective than the two techniques taken separately. We normalised term weights produced by PRF and NRF to the range $[0, 1]$ and for each RF run we merged the two ordered lists of terms. For terms appearing in both lists with different weights, the highest weight was chosen. We then used for RF the m highest ranked term (with $m = 10$ as in the previous tests for comparative reasons). We called this combination of PRF and NRF *neural-probabilistic relevance feedback* (NPRF). We performed a few tests using training sets of different sizes, in the same way described in the previous section. The results of this new RF device obtained by combining PRF and NRF on the CACM test collection are reported in Figure 7. Results show that NPRF is more effective that NRF at every level of training, moreover NPRF is also more effective that PRF at low training levels. Since PRF and NRF could be run in parallel on an IR system, without delaying the response of the RF to the user, we believe that we this is an effective way of performing RF.

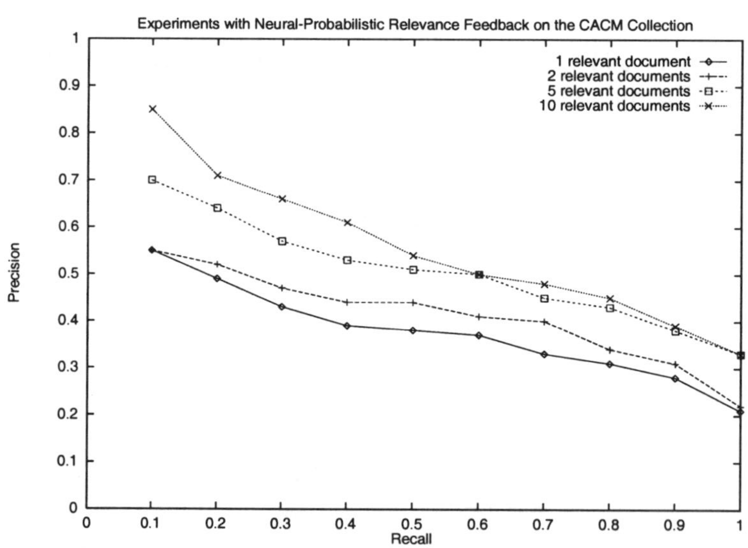

Fig. 7. Performance of Neural-Probabilistic Relevance Feedback.

The graphs reported in this section only refer to the CACM test collection. The results obtained with the other two collections have not been reported for reasons of space, but were very similar. This paper extends the experimental analysis reported in [6] by using different and larger test collections.

7 Conclusions and Future Work

The results of this investigation, briefly summarised in this paper, demonstrate that a RF device based on PRF is more effective that NRF for low level of training. A low level of training (i.e., a small number of documents indicated as relevant by the user) is typical of real life IR applications. However, since at any level of training PRF and NRF identify different sets of terms to be added to those present in the original query, a combination of PRF and NRF could prove effective. The results in this direction reported in this paper seem to indicate that the combination is indeed effective. Nevertheless, more tests with larger collections of documents and with different algorithms for PRF and NRF are necessary to validate these results and fully exploit their usefulness.

References

1. L. Almeida. Bacpropagation in perceptrons with feedback. In R. Eckmiller and Ch.v.d. Malsburg, editors, *Neural Computers*, NATO ASI. Springer-Verlag, Berlin, Germany, 1988.
2. C. Cleverdon, J. Mills, and M. Keen. *ASLIB Cranfield Research Project: factors determining the performance of indexing systems*. ASLIB, 1966.
3. F. Crestani. Comparing neural and probabilistic relevance feedback in an interactive Information Retrieval system. In *Proceedings of the IEEE International Conference on Neural Networks*, pages 3426–2430, Orlando, Florida, USA, June 1994.
4. F. Crestani. Domain knowledge acquisition for Information Retrieval using neural networks. *Journal of Applied Expert Systems*, 2(2):101–116, 1994.
5. F. Crestani. Implementation and evaluation of a relevance feedback device based on neural networks. In J. Mira and J. Cabestany, editors, *From Natural to Artificial neural Computation: International Workshop on Artificial Neural Networks*, volume 930 of *Lecture Notes in Computer Science*, pages 597–604. Springer-Verlag, Malaga, Spain, June 1995.
6. F. Crestani. Experiments of an effective combination of probabilistic and neural relevance feedback. In *Proceedings of the Seventh Conference on Information Processing and Management of Uncertainty in Knowledge-Bsed Systems (IPMU)*, pages 1446–1451, Paris, France, July 1998.
7. F. Crestani, M. Lalmas, C.J. van Rijsbergen, and I. Campbell. Is this document relevant? ...probably. A survey of probabilistic models in information retrieval. *ACM Computing Surveys*, 30(4):528–552, 1998.
8. F. Crestani and G. Pasi. Soft information retrieval: applications of fuzzy sets theory and neural networks. In N. Kasabov and R. Kozma, editors, *Neuro-fuzzy Techniques for Intelligent Information Systems*, pages 287–315. Physica Verlag, Heidelberg, Germany, 1999.
9. W.B. Croft. Approaches to Intelligent Information Retrieval. *Information Processing and Management*, 23(4):249:254, 1987.
10. M.D. Dunlop. The effect of accessing non-matching documents on relevance feedback. *ACM Transactions on Information Systems*, 15(2):137–153, 1997.
11. W.R. Frakes and R. Baeza-Yates, editors. *Information Retrieval: data structures and algorithms*. Prentice Hall, Englewood Cliffs, New Jersey, USA, 1992.
12. D. Harman. Ranking algorithms. In W.B. Frakes and R. Baeza-Yates, editors, *Information Retrieval: data structures and algorithms*, chapter 14. Prentice Hall, Englewood Cliffs, New Jersey, USA, 1992.
13. D. Harman. Relevance feedback and other query modification techniques. In W.B. Frakes and R. Baeza-Yates, editors, *Information Retrieval: data structures and algorithms*, chapter 11. Prentice Hall, Englewood Cliffs, New Jersey, USA, 1992.

14. D.J. Harper and C.J. van Rijsbergen. An evaluation of feedback in document retrieval using co-occurence data. *Journal of Documentation*, 34(3):189–216, September 1978.
15. A. Jennings and H. Higuchi. A personal news service based on a user model neural network. *IEICE Transactions on Information and Systems*, E75-D(2):198–209, 1992.
16. Y. Miyata. *A user's guide to PlaNet version 5.6: a tool for constructing, running and looking into a PDP network.* Computer Science Department, University of Colorado, Boulder, USA, December 1990.
17. S.E. Robertson and K. Sparck Jones. Relevance weighting of search terms. *Journal of the American Society for Information Science*, 27:129–146, May 1976.
18. D.E. Rumelhart, J.L. McClelland, and PDP Research Group. *Parallel Distributed Processing: exploration in the microstructure of cognition.* MIT Press, Cambridge, 1986.
19. G. Salton. *Automatic information organization and retrieval.* Mc Graw Hill, New York, 1968.
20. M. Sanderson and C.J. van Rijsbergen. NRT: news retrieval tool. *Electronic Publishing*, 4(4):205–217, 91.
21. J.C Scholtes. Neural networks in information retrieval in a libraries context. EC/PROLIB/ANN Contract, M.S.C. Information Retrieval Technologies B.V., The Netherlands, 1994.
22. K. Sparck Jones and C.J. van Rijsbergen. Information Retrieval test collections. *Journal of Documentation*, 32(1):59–75, March 1976.
23. C.J. van Rijsbergen. *Information Retrieval.* Butterworths, London, second edition, 1979.

GA-P based Feature Selection and Classification combining different Methods of Texture Analysis

Fernando Cano, Luis Junco, Luciano Sánchez

Departamento de Informática
Universidad de Oviedo (España)
fcano@etsiig.uniovi.es, junco@lsi.uniovi.es, luciano@lsi.uniovi.es

Abstract: In some classification problems, the most costly phase consists in associating the object we wish to classify with a vector of numerical attributes. In these cases, a good feature extraction procedure is important, because it will benefit the generalization properties of the classifier and also because it can reduce noticeablily the process time if the most relevant attributes are selected.

We have applied a new classification methodology, based upon genetic programming (GA-P algorithms) that structures the classification so that we do not need to calculate the values of all attributes of the texture in all cases. We calculate first the minimal set of attributes that allow us to discriminate between the most frequent class and the other ones, and then we continue calculating attributes only if we need them. This method serves us to achieve two objectives: classificating textures in an efficient manner and providing us with a selection of the most powerful attributes that, as we will see, can be used to feed another classification system and to enhance its performance.

1 Introduction

In a classification system an object is usually characterized by a vector of scalar measures of properties of the object, so called *feature vector*. Determining witch measures are relevant to the classification is not a trivial task. The feature vector usually contains redundant information (i.e. correlated features or features that statistically depend on others) and it is well known [] that an excess of features carries a descent in the generalization capabilities of the classifier. It is also important to notice that the process time needed to calculate the feature vector is proportional to the dimension of this vector.

Therefore it is desirable to design the smallest feature vector that completely characterizes the object for a given classifier, thus performing a *feature selection* over the set comprising all possible characteristics of the object being classified. It is a remarkable that this selection process is highly dependent on the kind of classifier used. For instance, most statistical methods for selecting characteristics are intrinsically inadequate for working with non lineally separable classes (see [9], pg. 339).

The methodology proposed in this paper will be illustrated with texture classification problems in computer vision. For this reason we will describe the general framework for the design of texture classifiers and the new solution proposed for the feature selection task and the classifier design. All the samples we will use in this paper are natural or pseudoramdon textures, like the textures of the Brodatz Album [3].

Our Methodology pretends to solve the above problems. We propose a methodology with the following characteristics

- It performs the feature selection simultaneously with the construction of the classifier
- The features are calculate when it necessary for the classification proccess.

Although our methodology can construct the classifier we go to show that the results of the feature selection independently improve the outcome of others classifiers like K-neighbors or neural networks.

2 Methodology of the classification

The methodology that we were applying up to now for the construction of texture classification systems comprised the following steps and is based on Texel [16] [17] an Integrated environment for developing and testing texture classification systems and algorithms. The steps are:

1. Determination of the conditions of image acquisition (illumination system, camera type, etc.)
2. Acquisition of the digitalized images.
3. Choosing of the pre-processing techniques.
4. Extraction of texture samples from images (windows of 32x32 or 64x64 pixel).
5. Application of TA methods to each sample: Generation of examples set and generation of the input datasets that will be used as training and validation sets of the supervised classifier. Each example is represented by a big characteristic vector composed by the corresponding statistics and the class label which it belongs to.
6. Selection of the characteristics that combine high power discrimination and low correlation between them. The objective of this step is the selection of those statistics that can provide better results in the classification phase and the reduction of the search space.
7. Training and validation of different classifiers (distances, neural net, entropy trees, K-neighbours) in order to select the best one.

When we don't obtain satisfactory results we must carry out a backtracking, modifying some of the previous processes and repeating the later steps. This methodology has been satisfactory applied in [7] and [8].

2.0.1 Methods of texture characterization

A great variety of Texture Analysis Methods (TAM) can be chosen for texture discrimination. The methods that now we describe usually provide good results in textures with high degree of randomness, well-known as natural textures or pseudorandom textures.

- Histogram Method: One of the defining qualities of texture is the distribution of gray values. This distribution can be represented by an Histogram, and we can calculate some general statistical properties from it such as mean, variance, entropy, energy, etc.

- Gray level co-ocurrence matrices method (GLDM): It estimates image properties related to second-order statistics. Matrices are built from the gray level co-ocurrences among pairs of pixels, once certain distances and orientations are fixed. Some functions calculated from these matrices [4, 5] are correlation, cluster shade, cluster prominence, local homogeneity, etc.

- Co-ocurrence generalized matrices Method (CGM): This method is quite similar to GLDM. We do not study gray level coocurrences but different characteristics that define the pixel. The statistics are the same ones that those calculated previously.

- Fractal Dimension Method (FD): It is based upon original Mandelbrot's works in geometry. The fractal dimension gives a measure of the roughness of a surface and self-similarity at different scales.

- Gabor Energy Method: We apply some convolutions to the image. These convolutions represent the corresponding gabor filters at different frequencies, orientations and phases. The energy function is calculated from the resulting image.

There are many other methods such as Run-length, Wavelets, Markov Random Fields (MRF), Gibbs Random Fields (GRF) and several versions of those previously referred. The number of possible methods is high and the set of statistics generated from them is even higher. Many of these methods also depend on certain parameters (for example, the distance or orientation in co-ocurrence matrices) so we can generate hundreds of features from one image. Not all the methods have been included in our study since we do not intend to make a comparative study of the TAM.

Certain approaches allow to reject some type of methods a priori. They are based upon the study of the characteristics of the problem. We can distinguish between methods that are scale or orientation invariant, high dependent of the illumination conditions or camera type, or tuned to certain type of textures.

3 The GA-P classifier

Complex classification problems presents some inconveniences:

1. The design of a good system depends excessively on the user experience.
2. Feature selection is a complex process
3. The computational cost is not usually kept in mind in all these feature choice methods.
4. The automation of the process is a complex task.

In some simple problems, we can solve these last three inconveniencies without resorting to statistical techniques. We can do an exhaustive search for the discriminating functions in the whole characteristic space. We search for discriminating functions that provide a high classification rate and low calculation cost.

This approach can be excessively expensive in texture classification problems: there are too many possible arguments (texture features) and the kinds of the searched functions are a priori unknown.

The GA-P algorithm is an hybrid method that combines genetic algorithm and genetic programming principles. They were originally optimized to carry out symbolic regressions. However, they are well suited to our model: they try to find generic functions that maximize a certain objective in spaces with a high number of variables.

Like any other evolution programming methods, this algorithm maintains a set of possible classification problem solutions (set known as population) and combining certain evolution operators creates new solutions that replace in many cases to the old members. The population evolves until a good solution is found. The function that evaluates the quality of a member of the population is named fitness function and usually it depends on the classification rates.

We shall intend to reduce the size of the solutions including this size as a parameter of the fitness. This causes the number of variables that appears in the solutions to be lower.

The complete description of the method can be found in [10], and some of its applications to other problems in [11, 13].

The use of GA-P algorithm is a very convenient option compared to GP. The reason is that this option deals with the values of the numeric constants in such a way that the codification of the solutions is usually more compact and allows the speeding up of the seach process by means of local optimization algorithms (p.e. simplex method).

The details of the implementation with GA-P algorithms of the classifier that we are applying here can be consulted in [12]

4 Discriminant functions

Let us imagine a situation like the one outlined in the figure 3. We want to classify some objects that can be described by two features each. There are

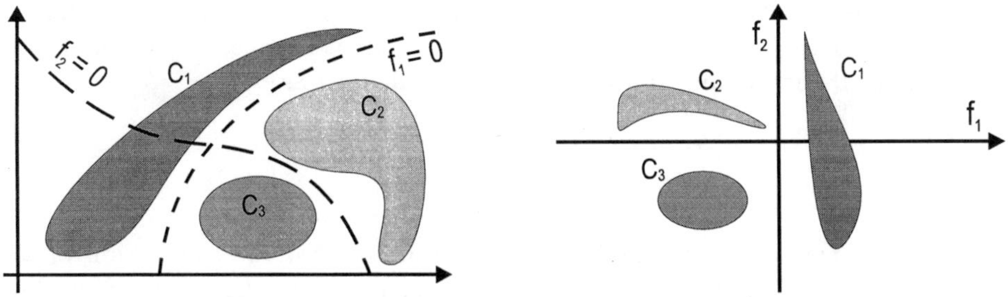

Figure 1: Structure of the classification process

```
if f_1(a)>0 then a is in class 1
else
   if f_2(a)>0 then a is in class 2
   else
   ...
     if f_N-1(a)>0 then a is in class N-1
     else
      a is in class N
     end if
  end if
end if
```

Figure 2: Pseudocode of the classifier

three different classes of objects, that we will name C_1, C_2 and C_3. We have shadowed the areas in which we expect an object of class C_1, C_2 or C_3 is.

We can structure the classification problem in succesive phases:

- Searching for a function f_1 such that $f_1(a) \geq 0$ if a belongs to C_1 and $f_1 < 0$ otherwise. This function can be viewed as a variable change followed by a projection, and it will send all the class 1 points to the half space of the positive abscissas (b). Once we apply the function f_1, we will eliminate of the search space the points belonging to this class.
- Searching for a new function f_2 with similar properties to find the elements of C_2, and so forth. The arguments that each function needs are calculated as the classification process advances (see figure 2)

The gain obtained by this procedure is obvious. Moreover, this gain can be much more important if the functions do not use all input arguments. This methodology allows us to considerably reduce the average processing time. We will show practical results that justify this assertion.

We are assuming that the classes are separable but it will be convenient to extend the problem to non separable classes. This can be done with the help of an easy simpler bayesian formulation [14]. If $\mathbf{a}$ is the vector of attributes and $C_1, \ldots C_N$ are the classes, defined in the attribute space, we will look for N functions f_i that minimize the error rates ϵ_i defined as

$$\epsilon_i = P\{f_i(\mathbf{a}) < 0 \ \wedge \ \mathbf{a} \in C\} +$$

$$P\{f_i(\mathbf{a}) \geq 0 \ \wedge \ \mathbf{a} \in C - \cup_{j=1\ldots i} C_j)\}.$$

where P is a measure of probability. We will admit that the calculation of all the attributes has the same computational cost and that the most favourable ordering of classes is obtained when $P(C_1) > P(C_2) > \ldots > P(C_N)$.

To solve a problem of classification of multiple classes we will look separately for N functions f_i that maximize a value of *fitness* defined as

$$\#\{\mathbf{a}^k \in C_i \mid f_i(\mathbf{a}^k) \geq 0\}$$

restricting the search to the functions that complete

$$\#\{\mathbf{a}^k \in C - \cup_{j=1\ldots i} C_j \mid f_i(\mathbf{a}^k) > 0\} = 0$$

where $M = \{\mathbf{a}^1, \mathbf{a}^2, \ldots, \mathbf{a}^m\}$ is a sample of classified objects. The expression that is minimized, therefore, is

$$N_i - \#\{\mathbf{a}^k \in C_i \mid f_i(\mathbf{a}^k) \geq 0\} +$$

$$\lambda \, \#\{\mathbf{a}^k \in C - \cup_{j=1\ldots i} C_j \mid f_i(\mathbf{a}^k)) > 0\}$$

where N_i is the number of elements of the class i and λ is a penalty factor that affects the misclasificated points.

When the fitness of two individuals are the same, we discriminate between them on the basis of the number of attributes they use. In other words, when we are confronted with two classifiers of the same power we choose the most simple of them, having in mind that we prefer complex functions depending on a few attributes than simple functions that use many attributes.

5 A Texture Classification Problem

The problem that we have chosen to validate our classifier consists on discriminating between two different types of textures with three different orientations (0, 45 and 90), so the system must differ between a total of six classes.

We have chosen textures named "Insulation" and "Straw". The images showing these textures are sample27.gif and sample40.gif, included in Columbia-Utrecht Reflectance and Texture Database [15].

These textures show a strong orientation and we have applied two rotations to each one of them (45 and 90 degrees), obtaining six different images of 256 gray levels. In each one of these images we selected a region and got a total amount of 1024 samples using windows of 32x32 pixels with a displacement in horizontal and in vertical of 20 pixels. For each set of samples we made two groups: one for training (80%) and one for test (20%), as can be seen in Table 1.

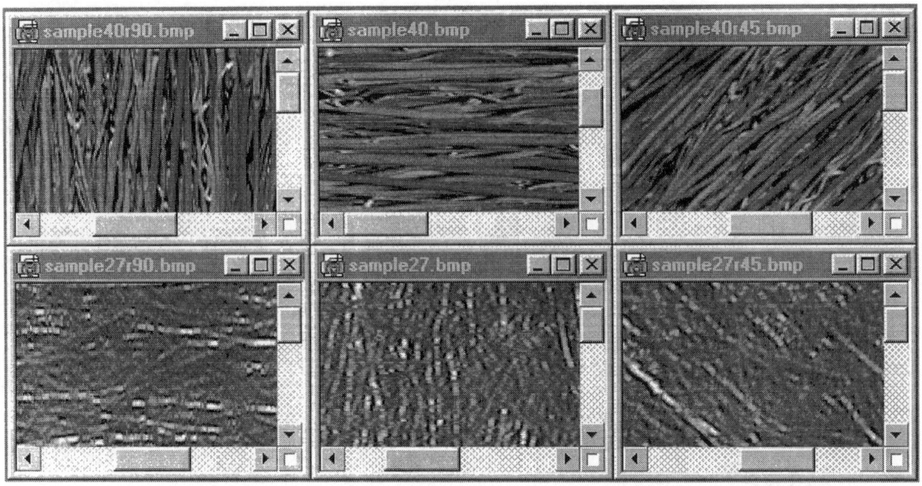

Figure 3: Textures being classified

Table 1: Characteristics of Datasets

Class	1	2	3	4	5	6
Description	Straw	Straw	Straw	Insulation	Insulation	Insulation
Rotation	90	0	45	0	45	90
Total Samples	199	186	168	165	146	160
Master	159	148	134	162	116	128
Test	40	38	34	33	30	32

Table 2: Classification Rates of individual methods

Class	1	2	3	4	5	6	Total
Histogram	50	42.1	29.4	30.3	36.7	9.4	33.9
DF	17.5	18.4	38.2	24.2	16.7	21.9	22.7
CGM	100	100	79.4	84.9	86.7	90.7	90.8
SGLDM	20	94.7	35.3	24.2	36.7	43.8	43
Gabor	70	81.6	94.1	90.1	86.7	75	82.6

Table 3: Classification Rates for different classifiers (32 features)

Class	1	2	3	4	5	6	Total
Neural Net.	97.5	100	97.4	100	96.7	96.9	98.1
Distances	90	97.4	100	87.9	96.7	100	95.2
K-Neighbours	100	100	100	93.9	96.7	90.6	97.1

We have tried three different approaches to solve this problem. The rate of successes of the classifier was computed for each class (successes in the class i divided by the number of examples class i) and for all of the classes (total successes divided by the total number of examples).

In the first approach, we have applied the next methods: Histogram, Fractal Dimension, CGM, GLDM and Gabor, in an independent way, generating for each sample a vector of textural features. From the Histogram we computed the mean, variance, asymmetry, kurtosis, energy, entropy and synergy. Three features were based on the fractal dimension. Two co - ocurrence matrices were generated: one with GLDM and one with CGM, both of them with distance 8 and orientation 0. We obtained 10 second order statistics (Autocorrelation, Correlation, Cluster Shade, Cluster Prominence, Covariance, Energy, Entropy, Inertia, Local Homogeneity and Modular Value) and 12 values of Gabor Energies for distances 1,2 and 4 and orientations 0, 45, 90 and 135. The employed classifier was a K-neighbours with K=5. The results are shown in the Table 2.

As shown in table 2, the methods which are independent of the orientation (Histogram and Fractal Dimension) obtained very bad results, so we discarded them for later approaches. GLDM method was kept in spite of his bad results. This method is orientation dependent and is possible that some of the features generated by him could offer a discriminant measure.

In our second approach, we simultaneously applied CGM, GLDM and Gabor methods to feed three different classifiers: a three-layered perceptron with 32 input elements, 8 process elements in the hidden layer, and 6 output elements an euclidean-distance-based classifier and a K-neighbours with K=5. The results were those that are shown in the Table 3.

In the third approach, our proposed GA-P based method was applied. It was proved on the same master and of test sets of samples as the former approach. Table 2 shows the final results.

Table 4: Classification Rates for GA-P

Class	1	2	3	4	5	6	Total
GA-P	100	100	97.1	87.9	90.0	96.9	95.7

Table 5: Classification Rates for different classifiers (15 features selected)

Class	1	2	3	4	5	6	Total
Neural Net.	100	100	100	97	100	94	98.6
Distances	100	97.4	100	98	96.7	100	98.6
K-Neighbours	100	100	100	97	93.3	97	98

Fifteen of a total of 32 features have been selected. If the computational cost of all the features is the same and the frequency of the classes is identical, we only have to compute 29.37 percent of calculations to generate the features vector of each sample. We have proven that our method is good enough to be used like a selector method (without the classifier). We have generated a new training and test sets using only the 15 features selected by our method. All classifiers improved their rates, like table 5 shows.

In this example, our classifier uses only two parameters to discriminate class 2, Covariance CGM (distance=8 dir=H) and Modular Value SGLDM (distance=8 dir=H). These two descriptors are among the best five that have been measured with the methods indicated in **??**.

In many texture inspection systems like defects detection and classification systems [8], it is very usual that the class "no defect" has a considerably greater frequency than the other classes (defects). It is very important that, in this case, the discriminant function depends on a few number of parameters, and that these parameters have a low computational cost.

For example if the class "no defect" frequency is over 99 percent, and for computing the discrimination function for this class we only need to calculate two features, we can reduced highly the computational cost.

Table 6: Some Feature Discriminant Power Values for Class 2

Feature	Run Test	Tchebycheff
Modular Value SGLDM	91.8	74.8
Cluster Prominence CGM	90.5	67.3
Cluster Shade CGM	88.5	64.3
Energy CGM	87.8	70.3
Covariance CGM	87.8	69.3
Local Homogeneity SGLDM	83.7	58.4

6 Conclusions

The GA-P based method proposed in this paper obtains results that are similar to another well known classifiers, but using a significantly lower number of texture features, with less computational cost. This method provides also an automatic, unsupervised and not statistical feature selection technique.

This feature extraction and classification method will be improved when a method for sorting the classes in a more efficient manner is developed. The most probable class is not always the best to begin with; that is only true when all functions f_i depend on the same number of attributes. Moreover, since examples are dropped each time we search for a new function, the percentages of classification will be better when we examine firstly the most easily separable class. Much work remains to be done in this field but, at this preliminary stage, we fell that this is a very good feature extraction procedure and a moderately good classifier system.

References

[1] R.M. Haralick and L.G. Shapiro. "Computer and Robot Vision", Addison Wesley.

[2] Mihran Tuceryan, Anil K. Jain, "Texture Analisis", The Hand book of Pattern Recognition and Computer Vision, World Scientific Publishing Co., 1993

[3] Brodatz P., Textures: A Photographic Album for artists and Designes. New York, Dover Publications, 1966

[4] R.M Haralick and K. Shanmugan, "Computer Classification of Reservoir Sandsttones", IEEE Trans. Geosci. Electron., vol. GE-11, pp. 171-177, Oct. 1973.

[5] R.W. Conners, C.W. McMillin, Kingyao Lin, and R.E. Vasquez-Espinosa, "Identifying and Locating Surface Defects in Wood: Part of an Automated Lumber Processing System", IEEE Transactions on pattern analysis and machine intelligence, Vol. PAMI-5, No. 6, Nov 1983, pp. 573-584

[6] Ohanian, P.P. and R.C. Dubes, "Performance Evaluation for Four Classes of Textural Features", Pattern Recognition, V25(8), pp. 819-833, 1992

[7] A. Ruiz. "Un sistema de integración multi-sensorial", Dpto. Informática y Automática, Facultad de ciencias Físicas, Madrid 1990.

[8] Fernando Cano Espinosa, "Sistema de percepción visual de defectos en pieles". Universidad Politécnica de Madrid, 1992.

[9] Looney, C. G. "Pattern Recognition Using Neural Networks". Oxford University Press, 1997.

[10] Howard, L.; D'Angelo, D. "The GA-P: A Genetic Algorithm and Genetic Programming Hybrid". IEEE Expert. June 1995. pp 11-15.

[11] Sanchez, L.,Couso, I. "Modelado a partir de ejmplos imprecisos mediante algoritmos GA-P" ESTYLF'97. VII Congreso Espaol sobre tecnologias y Logica Fuzzy. Tarragona.

[12] Sanchez, L. y Couso, I. "Clasificacion y Seleccion de Caracteristicas mediante Algoritmos GA-P". First Seminar "Computacion Evolutiva: Teoria y Aplicaciones". VII Conference of the Spanish Association of Artificial Intelligence. 1997.

[13] Cordón O., Herrera F., Sanchez L. "Evolutionary learning processes for data analysis in engineering applications". En Quagliarelli D., Perinaux J., Poloni C. y Winter G. (Eds.) Genetic Algorithms in Engineering and Computer Science. Jhon Wiley and Sons.

[14] Hand, D.J., "Discrimination and Classification". Wiley, 1988.

[15] Textural images bank at http: //www. cs. columbia. edu /CAVE /curet /html /sample.html

[16] Muiz R., Cano F., "Texel: A Methodology and an Integrated environment for Developing Automated Systems for Texture Classification". Proceedings from the IEEE International Joint Symposia on Intelligence and Systems, 1998.

[17] Muiz R., Cano F., "An extensible framework for developing and testing texture classification systems and algorithms". Proceedings from CISST'99 Las Vegas, Julio 1999.

Applications

Data fusion using a multi-agents architecture Application to artillery localization*

Sylvain Gatepaille **Antoine Kelman** **Sylvie Brunessaux**

MATRA Systèmes & Information

Laboratoire de Traitement de l' Information, de l'image et du Signal

parc d'affaires des Portes - BP613

27106 Val de Reuil Cedex

{sgatepaille,sylvie}@mcs-vdr.fr

Abstract: In the field of military intelligence, data to be fused are numerous and heterogeneous. Therefore an automatic decision aid method to reproduce intelligence officer reasoning is useful. We model data as fuzzy sets and we use an aggregation method based upon management of priorities between criteria. On top of that, a multi-agents architecture lying on modelisation of processes as competing agents provides an efficient and adaptive implementation. As an example, we describe hereafter an application aimed at helping artillery localization.

Keywords: fuzzy sets, aggregation, multi-agents systems, hybrid architecture.

1 Introduction

Means to collect intelligence data are increasing as well as their reliability but data flow to be analysed is also growing. To help officers during this task, some automatic data fusion applications should be provided. Due to complexity of input data, this kind of application is rare. Complexity comes from heterogeneity (imaging information, communication, radar, human data,...). Data collected are to be continuously fused to produce a synthetic and reliable situation to the intelligence officer.

We present hereafter a method to help the officer in this task. We did not studied the situation assessment problem. We focused indeed on the "relance" problem which consists in determining the next areas on the battlefield where intelligence means (UAVs, reconnaissance aircraft) should watch. The areas chosen depend upon known information and intelligence objectives.

We propose to describe an artillery localization help application which aim is to automatically provide to the intelligence officer the areas where it is possible to find artillery. Thanks to that, the intelligence officer could manage more rapidly and accurately his intelligence means.

This application relies on two complementary technologies which are fuzzy sets modelisation and multi-agents systems.

Fuzzy sets theory allows us to quickly model data received by the intelligence officer in a homogeneous manner. Moreover, data fusion processing is easily reproduced

* research work done under study "Fusion Multi-Sources", DRET funding, contract number 94 34 469.

thanks to fuzzy aggregation techniques. These techniques should be implemented and assessed.

Multi-agents systems help us to incrementally complete these tasks. The several steps of reasoning needed to perform data fusion processing are indeed implemented through several collaborative agents (each of them being responsible of a small task). Some of them could be shared among fusion processing. On top of that, agents could be used to design more than one artillery localization method which could then be concurrently activated. This helps in validating and optimizing such methods.

In the following chapters, these two techniques will be presented as well as the artillery localization application.

2 General fusion methodology

2.1 Homogeneous representation of relevant information

A straightforward fusion of heterogeneous data is generally impossible. Instead, we first apply a preprocessing on data to make them homogeneous. Then, we can aggregate data with standard fusion operators. We consider this preprocessing as an important and necessary step to fuse data. However it is usually not useful to process all the data available. Only relevant information should be kept.

Therefore, the application domain should be well known in order to identify relevant data. This knowledge is usually retrieved through a requirement analysis step. Though it is indeed a difficult step, it is easier than for an expert system. A precise reasoning description is not useful. Only inputs and outputs should be clearly stated.

Representing data as homogeneous information is application dependant. However, the chosen representation should allow to:

- model all the information contained in the relevant data. This criteria, which sounds natural, could reveal indeed advantages (as for fuzzy sets) or drawbacks of given representations.
- apply efficient aggregation tools to model expert reasoning. We would describe hereafter (chapter 2.3) how fuzzy sets representation offers such tools.

2.2 Information aggregation

The general principle of data aggregation is described in figure 1. It allows us to obtain a synthetic view of the available information from modified data (filtered as relevant data and preprocessed to an homogeneous information).This operation should model expert reasoning and is therefore delicate.

Indeed numerous artificial intelligence techniques showed that they were too strict to model precisely human reasoning. Practically, use of fuzzy terms is often noticed, thus leading to identify fuzzy logic as a valuable processing and representation mean. Numerous fuzzy sets aggregation tools are indeed available [2], even if a choice is sometimes difficult. Some authors propose operators classification, from their theoretical properties point of view ([7] and [8]) or from a user requirement point of view [1].

All of these operators have a broad range of action and it is possible to find such operators that can tackle with most of existing cases (criteria in accordance or not [3] weighting, partial aggregation and compatibility [15],...).

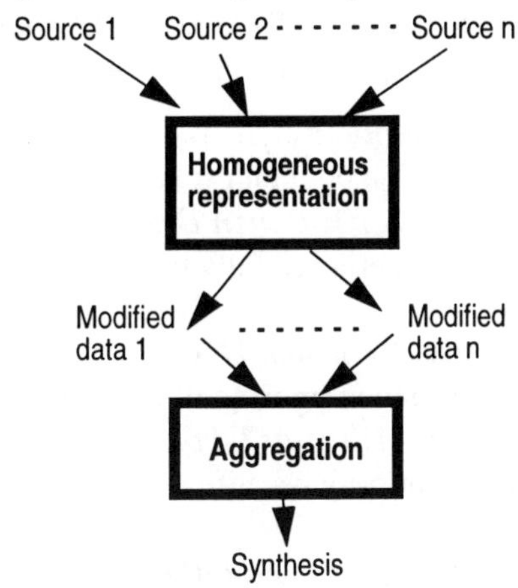

Figure 1: global process of aggregation

2.3 Tool to manage priorities between fuzzy criteria

Experts are often using priorities between criteria when they are facing numerous data and their associated criteria. Some data are therefore more important than others and this type of processing could lead to time savings when low priority processing are not used. This type of reasoning is hard to tackle with when you are using an expert system formalism but is possible when using fuzzy sets.

We present hereafter synthetically what has been done in [9] and [10] so that chapter 4 could be fully understood.
In [14] the definition of second order criteria has been introduced and linked to fuzzy sets as well as a first method to manage these criteria. A modification of these operators allows a good management of priorities between criteria.

2.3.1 Second order criteria

Let A and B be two decision criteria, defined as fuzzy sets. Let χ be the set representing all possible solutions to the problem. We know how an element of χ is satisfying A or B through its membership function.
We want to find an aggregation method such that A has priority over B. Thus a solution to the problem should first satisfy A and then B (if it is not in contradiction with satisfaction of A).
Let D be the global criteria. It can be defined as
$D = (A)$ and (if B is compatible with A then B)
Compatibility can be defined as a satisfaction of A and B simultaneously and is noted *Poss(A,B)*:

$$Poss(A, B) = max_{x \in \chi}(A(x) \wedge B(x))$$

where $\wedge$ represents a t-norm.
Thus, D can be defined as:

$$\forall(x \in \chi),\ D(x) = A(x) \wedge ((1 - Poss(A,B)) \vee B(x))$$
$$therefore,\ D(x) = (A(x) \wedge (1 - Poss(A,B))) \vee (A(x) \wedge B(x))$$

If B is totally incompatible with priority criteria A, then this second order criteria does not interfere in the choice of an optimum solution:

$$\text{if } Poss(A,B)=0 \text{ then } D(x)=A(x)$$

On the contrary, when the two criteria are fully compatible, the solution should satisfy A and B simultaneously:

$$\text{if } Poss(A,B)=1 \text{ then } D(x)=A(x) \wedge B(x)$$

We could finally introduce a degree of priority of A over B. We could consider [14]:

$$D(x)=A(x) \wedge (B(x) \vee ((1-Poss(A,B)) \wedge \alpha))$$

α represents indeed a degree of priority because if $\alpha=1$, we find again that A has priority over B:

$$D(x)=A(x) \wedge (B(x) \vee (1-Poss(A,B))),$$

However, if $\alpha=0$, A and B are equally important.

2.3.2 Aggregation through priority management

Taken into account results of the last paragraph, we propose hereafter an aggregation method consisting of defining a global criteria D from two criteria A and B defined as:

- A has priority over B with a degree α
- B has priority over A with a degree β

We obtain the following aggregation operator:

$$D(x) = [A(x) \wedge (B(x) \vee ((1 - Poss(A,B)) \wedge \alpha))] \vee [B(x) \wedge (A(x) \vee ((1 - Poss(A,B)) \wedge \beta))]$$

$\wedge$ et $\vee$ could be any operator from t-norms and t-conorms. Some properties of D could depend on this choice.

It has to be noticed that, in case where A and B are very important ($\alpha = \beta = 1$), we obtain an aggregation operator which is near from which proposed by Dubois & Prade [3] which was:

$$D_2(x) = \left[\frac{A(x) \wedge B(x)}{Poss(A,B)}\right] \vee [A(x) \wedge (1 - Poss(A,B))] \vee [B(x) \wedge (1 - Poss(A,B))]$$

2.3.3 *n* criteria generalisation

When faced to numerous criteria with different priorities, we should choose an aggregation strategy.
I we choose to compare each criteria to the others, a big number of comparisons is necessary (*n!*).

It could be simpler to complete aggregation by pairs. It is therefore necessary to aggregate all the criteria with the same priority together so that we obtain a unique criteria for each priority level. We then aggregate these criteria in pairs on a descending order, thus satisfying the more important criteria first. The method could be summarized through the following figures:

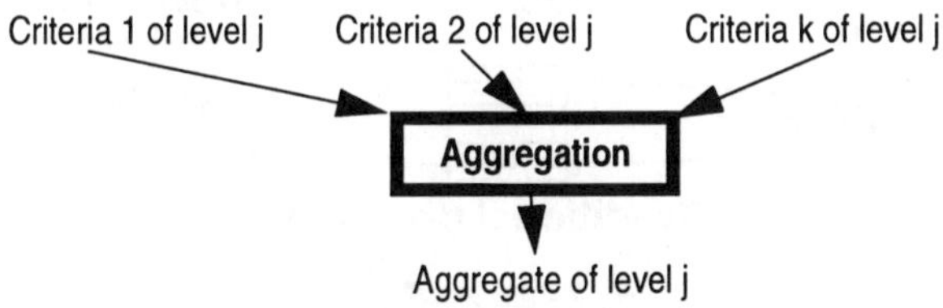

Figure 2: Aggregation of level j

then

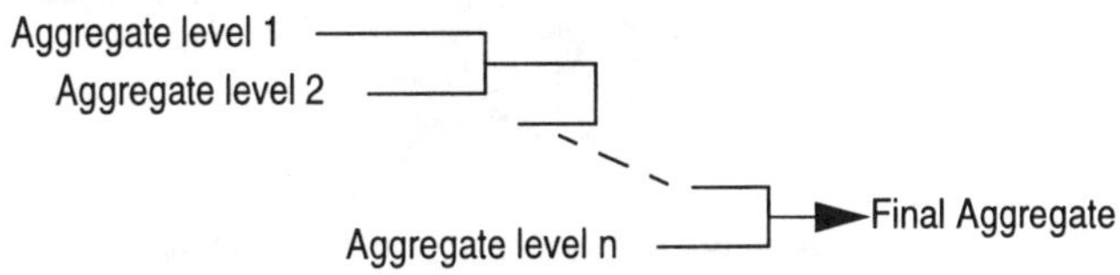

Figure 3: Final cascading aggregation

This method will be used in the example described in paragraph 4.

3 A multi-agents system for data fusion

The representation and criteria aggregation methods should now be implemented, tested and validated. Using a multi-agents system allows us to do it through an iterative, adaptive and efficient way.

3.1 Introducing multi-agents system concept

A multi-agents system (MAS) can be seen as a set of software components, called "agents" which cooperate through complex interaction protocols to achieve a common goal. In such a system, all can be distributed: knowledge, control, skills, activity [5]... (see fig. 4).

We describe hereafter some characteristics that support agents cooperation.

Agents can communicate together through different means (direct communication through message passing, indirect communication through acting on the environment). They can be organized as different structures (specific role for each of them or no precise role, hierarchical structure or not,...). Several types of collaboration can also exist (agents multiplied to enhance performance, task shared among agents, conflicts resolution...).

These criteria help in classifying MAS model used. Some other criteria could be found in [4].

Another level of characterization exists at the agent level. Indeed, some agents are designed to be deliberative such that they are reasoning about their world representation, their goals, their plans through explicit processing. Reactive agents are, on the contrary, not using any explicit representation. Most of the time, they act spontane-

ously to events [6]. Other criteria exist to distinguish between agents such as cooperation, autonomy, learning. All these criteria can be combined [12].
Therefore, MAS are not fixed software architecture components but they allow us to obtain specific properties through organization of the MAS and modelisation of agents and their cooperation.

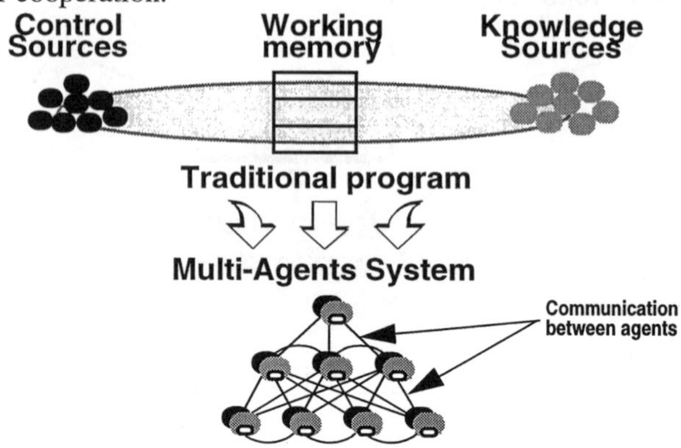

Figure 4: Difference between multi-agents System & traditional program

In the context of artillery localization, MAS are interesting because the building of the solution is iterative. Moreover, addition or modelisation of agents is easy, thus leading to tuning or adaptive capabilities. Besides, several fuzzy aggregation strategies could be tested through a single and simple modification of agents which collaborate together. Moreover, processing is dynamic, i.e. to solve two identical problems, different agents can be used. Therefore, some agents could be highly specialized and very efficient in a specific context.
Different processing chains could also be in action simultaneously (working concurrently). This capability is useful for validation or optimization steps of application building.
In the following paragraph we present a MAS architecture which is well integrated in the intelligence information fusion problem. We describe the MAS organization, the agent model and way of collaborating.

3.2 A multi-agents system for intelligence information fusion: AGB (AGent Builder)

3.2.1 The agent model

AGB lies on the deliberative agent concept. Each agent has the necessary information and knowledge to complete its task and manage interactions with the other agents and the environment. Agents in AGB are modelled as specialists of a specific problem solving situation. They own either all services and resources needed to complete this task or the necessary knowledge to separate this problem into several subproblems and the means to make them completed.

3.2.2 Organization

Agents belong to a hierarchical organization comprising several levels. They can only emit messages to their level or to the lower levels. This organization is suited to the hierarchy of fusion processes described in chapter 4.

3.2.3 Collaboration between agents

Agents are collaborating through the use of the "Contract Net" protocol [13]. The client (an agent) is offering a problem to be solved through a request of "Who can?" type. The agents which can a priori solve this problem emits a "I can" request with their a priori success scoring to complete this task. Then, the client is choosing one or more agents to actually perform the task and send them a "You do that" request. The client can afterwards retrieve the results through a "give me" request.
We add to the basic protocol a way to retrieve partial results, thus leading to a better efficiency.
Agents from a specific level could therefore delegate their problem solving request to other agents of the same or lower levels. This protocol is well suited to intelligence information fusion problems which are well modelled as subproblems.
Several concurrently processing chains could also be used to solve a unique problem. This can be useful to compare different expert opinions implemented as processing chains or to obtain "anytime" results through the carrying out of several processing chains at different levels of quality.
We describe in paragraph 4.5 the application of this MAS to artillery localization.

4 Artillery localization application

We now describe the application of scientific methods presented in the chapters 2 and 3 in the specific case of artillery localization on a battlefield. As already presented in the introduction, the aim of this application is to help the intelligence officer to rapidly localize on a map the possibility of presence of artillery pieces. This information should help him to use more efficiently his means to gather information (UAVs).

4.1 Sources to be taken into account

There are different data to be taken into account:

- knowledge about the enemy: the way it is usually organized, how units are deployed on the field, what is the hierarchy.
- knowledge about materials: for artillery, it consists mainly of minimum and maximum ranges.
- the terrain relief: which is described in NMT (Numerical Model of the Terrain) files.
- Vectorized data related to the terrain: indeed, forests and road network are relevant data for the artillery localization problem.
- Tactical situation perceived: observations already done by UAVs, communication intelligence or radar information gathered and processed should be integrated in the reasoning process to prevent redundancy of information.

One can notice that these data are numerous and heterogeneous. Their use is dependant upon the human reasoning process presented hereafter.

4.2 Domain expert reasoning process

The aim of this step is to gather knowledge used by the expert to analyse data available in order to localize areas where artillery should be. This knowledge is based upon constraints used by the enemy to install its artillery. Some criteria should be satisfied as much as possible. There exists also some priority levels between these criteria. The following criteria have been identified (by descending order of importance):

- Mission success: artillery should be localized so that it could hit its objective.
- Support: artillery should be placed near roads to allow easier ammunition support.
- Security: artillery should not be seen by the opponent when it is firing or in position. Relief is therefore important.

In addition to these criteria, observations already gathered and processed provide valuable information about artillery possible localization. Therefore, this type of information, denoted by "Tactical situation" criteria should be the more important criteria. This knowledge should now be linked to the available data to calculate and represent the different criteria. The type of chosen representation constitutes the link.

4.3 Chosen representation

This kind of choice is difficult because not only we define the representation of the available date but also we choose what kind of aggregation operators we could use. Our goal is to present to the operators areas where there is potentially artillery. Some of these areas will offer a greater chance to find artillery. The fuzzy set representation is therefore naturally chosen. For a given criteria, we will represent possibility of presence of the artillery through the membership function defined on a set of dimension 2 (the battlefield). If it is possible to find artillery on position (x,y), then the function value is 1 on (x,y), otherwise its value is 0.

Once the representation is chosen, we are now linking the available data to the criteria defined by the expert.

- knowledge about the enemy: relevant information are for these data the number of artillery basic units used for each higher level unit, their global hierarchy and their typical deployment (Order of Battle). With the information already gathered (tactical situation), we can define some areas where some artillery units should be (areas of higher units already perceived for which not all the artillery basic units have been perceived) and define some areas to be investigated. This information should lead to the fuzzy set corresponding to the "Tactical Situation" criteria, named Map_1.
- knowledge about materials: only minimum and maximum range information about artillery is useful here. The objective of the enemy is defined by the user of the application. These information are processed together to indicate us areas where artillery should be located to hit the objective.
- forest localization is also important to determine if an artillery piece could hit its objective. Indeed, if the artillery is inside a forest or very near of a forest, it can

not hit its objective. Therefore, the fuzzy set representing "Mission success" criteria is a conjunction of the fuzzy set depicting areas between minimum and maximum ranges described previously and the fuzzy set depicting areas outside forests.The resulting fuzzy set is named Map_2 (cf. fig. 5).

Figure 5: example of Map_2 (outside forests and hit areas)

- road network is important to determine whether an artillery piece could be supported or not. The artillery should be very near of the road, which is a fuzzy distance. The fuzzy set describing the "Support" criteria (Map_3) is described in figure 6.

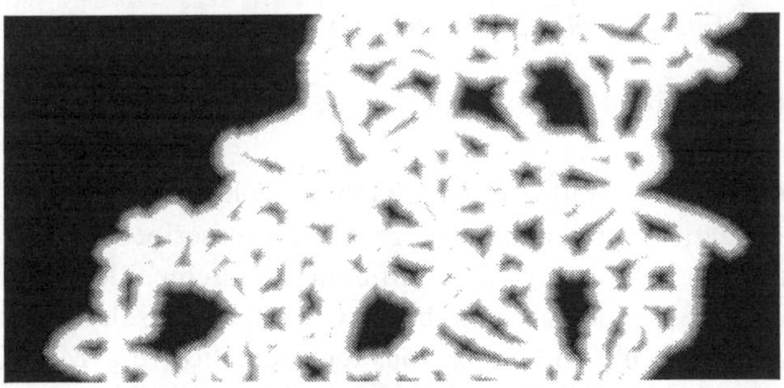

Figure 6: example of Map_3 (near from roads)

- Eventually, "Security" criteria defines that artillery should not be seen by the opponent. To calculate this last fuzzy set, we use NMT and objective information to determine areas not seen by the opponent (Map_4).

We described how to homogeneously represent relevant input information linked to each criteria as fuzzy sets. These different maps could be now aggregated to lead to a synthetic information about artillery localization.

4.4 Data fusion

Each criteria is defined by a level of priority and represented as a map. We should now define a global criteria represented as a map which aggregates all the criteria defined depending upon their priority. As it has been described in paragraph 2.3.3, we use a cascading aggregation strategy. We therefore fuse Map_1 with Map_2 (which leads to Map_12), then the result with Map_3... This enhances areas which satisfy the most important number of high priority criteria. A level of priority should be defined for each aggregation. This parameter should be chosen to suit best to the operational reality. Depending on the situation, these parameters could be easily changed to take into account new situations.

The synthetic map obtained (see fig. 7) could be overlaid on a cartographic map to help the user to localize areas where artillery could be. Then, intelligence means such as UAVs could be launched to investigate a particular area. The information gathered is afterwards integrated into the "Tactical Situation" map and the application can be reused to promote different areas till all artillery units localization are known.

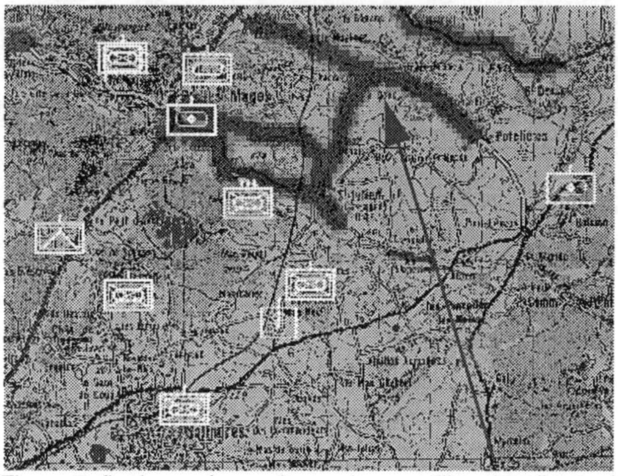

Figure 7: final map (areas in overlay = artillery localization)

4.5 Application to multi-agents system

The multi-agents system detailed in paragraph 3 has been instantiated to implement the artillery localization application. The processing described in the previous paragraphs have been modelled as agents of different hierarchical levels (cf. fig. 8). The roles of the agents are dependant upon their level in the MAS. Indeed, agents at level 3 are capable of completing an homogenous representation (e.g. Map_3 described in §4.3) by using results of processing by agents of level 4. We give an example of processing chain which leads to potential areas through the use of two criteria, "Tactical situation" and "Mission success" (follow arrows).

The advantages of using such a model are numerous: modularity of implementation, adaptiveness of the model (we can redefine an agent without modifying the others) and ease of tuning. The possibility which consists in launching more than one processing chain simultaneously should allow to test different ways of aggregation (i.e. different strategies) on the same input data. We could also use this technique to calculate successive results with an increasing quality depending on the number and order of the criteria used.

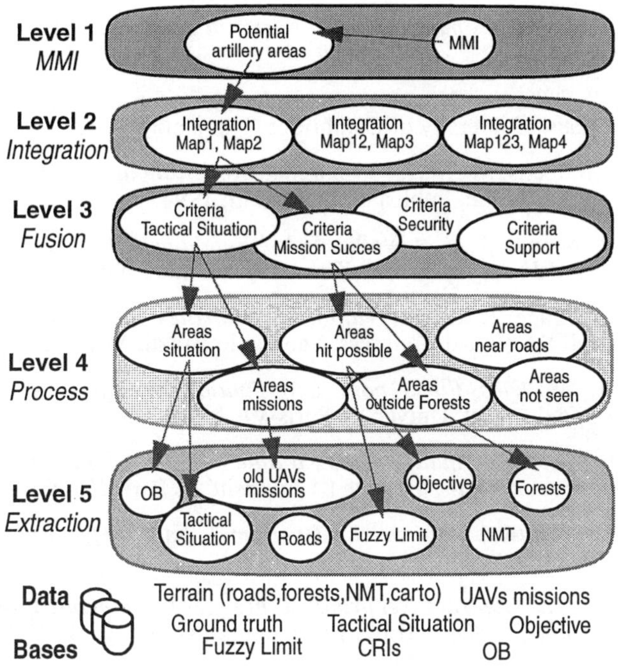

Figure 8: agents organization

5 Conclusion

We described the main steps of a general methodology of data fusion: determining relevant data, homogenous representation of these data and then aggregation thanks to operators as those used on fuzzy sets. The use of fuzzy sets allow us to obtain and present results to the intelligence officer as if they were processed "by hand". Moreover, modification of priority between criteria is very easy.

The implementation of this method as a multi-agents system show us that such a technique allows modularity, adaptiveness and validation opportunity. Besides, this multi-agents system could be applied to other domains thanks to a generic approach. This application has been operationally validated by an intelligence expert.

Bibliography

[1] Bloch,I.,"*Information Combination Operators for Data Fusion: a Comparative Review with Classification*", IEEE Trans. on Syst.,Man and Cyber.,Vol 26, 1, January, 52-67, 1996.

[2] Dubois,D. et Prade,H.,"*A Review of Fuzzy Sets Aggregation Connectives*", Information Sciences, 36, 85-121, 1985.

[3] Dubois,D. et Prade,H.,"*Combination of Information in the Framework of Possibility Theory*", dans "Data Fusion in Robotics and Machine Intelligence",Al Abidi (eds), Academic Press, New-York, 1991.

[4] Ferber,J.,"*Les systèmes multi-agents, vers une intelligence collective*",

Interéditions, 1995.

[5] Ferber,J.,"*Les systèmes multi-agents: un aperçu général*", TSI (16, 8/1997), 979-1012, Octobre 1997

[6] Ferguson,I.A.,"*Touring Machines: an architecture for dynamic, rational, mobile agents*", PhD Thesis, University of Cambridge, Novembre 1992.

[7] Fodor,J. et Roubens, M.,"*Fuzzy Preference Modelling and Multicriteria Decision Support*",Kluwer Academic Publisher, Dordrecht, 1994.

[8] Grabisch,M.,Nguyen,H.T. et Walker,E.A.,"*Fundamentals of Uncertainty Calculi with Applications to Fuzzy Inference*",Kluwer Academic Publisher,Dordrecht,1995.

[9] Kelman,A. et Yager,R.R.,"*Integration of Priorities in Aggregation Methods*", Proc. of the VIth IFSA World Congress, Sao Paulo,Brazil, Vol 1, 293-295, 1995.

[10] Kelman,A.,"*Modèles Flous pour l'Agrégation de Données et l'Aide à la Décision*", thèse de doctorat, Université Paris VI, 1996.

[11] Lefèvre,V.,"*Système multi-agents d'aide à la photo-interprétation sur architecture multiprocesseur*", thèse de l'Université de Paris XI, Novembre 1994.

[12] Nwana,H.S.,"*Software Agents: an Overview*", Knowledge Eng. Review (11), 205-244, Oct/Nov 1996.

[13] Smith,R.G.,"*The Contract-Net protocol: high level communications and control in a distributed problem solver*",IEEE Tr. on comp., vol C-29, 12, 1980.

[14] Yager,R.R.,"*Non-monotonic set theoretic operations*", Fuzzy Sets and Systems, 42, 173-190, 1991.

[15] Yager,R.R.,"*Aggregation operators and fuzzy systems modeling*", Fuzzy Sets and Systems, 67, 129-146, 1994.

Fuzzy Decision Trees to Extract Features of Odorous Molecules

Christophe Marsala
LIP6 – UPMC
mailbox 169, 4 place Jussieu
75252 Paris cedex 05, France
Christophe.Marsala@lip6.fr

Mohammed Ramdani
F.S.T de Mohammadia
BP146
Mohammadia, Maroc
ramdani@deneb.uh2m.ac.ma

Driss Zakarya
F.S.T de Mohammadia
BP146
Mohammadia, Maroc

Mustapha Tollabi
Faculté des Sciences
Av. Ibn Batouta Agdal
Rabat, Maroc

Abstract:
In this paper, an application of fuzzy decision trees to the recognition of odors is presented. Fuzzy decision trees are used to extract and highlight associations in the chemical structure of the smelling and the quality of their odors. Experiments have been conducted with the system *Salammbô* on data related to the description of molecules, modelized by means of the GESDEM (GEneration and Selection of Descriptor and pattern Elaboration Method). Beside the discontinuous descriptors generated by GESDEM method, we have used another type of descriptors which are continuous: the dimensions of each molecule and theirs ratios as geometric descriptors and logP, Molecular refraction and density as physico-chemical descriptors. These descriptors were measured on the most stable conformation of the molecules.

1 Introduction

In order to be discerned, volatile compounds, pure chemicals or miscellanies, are elated by the air to the nose where they are warmed and humidified. The birth of olfactory message results from the adsorption of the arriving smelling molecules to the nasal mucus on some glycoproteic receptors of the membrane of the olfactory lashes. Several theories of olfaction were suggested [2, 21], but, until now, the mechanism of perception stays unrecognized although progresses have been achieved in different disciplines annexed to the chimioreception. The chemists attempt to contribute to the understanding of the mechanisms implied in the olfaction by the investigation of the links that bind the chemical structure of the smelling to the quality of their odors.

To this academic goal, a convenient and commercial interest can be added as the rational design of new molecules which could be used in the industry of fragrance, aromas and cosmetic. Research for relationships between an odor and its structure is not an easy task. The first difficulty deals with the translation of the structure of chemicals in a set of parameters containing the usable information to solve the problem. Beyond methods based on some molecular properties [2, 21], ..., the topological methods [7], the auto correlation [24] and the fragmentation methods [6, 11] have been applied and obtained a satisfactory degree of success. Some parameters of various types (steric, electronic, geometric, energetic, lipophilic...), as well as a multiplicity of tools for the treatment of data (linear multiple regression, principal components analysis, discriminate analysis, and pattern recognition...) were used according to the aim of each study.

More recently, other approaches to determine the odor structure relationships have been developed using artificial neural networks [8]. Nevertheless, neural networks allow neither to establish mathematical equations between the studied odor and the used descriptors, nor to give off any rules allowing to know the role and the influence of every used descriptor. While descriptors generally used in this domain are of precise nature -continuous or discrete- the made decisions are shaded. Experts always classify the quality of an odor by some symbolic descriptors on some numeric ladders such as "strong or weak odor of musk", or "absence or presence of studied odor". However, classic systems do not allow the treatment of this double description of the odor.

In this contribution, we present and test an approach based on fuzzy decision trees. This approach is more explanatory and more adapted to treat this kind of data than classical ones. It is based on the use of the software *Salammbô* of construction and utilization of fuzzy decision trees [12, 15, 16].

This paper is composed as follows. In Section 2, we introduce the method to construct and to use fuzzy decision trees, implemented in the software *Salammbô*. In Section 3, the description of the chemical data is presented. In Section 4, the expected results and those obtained are shown. Finally, we conclude thereafter on some perspectives.

2 Fuzzy Decision Trees

A decision tree is a natural structure of knowledge. Each node in such a tree is associated with a test on the values of an attribute, each edge from a node is labeled with a particular value of the attribute, and each leaf of the tree is associated with a value of the class. Each path in the tree is associated with a production rule, where premises are composed by the tests of the encountered nodes, and the conclusion of the rule is composed by the class associated with the leaf of the path.

Edges can be labeled by so-called numeric-symbolic values. A numeric-symbolic attribute is an attribute whose values can be either numeric (*1.72 meters*) or symbolic (*tall*) linked with a numerical variable. Such kind of values leads to the generalization of decision trees into *fuzzy decision trees* [3, 5, 18,

20, 22].

Fuzzy decision trees (*cf.* Figure 6) enable us to use numeric-symbolic values either during their construction or when classifying new cases. The use of fuzzy set theory enhances the understandability of decision trees when considering numerical attributes. Moreover, it can be prove that fuzziness leads to a better robustness when classifying new cases [12, 13].

2.1 Learning Phase: Construction of a Fuzzy Decision Tree

A decision tree can be constructed from a set of examples by *inductive learning* [17]. Inductive learning is a process to generalize knowledge obtained from the observation of a given phenomenon. It is based on a set of *examples*, called the *training set.* Each example is a case already solved or completely known, associated with a pair [description, class] where the *description* is a set of pairs [attribute, value].

Most of the algorithms to build decision trees, the Top Down Induction of Decision Trees (TDIDT) algorithms, proceed in the same way. The decision tree is built from its root to its leaves. The training set is successively split by means of a question on the value of a chosen attribute.

Let $\mathcal{E}$ be a training set composed by a set of examples t_i. Each t_i is defined by a value $t_i[A_j]$ for each attribute A_j of a set of attributes $\mathcal{A}$. A particular attribute $C \in \mathcal{A}$ is highlighted and considered as the class to learn. The TDIDT algorithm to build decision trees is the following:

1. *Select* an attribute $A_j \in \mathcal{A}$, $A_j \neq C$, with m_j modalities $\{v_{j1}, ..., v_{jm_j}\}$. This attribute will be used to split the training set $\mathcal{E}$ into several subsets. A node $\eta(A_j)$ is created in the tree. It is labeled with a test on the value of A_j.

2. *Split* the training set $\mathcal{E}$ by means of the selected attribute A_j. As many subsets $\mathcal{E}_{jl}$ as modalities v_{jl} are created:

$$\mathcal{E} = \bigcup_{l=1,\ldots,m_j} \mathcal{E}_{jl} \quad \text{with} \quad \mathcal{E}_{jl} = \{t_i \in \mathcal{E} \mid t_i[A_j] = v_{jl}\}$$

   Each value v_{jl} of the attribute labels an edge from the node $\eta(A_j)$, this edge leads to the corresponding subset $\mathcal{E}_{jl}$. In the case of numeric-symbolic attributes, the partition of $\mathcal{E} = \mathcal{E}_{j1} \cup \ldots \cup \mathcal{E}_{jm_j}$ can be fuzzy when each $\mathcal{E}_{ji}$ is a fuzzy set of the set $\mathcal{F}$ of elements of $\mathcal{E}$ in adequation with the value v_{ji} of attribute A_j (i.e. $\mathcal{F} = \{t_i \in \mathcal{E} \mid \mu_{v_{jl}}(t_i[A_j]) > 0\}$ if $t_i[A_j]$ is numerical) and examples belonging to the intersection $\mathcal{E}_{ji} \cap \mathcal{E}_{jk}$ should be distributed by means of a splitting strategy.

3. *Check* if the stopping criterion is fulfilled by each subset $\mathcal{E}_{jl}$. A leaf is created from a subset that fulfills this criterion. This leaf is associated with the class of this subset.

4. Start again in step 1 with all the subsets that do not fulfill the stopping criterion.

Parameters related to each step of this algorithm must be selected: a measure of discrimination, a splitting strategy, a stopping criterion.

2.1.1 *Measure of Discrimination.*

A measure of discrimination enables us to measure the *power of discrimination* of an attribute A_j relatively to the class C. It evaluates to which extent the values of this attribute are linked with each modality of the class. In the process of construction of decision trees, the choice of the best attribute by means of a measure of discrimination is a heuristic that enables us to optimize the tree being built. This heuristic should minimize the size of the tree and introduces a semantic coherence of the tests that label the nodes of the tree. The question associated with a node will be the more pertinent in order to discover the value of the class.

A measure of discrimination must be defined specifically in order to construct fuzzy decision trees from a set of examples described by means of numeric-symbolic attributes. It has to take into account the degrees of membership to a fuzzy value for each example of the training set. The most commonly used measure of discrimination in the presence of fuzzy values is an extension of the Shannon entropy, the so-called star entropy [18]:

$$H_S^*(C|A_j) = -\sum_{l=1}^{m_j} P^*(V_{jl}) \sum_{k=1}^{K} P^*(C_k|V_{jl}) \log(P^*(C_k|V_{jl}))$$

where $V_{jl} = \{t_i \in \mathcal{E} \mid t_i[A_j] = v_{jl}\}$ and $C_k = \{t_i \in \mathcal{E} \mid t_i[C] = c_k\}$. This measure is obtained from the classical Shannon measure of entropy by substituting the Zadeh's probability measure P^* of fuzzy events [23] to the classical probability. Let $\mathcal{V} = \{x_1, ..., x_n\}$ be a fuzzy set defined by its membership function μ, each element x_i from $\mathcal{V}$ is associated with a classic probability measure of occurrence $P(x_i)$. $\mathcal{V}$ is considered as a fuzzy event. The *probability of the fuzzy event* $\mathcal{V}$ is defined by Zadeh as:

$$P^*(\mathcal{V}) - \sum_{i=1}^{n} \mu(x_i)P(x_i)$$

2.1.2 *Splitting Strategy.*

The splitting strategy defines how the training set will be split by a question on the value of an attribute. In the case of numerical or symbolic attribute, each modality v_{jl} of an attribute A_j defines a subset $\mathcal{E}_{jl}$ of the training set, composed by the examples that possess value v_{jl} of A_j for $l = 1...m_j$.

In the case of numeric-symbolic attributes, a common solution is to distribute the examples in all the subsets $\mathcal{E}_{ji}$ with their degree of membership to the fuzzy value v_{ji}. Another close strategy is to distribute the examples in the same way but to give a membership degree equal to 1 to all the examples in the intersection $\mathcal{E}_{jl} \cap \mathcal{E}_{jk}$ to reflect their membership to both subsets. However, a drawback of this strategy is to duplicate the most imprecise, uncertain or noisy examples of the training set. A third strategy is to use α-cuts for each fuzzy set. For instance, with $\alpha = \frac{1}{2}$, the following crisp partition is created: $\forall l = 1, ...m_j$, $\mathcal{E}_{jl} = \{t_i \in \mathcal{E} \mid \mu_{v_{jl}}(t_i[A_j]) \geq \frac{1}{2}\}$. A last solution can be to create an additional specific subset with all examples from this intersection. Thus, it will lead to the construction of a specific edge from the current node, and so, to the construction of a specific subtree to discriminate these examples.

2.1.3 Stopping Criterion.

The stopping criterion T enables us to know if a subset of $\mathcal{E}$ is homogeneous with regard to the class. The process of construction of the decision tree will stop the development of a path on a suitable set. The stopping criterion can be for instance defined as one of the following strategies:

- All the examples of $\mathcal{E}$, or at least a *majority* of examples, are associated with the same class. Usually, the stopping criterion T is linked with the measure of discrimination used in step 1 of the algorithm. The notion of *majority* is evaluated by means of a threshold for the value of the measure of discrimination. The smaller the value of the measure of discrimination, the more homogeneous the training set with regard to the class.
- The number of examples in $\mathcal{E}$ is too small to justify a split of $\mathcal{E}$.
- There is no more attribute to use. This stopping criterion is used when we accept only one node associated with an attribute on a path of the tree.

The stopping criterion for the construction of fuzzy decision trees is very similar to the stopping criterion in the classic case. The impurity of the current training set with respect to the repartition of the classes can be measured either by the measure of discrimination used in step 1 of the algorithm, which is fuzzy, or by another one, fuzzy or not.

2.2 Classification phase: Utilization of a Fuzzy Decision Tree

As mentioned, a path of the tree is equivalent to a production rule. The premises for such a rule r are composed by tests on values of attributes, and the conclusion is the value of the class that labels the leaf of the path:

$$\texttt{if } A_{l_1} = v_{l_1} \texttt{ and } \ldots\texttt{and } A_{l_p} = v_{l_p} \texttt{ then } C = c_k$$

In a fuzzy decision tree, a leaf can be labeled by a set of values $\{c_1, ..., c_K\}$ for the class, each value c_j associated with a weight computed during the learning phase. Thus, a path of a fuzzy decision tree is equivalent to the following rule:

$$\texttt{if } A_{l_1} = v_{l_1} \texttt{ and } \ldots\texttt{and } A_{l_p} = v_{l_p} \texttt{ then}$$
$$C = c_1 \texttt{ with the degree } P^*(c_1|(v_{l_1}, v_{l_2}, ...v_{l_p})) \texttt{ and } \ldots \texttt{ and } C = c_K \texttt{ with the degree } P^*(c_K|(v_{l_1}, v_{l_2}, ...v_{l_p}))$$

A new example e to classify is described by means of values for each attribute $\{A_1 = w_1; ...; A_n = w_n\}$. This description is compared with the premises of the rule r by means of a measure of satisfiability [4] enabling us to value the satisfiability of any observed modality w to the edge modality v. The measure of satisfiability used in the software *Salammbô* is:

$$\mathbf{Deg}(w, v) = \frac{\int_X \mu_{w\cap v} dx}{\int_X \mu_w \, dx} \quad \text{if} \quad \int_X \mu_w \, dx \neq 0 \tag{1}$$

where μ_w is the membership function associated with the modality w, $\mu_{w\cap v}$ is the membership function associated with the intersection $w \cap v$ between the modality w and the modality v, X is the universe of values where μ_w and $\mu_{w\cap v}$ are defined. When $\int_X \mu_w dx = 0$, we define $\mathbf{Deg}(w, v) = 0$.

For each premise, a degree of satisfiability $\mathbf{Deg}(w_{l_i}, v_{l_i})$ is computed for the corresponding value w_{l_i}. Finally, given a rule r, a description is associated with the class c_j with a *final degree* of satisfiability $\mathbf{Fdeg}_r(c_j)$ that corresponds to the satisfiability of the description to the premises of the rule r weighted by the conditional probability for c_j according to the rule r in order to take into account the confidence of the rule. These values are aggregated by means of a *triangular norm* $\top$:

$$\mathbf{Fdeg}_r(c_j) = \top_{i\,=\,1...p}\mathbf{Deg}(w_{l_i}, v_{l_i}).P^*(c_j|(v_{l_1}, v_{l_2}, ...v_{l_p}))$$

Final degrees computed from all the rules are aggregated by means of a triangular conorm $\perp$ (for instance, the *maximum* triangular conorm or the Łukasiewicz triangular conorm) to obtain a single degree of satisfiability $\mathbf{Fdeg}(c_j)$. If n_ρ is the number of rules given by the fuzzy decision tree:

$$\mathbf{Fdeg}(c_j) = \perp_{r\,=\,1...n_\rho}\mathbf{Fdeg}_r(c_j)$$

For each value of the class, the description e is associated with such a degree of satisfiability $\mathbf{Fdeg}(c_j)$ for each class c_j computed from the whole set of rules. The class c_e associated with e can be chosen as the class with the higher degree of satisfiability:

$$\mathbf{FDeg}(c_e) = \max_{j=1...K} \mathbf{FDeg}(c_j)$$

We used such a process of aggregation of degrees in order to have meaningful values of degrees for each class.

2.3 The software *Salammbô*

We have implemented the software *Salammbô* to construct and use fuzzy decision trees. In this system, from a training set, a fuzzy decision tree is constructed by means of the method presented in the first part of section 2.1.

Several kinds of parameters can be chosen by the user to construct the tree. For instance, the measure of discrimination is the star entropy, the splitting strategy is the $\alpha-$cut strategy (with $\alpha = \frac{1}{2}$) and the stopping criterion is based on the Shannon measure of information and the number of examples in the local training set.

Moreover, a new method of construction of fuzzy modalities is implemented in Salammbô. This method enables the system to deduce fuzzy modalities on the universe of values of continuous attributes related to the distribution of the classes [14].

3 Description of the chemical data

The set of studied compounds is constituted by 99 aliphatic alcohols; among them, 29 are primary, 52 are secondary and 18 are tertiary. They are composed by 1 to 12 atoms of carbon. The odor of these alcohols was described in details by Schnabel et al. [19] using 16 qualitative descriptors on an active scale valued of 1 to 5.

We focus here on the odor of camphor described as "etherisch" by Schnabel et al. In order to describe the molecules, we choose the GESDEM method

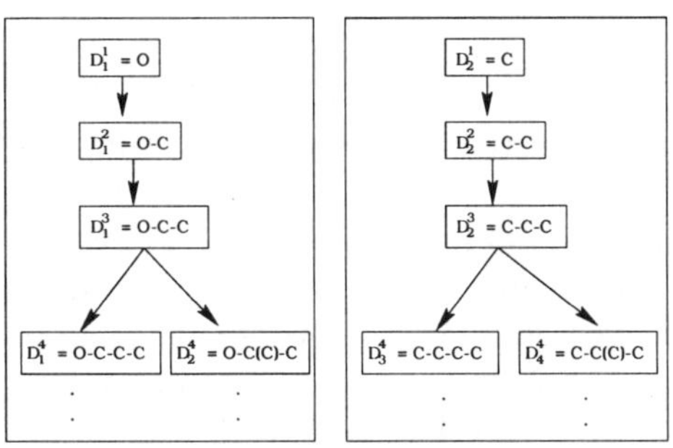

Figure 1: Method to generate GESDEM description

(Generation and selection of descriptor and pattern elaboration) described by Zakarya [25]. This method suits perfectly the description of the studied compounds in the sense that they are saturated aliphatic and monofunctional alcohols. In the GESDEM methodology, the used descriptors are only made up from groups of atoms held together by bonds and constituting specific subgraphs. The number of atoms in fragments is progressively increased, until descriptors giving an acceptable discrimination are obtained. The order n of a given descriptor is defined as the number of atoms (excluding hydrogen atoms) that it contains. Thus, descriptors of order one D_1^i are simply the different types of atoms found in the sample. Descriptors of order two D_2^i are elaborated by adding an atom existing in the studied molecules, in all possible ways, to descriptors of order one. Descriptors of order n are generated from descriptors of order $n-1$ using the same procedure. A set of descriptors of the same order n represents all possible arrangements of n atoms of all types, existing in the studied sample. Figure 1 shows how the descriptors of every order are generated, starting from those of the low order.

Each molecule is described by a vector composed by the number of descriptors of each type encountered in the molecule and by a set of geometric features.

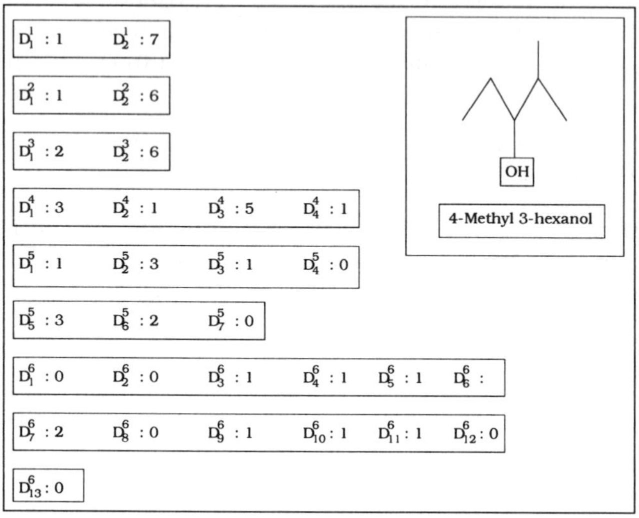

Figure 2: Descriptor counting

To calculate the geometries of the lowest energy conformations we used the method of molecular mechanics. This empirical method seems to be convenient for the calculation of the molecular geometries in gas phase. Several sets of force field parameters are available in the literature, in this study we used the MM+ parametrization [1]. As molecular mechanics give no information on either electron densities or electron charge on the atoms, semi-empirical methods on the minimized geometries were performed using Dewar's AM1 program [9]. All computations were performed using the Hyperchem© program package.

In order to take into account the form of each molecule, from the structural representation of the molecule (Figure 3), the molecule's maximum length was oriented along the x axis and the molecule's maximum width along the y axis, we have measured on the most stable conformations the dimensions of the molecule:

- the molecular length R is measured as the distance along the screen x axis between the extreme left and the extreme right atoms plus their Van der Waal's radii.
- the molecular width r is the distance along the screen y axis between the atoms at the top and the bottom plus their Van der Waal's radii.
- the molecular depth p is the distance along the screen z axis between the nearest and farthest atoms plus their Van der Waal's radii.

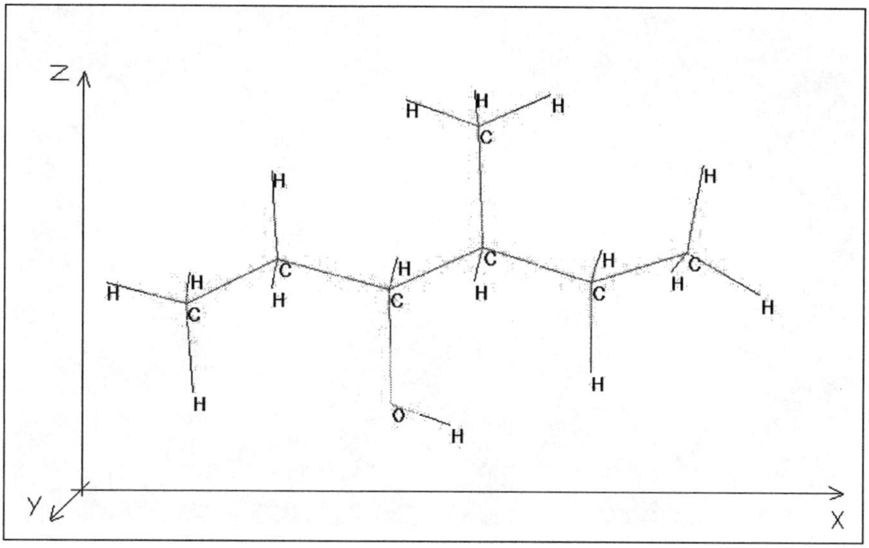

Figure 3: Example of molecular structure: 4-Methyl hexan-3-ol

- $a \log P$, the atomic based log of the partition coefficient between n-octanol and water, sometimes referred to as log Kow. This number is thought to be a good indicator of the relative lipophilicity of a molecule. It has been related to things like diffusion of drugs through biological lipid membranes. The use of $\log P$ in structure-effect work was pioneered by Hansh and his coworkers [10].
- the molar refraction aMR based on the contribution of the atoms constituting the molecule.
- the density d of the molecule (weigth / volume).
- the aqueous solubility Saq of the molecule in g/l.
- the ratios R/r, R/p, and r/p were also computed.

Thus, a data matrix containing all these vectors and geometric features is built and is associated with a value of the class (camphoraceous or non-camphoraceous).

For instance, let the molecule be the 4-Methyl hexan-3-ol molecule (Figure 4). The descriptor counting (Figure 2) and the geometric feature computations are done from its skeleton representation (Figure 3) to obtain the description of the molecule.

This description is associated with the value camphoraceous of the class to obtain a training example (Figure 5).

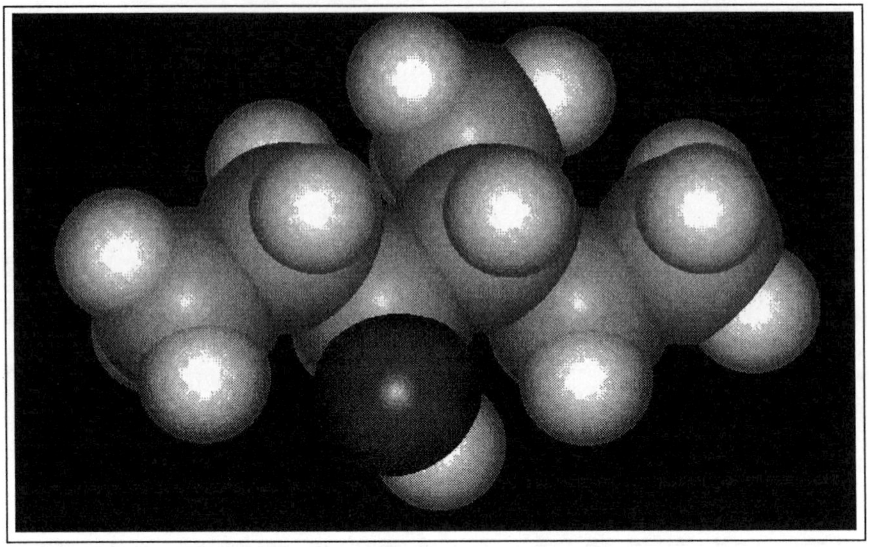

Figure 4: Example of molecule

1D2	2D2	3D1	3D2	4D1	4D2	4D3	4D4	5D1	5D2
7	6	2	6	3	1	5	1	1	3
5D3	5D4	5D5	5D6	5D7	6D1	6D2	6D3	6D4	6D5
1	0	3	2	0	0	0	1	1	1
6D6	6D7	6D8	6D9	6D10	6D11	6D12	6D13	R	r
0	2	0	1	1	1	0	0	10.39	6.95
R/r	p	R/p	r/p	alogP	aMR	d	Saq(g/l)		class
1.49	5.66	1.836	1.228	2.23	35.55	0.753	9.54		Camph.

Figure 5: Description and class of the 4-Methyl hexan-3-ol

4 Analysis of results

In this work, we considered as camphoraceous all compounds having a score between 1 and 5 on the Schnabel's scale [19]. The 58 molecules verifying this condition are assigned to the class 2. The non-camphoraceous compounds are those with score 0. There are 41 such compounds, all assigned to class 1.

The database is represented by means of 38 descriptors, 28 of which are generated by the GESDEM method, each one belonging to one of the 6 orders. Attributes with more than four values are discretized and those which present less than 4 values are considered as continuous attributes. The later 10 descriptors represent the geometrical and physico-chemical characteristics of the molecules.

Several tests were conducted. First of all, a fuzzy decision tree was build with the whole database, where each molecule was described by the whole set of attributes (38). The obtained tree is given in Figure 6. In this figure, within each node of the tree, the number of molecules pertaining to this node is given.

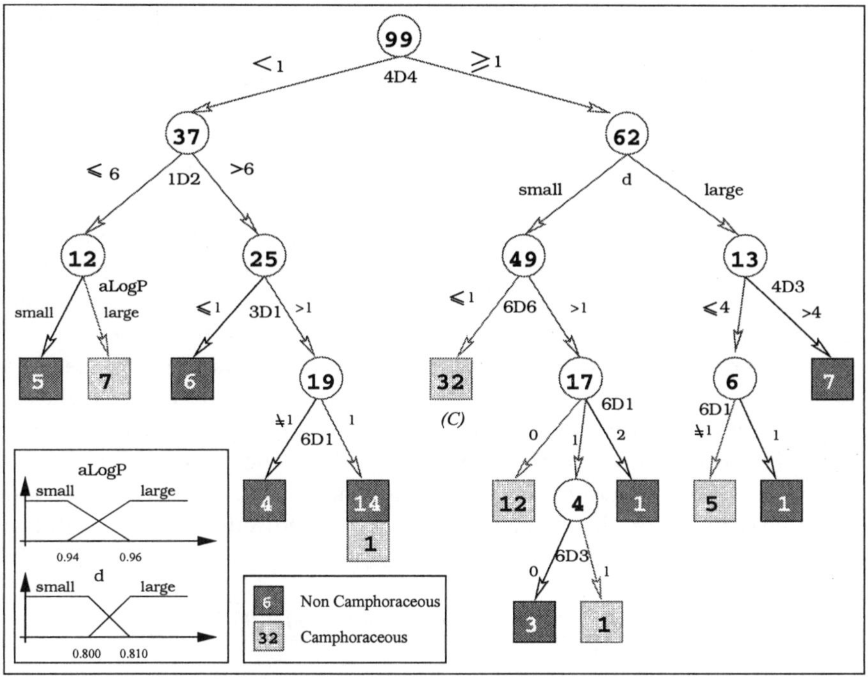

Figure 6: Fuzzy decision trees to classify camphoraceous data

On each vertex going out of a node, a test on the value of an attribute is given. This test can be a crisp one (e.g. ≤ 1) or a fuzzy one (e.g. *small*), in this case, the membership partition constructed by the Salammbô system is shown.

To validate such kind of tree, cross-validation tests were also conducted. The whole database was split into 4 subsets (S1, S2, S3 and S4), each one with 24 or 25 molecules with the same repartition of classes than in the whole database. The cross-validation was done by building a fuzzy decision tree with 3 subsets altogether (for instance, S1+S2+S3) and a classification rate was measured on the fourth base (in the previous case, S4).

Results are given in table 1.

	Strict	*Lukas.*	*Root*	*#paths*	*Avg.*
S1	88.5%	88.5%	4D4	10	3.5
S2	72.0%	76.0%	R/r	17	4
S3	95.8%	95.8%	4D4	14	3.5
S4	91.7%	91.7%	4D4	15	3.6
Mean	87.0%	**88.0%**		14	3.7

Table 1: Results – All attributes (38)

In this table, the first two columns (*Strict* and *Lukas.*) show the good classification rate when testing the corresponding subset. The column *Strict* corresponds to the classification when considering the test in the fuzzy tree as crisp tests (non fuzzy). The column *Lukas.* corresponds to the classification when considering the test in the tree as fuzzy tests and so, using the Lukasiewicz t-norm and t-conorm to aggregate the intermediate degrees. The column *Root* shows the attribute selected during the construction of the fuzzy decision tree as the root attribute. In the column *#paths*, the number of paths in the tree is given, and its average number of nodes is given in the column *Avg.*. In this table, it can be shown that the fuzzy method is efficient to classify new cases. Moreover, the attribute 4D4 is chosen (as in the global tree (Figure 6)) very often. The attribute R/r (which can be considered as the compacity of the molecule, an usually known discriminant attribute to predict the odor) is chosen once but gives poor results in classification relatively to the results obtained with the 4D4 attribute. We recall that the 4D4 attribute (related to C-C(C)-C), indicates the number of atoms of tertiary carbons and quaternary carbons. It gives an idea on the global shape of the molecule.

Another test was conducted to study advantages or drawbacks when using only the attributes of the descriptive model of molecules. Cross validation results are given in table 2.

	Strict	*Lukas.*	*Root*	*#paths*	*Avg.*
S1	84.6%	88.5%	4D4	14	3.5
S2	84.0%	80.0%	4D4	19	4.16
S3	87.5%	95.8%	4D4	19	3.84
S4	75.0%	75.0%	4D4	19	3.58
Mean	**82.8%**	81.8%		17.8	3.8

Table 2: Results – Descriptive Model (28 attributes)

Here, it can be shown that the strict method is more efficient than the crisp one. We can remark that the root attribute is always the 4D4 attribute, that is coherent with the previous test. However, the results here are worse than the previous results. It shows the advantages of using geometric attributes even if these attributes are not chosen as primary attributes in the tree. The size of the fuzzy tree is bigger here that reflects another advantage to use geometric attributes.

Finally, a cross validation test was conducted with only the geometric attributes to describe the molecules. Cross validation results are given in table 3.

Here, the fuzzy classification method (fuzzy aggregation with Lukasiewicz operators) is highly efficient. This can be due to the continuous nature of the attributes. However, the results are worse than previous results (although the trees are smaller).

From the results given here, it can be shown that the descriptive model is highly efficient to determine attributes to predict the camphoraceous odor of a molecule. Moreover, such attributes are more easily evaluated than geometric attributes which are more complex to measure and that do not improve greatly

	Strict	*Lukas.*	*Root*	*#paths*	*Avg.*
S1	73.1%	69.2%	d	6	2.67
S2	84.0%	84.0%	R/r	6	2.67
S3	87.5%	87.5%	R/r	7	3
S4	58.3%	70.8%	r	4	2.25
Mean	75.7%	**77.9%**		5.8	2.6

Table 3: Results – Geometric attributes (10)

the prediction of the odor.

5 Conclusion

In this paper, an application of the method to construct and use fuzzy decision trees is presented. In this application, fuzzy decision trees enable us to extract and highlight association in the chemical structure of the smelling and the quality of their odors.

Thanks to the software *Salammbô*, experiments have been conducted on data related to the description of molecules, modelized by means of the GES-DEM method. It enables us to highlight relationship between the molecule descriptors and the odor characteristics.

In future work, new experiments will be conducted on several smelling compound.

Acknowledgment

This work has been supported by a cooperation CNRS/CNCPRST n°5188 between France and Morocco.

References

[1] N. L. Allinger. Conformation analysis. *Journal of American Chemical Society*, 99(25):8127–8134, 1977.

[2] M. G. J. Beets. *Structure -Activity relationships in human chemoreception.* Applied Science Publishers, London, 1978.

[3] B. Bouchon-Meunier, C. Marsala, and M. Ramdani. Learning from imperfect data. In D. Dubois, H. Prade, and R. R. Yager, editors, *Fuzzy Information Engineering: a Guided Tour of Applications*, pages 139–148. John Wileys and Sons, 1997.

[4] B. Bouchon-Meunier, M. Rifqi, and S. Bothorel. Towards general measures of comparison of objects. *Fuzzy Sets and Systems*, 84(2):143–153, 1996.

[5] X. Boyen and L. Wehenkel. Automatic induction of continuous decision trees. In *Proceedings of the 6th International Conference IPMU*, volume 1, pages 419–424, Granada, Spain, 1996.

[6] W. E. Brugger and P. C. Jurs. Extraction of important molecular features of musk compounds using pattern recognition techniques. *J. Agric. Food Chem.*, 25(5):1158–1164, 1977.

[7] M. Chastrette, D. Zakarya, and A. Elmouaffek. Relations structure-odeur dans la famille des muscs benzéniques nitrés. *Eur. J. Med.-Chim. Ther.*, 21(6):505–510, 1986.

[8] M. Chastrette, D. Zakarya, and J. P. Peyraud. Structure-musk odor relationships for tetralins and indans using neural networks. *Eur. J. Med. Chem.*, 29:343–348, 1994.

[9] M. J. S. Dewar, E. G. Zoebisch, E. F. Healy, and J. J. P. Stewart. A new general purpose quantum mechanical molecular model. *Journal of American Chemical Society*, 107:3902–3909, 1985.

[10] C. Hansch and A. Leo. *Substituent constants for correlation analysis in chemistry and biology.* Wiley-intersciences, New York, 1979.

[11] G. Klopman and D. Ptchelintsev. Application of the computer automated structure evaluation methodology to a QSAR study of chemoreception. aromatic musky odorants. *J. Agric. Food Chem.*, 40:2244–2251, 1992.

[12] C. Marsala. *Apprentissage inductif en présence de données imprécises : construction et utilisation d'arbres de décision flous.* Thèse de doctorat, Université Pierre et Marie Curie, Paris, France, Janvier 1998. Rapport LIP6 n° 1998/014.

[13] C. Marsala. Stability of fuzzy decision trees when classifying evolving observations. In D. Ruan, H. Aït Abderrahim, P. D'hondt, and E. E. Kerre, editors, *Fuzzy Logic and Intelligent Technologies for Nuclear Science and Industry*, pages 83–90, Antwerp (Belgium), September 1998. World Scientific.

[14] C. Marsala and B. Bouchon-Meunier. Fuzzy partioning using mathematical morphology in a learning scheme. In *Proceedings of the 5th IEEE Int. Conf. on Fuzzy Systems*, volume 2, pages 1512–1517, New Orleans, USA, September 1996.

[15] C. Marsala and B. Bouchon-Meunier. Construction methods of fuzzy decision trees. In *Proceedings of the JCIS'98 Conference*, volume 4, pages 17–20, October 1998.

[16] C. Marsala and B. Bouchon-Meunier. An adaptable system to construct fuzzy decision trees. In *Proc. of the NAFIPS'99 (North American Fuzzy Information Processing Society)*, New York (USA), June 1999.

[17] J. R. Quinlan. Induction of decision trees. *Machine Learning*, 1(1):86–106, 1986.

[18] M. Ramdani. Une approche floue pour traiter les valeurs numériques en apprentissage. In *Journées Francophones d'apprentissage et d'explication des connaissances*, Dourdan, 1992.

[19] K. O. Schnabel, H. D. Belitz, and C. Ranson. Untersuchungen zur struktur-activitäts-beziehung bei geruchsstoffen. *Z. Lebensm Unters Forsch*, 187:215–233, 1988.

[20] M. Umano, H. Okamoto, I. Hatono, H. Tamura, F. Kawachi, S. Umedzu, and J. Kinoshita. Fuzzy decision trees by fuzzy ID3 algorithm and its application to diagnosis systems. In *Proceedings of the 3rd IEEE Conference on Fuzzy Systems*, volume 3, pages 2113–2118, Orlando, june 1994.

[21] R. H. Wright. Odor and molecular vibration. quantum and thermodynamic consideration. *J. Appl. Chem.*, 4:611–615, 1954.

[22] Y. Yuan and M. Shaw. Induction of fuzzy decision trees. *Fuzzy Sets and systems*, 69:125–139, 1995.

[23] L. Zadeh. Probability measures of fuzzy events. *Journal Math. Anal. Applic.*, 23, 1968.

[24] D. Zakarya. Use of autocorrelation components and Wiener index in the evaluation of the odor threshold of aliphatic alcohols. *New J. Chem.*, 16:1039–1042, 1992.

[25] D. Zakarya, M. Chastrette, M. Tollabi, and S. Fkih-Tetouani. Structure-camphor odor relationships using the generation and selection of pertinent descriptors approach. *Chemometrics and Intelligent Laboratory Systems*, 48:35–46, 1999.

Document Retrieval from Multiple Sources of Information

Gabriella Pasi* and R.R. Yager+

*CNR-ITIM via Ampére 56
20131 Milano Italy
e-mail: gabriella.pasi@itim.mi.cnr.it

+Dept. of Machine Intelligence - IONA College
New Rochelle, NY 10801
e-mail: RYager@Iona.edu

Abstract: When retrieving documents from distinct multiple sources of information a user query is evaluated by different IRSs residing on distinct servers. In response to the user query an overall list of documents has to be obtained. One problem that arises is the merging of the results produced by the different IRS. In solving this problem two main issues are involved. The first issue concerns the decision of how many retrieved documents to select from each information source located on a different server. The second aspect is to define a procedure to fuse the individual lists of retrieved documents into an overall ordered list. In this paper some flexible approaches to solve the first issue are proposed.

1 Introduction

The problem of retrieving documents from multiple sources of information located on different servers characterizes information retrieval from archives distributed on a network [1, 14, 19]. It is assumed that each server is provided with its own Information Retrieval System (IRS): a user query is independently evaluated by each IRS which produces a list of documents ordered on the basis of a score indicating the estimated relevance of each document with respect to the query (this score is called the Retrieval Status Value - RSV). The computation of the RSVs depends on the model on which the IRS is based. What the user would expect is an overall list of documents, which must be obtained by the fusion of the individual lists produced by each server. This is not an easy task, as the retrieval engines may be based on different retrieval models, which apply different matching mechanisms, with the consequence of producing not comparable RSVs. The main problem related with list fusion is then to compare the ordered lists and construct an overall list which preserves the retrieval results produced by the servers and approximates the effectiveness of searching the entire set of documents as a single collection [15].

In [14,15] a three steps startegy for solving the problem of retrieval from multiple sources of information has been proposed. In the first step a query Q is submitted to the IRSs of the *m* different servers, which evaluate it; the result of this step is m ordered lists of documents, one for each server. It is assumed that in the m lists each document has an RSV associated. In the second step a procedure is applied to establish the number of documents that each server should contribute; this is the problem addressed in this paper. The third step concerns the problem of fusing the individual ordered lists into an overall list which is presented to the user.

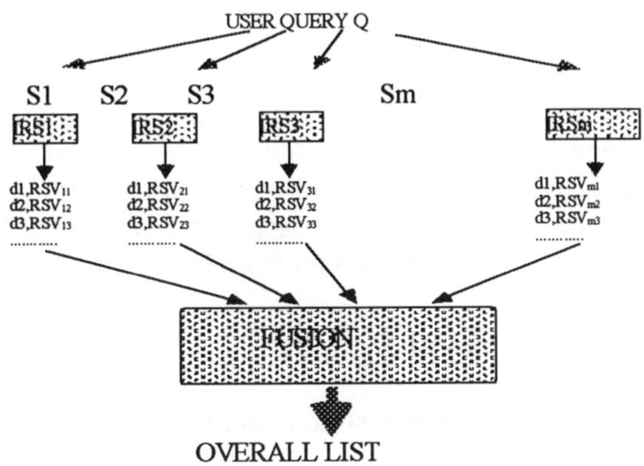

Figure 1: a scheme of IR from multiple information sources

To determine how many documents to select from a given server S_i, first the number N of relevant documents to be presented to the user has to be identified; this number can be directly specified by the user, who selects in this way a threshold on the number of documents he/she desires to analyze. Let us denote by N_i the number of documents which should be contributed by server S_i; we have then that $\sum_{i=1}^{m} N_i = N$. The process of determining the numbers N_i is "knowledge intensive", as it depends on many factors, among which the type and the nature of the information contained in the server S_i, the topics investigated by the user and formalized in her/his query, an evaluation of how the information source S_i fits the searched topics, etc. In the literature some approaches have been proposed to face this problem [14,15,18,19]. In particular, in [18, 19] a general approach has been proposed which is based on the computation of a score for each server indicating its *fitness* with respect to the considered query [18,19]. Based on this approach, the number N_i of documents to be selected from S_i is computed as: $N_i = \alpha_{ij} * N$, where α_{ij} is the normalized fitness score of server i with respect to query j.

In this paper we retain the approach based on the use of fitness scores, and we address the problem of computing these fitness values. To this aim we propose three different approaches:

- a first approach is based on the evaluation of the "appropriateness" of the topics describing the information source with respect to query terms. To this purpose a fuzzy set of terms is defined for each server as the descriptor of the topics dealt with in the server. This fuzzy set can be interpreted as a "prototypal-document" representing the documents on the server. The fitness score of a server for a given query is obtained by matching the query against this fuzzy set;

- the second approach is based on the specification of a set of "query type" (prototypical queries) for each server, and on the evaluation of the similarity between the query type and the actual query;
- an application of the rule based approach proposed in [18,19] is finally proposed; with this approach a weighted query language is considered, and rules evaluating the importance of topics in a given server are defined. Rules are fired by a query and produce the fitness scores to be associated with each server for the considered query.

The paper is structured as follows: in section 2. a synthetic presentation of information retrieval systems is introduced. In section 3. the problem of information retrieval from multiple sources of information is sketched, and in section 4. the previously mentioned approaches to compute the fitness scores of the servers with respect to a user query are presented.

2 Information Retrieval Systems

An Information Retrieval System is structured in three main components:

- the indexing mechanism;
- the query language;
- the matching mechanism.

The indexing mechanism produces surrogates of the information content of textual documents, formally organized in the so called document representations [10,12]. The basic elements of the document representations are generally terms, called the *index terms.*

Users queries are expressions of the system's query language; the atomic selection criteria are either terms or weighted terms, and the aggregation operators can be implicit in the query, as in the Vector Space model, or explicit as in the Boolean model [10].

The matching mechanism evaluates a user's query against the representations of documents, and estimates the relevance of the documents to the query. The relevance estimates, called the Retrieval Status Values (RSVs), are computed by a function which is peculiar to each IR model. In the following some IR models are briefly described.

The Boolean information retrieval model constitutes the basis of the majority of current commercial systems. It offers an oversimplified interpretation of the information retrieval activity. The Boolean indexing procedure performs a binary decision, indicating whether a term t is either *significant* or *useless* in synthesizing the content of document d. Therefore, a document is represented as a set of index terms $R(d) = \{t_1, t_2, \ldots, t_n\}$. A Boolean query is constituted by selection criteria consisting of single terms, aggregated by the Boolean operators AND and OR, and negated via the NOT operator, which are interpreted as the intersection, the union and the complement in set theory respectively. Not negated query terms must appear in the representation of desired documents, while negated query terms must not appear. The main limitation of this simple model is that it is unable to assess a partial relevance estimate. Moreover, the query language gives users a crisp way of specifying their information needs: a term is either definitely significant or completely undesired in synthesizing the content of the interesting documents.

To overcome the limitations of the Boolean model some extended Boolean models have been defined within fuzzy set theory [2,3,4,5,6,7,9,16]. The representation of documents has been extended by associating with each index term of a document a numeric weight, called the index term weight, which indicates the degree of *aboutness* or *significance* of the term with respect to the document [5,9,16]. The computation of the index term weight is generally based on the number of occurrences of the term in the document and in the whole archive D [11,12]. A document is then represented as a fuzzy set of terms: $R(d) = \{\mu_d(t)/t, t \in T\}$. Based on this representation the retrieval mechanism is able to rank the retrieved documents in decreasing order of their significance with respect to the user query.

To make the Boolean query language more user friendly and less limited in its expressiveness some extensions have been proposed to enrich the atomic selection criteria and to introduce more flexible aggregation operators [2,3,4,6,7]. Numeric query weights have been introduced to make the selection criteria more expressive, thus introducing the following structure of queries:

$$<t_1,w_1> \text{AND} <t_2,w_2> \text{OR} <t_3,w_3>$$

in which t_1,t_2,t_3 are search terms and w_1, w_2, w_3 are either numeric weights (in the set [0,1]) or linguistic weights (such as *important*, *very important*, etc.) [4]. Different semantics have been defined for query weights, among which the relative importance, the threshold and the ideal semantics [2,6,7,9,16]. The matching mechanism applies a two steps evaluation of weighted queries. In the first step, the selection criteria are evaluated by a matching function E, $E: D \times Q' \rightarrow [0,1]$, in which D is the set of documents in the archive and Q' is the set of selection criteria $<t,w>$. The function E computes the degree to which document d matches the query $q = <t,w> \in Q'$, consisting of a weighted term. The semantics adopted for query weights determines the definition of function E. In the second step, a function E^* is applied, $E^*: D \times Q \rightarrow [0,1]$, (where Q is the set of all the legitimate queries) which evaluates the final RSV of a document. If Boolean aggregation operators are adopted, the evaluation of E^* is performed by interpreting the operators AND, OR and NOT, as fuzzy intersection, union and complement respectively. In [3] a query language has been defined in which single selection criteria are aggregated by means of linguistic quantifiers formally defined as OWA operators [17].

Another important retrieval model is the Vector Space model, which has been defined to overcome the main disadvantage of the Boolean model consisting in the inability to rank the retrieved documents. In the vector space model the documents are represented as vectors of numeric weights in a multidimensional term space of dimension *s*, with *s* being the number of index terms. In this space each axis corresponds to a different term; the jth element of the vector representing a document d is the significance degree of term j in d. The weight can be either a binary value or a value in [0,1]. Also queries are expressed as vectors of weights in which the jth weight represents the importance of the corresponding term in the query. Differently from the Boolean model in which nothing is assumed about terms not explicitly specified in a query, in the vector space model they are considered not desired in the documents to be retrieved. Thus, all the index terms not appearing in the query are assumed with an importance weight equal to 0. The retrieval function evaluates the similarity of the query vector q and the document vector d. The most commonly used similarity measure is the cosine measure, which measures the cosine of the angle between the vectors representing the document and the query.

Another important class of retrieval models is constituted by the probabilistic models. By assuming that a document is either relevant or not relevant to a query, the task of a probabilistic IR system is to rank documents according to their estimated probability of relevance [13]. The problem of estimating the probability of relevance for every document in the collection is difficult because of the large number of variables involved in the representation of documents in comparison to the small amount of information about the relevance of documents. The various models differ, primarily, in the way they estimate this or related probabilities. Probabilistic inference models apply concepts and techniques originating from areas such as logic and artificial intelligence. For a survey of probabilistic models see [8].

3 Retrieving Information from multiple sources

An important and up to date problem in the area of information retrieval concerns the inquiry of information distributed over multiple sources, each of which resides on a server. The rapid and increasing development of the Internet makes urgent to define effective solutions to this problem. An example of document search from multiple information sources is offered by the inquiry of archives of newspapers: a user looking for the market trend in U.S.A. could be interested in inquiring the archives of the articles maintained for example by the New York Times, the Wall Street Journal and the Chicago Tribune.

Let us consider m information servers, denoted by S_i, with i = 1...m; a distinct collection of documents resides on each server, which is provided with its own IRS, possibly based on a distinct retrieval mechanism. We assume here that the retrieval engines produce weighted lists of retrieved documents, like the IRSs on the Internet. As outlined in the previous section the weight is an indicator of the estimated relevance of each document with respect to the query. In order to propose to a user a unique ordered list of relevant documents as a result of her/his query, the individual lists produced by the servers have to be fused. The fusion of the results produced by the local IRSs is a difficult problem, as they can produce lists of documents with relevance estimates based on different criteria.

Several works in the literature have faced this problem [1,14,15,18,19]; in particular, in [14,15] an approach for solving it has been suggested, which essentially consists of a three step process. In the first step a query Q is submitted to the m different servers, which evaluate it; the result is constituted by m lists of documents, one for each server. It is assumed that in the m lists each document has a score associated, which indicates its relevance with respect to the query. In the second step a procedure is applied to establish the number N_i of documents that each server has to contribute. If N is the total number of documents to be proposed to the user we have that $\sum_{i=1}^{m} N_i = N$. From each server a sublist L_i can then be constructed, which contains the N_i documents with the highest score. The third step concerns the fusion of the m individual ordered lists L_i into an overall list which is presented to the user.

In the next section we propose some solutions to the problem of computing the N_i values; some solutions to the problem of the lists fusion can be found in [1,14,15,18].

A strategy for deciding how many documents to select from a given server is to evaluate the appropriateness of the server as collector of documents relevant to the considered query. This is a knowledge intensive problem, as some meta information about the content of the server is needed, as well as some information about the nature of the considered query.

In [14,15] the authors have proposed an approach to determine the numbers N_i, which is based on the use of training queries to build both the content and search behaviour of each collection.

In [18,19] a knowledge based approach to determine the N_i has been proposed. This approach is based on the computation of a fitness score for each server with respect to a user query. A fitness score indicates how much a server is a good collector of the relevant documents for a given query. In order to compute the fitness scores for a considered query the authors propose a rule based approach. First a set of query type is defined; with each query type a set of fitness scores (one per server) is associated. A query type is formalized by means of a rule in which the antecedent is the description of the query by means of a set of properties, and the consequent specifies the fitness of each server with respect to this query type. Formally, the properties useful to characterize the subject matters of queries are denoted as U_j ($j=1..s$); the fitness scores are the values associated with variables V_i (i=1..m), one for each server S_i. The fuzzy rules identifying query types are formalized as:

$$\text{if } U_1 \text{ is } A_{k1} \text{ and ... and } U_s \text{ is } A_{ks} \text{ then } \mathbf{V} \text{ is } \mathbf{B}_k$$

in which k is the index of the rule, the A_{kj} are fuzzy subsets constituting the values of variables U_j, $\mathbf{V}$ is an m dimensional vector whose components are the V_i, and $\mathbf{B}_k$ is also an m dimensional vector whose components, b_{ki}, correspond to the fitness of server S_i as an appropriate source of documents for the type of query described in the antecedent of rule k. Once a user query has been evaluated by the IRSs on the servers, a "matching" between it and the query types rules is performed, in order to compute the fitness scores for the considered query on the basis of the scores of the query types. The first step is to obtain a unique fitness score per server for the considered query. To this aim the user query is also described in terms of properties U_j; a value a_j is associated with each U_j and for each rule k a firing level τ_k is computed: $\tau_k=\min_j[A_{kj}(a_j)]$. To combine the fitness scores in the distinct rules, the obtained information is employed as follows:

$$\mathbf{B}* = \frac{\sum_{k=1}^{p} \tau_k \, \mathbf{B}_k}{\sum_{k=1}^{p} \tau_k} \tag{1}$$

in which p is the number of query types.

The components b_i* of vector **B*** denote the fitness values of the servers for the considered query.

Finally, to obtain the values N_i of documents to be contributed by each server, first the fitness values are normalized:

$$\alpha_i = \frac{b_i^*}{\sum_{i=1}^{m} b_i^*} \tag{2}$$

At this point the normalized values are used to compute the number of documents to be retrieved from each server:

$$N_i = \alpha_i N \tag{3}$$

The number of documents to be selected from each server is proportional to the fitness of that server to the query.

4 Some approaches to compute the fitness scores of the servers

In this section we propose three approaches to compute the number of documents to be contributed by each server. The common basis of these approaches is the computation for a given query of a fitness score with respect to each server, as proposed in [18,19] and described in the previous section. Each approach proposes a distinct way of computing fitness scores. Starting from the obtained fitness scores the numbers of document to be selected from each server is determined by applying formulas (2) and (3) in the previous section.

4.1 Approach based on the association of a fuzzy prototypal set with each server

The idea at the basis of this approach is to associate with each server a fuzzy set of key terms; the key terms are those which best represent the topics in the considered archive, and their associated membership values are interpreted as their importance as descriptors of the server. In other words the weights represent the fitness of the server with respect to the topic expressed by the associated term. The fuzzy set can be interpreted as a "prototypal document" or "document type" constituting a representative of the documents in the archive of the server. The terms and their "fitness" weights can be either manually defined or automatically computed. An automatic selection of the key terms can be obtained on the basis of their normalized occurrences in the archive on the considered server; the computed occurrences can then be used as terms membership values. Let us denote by $TOTOCC(t)_i$ the total number of occurrences of a given term t in the archive of a server i, and by $TOTOCC_i$ the highest number of occurrences among all the terms in the archive. For each term t the following "importance" weight can then be evaluated:

$$IMP_i(t) = TOTOCC(t)_i \, / \, TOTOCC_i.$$

The terms considered as the key concepts are selected as the ones with an importance weight over a given threshold τ. For a given server S_i then a prototypal fuzzy set is defined:

$$PROT(S_i) = \sum IMP(t)_i / t$$

When a query has to be evaluated, the process of estimate of the appropriateness of each server as the collector of relevant information for the query can be done on the basis of a procedure which performs a matching between the query and the "prototypal" fuzzy set of terms. The matching procedure of a Boolean query against the fuzzy prototypal term set proceeds in a bottom up way: first, the membership of each query term to the prototypal fuzzy set is computed. The obtained values (indicating the fitness of the server for each query term) are then aggregated by applying the connectives specified in the query (the AND is interpreted as a min, the OR as a max, and the NOT as a complement).

$$Q = t_1 \text{ AND } (t_2 \text{ OR } t_3)$$
$$\Downarrow$$
$$b_i^* = \min(IMP_i(t_1), \max(IMP_i(t_2), IMP_i(t_3)))$$

Figure 2: example of computation of b_i* for a given query Q

The obtained value represents the fitness b_i* of the server S_i with respect to the considered query (see the example in Figure 2).

4.2 Approach based on the specification of a set of "query type" for each server.

This approach is based on the definition of a set of "prototypal queries" for each server. A "prototypal query" is conceived as a high level description of the key-concepts summarizing the information in the archive on the server. A prototypal query is simply defined by means of two sets of terms; the first set (denoted as NNT) contains the key terms that the server deals with, while the second set (denoted as NT) contains the key terms that the server does not deal with. If for example the documents in the archive deal with the applications of computer science to medicine, but not with the applications related with image processing, the two following sets could be defined: NNT={computer-science, medicine, medical-applications, expert systems} and NT={image, image-processing, image-analysis}. To make more refined the role of prototypal queries as carriers of the information contained in the server, a fitness score is associated with each of them. This score expresses the degree of concern of the considered server with the topics highlighted in the prototypal query. As described before, the fitness score is defined as a numeric value in [0,1].

We consider queries formulated by means of the Boolean query language. When a given query is considered, to evaluate the fitness of server S_i with respect to it the following process is applied. First two sets are defined: the set NNT which contains the terms not negated in the query, and the set NT which contains the terms negated in the query. As a second step, for each prototypal query Pq_k in the server the intersection of NT with the set of negated terms in the prototypal query ($PQNT_k$) is computed, thus obtaining the set INT_k, and the intersection of NNT with the set of not negated terms in the prototypal query ($PQNNT_k$) is also computed, thus obtaining the set $INNT_k$. To obtain a fitness score for the considered query with respect to a prototypal query the following rule is applied:

If *most*($|INNT_k| / |PQNNT_k|$) AND *most*($|INT_k| / |PQNT_k|$) then $V_{ik} = b_{ik}$

in which $|S|$ is the cardinality of the set S, and b_{ik} is the fitness score of server S_i for the prototypal query Pq_k. This rule verifies if most of the query terms are contained in the prototypal query. *most* is a proportional increasing linguistic quantifier formally defined as a fuzzy set on the interval [0,1] [21]. The evaluation of the antecedent of a rule produces a firing level τ_{ik}. To obtain the overall fitness score b_i^* of the server S_i for the considered query, the following formula is applied:

$$b_i^* = \frac{\sum_{k=1}^{p} \tau_{ik} b_{ik}}{\sum_{k=1}^{p} \tau_{ik}}$$

in which p is the number of prototypal queries defined for a given server S_i.

4.3 Rule based approach

As explained in section 3., the kernel of this approach is the identification of a set of variables useful to characterize a query in terms of "properties". The definition of a prototypal query is obtained by instantiating each variable with a selected value. For each prototypal query each server has a corresponding fitness score. In the approach proposed by Yager and Rybalov, the score is selected "a priori" for each prototypal query, and encodes the appropriateness of the source as a collector of the relevant information with respect to the prototypal query. In this way the information role played by each information source is directly encoded in the numeric fitness score. A more flexible but complex approach could also model the preliminary phase of computation of these scores.

The main difficulty related to the knowledge-based approach is the identification of properties useful to characterize queries. A consideration useful to identify some properties is that they are strongly related with the adopted query language. In particular the properties should be selected in order to highlight the information content of the query. To this aim, it is necessary to consider the level of the "information carriers" in the query expressions; in the query languages of current IRSs this role is played by terms.

In this subsection we present an example of application of the knowledge based approach synthesized in section 3. [18,19]; we refer to the specific case in which a weighted query language is adopted (like in the extended Boolean models and the vector space model). In a weighted query language (as seen in section 2.) numeric weights are employed as indicators of the importance of terms as descriptors of user's needs.

The property which can be considered to define the prototypal rules is the *importance* of terms as descriptors of relevant topics. The antecedent of a rule is then defined by first selecting a set of terms useful to characterize a given topic. A linguistic importance value is then associated with each term. For evaluating a prototypal rule first the terms in the query contained in the antecedent of the rule are selected, then the compatibility between the query term weights and the linguistic weights is performed.

From a formal point of view, the variable considered is one, referring to the "importance" of a term as a descriptor. The linguistic values of the variable *Importance* belong to a term set like {*important*, *very important*, ...} [20], and their meaning is formally defined with respect to the domain of the numeric values of importance which are associable to the query term. By following the approach specified by Yager and Rybalov each prototypal query corresponds to a rule; in the antecedents of each rule the variables with their associated values are specified. An example of rule defined by considering the variable "term importance" is the following:

If t_1 is *important* and t_2 is *very important* and t_3 is *not very important* **then V** is $\mathbf{B}_k$

in which the t_i are terms, k is the index of the rule, **V** is an m dimensional vector whose components are the V_i, and $\mathbf{B}_k$ is also an m dimensional vector whose components, b_{ki}, correspond to the fitness of server S_i as an appropriate source of documents for the type of query described in the antecedent of rule k.

If the query language considered is an extended Boolean language, a query is formulated by applying the Boolean connectors to pairs <term,numeric weight>, as seen in section 2.

To match the antecedent of a rule with a query, the compatibility between the numeric query term weights (of query terms appearing in the antecedent) and the linguistic weights is evaluated on the basis of the weight semantics.

To obtain a more flexible modeling the antecedents of rules could be specified by applying a linguistic quantifier to aggregate the single terms considered, like in the following example:

If *most*(t_1 is *important*, t_2 is *very important*, t_3 is *not very important*) **then V** is $\mathbf{B}_k$

in which *most* is defined as an ordered weighted averaging operator [17].

$<t_1,w_1>$ AND $<t_2,w_2>$ OR $<t_3,w_3>$)

⇓

$\min(\mu_{important}(w_1), \max((\mu_{not\ very\ imp}(w_2), (\mu_{very\ imp}(w_3)))$

Antecedent: if t_1 is *important* and t_2 is *not very important* and t_3 is *very important* then ....

Figure 3: example of query evaluation.

5 Conclusions

In this paper the problem of retrieving document from multiple collection sources has been addressed. In particular three approaches have been proposed to compute the number of retrieved documents which have to be contributed by each distinct server. The three approaches are based on the preliminary computation of a fitness score for each server with respect to the considered query; the fitness scores give an indication of the appropriateness of the servers with respect to the information needs expressed in the user query.

References

[1] Belkin, N.J., Kantor, P., Cool, C. and Quatrain, R., Query combination and data fusion for information retrieval, Proceedings of the second Text Retrieval Conference (TREC-2), 35-44, 1993.

[2] Bordogna, G., Carrara, P., and Pasi, G., Query term weights as constraints in fuzzy information retrieval, *Information Processing & Management.* 27(1), 15-26, 1991

[3] Bordogna, G., Pasi, G., Linguistic aggregation operators of selection criteria in fuzzy information retrieval, *Int. J. of Intelligent Systems,* 10, 233-248, 1995.

[4] Bordogna, G., and Pasi, G., A fuzzy linguistic approach generalizing Boolean Information Retrieval; a model and its evaluation, *J. of the American Society for Information Science.* 44(2), 70-82, 1993.

[5] Buell, D.A., An analysis of some fuzzy subset applications to information retrieval systems, *Fuzzy Sets and Systems.* 7, 35-42, 1982.

[6] Buell, D.A., and Kraft, D.H., A model for a weighted Retrieval System, *J. of the American Society for Information Science.* 32(3), 211-216, 1981.

[7] Cater, S.C., and Kraft, D.H., A generalization and clarification of the Waller-Kraft wish-list, *Information Processing & Management.* 25(1), 15-25, 1989.

[8] Crestani, F.,Lalmas, M., Campbell, I., and van Risbergen, C.J. Is this document relevant? ...probably. A survey of probabilistic models in Information Retrieval. *ACM Computing Surveys*, 1998, in press.

[9] Radecki, T., Fuzzy set theoretical approach to document retrieval, *Information Processing & Management.* 15, 247-260, 1979.

[10] Salton, G., and McGill, M.J., *Introduction to modern Information Retrieval.* McGraw-Hill International Book Company, 1983.

[11] Salton, G., and Buckley, C., Term weighting approaches in automatic text retrieval, *Information Processing & Management.* 24(5), 513-523, 1988.

[12] Salton G., *Automatic text processing. The transformation, analysis and Retrieval of Information by computer.* Addison Wesley series in Computer Science, 1989.

[13] van Rijsbergen C.J., *Information Retrieval.* Butterworths & Co Ltd., 1979.

[14] Voorhees, E.M., Gupta, N.K. and Johnson-Laird, B., The collection fusion problem, Proceedings of the third Text Retrieval Conference (TREC-3), 95-104, 1994.

[15] Voorhees, E.M., Gupta, N.K. and Johnson-Laird, B., Learning collection fusion strategies, Proceedings of the 18th ACM SIGIR Conference on Research and Development in Information Retrieval, Seattle, 172-179, 1995.

[16] Waller W.G., and Kraft, D.H., A mathematical model of a weighted Boolean Retrieval System, *Information Processing & Management*. 15, 235-245, 1979.

[17] Yager, R. R., On Ordered Weighted Averaging aggregation Operators in Multi Criteria Decision Making, *IEEE Trans. on Systems, Man and Cybernetics*. 18(1), 183-190, 1988

[18] Yager, R. R. and Rybalov, A., "On the fusion of documents from multiple collection information retrieval systems," *Journal of the American Society for Information Sciences*, 49, 1177-1184, 1998.

[19] Yager, R. R. and Rybalov, A., "Retrieving documents from multiple information sources," in New Trends in Fuzzy Systems, edited by Mancini, D., Squillante, M. and Ventre, A., World Scientific Publishers: Singapore, 3-22, 1998.

[20] Zadeh, L.A., The concept of a Linguistic Variable and its application to Approximate Reasoning-I,II, *Information Science*. 8, 199-249, 301-357, 1975.

[21] Zadeh, L.A., A computational approach to fuzzy quantifiers in natural languages, *Computing Math. Appl.* 9, 149-184, 1983.

THE PROGRESSING OF FUZZY-LOGIC CONTROL APPLICATIONS TO THE BELGIAN REACTOR 1

DA RUAN
Belgian Nuclear Research Centre (SCK•CEN)
Boeretang 200, B-2400 Mol, Belgium
E-mail: druan@sckcen.be

We present the progressing of an on-going R&D project on fuzzy-logic control applications to the Belgian Nuclear Reactor 1 (BR1) at the Belgian Nuclear Research Centre (SCK•CEN). The project started in 1995 and aimed at investigating the added value of fuzzy logic control for nuclear reactors. We first review some relevant literature on fuzzy logic control in nuclear reactors, then present the state-of-the-art of the BR1 project.

1 Introduction

Fuzzy logic [24] is designed to handle imprecise linguistic concepts such as *small, big, low, or high.* Systems based on fuzzy logic exhibit an inherent flexibility and have proven to be successful in a variety of industrial control and pattern-recognition tasks ranging from handwriting recognition to traffic control. Central to the flexibility that fuzzy logic provides is the notion of fuzzy set. Fuzzy reasoning or approximate reasoning is an application of fuzzy logic to knowledge processing. Fuzzy control is an application of fuzzy reasoning to control. One of the main strengths of fuzzy logic compared with other schemes to deal with imprecise data is that their knowledge bases, which are in a rule format, are easy to examine and understand. This rule format also makes it easy to update and maintain the knowledge base. As for the limitations of fuzzy logic, the main shortcoming is that the membership functions and rules have to be specified manually. Determining membership functions can be a time-consuming, trial-and-error process. Moreover the elicitation of rules from human experts can be an expensive, error-prone procedure.

Nuclear reactor control is one of the nuclear areas with a large potential for applications of fuzzy logic. The Chernobyl accident and its cross-border consequences have reminded us that nuclear safety remains a short-term priority, both at home and abroad, as nuclear technology has not reached the same maturity in all countries. The need of on-line decision-support systems for reactor operators has become evident after the Three Mile Island accident in 1979. Since then, considerable attention has been paid by the engineering, scientific, economic, political communities and by society at large to prevent these types of event by using state-of-the-art artificial intelligence techniques.

Nuclear engineering is different from many other engineering areas, for instance, an experimentation is only possible to a certain degree which does not provide a safe basis for stochastic models or the validity of the law of large numbers; the consequences of misjudgement, wrong decisions or bad design can be such horrendous that one is hesitant to accept even a tiny probability for such an event to happen, and the public opinion with respect to nuclear energy and related issues is much more controversial and influential than in other engineering disciplines [25].

Fuzzy logic applications in nuclear reactors present a tremendous challenge due to its strict nuclear safety regulation. The fields of nuclear engineering and fuzzy logic have nevertheless matured considerably during the last decade [18,19,20]. We list here part of references from the literature concerning nuclear engineering applications of fuzzy logic: A fuzzy-logic approach to HTR nuclear power plant model control [4], to a rule-based system for process control [2], to a nuclear reactor control [7,17,9,12,14,21], to nuclear reactor system dynamics [15], to a PWR-type nuclear power plant [1,8], to a site selection for nuclear plants [6], to control of steam generator water-level in PWR [13,16,5], to nuclear technology [22], and to the redundant sensor validation [10].

2 Fuzzy Control Applications at the BR1 Reactor

FLINS is an acronym for **F**uzzy **L**ogic and **I**ntelligent Technologies in **N**uclear **S**cience. The main task for FLINS for the coming years is to solve many intricate problems pertaining to the nuclear environment by using modern technologies as additional tools and to bridge a gap between novel technologies and the industrial nuclear world. Specific prototyping of fuzzy logic control of the BR1 research reactor has been chosen as FLINS' first priority. The accumulated knowledge at BR1 during this time has lead to the best calibration conditions for applying FLC for nuclear reactor control [21].

The mathematical model presently used for the BR1 graphite-moderated research reactor actually is the point kinetics model. It can be described by a non-linear system with a set of differential equations with six delayed neutron groups [3]:

$$\frac{dn}{dt} = \frac{\rho - \beta}{\Lambda} n + \sum_{i=1}^{6} \lambda_i c_i$$

$$\frac{dc_i}{dt} = \frac{\beta_i}{\Lambda} n - \lambda_i c_i, i = 1, \ldots, 6$$

Where
n is the neutron density at rated power (%);
c_i is the ith group precursor concentration;
β_i is the ith group delayed neutron fraction;
β is the total delayed neutron fraction;
λ_i is the ith group delayed neutron decay constant (s^{-1});
Λ is the neutron generation time (s);
ρ is the reactivity due to the control rod ($\Delta k/k$). (Note: Reactivity is defined as the difference between the effective multiplication factor and unity divided by the effective multiplication factor).

The neutron density is related to the power level, and depends on the reactivity of the reactor and the number of delayed neutrons. The control requirements of BR1 are to keep the reactivity ρ near zero or to exhibit a certain transient behaviour for a required power transient. At the required steady-state conditions, if ρ is different from zero, the controller inserts or withdraws the regulating rods to return ρ to zero. However, since ρ is not easily measurable, we use input signals such as the difference of power (DP) (difference between the actual and the desired power) and the reactor period (T). In steady state, T remains infinitely large. Basically, the controller reads DP as input. This input signal is electronically transformed into an analogue command signal. Its sign and magnitude command the selection of the direction and speed of A-rods (the rods for fine-tuning the reactivity). The controller is efficiently limited by a certain delay due to neutronics and the thermal behaviour of the reactor. Whereas the fuzzy logic control (FLC) no longer requires an explicit model of the reactor, it can take into account the knowledge of the operators for controlling the reactor. Figure 1 is a simplified version of the BR1 controller.

Figure 2 shows the testing environment schematically. In addition the control initially focuses exclusively on the movement of A-rods, thereby mimicking the classical controller. The full rule base controlling both A- and C-rods simultaneously, thereby eliminating the manual movement of C-rods by the operator, is of course the ultimate goal of this work.

The hardware configuration of fuzzy-logic control scheme for BR1 is shown in Figure 3.

In the experience of the author it is wise to rely on certified, proven industrial hardware instead of developing *ad hoc* software when developing a controller for use in an environment that presents a potential high risk if control breaks down. It also makes it easier to exchange rule bases, because it is the responsibility of the PLC manufacturer to provide state-of-the-art tools that work in modern operating system environments. In taking this strategy,

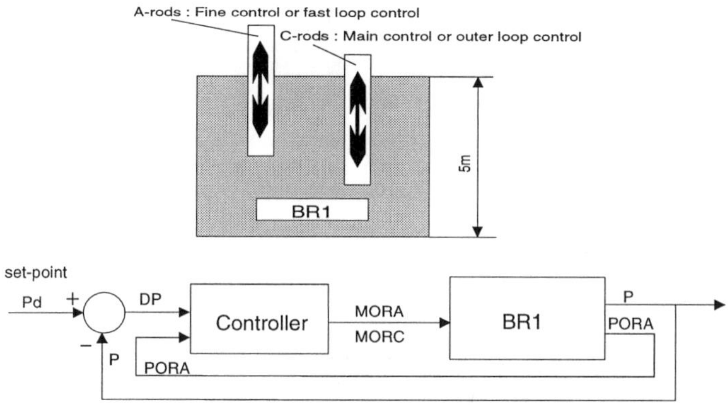

Figure 1. A-rods for the fine-tuning of reactivity, and C-rods mainly for the compensation of other reactivity effects.

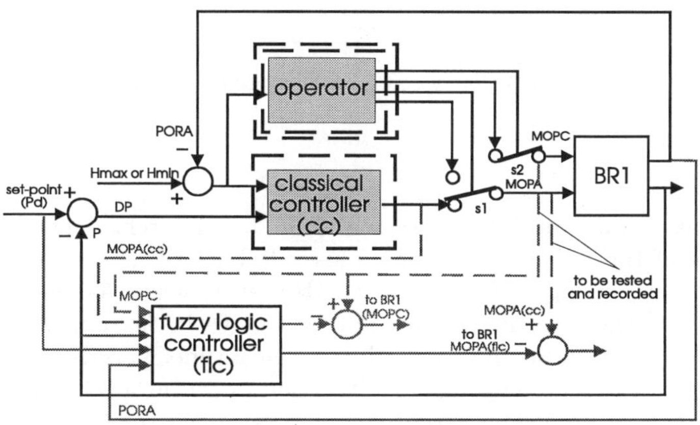

Figure 2. Safe testing environment for FLC on-line experiments at BR1.

it is straightforward to extrapolate the present results to similar industrial reactors without having to repeat all safety tests.

The kernel of FLC is a fuzzy knowledge base in fuzzy control applications. Our current aim is to control the reactor in steady-state operation. According to observations and experience, if the difference between the real and the desired power (DP) is larger than 0.2 % but smaller than 0.8 %, A-rods do not insert as far; by contrast, if DP is larger than 0.8 %, A-rods insert further.

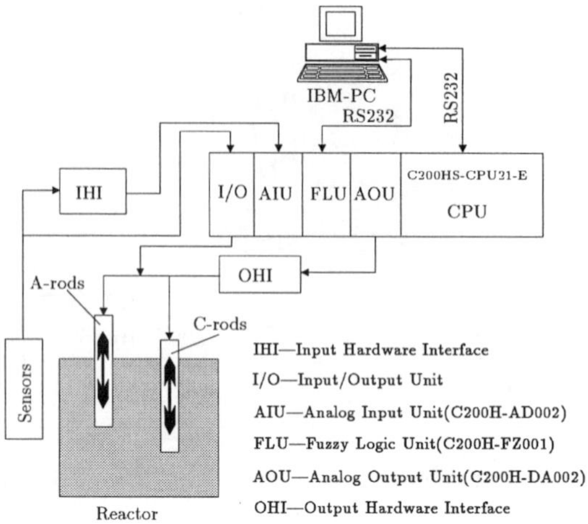

Figure 3. Fuzzy control configuration for BR1.

For a negative value of DP, A-rods withdraw to an extent depending on the magnitude of the DP perturbation. This rule base remains true for as long as A-rods have enough space to move. However, when A-rods reach their insertion or withdrawal limit, they start to move in the opposite direction to return to their initial position. In the meantime, C-rods are controlled to equilibrate the reactivity by slow insertion or withdrawal. This sequence of actions can be modelled in the more sophisticated rule base presented in Table 1.

Table 1: Rule base of FLC with two inputs and two outputs

PORA	IL		NIL		AC		NWL		WL	
DP	MOPA	MOPC	MOPA	MOPC	MOPA	MOPC	MOPA	MOPC	MOPA	MOPC
NL	WB	NA	WB	NA	WB	NA	WS	WS	NA	WB
NM	WM	NA	WM	NA	WM	NA	WS	WS	NA	WS
NS	WS	NA	WS	NA	WS	NA	WS	NA	NA	WS
NZ	NA	NA	NA	NA	NA	NA	NA	NA	NA	NA
PS	NA	IS	IS	NA	IS	NA	IS	NA	IS	NA
PM	NA	IS	IS	IS	IM	NA	IM	NA	IM	NA
PB	NA	IB	IS	IS	IB	NA	IB	NA	IB	NA

3 BR1 as a Test Bed for Applying Fuzzy Logic

To build a controller for BR1 in the steady-state operation, two inputs are selected in our current study: DP, and POR (the current position of the control rod: PORA is for A-rods, and PORC for C-rods, respectively). DP is the power mismatch between the actual power and the desired power. In the steady-state operation, DP is free to vary within 0.2 %. It is expressed by 7 linguistic values from -2 to 2 %: Negative Large (NL), Negative Medium (NM), Negative Small (NS), Near Zero (NZ), Positive Small (PS), Positive Medium (PM), and Positive Large (PL). The rod position is expressed by 5 linguistic values from 0 to 4 m: Insertion Limit (IL), Near Insertion Limit (NIL), Around Centre (AC), Near Withdrawal Limit (NWL), and Withdrawal Limit (WL).

Two outputs in terms of MOPA (Motion of Position for A-rods) and MOPC (Motion of Position for C-rods) are set up regarding the speeds of the A- and C-rods, respectively. MOPA is expressed by 7 singletons from -100 to 100 mm/s: Insertion Big (IB), Insertion Medium (IM), Insertion Small (IS), No Access (NA), Withdraw Small (WS), Withdraw Medium (WM), and Withdraw Big (WB). In the same way, 5 singletons are used to represent MOPC (from -35 to 35 mm/s). Although the definition of MOPA and MOPC are similar, their effects on the resulting reactivity are not the same. Generally, the amount of reactivity controlled by the C-rods is 8 times larger than that of A-rods. Figures 4 and 5 are membership functions presently used for this BR1 project.

At our current stage, we aim at realizing a real on-line control at BR1. This is very important for us to be sure that everything, including both hardware and software, can work properly. Afterwards we are confident of carrying out some basic experiments at BR1. We briefly outline the plan of our early experiments at BR1. Given a desired power of BR1, we ask the FLC system to control the reactor's power output at this desired value while we turn the FLC system on. To ensure the maximum reactor safety during FLC experiments, we design an automatic switch between an FLC experimental operation and a normal control (NC) operation [a]. The switch can only be automatically connected with either FLC or NC in order to at least keep the NC operation of BR1. Figure 6 illustrates the electrical circuit connection of FLC and NC.

As shown in Figure 7, we require an extra support software for our safety design of FLC at BR1.

The software environment of PLC guarantees to the realization of the

[a] a normal control (NC) has the same meaning as a classical control (CC) in this paper, i.e., this is the current control at BR1.

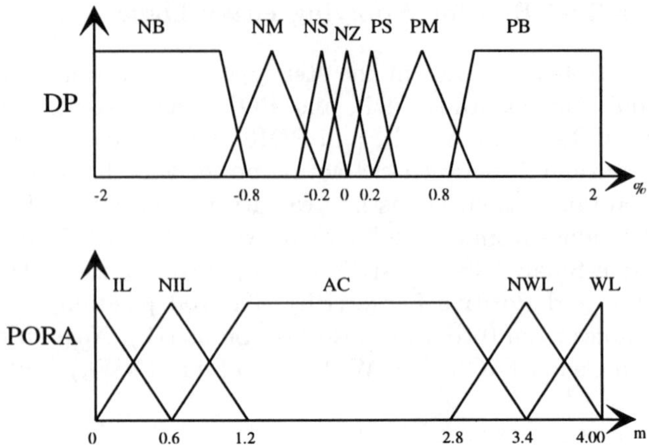

Figure 4. Membership functions for DP and PORA.

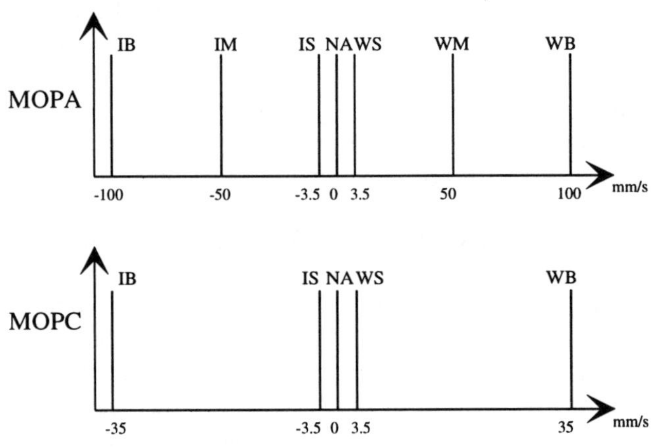

Figure 5. Membership functions for MOPA and MOPC.

programme. After turning the power on, the PLC will always first read each input signal from the A/D unit, i.e., P, Pd, T, PORA, and PORC. Then the PLC checks each signal with its corresponding alarm boundary. If any of the above-mentioned parameters is outside the alarm boundary, the FLC will stop running and NC will automatically take over. Otherwise, the FLC will proceed with outputs of motion of the A-rods (MOA) and that of the C-rods

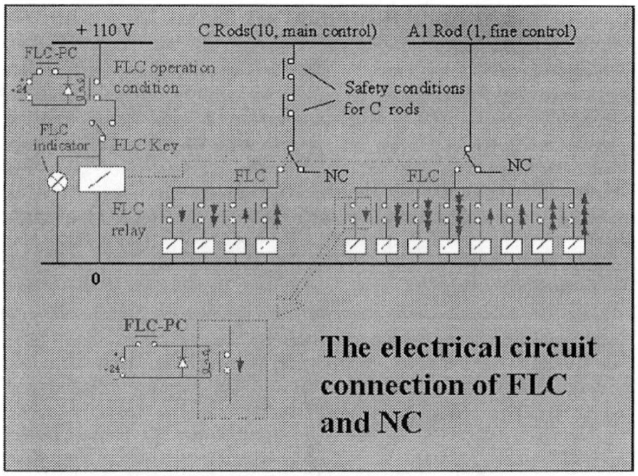

Figure 6. Electrical circuit connection of FLC and NC.

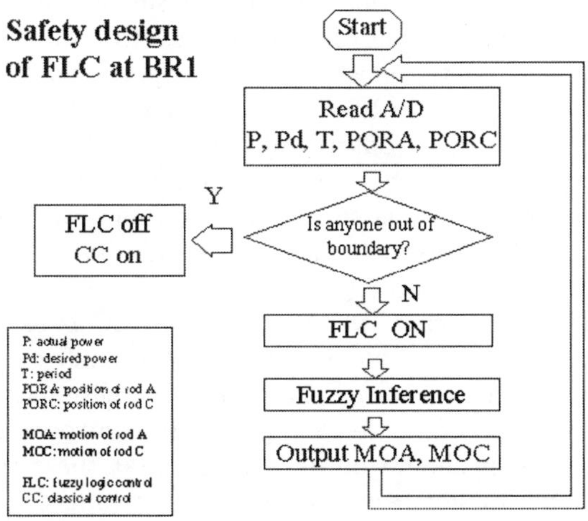

Figure 7. Extra support software for safety design of FLC at BR1.

(Mc) to control the A-rods, and C-rods, respectively.

4 Fuzzy Logic Control On-line at BR1

By July 1998, we obtained a permission to carry on our FLC on-line test at the BR1 reactor. The very first on-line experiment was successfully carried out in September 1998. Figure 8 recorded that experiment.

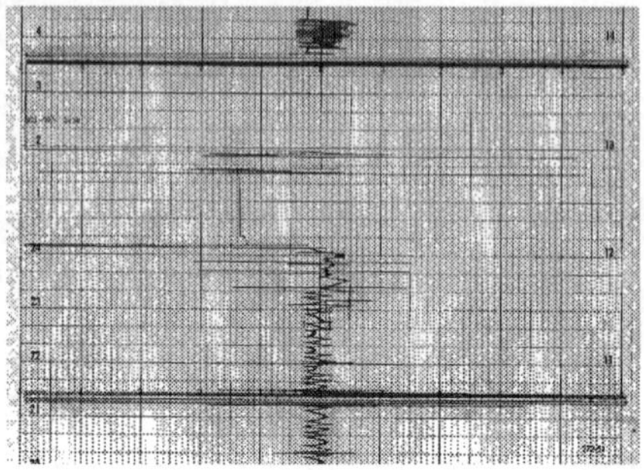

Figure 8. The first fuzzy control on-line experiment at BR1 (September 1998).

We had a dual aim for this on-line experiment. First of all we wanted to show that the FLC is able to keep the reactor stable for different power levels. This is of course the most essential property the FLC must have. The second part of this experiment was to show that FLC can handle a (manually invoked) disturbance of C-rods (resulting in a sudden power change). For every experiment, we show how classical control (CC) and FLC behave. We have carried out over ten tests so far. Among them, we illustrate two cases in Figure 9: (1) Test FLC up to 400 kW at its stability, and (2) Test FLC up to 400 kW with a disturbance.

With these experiments, we showed that FLC is as good as CC in the stable situation and in the compensation of a small disturbance. Though the results reported here are very limited and preliminary, they have clearly demonstrated that it is feasible to apply fuzzy control in the nuclear reactor domain. Moreover, it should be understood that these results are obtained under an issued permission from the nuclear safety authority, which is different from other academic study.

5 Concluding Remarks

As pointed out in [23], the nuclear power industry puts special demands on plant safety, surpassing all other industries in its safety culture. The regulatory environment in which nuclear power plants operate reflects these needs, and

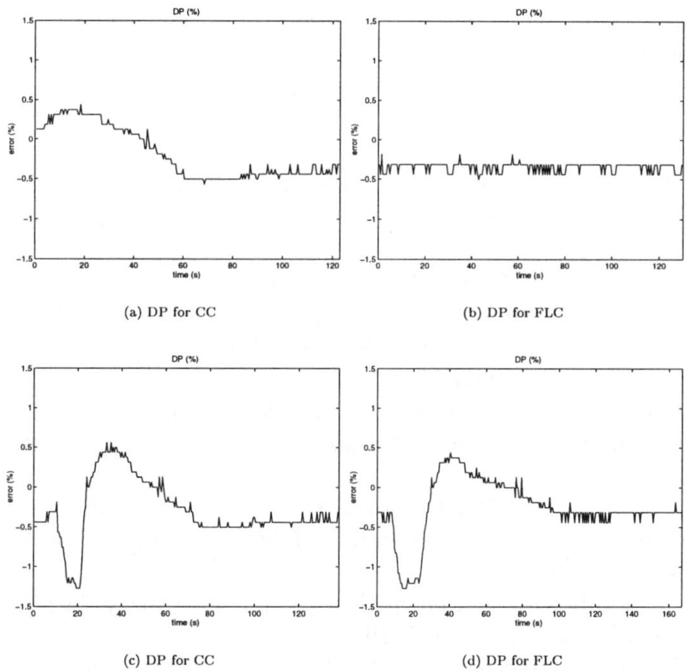

(a) DP for CC

(b) DP for FLC

(c) DP for CC

(d) DP for FLC

Figure 9. The error DP up to 400 kW at its stability (a) and (b), and with a disturbance (c) and (d), respectively.

also the demands of the public for high levels of assurance about safety and regulatory compliance. This culture is not one that encourages innovation in control systems and philosophy, yet nowhere are there greater potential benefits from high reliability systems, automated fault recognition and rationally supported decision-making. A demonstration of the use of intelligent control in an actual plant is a vital step in prototyping the next generation of nuclear power plants. These demonstrations must prove not only the ability to safely survive major disturbances, but also the ability to operate efficiently and reliably in normal operation and to recover smoothly from the minor events that will occur on a regular basis, without challenge to future operations.

In this paper, we report a real R&D project on fuzzy logic application to the BR1 research reactor as a test bed. We aim at being of benefit to the existing control systems by applying fuzzy logic as an additional tool for both the safety and economic aspects in nuclear power plants (NPPs). The final goal of this research is to obtain a license for designing or using fuzzy logic based approach in NPPs.

References

1. H.L. Akin and V. Altin, Rule-based fuzzy logic controller for a PWR-type nuclear power plant, *IEEE Transaction on Nuclear Science* **38** (2), 883–890, 1991.
2. J.A. Bernard, Use of a rule-based system for process control, *IEEE Control Systems Magazine* **8** (5), 3–13, 1988.
3. Bell, G. I. and S. Glasstone: *Nuclear Reactor Theory.* Van Nostrand Reinhold Company, New York, 1970.
4. M. Bubak and J. Moscinski, A fuzzy-logic approach to HTR nuclear power plant model control, *Annals of Nuclear Energy* **10** (9), 467–471, 1983.
5. B.H. Cho and H.C. No, Design of stability-guaranteed fuzzy logic controller for nuclear steam generators, *IEEE Transaction on Nuclear Science* **43** (2), 716–730, 1996.
6. S. Gencay, Site selection for nuclear plants using fuzzy decision analysis, *Kerntechnik* **56** (5), 320–327, 1991.
7. M.A.S. Guth, Some uses and limitations of fuzzy logic in artificial intelligence reasoning for reactor control, *Nuclear Engineering and Design* **113**, 99–109, 1989.
8. Y.-J. Hah and B.-W. Lee, Fuzzy power control algorithm for a Pressurized Water Reactor, *Nuclear Technology* **106**, 242–253, 1994.
9. A.S. Heger, N.K. Alang-Rashid, and M. Jamshidi, Application of fuzzy logic in nuclear reactor control. Part I: an assessment of state-of-the-art, *Nuclear Safety* **36** (1), 109–121, 1995.
10. K.E. Holbert, A. Sharif Heger, and N.K. Alang-Rashid, Redundant sensor validation by using fuzzy logic, *Nuclear Science and Engineering* **118**, 54–64, 1994.
11. H.G. Kim, S.H. Chang, and B.H. Lee, Optimal fuel loading pattern design using an artificial neural network and a fuzzy rule-based system, *Nuclear Science and Engineering* **115**, 152–163, 1993.
12. D.Y. Kim and P.H. Seong, Fuzzy gain scheduling of velocity PI controller with intelligent learning algorithm for reactor control, *Annals of Nuclear Energy* **24** (10), 819–827, 1997.
13. C.C. Kuan, C. Lin, and C.C. Hsu, Fuzzy logic control of steam generator water level in Pressurized Water Reactors, *Nuclear Technology* **100**, 125–134, 1992.

14. C. Lin and D.-H. Yang, Design of a fuzzy logic controller for water level control in an advanced Boiling Water Reactor based on input-output data, *Nuclear Technology* **122**, 318–329, 1998.
15. H. Matsuoka, A simple fuzzy simulation model for nuclear reactor system dynamics, *Nuclear Technology* **94**, 228–241, 1991.
16. N. Na, K. Kwon, C. Ham, and Z. Bien, A study on water level control of PWR steam generator at low power and the self-tuning of its fuzzy controller, *Fuzzy Sets and Systems* **74** (1), 43–51, 1995.
17. P. Ramaswamy, R.M. Edwards, and K.Y. Lee, An automatic tuning method of a fuzzy logic controller for nuclear reactors, *Transactions on Nuclear Science* **40** (4), 1253–1262, 1993.
18. D. Ruan, Fuzzy logic in the nuclear research world, *Fuzzy Sets and Systems* **74** (1) (1995) 5–13.
19. D. Ruan, H. Aït Abderrahim, P. D'hondt, and E.E. Kerre, Eds., *Fuzzy Logic and Intelligent Technologies for Nuclear Science and Industry*, World Scientific, 1998.
20. D. Ruan, Intelligent systems in nuclear applications, *Int. J. of Intelligent Systems* **13** (2/3), 115–125, 1998.
21. D. Ruan and A.J. van der Wal, Controlling the power output of a nuclear reactor with fuzzy logic, *Information Sciences* **110**, 151–177, 1998.
22. L. Tsoukalas and M. Modarres, Artificial intelligence, expert systems, and fuzzy logic in nuclear technology, *Transactions on America Nuclear Society* **68**, 133–139, 1993.
23. J.G. Williams and W.C. Jouse, Intellgent Control in Safety Systems: Criteria for Acceptance in the Nuclear Power Industry, *IEEE Transactions on Nuclear Science* **40** (6), 2040–2044, 1993.
24. L.A. Zadeh, Fuzzy Sets, *Information and Control* **8** (3), 338–353, 1965.
25. H.-J. Zimmermann (1998), Computational intelligence and nuclear engineering, in: [19], 1–18.

Audit Risk Assessment : An Imperfect Knowledge Based Model

Cédric Lesage
CREREG (UMR CNRS C6585)
Institut de Gestion de Rennes
Université de Rennes 1, France
cdlesage@club-internet.fr

Abstract

The reliability of the financial Statements is obtained by the aggregation of the elementary risk assessments of numerous audit tasks. But the available numerical models do suit the auditors who tend to express their judgments by words when confronted with uncertainty. Therefore we have conceived a fuzzy model, that appears to be more reliable than the numeric models.

1. Introduction

The financial Statements must be established by respecting the accounting standards into force, which the auditor commits himself to checking during the certification of the accounts. In this context, two opposite constraints delimit the action of the auditor :

- Carrying out sufficient work to be able to justify of an opinion on the accounts (Quality Constraint)
- Keeping a cost (for the company) and a time reasonable for a relevant use by the thirds (Economic constraint).

The existence of professional standards makes it possible to justify the quality of the work carried out under the economic constraint. Some standards propose true models of audit risk evaluation (i.e. risk that the auditor makes a mistake by expressing his opinion), thus constituting a sure guide for the development of the opinion of the auditor. In this respect, the American standards (Statements on Auditing Standards, or SAS,[2]) are exemplary by two respects : they present an extremely formalized model of evaluation, and they found the methodologies adopted by the large international audit firms. Therefore they are a natural support of any design of audit risk assessment model.

According to these standards [1], audit risk results from the following events :

$$IR \cap CR \cap DR = AR$$

with :

- AR (Audit Risk) : final risk that an error remains into the financial Statements. AR is not explicitly quantified by the SAS, the auditor being the best qualified to evaluate the tolerable risk level,
- IR (Inherent Risk) : evaluation concerning the environment and measuring the risk for a company to book false information,
- CR (Control Risk) : evaluation of the inability of the internal control to detect and correct the existing error into the system of booking,
- DR (Detection Risk) : evaluation of the inability of the auditor to detect and correct the remaining errors. DR can be detailed according to the kind of audit tasks :
    - ◊ Ra : inability of the analytical review to detect the error,
    - ◊ KI : remaining risk after the exhaustive control of some Key-Items,
    - ◊ Stat : remaining risk after the control on a sample, selected by some statistical methods.

For each account or class of transaction, this chain of events must be applied at the *assertion* [2] level :

- *Existence* or *Occurrence* : which is recorded is correctly recorded,
- *Completeness* : all that must be recorded is actually recorded,
- *Rights and Obligations* : all the commitments are respected,
- *Valuation or Allocation* : valuation methods are correctly applied,
- *Presentation and Disclosure* : the standards of presentation and disclosure are correctly applied.

In the practice, this model constitutes the basis for the methodologies and expert systems developed by the audit firms in order to meet the double requirement of the quality constraint and the economic constraint. The problematic consists in the assessment, then the aggregation of pieces of information in order to calculate the final error risk level and to compare it with the risk considered as tolerable.

2. SAS 47 model : limits and discussions

Numerous theoretical and practical limits have been raised by practitioners and researchers upon the actual application of the SAS 47 model, from the evaluation and from the aggregation point of view.

a) *Evaluation : numerical or linguistic ?*
This first point arises the question of the nature of the assessment of the risk of error by the auditor. A numerical evaluation implies precision, whereas in practice,

---

[1] The SAS 47 (AU § 312) defines IR , CR and AR. The SAS 39 (AU § 350) defines the others elements.

[2] SAS 31 (AU § 326) and SAS 55.

most of the audit firms resort to linguistic evaluations of some risks (IR, CR and RA primarily) [9], because of a great part of judgments involved in their opinion on these risks. However, in spite of the reluctance of the practitioners to use numerical evaluations, the question continues to divide the researchers. Indeed, the studies reveal that :

1) the linguistic evaluation allows [13] :
   - a better communication,
   - a better link cost/justification.
2) the numerical evaluation should allow [3] [3] :
   - a better justification for the use of statistical sampling procedures,
   - less error of judgments,
   - a better justification between the decisions about the extend of audit tasks and the global risk level,
   - a greater coherence of judgments between auditors.

Some studies decided to tackle the problem by comparing their respective advantages in experiments. The results obtained are the following [4] :

- the auditor have more confidence in a judgment expressed by words rather than by numbers [20],
- the auditors who use words are more conservative that those who use numbers [15],
- the auditors show a better constituency of judgment when they use numbers rather than words [18].

b) Aggregation

The mode of aggregation of the various components of the risk is crucial in the evaluation of the audit risk because it establishes the formal link between the quality constraint and the economic constraint. Let us suppose a mode of aggregation **A** of the various components of the audit risk (IR, CR, DR). You only have to fix the final risk AR at a level considered as tolerable to obtain :

$$\mathbf{A}\,(IR, CR, DR) = AR$$

AR being fixed, and IR and CR imposed by the accountable context of the company, then the auditor, if he has a relevant and reliable mode of aggregation, can calculate DR. It enables him thus to determine the necessary quantity of work (economic constraint) to reach the objective of final risk (quality constraint). As given its significance, the mode of aggregation has been studied by many contributions. They are based on various mathematical frameworks.

1) Probability-based aggregation

According to this approach all the components are probabilities. The subjective nature of some evaluations, underlined many times by the SAS, requires to use subjective probabilities :

---

[3] Unlike studies on linguistic evaluations, these one have not been experimentally tested but just postulated.

[4] Apart from the first result, some biases seem to hind the generalization of these conclusions [16].

$$p_K(AR) = p_K(IR) \times p_K(CR) \times p_K(DR)$$

Detailing *DR* by its components :

$$p_K(AR) = p_K(IR) \times p_K(CR) \times (P_{Ra} \times P_{KI} \times P_{Stat})$$

This aggregation is suggested, but not imposed, by the standards SAS to formally link the quality constraint and the economic constraint. Although the standards SAS do not impose a quantified risk, their examples, as well as the methodologies and the expert systems used by the firms of audit, set AR = 0,05.

Many criticisms [6], [21] have been made against this probabilistic processing, specially relating to :

- the independence conditions of the variables (for example: although preventive and detective effects are both defined by the SAS as components of CR, preventive effect is also unconsciously taken into account when assessing IR)
- the difficulty in assessing a conditional probability.

Others critics [7] are focused on the unavoidable complexity of the model to :

- evaluate at the assertion level, because of the multiple connections due to a Bayesian structure of inference (see for example [11]),
- consider qualitative data.

In spite of its success, the probability-based audit risk model appears then to include severe theoretical as well as practical limits.

2) Belief-based aggregation

The reason for using this approach comes from the inability of the model SAS 47 to distinguish between the total ignorance that the system works (for example because the system has not been tested), and the certainty that it does actually not work : for both cases, SAS 47 forces to hold a probability of risk of errors of 100%. However both events have a very different nature. Srivastava and Shafer [17] have thus developed a model of evaluation of the audit risk based on the Belief theory. The basic idea of this theory is to evaluate, not directly an element A, but each part of the set $\{A; \bar{A}\}$, where A = " absence of error " et $\bar{A}$ = " presence of error " :

Figure 1 : Belief-Based ARM Model

IR		CR		RA		KI		AR
m_1		m_1		m_1		m_1		0,95
m_2	⊕	m_2	⊕	m_2	⊕	m_2	=	m_2
m_3		m_3		m_3		m_3		m_3

m_1 = belief that no error exists m_3 = uncommitted belief

m_2 = belief that an error exists   ⊕ : Dempster's rule of combination

Thus, by replacing the probability by a function of belief, this model makes it possible to distinguish assessments of quite different situations as for their impact on the real reliability of the financial Statements. This improvement is carried out by the acceptance of the subjectivity of the evaluation. Since its publication, this model is the subject of many experiments [7], [8]. However this approach, on the contrary to the probabilistic processing, is not applied within the audit firms.

Both Probability- and Belief- based models present two major characteristics :

- numerical evaluation,
- probabilistic aggregation (using the product)

Aggregation of the probabilistic type arises the problem of the knowledge of aggregation structure. It supposes a network in the tree form, where connections are clearly identified, thus allowing to precisely measure the impact of an element of proof at the assertion, account, or financial Statements level. However, no element proves to date the perfect knowledge of these interrelationships [10], [12]. On the contrary, the difficulty in connecting for instance the assertions to the evaluations of the accounts [21] has been highlighted.

Another question, (that has never been tackled as far as we know) deals with the commutative property of the product aggregator. Its use involves a strict equivalence of impact on AR between two elements evaluated on the same level (It is thus equivalent for AR that IR = 0,5, other components = 1, or equally that KI = 0,5, other components = 1 : in both cases AR = 0,5). However can we really assume that the various components of the risk affect AR in the same way ?
Can we for instance consider as equivalent IR, that assesses the context in which the auditor intervenes, and thus that he undergoes, and DR, assessing his work inscribed within this framework ? It does not appear necessary to us that the aggregation operator between these two components has the remarkable property of commutation.

Finally, this discussion leads us to adopt :

- an evaluation under a linguistic form, in order to conform to the practice, also allowing the processing of perfect information and statistical data when available,
- an aggregation of a partial ignorance type.

We thus propose to build and try out a model of evaluation of the risk of audit applying the principles above.

3. Design of an imperfect information audit risk model

Cooley and Hicks [5] have proposed a non numerical approach, based on fuzzy logic, of problems close to the evaluation of the audit risk : the evaluation of the internal audit (CR). Their model stands as follows :

$$E = S * P * R$$

with: S = Significance of the control objective P = Possibility of the risk
R =Reliance on the control procedure *: aggregating operator
and where :

- Evaluation : each variable is evaluated by a linguistic variable. Cooley and Hicks chose to use the canonical S (weak, strong) and P functions (moderate) of Zadeh, as well as the operator of concentration of Lakoff (very weak, very strong).
- Aggregation: by using the general principle of extension, the authors propose various types of aggregation, according to the aimed objective (the weakest link, the strongest component, the weighted average reliance, etc.).

This approach was the first attempt of a non-probabilistic formalization of an evaluation of internal control procedures. However, major drawbacks (in particular the theoretical membership functions) have prevented its actual use, explaining its non experimentation.

On the other hand, the representation of information characterized by uncertainty and imprecision by the means of linguistic variables allows both an evaluation respecting their nature, and an aggregation in a formal mathematical framework (fuzzy logic). These characteristics lead us to resort to this data processing for the resolution of the problem of the audit risk assessment.

a) Evaluation with context dependent linguistic variables

As suggested by Cooley and Hicks, we will use linguistic variables to represent the judgments of the auditor expressing his confidence in the tested procedure. For easy calculation purposes, we propose to use the trapezoidal fuzzy numbers (NFT) to define the forms of the linguistic variables, the parameters L_0, L_1, U_1, U_0 being determined by a psychometric questionnaire based on the expert method [3].

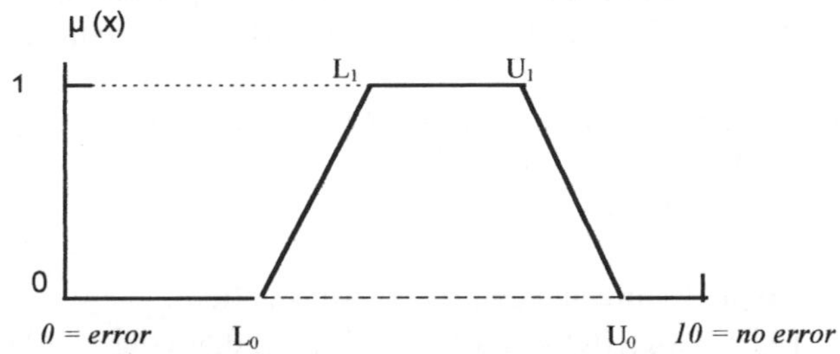

This list will be completed by the values [cer] (certainty : $\{x=10;\ \mu(x)=1\}$, and [stat] (membership function determined by statistical sampling procedures). The global opinion thus becomes an aggregation of judgments of confidence expressed by the practitioners by one of the 7 following evaluations:

very weak, weak, moderate, strong, very strong, cer and stat

b) Aggregation structure with partial ignorance

Our basic postulate is the ignorance of the real aggregation structure. Therefore we suggest that the detection procedures have no joined effects on the evaluation of the final risk : the global reliance will thus be given by the procedure with the highest confidence, which mathematically results in the use of the operator max (noted $\vee$) :

$$[CR] \vee [KI] \vee [Ra] \vee [Stat] = [ADR]$$

This first equation can be refined. Ignorance about what is recorded is not absolute : the percentage *t* of tested Key-items will be error free in an unquestionable way. We can therefore distinguish between :

- t % of the directly validated account balance :

$$[KI] = [ADR(t)]$$

- (1-t) % remaining, validated indirectly by the analysis of the procedures :

$$[CR] \vee [Ra] \vee [Stat] = [ADR(1-t)]$$

Both cases being exclusive one of the other, we thus obtain the following equation :

$$t\,[KI] + (1-t)\,[[CR] \vee [Ra] \vee [Stat]] = [ADR]$$

ADR thus represents the confidence in the accounts to correctly evaluate what is recorded, for a given IR. Indeed, the evaluation of the risk related to the environment equals to evaluate the informational context in which fits the financial Statements process. Therefore, we suggest to base our model on an operator of compensation, among which we chose the average (being the simplest one) :

$$[AR] = 0{,}5\,([IR] + [ADR])$$

$$\text{with: } [ADR] = t\,[KI] + (1-t)\,[[CR] \vee [Ra] \vee [Stat]]$$

This basic structure is completed by taking into account the results of the studies showing that the assertions play a key role in the evaluation of the risk by the auditor [14]. Moreover, it was shown that the 5 assertions did not have all the same importance according to the nature of the audited account : the asset accounts privilege reality, and liabilities accounts privilege completeness [21]. To represent this phenomenon, we propose to retain the following operator of aggregation :

$$A\,\Omega\,B = \lambda\,(A \vee B) + 0{,}5\,(1-\lambda)\,(A+B) \qquad \text{with } \lambda \in [0-1]$$

This operator is interpreted like a fuzzy OR [5], with the following limit cases :
when $\lambda = 1$, $A\,\Omega\,B = A \vee B$ = classical OR
when $\lambda = 0$, $A\,\Omega\,B = 0{,}5\,(A + B)$ = average

We thus come to the following comprehensive equation :

$$[AR] = \lambda_N\,([IR] \vee [ADR]) + (1 - \lambda_N)\,0{,}5([IR] + [ADR])$$

with : $[ADR] = t\,[KI] + (1-t)\,[[CR] \vee [Ra] \vee [Stat]]$
$\lambda_N \to 1$ when Occurrence is privileged (Assets),
$\lambda_N \to 0$ when Completeness is privileged

This equation constitutes our proposal for a linguistic-based audit risk model.

4. Experimentation and discussion

a) Methodology

We led a study into a large audit firm in Paris (Big 6). We obtained 69 field evaluations of accounts, detailed according to various components' risk. They were expressed according to one of the 7 assessments expressing the auditor's reliance on the tested audit task. The psychometric questionnaire made it possible to obtain the following values, thus defining the NFT of the linguistic variables from now on used by the model :

Variable	L_0	L_1	U_1	U_0
very weak	0,0	0,0	2,1	4,9
weak	0,5	2,1	4,3	6,2
moderate	2,8	4,4	6,4	7,7
strong	5,4	6,9	8,8	9,9
very strong	6,7	8,9	10,0	10,0

The tests carried out on the models consist in the comparison [5] between the theoretical final evaluation (theoretical aggregation of the real evaluations of the components (IR, CR, etc.), given by the auditor) provided by the model and the real final evaluation given by the auditor of the audit risk (AR) on the tested account.

b) Preliminary results

During the talks, two facts appeared, corroborating the remarks already made on the real process of evaluation of the risk of audit :

- The evaluation using words to indicate confidence in the procedure to detect an error has never raised difficulties amongst the tested auditors, thus illustrating their current use,
- The most used assessment for final reliance (AR) was « strong » (69,6 % of the answers). 21,7 % of the evaluations were « very strong », among which 46,5 % declare their certainty. Conversely, the remaining 8,7 % relate to a « moderate » evaluation, for which the accounts have been either certified with a reserve, or declared to require some internal procedures from the audited company before their acceptance. Consequently, it seems that the difficulty in expressing a final judgment encourages the auditors to be very cautious : the « strong » assessment seems to constitute the reference degree of confidence.

c) Test of SAS 47 Model

In a first step, we applied the data collected (after reprocessing transforming the linguistic values expressing a confidence into a probability of risk of error), with the probabilistic model suggested by the SAS standards. In spite of the inherent skews due such transformations, the results obtained are in conformity with the results of former studies [6] [7] :

---

[5] We suggest to calculate the difference E = theoretical - real as follows :

$$E = (L_{0(T)}+L_{1(T)}+U_{1(T)}+U_{0(T)})/4 - (L_{0(R)}+L_{1(R)}+U_{1(R)}+U_{0(R)})/4$$

We will present the averages $\bar{\mathbf{x}}$ et standard deviations σ of the calculated differences, and the % of items (noted **LV%**) having the same linguistic *AR* evaluation from the model and from the auditor. The linguistic equivalent of the theoretical TFN is the nearest linguistic value (as calculated by the distance between the centers of gravity).

[6] It should be noticed that this overvaluation noted on a non probabilistic problem remains in the case of subjective assessment of conjunctive probabilities applied to simple and probabilistic problems [21].

Figure 2 : SAS 47 Model

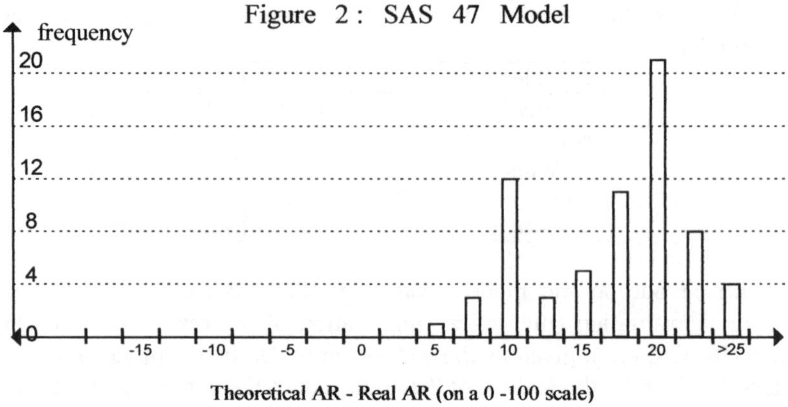

A significant over-estimate is actually noted (the average of the variations is 19 %, the standard deviation 8%). However the examples of the SAS standards suggest to retain a final risk of 5%, which is extremely restrictive (this value corresponds to a confidence closer to « certainty » than to « very strong »). Consequently, it appears that if the final objective is stricter in the standards than in practice (« strong » confidence instead of a risk of error of 5 %), on the other hand the real type of aggregation is more preserving than that suggested by the probabilistic model.

d) Linguistic Model test

Results of the experiment of the linguistic model stand as follows :

Figure 3 : Linguistic Model

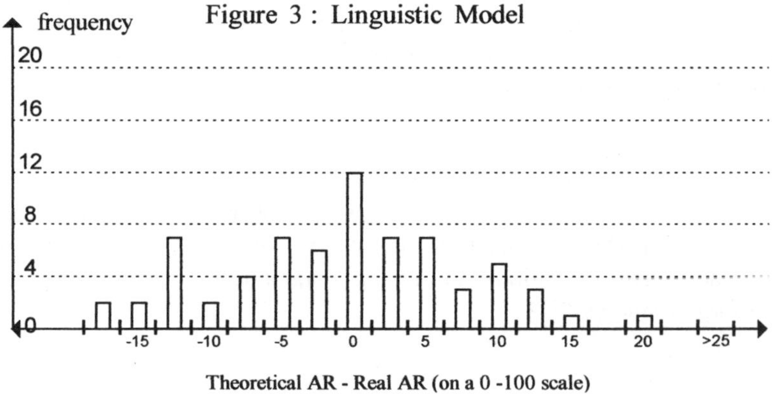

This model, built, let us recall it, on an aggregation structure partially unknown obtains the following results :

- The average of the variations is 0,0 % : the model is thus centered on the real results. It should be noted that the use of the parameter makes it possible to adjust the model as well on the Liabilities accounts as on the Credit accounts. Its optimization is carried out with the following values λ_{Assets} = 0,18 and $\lambda_{Liabilities}$ = 0,03 : the risk related to the environment thus is more importance for the Liabilities accounts than for the Assets accounts , in accordance with the preceding reasoning.

Moreover, these values make it possible to obtain a similar behavior (average, standard deviation) whatever the nature of the account is.

- The spread of the variations is comparable with the probabilistic model (Standard deviation of the variations = 8,8 %). It seems however that the most relevant indicator in the case of a linguistic model consists in the calculation of the number of identical evaluations provided by both the model and the auditor in terms of linguistic values. In 66,7 % of the cases, the model provides the same linguistic assessment as the auditor, the other cases being an assessment immediately above (23,2 %) and an assessment immediately below (10,1%).
- An analysis of the variations according to the evaluation of the environment (IR) shows a very heterogeneous behavior of the model :

IR Assessment	n	$\bar{x}$	σ	LV%.
« very weak » or « weak »	8	-9,9 %	10,2 %	58 %
« moderate »	17	-5,9 %	9,3 %	76 %
« strong »	39	1,8 %	5,9 %	67 %
« very strong »	5	9,4 %	6,6 %	40 %
Total	69	0,0	8,8 %	67 %

We notice that the more IR moves away from a value located between « moderate » and « strong » the stronger is the tendency to move away from the average. A possible explanation of this phenomenon could be related to the usual lack of habit for the auditor to intervene in an « extreme » environment, thus modifying his evaluation of the risk by overweighing the importance of the environment. Psychological effects [7] would thus occur, which is not considered by our linguistic model. Let us recall that we limited ourselves to a simple fuzzy operator of an average-type between IR and ADR. A better consideration of the environment would thus demand the modeling of a risk behavior, or a refinement of the effects of information redundancy between the evaluations of the various types of procedures.

5. Conclusion

Our approach consisted in a theoretical approach of the structure of aggregation of the audit risk, validated by an experiment on field data. It aimed to bring closer the practice (use of words for the representation of knowledge) and the theory (construction of models of evaluations to quantify the risk). Its originality is to highlight the prospects for a model of audit risk assessment registered within the framework of the fuzzy logic (evaluation by linguistic variables, aggregation by a fuzzy operator), which turns out to be able of a predictive capacity higher than the available numerical models.

[7] If research in decision making gives a significant place to the behavior faced to risk, this question is still to be studied on the audit field.

However some features of this study limit its the range, so much from the experimental point of view (field date coming from a single firm), than from the conceptual (the process of the evaluation of the couples procedures/assertions having been regarded as resulting from a standard " black box " process). Lastly, this model does not a priori claim to explain the phenomena in process during the evaluation of the audit risk. However, the robustness and the flexibility of a linguistic model could help to identify their nature and their impact on the behavior of the auditor. This study thus has highlighted the particular role of environment, as well as the non-symmetry of the reality- and completeness- assertions regarding the assets- and liabilities-accounts. It is a first attempt to formalize two well-known phenomena experienced in the daily practice of audit.
We propose to proceed in this way by testing other types of aggregation and modeling of these effects during next experiments led within other audit firms.

Bibliography

[1] Aladenise N., Bouchon-Meunier B.: « Acquisition de connaissances imparfaites : mise en évidence d'une fonction d'appartenance». *Revue internationale de systémique*, vol.11, n°1, 1997, pp. 109-127.

[2] American Institute of Certified Public Accountant: *AICPA Professionnal Standards*, vol.1, US Auditing Standards, AICPA , New York, 1992.

[3] Boritz J.E., Gaber B.G., Lemon W.M. : « Managing Audit Risk », *CA Magazine*, vol. 120, n°1, 1987, pp.36-41.

[4] Bühler H.R. : *Réglage par la logique floue*, Presses polytechniques et universitaires romandes, Lausanne, 1994.

[5] Cooley J.W., Hicks J.O. : « A fuzzy approach to aggregating internal control judgements » *Management Science,* vol 29, n°3 , 1983, pp. 317-334.

[6] Cushing B.E., Loebbecke J.K. : « Analytical approaches to audit risk : a survey and analysis »; *Auditing : Journal of Practice & Theory*, n°3 (Fall), 1983, pp.23-41.

[7] Dusenbury R., Reimers J.L., Wheeler S. : « An Empirical study of Belief based and Probability-based Specification of Audit Risk », *Auditing : A Journal of Practice & Theory*, vol.15, n°2,Fall, 1996, pp.13-27.

[8] Dutta S.K, Srivastava.R.P. : « Aggregation of Evidence in Auditing : A likelihood Perspective », *Auditing : A Journal of Practice & Theory*, vol.12, Supplement, 1993, pp.137-172.

[9] Janell P., Wright A. : « Inherent risk and control environment assessments practices of major auditing firms : Implications for practice and future research ». Working Paper. North-Eastern University, 1992.

[10] Krishnamoorthy K : « Discussion of Aggregation of Evidence in Auditing : A likelihood Perspective », Auditing : *A Journal of Practice & Theory*, vol.12, Supplement, 1993, pp.161-166.

[11] Lea R.B., Adams S.J., Boykin R.F. : « Modeling of the Audit Risk Assessment Process at the Assertion Level Within an Account Balance », *Auditing, A Journal of Practice and Theory*, vol. 11, Supplement, 1992, pp. 153-179.

[12] Loebbecke J.K. : « Discussion of Aggregation of Evidence in Auditing : A likelihood Perspective », *Auditing : A Journal of Practice & Theory*, vol.12, Supplement, 1993, pp.167-172.

[13] Macfadgen D.N.: «Discussion of When Numbers Are Better Than Words : The Joint Effects of Response Representation and Experience on Inherent Risk Judgments », *Auditing : A Journal of Practice and Theory*, vol.13 Supplement, 1994, pp.20-23.

[14] Nelson M.W., Bonner S.E., Libby R. : « Knowledge Structure and the Estimation of Conditional Probabilities in Audit Planning »; *The Accounting Review*, vol. 70, n°1, 1995, pp. 27-47.

[15] Reimers J., Wheeler S., Dusenbury R. : « The Effect of Response Mode on Auditors' Control Risk Assessments », *Auditing : A journal of Practice & Theory*, vol.12, n°2, 1993, pp.62-78.

[16] Rennie M. : « Discussion of When Numbers Are Better Than Words : The Joint Effects of Response Representation and Experience on Inherent Risk Judgments », *Auditing : A Journal of Practice and Theory*, vol.13 Supplement, 1994, pp.24-28.

[17] Srivastava R.P., Shafer G.R. : « Belief-Function Formulas for Audit Risk », *The Accounting Review*, vol. 67, n° 2, 1992, pp. 249-283.

[18] Stone D.N., Dilla W.N. : « When Numbers Are Better Than Words : The Joint Effects of Response Representation and Experience on Inherent Risk Judgments », *Auditing : A Journal of Practice and Theory*, vol.13, Supplement, 1994, pp.1-19.

[19] Tversky Amos., Kahneman D., Slovic P. : *Judgments under uncertainty : Heuristics and biases*, Cambridge University Press, Cambridge, 1984.

[20] Waller W.S. : Auditor's risk assessments : Effects of task experience, conditioning information, and precision on second order uncertainty, Working Paper , University of Arizona, 1995.

[21] Waller W.S. : « Auditor's Assessments of Inherent and Control Risk in Field Settings »; *The Accounting Review*, Vol. 68, n°4, 1993, pp. 783-803.

Operational Risk Measurement in Financial Institutions: A Fuzzy Logic Approach

Sergio Scandizzo
Canadian Imperial Bank of Commerce
scandizz@cibc.ca

Abstract: In this paper I discuss how to use fuzzy logic in the measurement of operational risk within a financial institution. After reviewing the theoretical basis and the main approaches to the assessment of operational risk in modern banking, I describe an application of fuzzy logic within an integrated risk management framework. A clustering algorithm is developed based on a fuzzy algebra that produces a ranking of the business units within a financial institution.

1 Introduction

Risk can be defined as the potential for realization of unwanted, adverse consequences to the measurable output of a system or a process. In financial markets this can happen because of the adverse move of market factors (market risk), because of the failure of a counterpart to comply with its obligations (credit risk) and because of whatever other occurrence - human error, fraud, system failure, new regulations, etc. - adversely affects the company's bottom line.

In banking, as in all other areas where the topic is relevant, risk analysis is not a discipline *per se*. It is an offspring of decision-making analysis. The decision-maker faces a number of alternative actions in achieving his/her objectives. The outcomes of these actions depend on one or more (usually more than one) variables whose behavior is often uncertain. If these variables are observable and if their statistical properties can be assumed to be stable (or at least to tend to become stable in the long run) the estimation of their probability distribution is a big step in estimating the distribution of the outcome (profits, return on capital, or whatever we are interested in) which we can assume to be statistically stable as well.

This approach works well in all those cases where the past can reasonably be used to predict the future - or at least in all those cases where information about the past is abundant and accessible, and it worked well so far in analyzing market risk, where market factors (interest and exchange rates, commodity and equity prices) can be modeled as random variable with known statistical properties.

It fails, though, whenever we cannot assume statistical stability or, in other words, in all those cases where the past is of no help in forecasting the future. This can happen for two main reasons: because we are not able to transform our knowledge about historical behavior in statistically meaningful, quantitative terms, or because there is no past whatsoever to analyze.

Let us consider the quantification problem first. Even if it is in principle possible to think of some events as being generated by an underlying random process, sometimes we may just not be able to collect the necessary data or the available information can be very difficult to express in a form suitable for risk analysis. Take credit risk for example. The traded debt of a rated financial institution can be quite satisfactorily treated in a statistical framework - as recent attempts like J.P. Morgan's CreditMetrics and Credit Swiss-First Boston's CreditRisk systems suggest - but other kinds of debt can be much more difficult to assess. Sometimes the information available is abundant, a very thorough analysis of the firm creditworthiness may have been conducted, but, although the result of this analysis can fill several pages of text, drawing an actual probability distribution may prove very hard to say the least. Most banks have now very sophisticated risk rating systems, that process information from the balance sheet as well as about the quality of management and the nature of collateral, but the output of these systems is usually nowhere near to provide a probability distribution.

Operational risk is another case in point. Take for example the risk of human error. There is no reason not to assume statistical stability in the generating process (at least under normal conditions), but trying to collect historical data may easily become a nightmare. Furthermore, given the likelihood of a human error, it is necessary to identify and estimate probability for risk factors like seniority in the position, training received, past track record for each employee and so on. Even if this is accomplished, how significant is the relationship between these factors and the actual risk? And how do we transform the likelihood of an error into the probability of loosing X dollars over a certain time period?

In other words risk management deals with uncertainty, but there is more than one kind of uncertainty. There is uncertainty due to randomness, like the one we face in dealing with market risk factors, which are driven by a mechanism that can be modeled as a random process, and there is uncertainty due to knowledge imperfection. The origin of this kind of uncertainty does not lie in the process generating the risk factor, but rather in our own inability to express our knowledge numerically [3].

The second problem - no history to analyze - is well known in project analysis where, more often than not, projects cannot be repeated under various conditions and are unique, with nothing in the past that can be used as a proxy. Here the difficulty is not in our ability to quantify a stable distribution, but rather in the existence itself of such a distribution. Even in the long run, an earthquake, a revolution, a fraud of unheard proportions can be just a singularity in the event horizon which is pointless to try to capture in a probability number.

It is also worth mentioning that in many cases the unrepeatable event is just a very peculiar combination of a great number of simpler occurrences. Project analysts often refer to this as the "Murphy Risk", or, in other words, the risk that "many things go wrong at the same time". Each of these events could very well be easier to analyze, but, as a combination, given also the senselessness of trying to estimate correlations among them, they constitute a singularity for which no underlying stable distribution can be assumed.

We present an attempt to overcome these difficulties by using fuzzy logic to express and process that kind of knowledge which is relevant, sometimes abundant within an organization, but very hard to quantify and, as a consequence, very difficult to use if our ultimate goal is to generate a numerical estimate (in monetary terms) of the operational risk faced by a financial institution.

In contemporary banking environment operational risk may be defined as the potential for loss incurred as a consequence of the breakdown of processes, human errors, technology and infrastructure failures, business interruptions, faulty reporting and non-compliance with regulations and laws. Operational risk is then the risk of loss originating from the normal operations within a financial institution. Therefore an obvious way to measure operational risk is to identify operational risk factors and to measure the impact of each factor on the operations of each business units within the bank. This analysis, though, is by no means straightforward since no statistical framework exists to estimate risk factors probability distributions and to link such distributions to earnings and value at risk.

2 Structure of the System

While an already considerable body of literature [1], [5] has been produced on operational risk understanding and management, practitioners are still far away from developing a consistent framework for the measurement of this kind of risk. We can identify two, strictly related, reasons for this lack of success. First, historical data on operational risk factors are very difficult to collect and organize in a meaningful manner. Unlike market risk factors which are quantitative in nature and easy to monitor and record, operational risk factors are, more often than not, very difficult to measure and extremely hard to observe. Second, no mathematical models or pricing equations are available that rigorously link the occurrence of a particular operational risk factor with the market value of a financial institution or with the amount of loss that can actually be incurred.

Therefore, some banks have resolved to a less ambitious approach by trying to recognize certain categories of risk, to rate each business unit within the bank according to such categories, and to establish a relative operational risk ranking not unlike what they are already doing while rating clients according to their credit risk.

Take for example a financial institution with a number of business units and consider the following components of operational risk (risk factors):

1. People risk: human errors, insufficient expertise, misconduct or fraud.
2. Process risk: inefficiencies of internal procedures and controls.
3. System risk: failures in computer and/or communication systems.
4. Business event risk: changes in competition, regulations, natural disasters.

Operational risk analysis within this framework may be thought of as a fuzzy multi-attribute evaluation problem where a number of attributes (risk factors) are assigned fuzzy linguistic labels, then weighted according to their relative relevance, and eventually aggregated into a single measure for each business unit. Therefore, in order to be able to rank the various business units, we have to rank the risk factors first.

Thomas Saaty's Analytic Hierarchy Process is a well-known analytical tool to support multi-objective decision-making. It has been used both in weighting the relative importance of multiple objectives to the decision-maker as well as in evaluating alternatives according to multiple objectives. In this application we will use AHP to develop a set of weights for our risk factors and will then follow an algebra-based approach to assess operational risk according to both risk factors and weights. The theoretical structure underlying AHP is addressed in [6]; here we will briefly describe it and will show how we have applied a fuzzy version of AHP to our problem.

In AHP the decision-maker is asked to rate every attribute relative to each other. For example, for attributes 1 and 2 a numerical value a_{12} is assigned. Then an nxn matrix A is built where a_{ij} is the relative weight of attribute *i* versus attribute *j*, $a_{ii}=1$ and $a_{ij}=1/a_{ji}$. It can be shown that the problem of finding the vector of normalized weights W consistent with the preferences expressed in A is equivalent to determine the eigenvector W which corresponds to the maximum eigenvalue λ_{max} from the equation

$$(M-\lambda I)W=0$$

such that $\max_i w_i=1$.

Although in traditional AHP method weights are normalized so that the sum is equal to 1, we will use fuzzy possibility measures denoted by linguistic expressions [8] which will result in a set of non-additive weights.
The traditional additivity condition can be easily removed by using a possibility (non additive) fuzzy measure such as Shafer and Bel's [7] measure: $Bel(A)=\Sigma_{B\subset A}m(B)$, $\forall A\subset B$,
which measures the certainty for $x\in X$ to be a member of A, and where $m:2^X\to[0,1]$.

3 Fuzzy Clustering

Then the task of classifying the various business units may be addressed in the framework developed by Loia and Scandizzo [4] where a fuzzy algebraic structure is expressly designed to implement multi-criteria analysis. This algebra originally developed in [2], acts on ordered strings generated by fuzzy attributes. In our application, ordered strings are the result of complex assessments such as: *high* people risk, *low* process risk, *average* system risk, *low* business event risk. Each of these attributes or criteria induces a partition in the set of business units. For each criterion we will have a string of the form $a_1^{\alpha 1}..a_n^{\alpha n}$, where Roman letters represent the various units and the Greek ones are linguistic (fuzzy) labels. By combining all these partitions together, our algebra generates a classification that is more refined than the initial ones and also consistent with all the original criteria.

Let **U** be a universe of discourse where each element **u** is represented by a k-uple $(A_1(u),\dots,A_k(u))$. The $A_i(u)$ are fuzzy measures of the elements of **U** whose values are ordered sets of fuzzy numbers. Each attribute A_i of the set $\{A_1,\dots,A_k\}$ is represented by an ordered string:

$$A_i = a_n^{\alpha n}\, a_{n-1}^{\alpha n-1} \dots a_1^{\alpha 1}$$

where the set $\{\alpha_1\dots\alpha_n\}$, with $\alpha_1 < \alpha_2 < \dots < \alpha_n$, represents the set of the linguistic labels, whereas the elements $a_j=A_j^{-1}(\alpha_j)$ are the possible subsets of **U** for which the attribute A_j takes` the value α_j . Since each element of **U** has a unique evaluation with respect to a single attribute, the set $\{a_n,a_{n-1},\dots,a_1\}$ is an ordered partition of **U**. Hence, each attribute generates a partition, or classification of elements of **U**.

For the structure to generate a classification we need to introduce an operation between the ordered strings associated with the attributes A_i such that it gives us a string which is a finer classification of the information contained in the original strings. The idea of such an operation can be intuitively understood if we consider the two-fold meaning of a digit in a number, i.e., the roles of value and position. In the case of our strings, the absolute value of the generic element a_i is the set of the elements of **U** which a_i represents, whereas the value corresponding to the position is given by the linguistic label α_i. Thus, being aware of the real nature of the elements of the strings (subsets of U as values, and fuzzy numbers as powers), the basic operation of our structure appears as a variant of the classical multiplication of natural numbers. The main difference from the classical operation is due to the fact that our string is made of two heterogeneous objects:

- the subsets of U, which constitute the first part of the string,
- the fuzzy sets, which constitute the second part of the string.

For this reason, it is necessary to define the operations on the two parts of the strings separately. Thus, given two strings, A and B, the operation between them, A Δ B, involves two different operations:

1. the operation * between the first parts of the strings (ordinary sets),
2. the operation ° between the second parts of the strings (fuzzy numbers).

The results of AΔB is an still an ordered string, in which the first part is obtained applying the operation * over the first parts of A and B; and the second part of AΔB is given by the application of ° on the corresponding second parts of A and B in an independent and asynchronous way. Specifically, given:

$$A = an^{\alpha n}\, an\text{-}1^{\alpha n-1} \dots\dots\dots a1^{\alpha 1} \qquad \text{and}$$
$$B = bm^{\beta m} bm\text{-}1^{\beta m-1} \dots\dots\dots b1^{\beta 1}$$

then

$A \Delta B = (an^{\alpha n}\ an\text{-}1^{\alpha n\text{-}1} \ldots\ldots a1^{\alpha 1})\ (bm^{\beta m}\ bm\text{-}1^{\beta m\text{-}1} \ldots\ldots b1^{\beta 1}) =$
$c_{m+n-1}{}^{\gamma m+n-1} \ldots\ldots c_1{}^{\gamma 1}$

where c_i (respectively γ_I), with I=1,....m+n-1, is obtained by applying * on the first parts (respectively ° on the second parts) of the strings A and B.

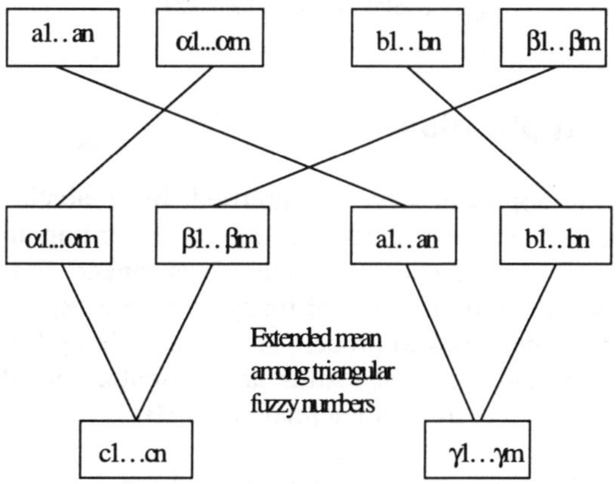

Figure 1. Structure of the Fuzzy Algebra

Within this framework the business units in a financial institution can be ranked according to the risk factors discussed above. The risk factors are themselves ranked and weighted according to managers' assessment in the form of fuzzy linguistic expressions. An analogous kind of appraisal is then used to process single factor's ranking through our fuzzy algebraic structure, and the final results are presented and discussed.

The proposed methodology can be represented graphically in the following diagram.

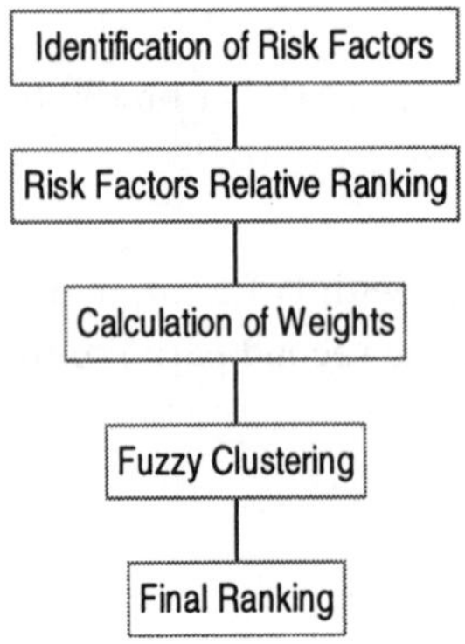

Figure 2. Structure of the Methodology.

4 A Simple Application

We develop an application for a simplified, but realistic financial institution where a number of business units are ranked according to the 4 risk factors discussed above. The risk factors are themselves ranked and weighted according to managers' assessment in the form of fuzzy linguistic expressions. An analogous kind of appraisal is then used to process single factor's ranking through our fuzzy algebraic structure, and the final results are presented and discussed. The three business units considered are Commercial Bank (B1), Investment Bank (B2), and Trading Room (B3).

Table 1 shows linguistic labels and associated fuzzy numerical values. Table 2 and 3 show how linguistic labels for each category are related to the 3 business units. Table 4 shows the three consecutive steps in the processing. Table 5 reports the final ranking.

Linguistic values	Triangular fuzzy numbers		
High	0.6	0.8	1.0
Medium	0.3	0.5	0.7
Low	0.0	0.2	0.4

Table 1. Labels and fuzzy numbers

People	Process	Systems	Events
High	Medium	Low	Low
Medium	High	Medium	Low
Low	Low	Medium	High

Table 2. Fuzzy labels for the 4 categories.

People	Process	Systems	Events
B1	B2		B3
B2	B1	B2B3	
B3	B3	B1	B1B2

Table 3. Business unit alignment in each category.

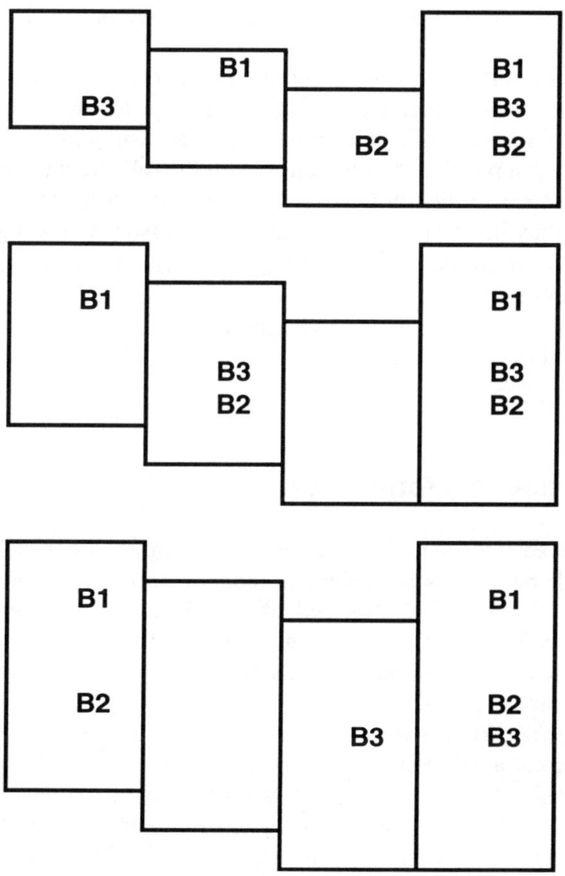

Table 4. Processing steps.

Rank	Business
1	
2	B1
3	
4	
5	B2
6	B3
7	
8	
9	

Table 5. Ranking results.

As we mentioned at the beginning of this article, the result of this analysis is a *relative* assessment of the risk to which the various business units are exposed. Therefore it falls short of providing a hard dollar number for how much money is actually at risk.

In a forthcoming paper I am suggesting a market data-based methodology to estimate the overall operational risk borne by a financial institution. The combination of such a synthetic estimate with the results of the clustering analysis discussed here can provide the institution with the reliable valuation it needs.

Weights are easily incorporated in this algebraic structure. If the jth risk factor generates the classification $a_n^{\alpha n}..a_1^{\alpha 1}$ and μ is the associated weight, then to the left of each class a_i we introduce $N_{ai}=int(m_{\alpha i}\mu)$ new classes, where $m\alpha I$ is the middle value of the corresponding fuzzy number.

Then we move the set a_i and the exponent α_i by $N_{\alpha i}$ classes to the left. The labels for the new classes will be:

$\sigma_{i-1}+j(\alpha_i-\alpha_{i-1})/(N_{\alpha i}+1)$.

5 Conclusion and future work

At least three important applications of this analysis can be identified. First, the ability to rank businesses according to their operational risk is a way to assess the effectiveness of the capital allocated to the management of operational risk itself. There is little point in spending millions of dollars to control the possibility of loosing tens or hundreds of thousands dollars in a business unit, while doing the exact opposite for another one.

Second, the ability to assess operational risk at the business units level is a critical step in the capital allocation process by which performance is evaluated on the basis of the contribution to both return and risk for the organization.

Finally, the striking similarities, in terms of implementation difficulties as well as of structure, between the operational risk and the credit risk problem suggest that a fuzzy logic approach could be developed in an integrated fashion for both problems. This would not only add a lot of soundness to most current practices, but would also help in designing a consistent frame of reference for risk measurement as a whole which would be certainly welcomed by both investors and regulators.

References

[1] Falkenstein E., "Value-at-Risk and Derivatives Risk", Derivatives Quarterly, Vol. 4, N. 1, fall 1997

[2] Gisolfi A., Loia V., "A Complete Flexible Fuzzy-based Approach to the Classification Problem", International Journal of Approximate Reasoning, 13, pp. 151-83, 1995.

[3] Jablonowski M., "Recognizing Knowledge Imperfection in the Risk Management Process", Proceedings of ISUMA-NAFIPS '95, College Park, MD, USA, September 17-20, 1995.

[4] Loia V., Scandizzo S., "Qualitative Selection Strategies in Genetic Based Evolutionary Economic Models", Proceedings of ISUMA-NAFIPS '95, College Park, MD, USA, September 17-20, 1995.

[5] Parsley M., "Risk Management' Final Frontier", Euromoney, pp. 74-79, September 1996.

[6] Saaty T.L., "The Analytic Hierarchy Process", McGraw-Hill, 1980.

[7] Shafer, G., "A Mathematical Theory of Evidence", Princeton University Press, Princeton, New Jersey, 1976.

[8] Terano T., Asai K., Sugeno M., "Applied Fuzzy Systems", AP Professional, Cambridge, MA, 1994.